DATE DUE

MY 18 01			

DEMCO 38-296

NATIVE AMERICANS
AND THE EARLY REPUBLIC

United States Capitol Historical Society

Clarence J. Brown, President

PERSPECTIVES ON THE AMERICAN REVOLUTION

Ronald Hoffman and Peter J. Albert, Editors

Diplomacy and Revolution: The Franco-American Alliance of 1778

Sovereign States in an Age of Uncertainty

Slavery and Freedom in the Age of the American Revolution

Arms and Independence: The Military Character of the American Revolution

An Uncivil War: The Southern Backcountry during the American Revolution

Peace and the Peacemakers: The Treaty of 1783

The Economy of Early America: The Revolutionary Period, 1763–1790

Women in the Age of the American Revolution

To Form a More Perfect Union: The Critical Ideas of the Constitution

Religion in a Revolutionary Age

Of Consuming Interests: The Style of Life in the Eighteenth Century

The Transforming Hand of Revolution:
Reconsidering the American Revolution as a Social Movement

Launching the "Extended Republic": The Federalist Era

The Bill of Rights: Government Proscribed

Native Americans and the Early Republic

Native Americans and the Early Republic

Edited by FREDERICK E. HOXIE

RONALD HOFFMAN

and PETER J. ALBERT

Published for the

UNITED STATES CAPITOL HISTORICAL SOCIETY

BY THE UNIVERSITY PRESS OF VIRGINIA

Charlottesville and London

THE UNIVERSITY PRESS OF VIRGINIA
© 1999 by the Rector and Visitors of the University of Virginia
All rights reserved
Printed in the United States of America

First published 1999

♾ The paper used in this publication meets the minimum requirements
of the American National Standard for Information Sciences—
Permanence of Paper for Printed Library Materials, ANSI Z39.48-1984.

Library of Congress Cataloging-in-Publication Data

Native Americans and the early republic / edited by Frederick E.
    Hoxie, Ronald Hoffman, and Peter J. Albert.
        p.   cm. — (Perspectives on the American Revolution)
    Includes bibliographical references and index.
    ISBN 0-8139-1873-1 (cloth : alk. paper)
        1. Indians of North America—Government relations—1789–1869.
    2. Indians, Treatment of—United States—History.   3. United States—
    Race relations.   I. Hoxie, Frederick E., 1947–   .   II. Hoffman,
    Ronald, 1941–   .   III. Albert, Peter J.   IV. Series.
    E93.N35   1999
    323.1'197073'09033—dc21   98-39823
                                                                      CIP

Contents

Contents

III. *Native American Images*

Afterword

Preface

With the publication of this volume, Peter J. Albert and I conclude the work with which Fred Schwengel, the late president of the United States Capitol Historical Society, charged us twenty years ago.

On countless occasions during the course of our collaboration, Fred reiterated to me the maxim he lived by—words first spoken to him in the late 1930s by Harry S. Truman: "You've got to know your history if you want to be a good citizen." Acting on his belief in the essential truth of that precept, Fred founded the United States Capitol Historical Society in 1962, and as he envisioned it, the organization's most important role would be to serve as "history teacher to the nation." Deeply disappointed that no sustained scholarly legacy had been created to mark the bicentennial of the Declaration of Independence in 1976, he raised with me in 1977 the possibility of organizing a conference and publication series that would commemorate in a substantial and enduring way the 200th anniversary of the Revolutionary, constitutional, and early federal eras of our country's history. Accordingly, the United States Capitol Historical Society's Symposia Series began in March 1978 with an examination of the Franco-American alliance and continued to explore the salient themes of the nation's formative years for the next decade and a half. To the last moments of his life, Fred took an enormous and entirely justified pride in the Society's sponsorship of these annual meetings and the books that developed from them.

Although his health had begun to fail by the spring of 1993, Fred attended the final conference of the series we created together that March. The vigorous and impassioned statement he made there about the influence of the Masonic order during the American Revolutionary era—a historical subject dear to his heart—was to be his last public performance. Within a month, physical problems overcame Fred's indomitable spirit, and he died on April 1, 1993.

The volumes in *Perspectives on the American Revolution* constitute a permanent memorial to Fred Schwengel's commitment to the critical importance of studying the past and his unwavering belief that the knowledge thereby gained enriches our understanding, deepens and broadens our perspective, and enables us to be better citizens of both our nation and the world. Peter Albert and I are deeply grateful that Fred gave us the chance to work with him in making his noble vision a reality.

The editors wish to acknowledge the contributions of the other participants at the United States Capitol Historical Society's symposium "Native Americans in the Early Republic," JoAllyn Archambault, A. Brian Deer, George R. Hammell, Robert W. Venables, Wilcomb E. Washburn, and Mary E. Young. We would also like to acknowledge the assistance of Diane Koch and Aileen Arnold in the preparation of this manuscript.

RONALD HOFFMAN
Omohundro Institute of Early
American History and Culture

Introduction

At the 1795 treaty council that sealed Anthony Wayne's victory at Fallen Timbers in northwest Ohio, the Wyandot leader Tarhe spoke for the assembled Native leaders when he admonished the American emissaries. "Take care of all your little ones," he implored the treaty negotiators; "an impartial father equally regards all his children."[1] Spoken two decades after the Minutemen's shots had echoed across Lexington green, Tarhe's words compel historians to reconsider the rosy truisms that customarily encircle the age of the Early Republic. Tarhe spoke as an embattled settler, determined to shield his freedom-loving community from the capricious acts of an imperial sovereign. He called on those who held the upper hand to set aside arbitrary power and embrace instead the role of wise and benevolent father. He could not imagine that his humiliation would someday be studied by schoolchildren as a happy chapter in the story of the founding of an empire of liberty.

Tarhe's words echo those of the patriots who had risen up a generation earlier to call the British Crown to account and who had followed up their petitions with war. His eloquence, quoted at length in Richard White's essay in this volume, provides inescapable evidence that American Indians were not defeated refugees who dutifully stood aside in the wake of the British defeat, nor were they passive victims of American expansion. When peace was made in Paris between the Crown and her former colonists, North America was largely Indian country. European settlement, while densely packed around prosperous seaports and their satellites, still hugged the Atlantic; most citizens of the new United States could not describe the geography of their new nation. The Ohio country and the Great Lakes had been seen by only a handful of American soldiers and settlers, while the territory west of the Smokies remained the domain

[1] Treaty of Greenville, Aug. 7, 1795, Speech of Tarhe, *American State Papers: Indian Affairs*, 1:580.

of French and Spanish merchants and their Native allies. An American navigating the Mississippi who spoke only English could have easily traveled the length of this national border without hearing his native tongue.

But the Treaty of Paris that ended the war between Britain and her former colonies had held to an imperial custom that began when Pope Alexander VI granted the New World to Spain: the Indian presence was ignored as an unpleasant detail. Following this habit, the former combatants who negotiated in Paris drew America's national boundaries without regard to native power. "It was an act of cruelty and injustice," Iroquois warriors gathered at Niagara declared, "that Christians only were capable of doing."[2] Not surprisingly, the Paris treaty marked only the midpoint in a generation of Indian warfare, and the founding of the American republic the beginning of a struggle for independence and equity that continues to the present day.

Looking behind the chauvinistic rhetoric of the half-century that followed the founding of the United States opens new dimensions of our past. Recreating Tarhe's world and that of the Native communities that stretched in a vast arc from northern New England to the western Great Lakes and back to the Tennessee Valley and the Gulf enables Americans to see their history as a complex mosaic through which cultural, political, and military tides pulsed and broke across one another. Forces of change in this vast arena ran not only from east to west, but also from south to north, west to east, and north to south. The essays in this book provide a guide to that mosaic and the beginnings of a history of those tides.

Three groups of essays lie between bookend discussions of the Revolutionary War itself and Indian affairs in the Jacksonian era. The first, made up of essays by Reginald Horsman on American policymaking, Richard White on the conceptions Indians and whites had of each other, and Theda Perdue on Native women, provide broad discussions of the interaction between American Indians and the United States in the postwar era. They paint three contrasting portraits of the political, cultural, and social conflicts that underlay relations between Na-

[2] Quoted in Colin G. Calloway, *Crown and Calumet: British-Indian Relations, 1783–1815* (Norman, Okla., 1987), p. 11.

tive people and the Europeans, who now thought of themselves as permanent residents on their land. The second group of essays—by Daniel K. Richter, R. David Edmunds, Daniel H. Usner, Jr., and Joel W. Martin traces the histories of specific tribal communities in modern New York, Pennsylvania, Ohio, and the Southeast. These studies provide vivid evidence of the variety of Indian traditions that were encompassed within the new nation as well as the equally various ways in which these communities were affected by—and affected—their neighbors. Finally, two essays—one by Elise Marienstras on literary images and one by Vivien Green Fryd on visual representations—discuss the powerful repertoire of stories and pictures Americans used to describe Indian people to themselves and their fellow citizens during an era of national expansion. Introduced by Colin G. Calloway's panoramic description of the Revolution in Indian country and drawn to a thoughtful conclusion by James H. Merrell's afterword, these eleven essays touch on events in every corner of the eastern American landscape.

The power of this volume's essays reaches far beyond the book's modest title. They do not fill in the missing words of a preordained narrative. Rather they remind us that our history is far richer than we have imagined, far older than we are told, and far more complex than we have so far been able to communicate. The eleven authors who write here mark out the dimension of a new and unsettled past, one that, once populated and described in detail by colleagues, might guide us more effectively into the future than tired slogans and shopworn stereotypes.

FREDERICK E. HOXIE
University of Illinois

NATIVE AMERICANS
AND THE EARLY REPUBLIC

Prologue

COLIN G. CALLOWAY

The Continuing
Revolution
in Indian Country

FOR MANY NATIVE AMERICANS, the American Revolution did not end in 1783; it was one phase of a Twenty Years' War that continued at least until the Treaty of Greenville in 1795. Before it was over, a whole generation had grown up knowing little but war. Whether they sided with rebels or redcoats, or neither, or both, Indians during the Revolution were doing pretty much the same thing as the American patriots—fighting for their freedom in tumultuous times. Indian people in the new republic continued their struggles for independence and attempted to adjust to the new world order. But, with the Revolution won, Americans reduced to a single adversarial role the diverse Indian experiences and varying degrees of involvement in that conflict. Native Americans became identified with the enemies of the republic. This image fueled ambivalence about the place of Indian people in the American future. In its simplest terms, while Anglo-Americans could imagine subordinate Indians as friends, they typically equated resistance with a national threat. Native Americans in the new Republic found that the American Revolution not only had created a new society; it also provided the justification for excluding them from it.

The "world turned upside down" for American Indians long before it did for Lord Cornwallis,[1] and many Indian nations

Since this essay was written the author has included and expanded many of its points in the book *The American Revolution in Indian Country: Crisis and Diversity in Native American Communities* (New York, 1995).

[1] Compare James H. O'Donnell III, "The World Turned Upside Down: The American Revolution as a Catastrophe for Native Americans," in Francis P.

were already shadows of their former selves by 1775. European emigration, European diseases, European firearms, and European imperial ambitions had produced political upheaval, economic dislocation, and demographic disaster throughout Indian country. Generations of contact had seen precedents established, attitudes ingrained, and patterns of coexistence worked out and fall apart. Indian communities in colonial America struggled to survive in a chaotic new world, and yet despite massive inroads in Indian country and Indian cultures, Indian people were still virtually everywhere in colonial America.[2]

The forces that had inverted their world intensified with the outbreak of the Revolution. At first the American Revolution had looked very much like an English civil war to Indian eyes, and most Native Americans tried to avoid becoming entangled in it. Throughout the eastern woodlands, and throughout the war, British and American agents solicited Indian support. An Abenaki woman in western Maine said her tribe was being constantly courted. "O, straing [strange] *Englishmen* kill one another," she said. "I think the world is coming to an end." In the spring of 1777 British agent William Caldwell warned the Senecas not to "regard anything the Bigknife [Americans] might say to them for tho he had a very smooth Oily Tongue his heart was not good." Two years later American commander Daniel Brodhead warned the Shawnees that the British would tell them fine stories but had come three thousand miles only "to rob & Steal & fill their Pockets."[3]

Jennings, ed., *The American Indian and the American Revolution* (Chicago, 1983), pp. 80–93.

[2] James H. Merrell, "Some Thoughts on Colonial Historians and American Indians," *William and Mary Quarterly*, 3d ser. 46 (1989):94–119.

[3] Letter from Henry Young Brown, May 16, 1775, U.S. Revolution Collection, American Antiquarian Society, Worcester, Mass.; Peter Force, ed., *American Archives*, 4th ser., 9 vols. (Washington, D.C., 1837–53), 2:621; Reuben Gold Thwaites and Louise Phelps Kellogg, eds., *The Revolution on the Upper Ohio, 1775–1777* (Madison, Wis., 1908), pp. 67–70; Robert L. Scribner et al., eds., *Revolutionary Virginia, the Road to Independence: A Documentary Record*, 7 vols. (Charlottesville, Va., 1973–83), 4:129–30; Draper Manuscripts, 1H54, Wisconsin State Historical Society, Madison.

Such competition produced confusion and division in Indian communities as people wrestled with how best to proceed in perilous and uncertain times. Fernando de Leyba told Governor of Louisiana Bernardo de Galvez in the summer of 1778 that the war was "causing a great number of Indian tribes to go from one side to the other without knowing which side to take."[4] Discourse and discord were part of the normal process by which most eastern woodland societies reached consensus, but the issues raised by the Revolution were such that consensus could not always be reached. The divisions of colonial society that John Adams summarized as one-third patriot, one-third loyalist, and one-third neutral were replicated with numerous variations in countless Indian communities in North America, and, as elsewhere on the frontier, the pressures imposed by the Revolution revealed existing fissures as well as creating new ones.[5] The Delawares in 1779 asked Congress to distinguish between their nation as a whole, which was still friendly, and the actions of a few individuals who, like the loyalists in the states, sided with the British and had been obliged to leave the nation.[6] As provocations increased, however, neutrality became increasingly precarious, even impossible, forcing Indians to choose sides.

The national mythology has assigned Indians a minimal and one-dimensional role in the Revolution: they chose the wrong side and they lost. But commitment was never unanimous, and in Indian country the American Revolution often translated into an American civil war. The League of the Iroquois—the confederacy of the Mohawks, Oneidas, Onondagas, Cayugas,

[4] Lawrence Kinnaird, ed., "Spain in the Mississippi Valley, 1765–1794," in *Annual Report of the American Historical Association for the Year 1945*, 4 vols. (Washington, D.C., 1946–49), 2:298.

[5] Compare Ronald Hoffman, Thad W. Tate, and Peter J. Albert, eds., *An Uncivil War: The Southern Backcountry during the American Revolution* (Charlottesville, Va., 1985), p. xii.

[6] Draper Mss., 1F50 and 1H91–93; Louise Phelps Kellogg, ed., *Frontier Advance on the Upper Ohio, 1778–1779* (Madison, Wis., 1916), p. 352; Papers of the Continental Congress (microfilm M247), roll 183, item 166, p. 446, National Archives, Washington, D.C.

Senecas, and Tuscaroras that stretched across upper New York state—had managed to maintain a pivotal position in North American affairs by preserving formal neutrality and essential unity of action in previous conflicts, but was unable to do so now. Samuel Kirkland, the New England Presbyterian missionary who himself generated significant divisions in Oneida society, heard Indians say that "they never knew a debate so warm & contention so fierce to have happened between these two Brothers, Oneidas & Cayugas, since the commencement of their union." The bitter divisions the Revolution produced *within* the Oneidas were "not yet forgotten" by 1796.[7] In 1775 both the Oneidas and Senecas took a neutral stance; two years later they were killing each other at the Battle of Oriskany and the league's central council fire at Onondaga was ritually extinguished. Pro-British warriors burned Oneida crops and houses in revenge; Oneidas retaliated by burning Mohawk homes. Most Tuscaroras also supported the Americans while the Cayugas lent their weight to the British. The Onondagas maintained a precarious neutrality until American troops burned their towns in 1779. For the Iroquois the Revolution was a war in which, in some cases literally, brother killed brother.[8]

In Massachusetts the Stockbridge Indians, a community of Christian Mohican and neighboring groups, had their own scores to settle against the British, having been deprived of

[7] Samuel Kirkland to Philip Schuyler, Mar. 11, 1776, Kirkland Papers, 64b, Hamilton College, Clinton, N.Y.; John C. Guzzardo, "The Superintendent and the Ministers: The Battle for Oneida Allegiances," *New York History* 57 (1976): 255–83; *Collections of the Massachusetts Historical Society*, 1st ser. 5 (1798): 16.

[8] Barbara Graymont, *The Iroquois in the American Revolution* (Syracuse, N.Y., 1972); idem, "The Oneidas and the American Revolution," in Jack Campisi and Laurence M. Hauptman, eds., *The Oneida Indian Experience: Two Perspectives* (Syracuse, N.Y., 1988), p. 39; George F. Stanley, "The Six Nations and the American Revolution," *Ontario History* 56 (1964): 217–32; James Everett Seaver, *A Narrative of the Life of Mary Jemison* (Syracuse, N.Y., 1990), pp. 49, 52; Papers of Sir Frederick Haldimand, Add. Mss. 21767:104 and 21773:101, British Museum; Draper Mss., 14:248–51; *Papers of the Continental Congress*, roll 183, pp. 387–93; Thomas S. Abler, ed., *Chainbreaker: The Revolutionary War Memoirs of Governor Blacksnake, as Told to Benjamin Williams* (Lincoln, Nebr., 1989), pp. 69, 87, 91, 144.

lands while warriors were away fighting *for* the Crown in earlier wars and having tried in vain to seek redress.[9] They volunteered at the outbreak of the Revolution and assisted the Americans steadfastly, despite suffering heavy losses.[10] William Apess, a Pequot Indian writing in the next century, said that the small Indian town of Mashpee on Cape Code furnished twenty-six men for the patriot service, all but one of whom "fell martyrs to liberty in the struggle for Independence." Pequots and Mohegans from Connecticut suffered similar high casualties. Indian women widowed by the war were forced to look outside their communities for husbands, intermarrying with Anglo-American and African-American neighbors.[11]

The situation elsewhere in New England and eastern Canada was less simple. The Abenakis, for generations the shock troops of New France against the New England frontier, displayed ambivalence, despite considerable British coercion. Some served the British; others offered their services to George Washington. About forty-five Abenaki families took up residence near American settlements on the upper Connecticut and supplied scouts

[9] Oscar Handlin and Irving Mark, eds., "Chief Daniel Nimham *v.* Roger Morris, Beverly Robinson, and Philip Philipse—An Indian Land Case in Colonial New York, 1765–1767," *Ethnohistory* 11 (1964): 193–246; William Coates, ed., "A Narrative of an Embassy to the Western Indians, from the Original Manuscript of Hendrick Aupaumut," part 1, *Memoirs of the Historical Society of Pennsylvania* 2 (1827): 128. On the history of Stockbridge, see Patrick Frazier, *The Mohicans of Stockbridge* (Lincoln, Nebr., 1992).

[10] Deirdre Almeida, "The Stockbridge Indians in the American Revolution," *Historical Journal of Western Massachusetts* 4 (1975): 34–39; *Journals of the Continental Congress, 1774–1789*, 34 vols. (Washington, D.C., 1904–37), 5:627, 9:840; Papers of the Continental Congress, roll 23, item 12A, vol. 1, p. 196, vol. 2, p. 14, roll 50, item 41, vol. 4, p. 422, roll 55, item 42, vol. 5, p. 451, roll 170, item 152, vol. 9, pp. 165–66; Force, ed., *American Archives*, 4th ser. 1:1347, 2:315–16, 1002–3, 1060–61; 5th ser., 3 vols. (Washington, D.C., 1848–53), 1:725, 903; John C. Fitzpatrick, ed., *The Writings of George Washington from the Original Manuscript Sources, 1745–1799*, 39 vols. (Washington, D.C., 1931–44), 20:44–45; *Papers of Horatio Gates, 1726–1828* (New York, 1978, microfilm), roll 3:248, roll 6:85, 720.

[11] Colin G. Calloway, "New England Algonkians in the American Revolution," in *Annual Proceedings of the Dublin Seminar for New England Folklife*, 1991 (Boston, 1993), pp. 51–62.

and soldiers for the American army. Those who remained in Canada became deeply divided, and some appeared to play both sides of the street. Most Abenakis seem to have restricted their role to watching the woods.[12] Other Canadian tribes displayed similar reluctance and ambivalence, while the village of Caughnawaga (Kahnawake) near Montreal became a hotbed of intrigue in the contest for Indian allegiance in the north.[13] In Maine and Nova Scotia the Passamaquoddies, Micmacs, and Maliseets were not eager to become involved in a war that had little to do with them or to offer them. Many sided with the Americans but then split as British power and British goods exerted increasing influence.[14]

In the strategically crucial Ohio country, the Indians were the prize in a diplomatic tug of war between Henry Hamilton, the British commander at Detroit, and George Morgan, the American Indian agent at Fort Pitt. The Delawares, neutral at the outbreak of the war, soon came under pressure from American and British agents and from other tribes, particularly the pro-British Wyandots under Half King to the north. A group of young Delaware warriors defected, but even General Hand's infamous "squaw campaign" did not destroy the tribe's commitment to

[12] Colin G. Calloway, *The Western Abenakis of Vermont, 1600–1800: War, Migration and the Survival of an Indian People* (Norman, Okla., 1990), chap. 11; idem, "Sentinels of Revolution: Bedel's New Hampshire Rangers and the Abenaki Indians on the Upper Connecticut," *Historical New Hampshire* 45 (1990):271–95; Papers of General Philip Schuyler, roll 7, box 14, New York Public Library; "List of St. Francis Indians, June 5, 1778," *The Remembrancer or Impartial Repository of Public Events* (London), 1775, p. 251.

[13] Paul Lawrence Stevens, "His Majesty's 'Savage' Allies: British Policy and the Northern Indians during the Revolutionary War: The Carleton Years, 1774–1778," Ph.D. diss., State University of New York at Buffalo, 1984.

[14] *Sir Guy Carleton Papers, 1777–1783* (microfilm), roll 5, no. 1690, roll 6, no. 2158; K. G. Davies, ed., *Documents of the American Revolution, 1770–1783*, 21 vols. (Shannon, Ireland, 1972–81), 13:266; Frederic Kidder, ed., *Military Operations in Eastern Maine and Nova Scotia during the Revolution, Chiefly Compiled from the Journals and Letters of Colonel John Allen* (Albany, 1867); *Dictionary of Canadian Biography*, s.v. Saint-Aubin, Ambroise, and Tomah, Pierre; James Phinney Baxter, ed., *Documentary History of the State of Maine: Collections of the Maine Historical Society*, 24 vols. (Portland, Maine, 1869–1916), vols. 14 and 15.

peace. The United States signed a treaty with the Delawares in 1778 in an effort to secure their neutrality and right of passage across their lands, but many Delawares complained they had been deceived into taking up the hatchet for the United States. White Eyes and John Killbuck of the Turtle clan displayed continued pro-American sympathies, but Captain Pipe and the Wolf clan moved to the Sandusky River, closer to the Wyandots and the British. The American murder of White Eyes, their strongest supporter in the Delaware National Council, and their failure to provide the trade goods the Delawares needed, allowed Pipe to gain influence among his hungry and disillusioned people.[15]

A detachment of Delawares served the United States through the final years of the war,[16] but in 1780 Daniel Brodhead declared the Delawares had "acted a double part long enough." American troops, guided by Killbuck and his men, burned the Delaware capital at Coshocton.[17] Killbuck's followers took refuge at Fort Pitt, where they not only suffered hunger and hardship but were exposed to danger at the hands of American frontiersmen to whom all Indians were the same. Those Delawares

[15] On the Delawares in the Revolution and the schisms within the nation, see C. A. Weslager, *The Delaware Indians: A History* (New Brunswick, N.J., 1972), chap. 13; Gregory Evans Dowd, *A Spirited Resistance: The North American Indian Struggle for Unity, 1745–1815* (Baltimore, 1992), pp. 65–89; The Brodhead Papers, Draper Mss., H ser., esp. 1H22–23, 47–48; Reuben Gold Thwaites and Louise Phelps Kellogg, eds., *Frontier Defense on the Upper Ohio, 1777–1778* (Madison, Wis., 1912), pp. 27–29, 95–97, 100–101, 215–20; Kellogg, ed., *Frontier Advance*, esp. pp. 20–21, 117–18; George Morgan Letterbook, esp. 1:18–22, 46, 49–51; 3:149–51, 162–65, Carnegie Library, Pittsburgh. John Heckewelder, *A Narrative of the Mission of the United Brethren among the Delaware and Mohegan Indians* (Philadelphia, 1820), provides a first-hand, pro-American account of developments in Delaware country.

[16] Pay Roll of the Delaware Indians in Service of the United States, June 15, 1780–Oct. 31, 1781, Revolutionary War Rolls, 1775–83 (microfilm M246), roll 129, Natl. Arch.

[17] Draper Mss., 3H19, 5D80, 86, 99, 142; *Pennsylvania Archives*, 1st ser., 12 vols. (Philadelphia, 1852–56), 8:640; 9:161–62; Kellogg, ed., *Frontier Advance*, pp. 337–43, 353, 376–81, 399; Neville B. Craig, ed., *The Olden Time*, 2 vols. (Cincinnati, 1876), 2:378–79, 389; Dowd, *Spirited Resistance*, pp. 82–83.

who lived in separate villages under the guidance of Moravian missionaries also clung to a neutrality that cost them dearly. In 1782 American militia marched to the Moravian Delaware town of Gnadenhutten, rounded up the inhabitants, and bludgeoned to death ninety-six men, women, and children.[18]

The neighboring Shawnees had been involved in long resistance against encroachment on their lands and had just fought a costly war against Lord Dunmore and Virginia. Shawnee emissaries were active in efforts to form a confederacy against American expansion, but the Shawnees themselves were divided over the question of further resistance and many migrated west of the Mississippi. The Shawnee chief Cornstalk tried to preserve his people's fragile neutrality but confessed he was unable to restrain his "foolish Young Men." Moreover, the Americans displayed their peculiar penchant for murdering key friends at key moments. After Cornstalk was killed under a flag of truce at Fort Randolph in 1777, his Maquachake peace party joined the still-neutral Delawares at Coshocton, but most of the Shawnees now made common cause with King George.[19]

In the South the Cherokees had already had grim experience of the consequences of becoming involved in the wars of their non-Indian neighbors, but, with settlers encroaching on their

[18] Papers of the Continental Congress, roll 73, item 59, vol. 3, pp. 49–51; *Pennsylvania Archives*, 1st ser. 9:523–25; Edmund de Schweinitz, *The Life and Times of David Zeisberger* (1870; reprint ed., New York, 1971), pp. 537–38; Consul Willshire Butterfield, ed., *Washington-Irvine Correspondence* (Madison, Wis., 1882), pp. 99–109, 179.

[19] Colin G. Calloway, "'We Have Always Been the Frontier': The American Revolution in Shawnee Country," *American Indian Quarterly* 16 (1992):39–52; Davies, ed., *Documents*, 12:199–203; Papers of the Continental Congress, roll 180, item 163, pp. 245–47; Draper Mss., 2YY92, 3D164–73; Thwaites and Kellogg, eds., *Revolution on the Upper Ohio*, p. 43; idem, *Frontier Defense*, pp. 157–63, 175–77, 188–89, 205–9, 243–47, 258–61; *Remembrancer*, 1780, pt. 1, pp. 154–58; *Collections and Researches Made by the Michigan Pioneer and Historical Society*, 40 vols. (Lansing, Mich., 1874–1929), 25:690; William L. Saunders, ed., *The Colonial Records of North Carolina, 1662–1776*, 30 vols. (Raleigh, 1886–1914), 10:386; Morgan Letterbook, 1:47–49, 57–59; 3:27, 56, 96. The Maquachake division of the Shawnees were consistently most amenable to peace with the Americans. See, for example, Edward G. Williams, ed., "The Journal of Richard Butler, 1775: Continental Congress' Envoy to the Western Indians," *Western Pennsylvania Historical Magazine* 47 (1964):45, 148.

lands, they fought this war for their own reasons. While the older chiefs watched in silent dejection, Dragging Canoe and younger Cherokees accepted a war belt from the northern nations and threw themselves into the fighting early in the Revolution. After expeditions from Virginia and North and South Carolina destroyed Cherokee towns and crops, the older chiefs sued for peace, and refugees fled to the Creeks, the Chickasaws, and to Pensacola. The nation split along generational lines as many younger warriors followed the lead of Dragging Canoe, seceding to form new communities at Chickamauga, which became the core of Cherokee resistance until 1795. Other Cherokees suffered as a result of Chickamauga resistance; some helped the Americans, and the Revolution assumed the look of a civil war in Cherokee country.[20]

Elsewhere in the South, Choctaw towns were divided between Britain and Spain; the majority supported King George, but British agents always feared losing them. The Chickasaws were basically pro-British, while the Catawbas, surrounded by settlers, supported the Americans.[21] At the beginning of the Revolution,

[20] Gary C. Goodwin, *Cherokees in Transition: A Study of Changing Culture and Environment prior to 1775* (Chicago, 1977), pp. 103–4; James Paul Pate, "The Chickamaugas: A Forgotten Segment of Indian Resistance on the Southern Frontier," Ph.D. diss., Mississippi State University, 1969; Saunders, ed., *Colonial Records of North Carolina*, 10:657, 659–61, 763–85; John P. Brown, *Old Frontiers: The Story of the Cherokees from Earliest Times to the Date of Their Removal to the West, 1838* (Kingsport, Tenn., 1938), pp. 163, 171; James H. O'Donnell III, *The Cherokees of North Carolina in the American Revolution* (Raleigh, 1976); idem, "The Virginia Expedition against the Overhill Cherokees, 1776," *East Tennessee Historical Society's Publications* 39 (1967):13–25; Robert L. Ganyard, "Threat from the West: North Carolina and the Cherokee, 1776–1778," *North Carolina Historical Review* 45 (1968):47–66; Archibald Henderson, "The Treaty of Long Island of Holston, July 1777," *North Carolina Historical Review* 8 (1931): 55–117; William P. Palmer, ed., *Calendar of Virginia State Papers and Other Manuscripts, 1652–1781*, 11 vols. (Richmond, 1875–83), 1:484–87, 495, 2:24, 679; Draper Mss., 30S66–73, 140–80, 31S170–71, 1U45–48, 12S19, 11S99–100; Davies, ed., *Documents*, 12:190, 200, 205–8, 229–30, 239–40, 247, 14:34–35, 94, 112–15, 194, 15:285, 17:181–82; Fred Gearing, "Priests and Warriors: Social Structures for Cherokee Politics in the 18th Century," *American Anthropologist* 64, no. 5, pt. 2 (1962):102–4.

[21] Davies, ed., *Documents*, 11:118, 19:62, 20:59–60, 149–50; James H. Merrell, *The Indians' New World: Catawbas and Their Neighbors from European Contact through the Era of Removal* (Chapel Hill, N.C., 1989), pp. 215–21.

the Creeks were at war with the Choctaws, and though the British now took measures to end a conflict they had previously encouraged, the Cherokee experience gave them ample reason to drag their feet. British Indian superintendent John Stuart complained they were "a mercenary People, Conveniency & Safety are the great Ties that Bind them." Most eventually sided with the British and about 120 Creeks and over 700 Choctaws fought alongside the British in the defense of Pensacola against Spanish attack early in 1781. But the war divided the Creeks into bitter factions.[22]

Any overview of Indian dispositions and allegiances is difficult and hazardous. Most tribes fluctuated in their sentiments, intertribal alliances formed at the cost of increased intratribal disunity, and participation was usually cautious and often relatively brief. One of the first communities to wage war against the Americans was Pluggy's Town, where Chippewas, Wyandots, and Ottawas joined Mingoes (Ohio Iroquois), and where Americans found it was often "difficult to tell what Nation are the Offenders." Pluggy's Mingoes caused consternation among neighboring tribes who blamed them for corrupting their young men and threatening to embroil everyone in the war.[23] In June 1778 Congress found that the nations at war against them in the West included "the Senecas, Cayugas, Mingoes and Wiandots in general, a majority of the Onondagas and a few of the Ottawas, Chippewas, Shawnese & Delawares, acting contrary to the voice of their nations," but the situation was not that simple and was constantly changing. A month later, delegates from the Shawnees, Ottawas, Mingoes, Wyandots, Potawatomis, Delawares, Mohawks, and Miamis accepted a war belt from Henry Hamilton

[22] David H. Corkran, *The Creek Frontier, 1540–1783* (Norman, Okla., 1967), pp. 316–25; Michael D. Green, "The Creek Confederacy in the American Revolution: Cautious Participants," in William S. Croker and Robert R. Rea, eds., *Anglo-Spanish Confrontation on the Gulf Coast during the American Revolution* (Pensacola, Fla., 1982), pp. 54–75; *Carleton Papers*, roll 3A, no. 925; Haldimand Papers, 21761:134.

[23] Draper Mss., 2D122; "In Congress, Dec. 3, 1777," Schuyler Papers, roll 7, box 14; Schweinitz, *Life and Times of Zeisberger*, p. 445; Thwaites and Kellogg, eds., *Revolution on the Upper Ohio*, pp. 236 -37; *Pennsylvania Archives*, 1st ser. 5:260; Morgan Letterbook, 1:23, 47–50, 56–59, 61, 71–73, 76; 2:45.

at Detroit. While Delawares, Oneidas, Tuscaroras, and other Indians friendly to the United States gathered "to guard against the impending Storm" and called on the Americans for protection, Thomas Jefferson and others advocated using friendly tribes to wage war against hostile ones.[24]

The American Revolution was not only a civil war for Indian people; it also amounted to a world war in Indian country, with surrounding nations, Indian and non-Indian, at war, on the brink of war, or arranging alliances in expectation of war. American history has paid little attention to the impact of this war on the Indians' home front. American campaign strategy aimed to carry the war into Indian country, destroy Indian villages, and burn Indian crops late in the season when there was insufficient time for replanting before winter. American troops and militia tramped through Indian country, leaving smoking ruins and burned cornfields behind them.[25] American soldiers and militia matched their British and Indian adversaries in the use of terror tactics. George Rogers Clark declared that "to excel them in barbarity was and is the only way to make war upon Indians and gain a name among them," and he carried his policy into effect at Vincennes by binding and tomahawking Indian prisoners within sight of the besieged garrison. Pennsylvania offered $1,000 for every Indian scalp; South Carolina £75 for male scalps, and Kentucky militia who invaded Shawnee villages dug open graves to scalp corpses.[26]

[24] *Papers of Gates*, 7:764–66; *Journals of the Continental Congress*, 11:587–88; *Collections by the Michigan Pioneer and Historical Society*, 9:442–58; Julian P. Boyd et al., eds., *The Papers of Thomas Jefferson*, 28 vols. to date (Princeton, 1950–), 3:276; Clarence W. Alvord, ed., *Kaskaskia Records, 1778–1790* (Springfield, Ill., 1909), p. 147. A better summary of limited tribal commitments is provided in Richard White, *The Middle Ground: Indians, Empires, and Republics in the Great Lakes Region, 1650–1815* (Cambridge, 1991), p. 399.

[25] Fitzpatrick, ed., *Writings of Washington*, 15:189; Kellogg, ed., *Frontier Advance*, p. 311; *Pennsylvania Archives*, 1st ser. 6:614.

[26] Milo M. Quaife, ed., *The Conquest of the Illinois* (Chicago, 1920), pp. 148–49, 167; *Pennsylvania Archives*, 1st ser. 8:167; Force, ed., *American Archives*, 5th ser. 3:32; Calloway, "'We Have Always Been the Frontier,'" p. 43.

Barely had the Cherokees launched their attacks on the back-country settlements than the colonists carried fire and sword to their towns and villages, bringing the nation to its knees. Even Dragging Canoe's villages were not invulnerable to attack: Evan Shelby burned eleven of them in 1779, forcing the Chickamau-gas to relocate in safer locations. John Sevier burned fifteen Middle Cherokee towns in March 1781, and the following sum-mer destroyed new Lower Cherokee towns on the Coosa River. American armies marching through Cherokee country in pur-suit of Chickamauga raiders did not always distinguish between Cherokee friends and Cherokee foes, thereby swelling Drag-ging Canoe's ranks with new recruits. A Cherokee headman summed up the cost of the Revolution for his people: "I . . . have lost in different engagements six hundred warriors, my towns have been thrice destroyed and my corn fields laid waste by the enemy." British reports claimed Cherokee women and children were butchered in cold blood and burned alive.[27]

In the spring of 1779, Col. Goose Van Schaick marched against the Onondaga settlements, laying waste their towns and crops, slaughtering cattle and horses, and carrying off thirty-three prisoners. In the fall Gen. John Sullivan led his famous ex-pedition into Iroquois country on a campaign of destruction that burned forty towns, 160,000 bushels of corn, as well as beans, squash, orchards, and cattle. Meanwhile, Daniel Brod-head devastated the Seneca and Munsee towns on the Alle-gheny. The Americans spent whole days systematically destroy-ing Iroquois fields and food supplies.[28] The Iroquois pulled

[27] Brown, *Old Frontiers*, pp. 173–75, 196; Pate, "Chickamaugas," pp. 93–95, 116, 119, 122–26; Papers of the Continental Congress, roll 85, item 71, vol. 1, pp. 45, 241–42; Carleton Papers, 30/55/60, no. 6742:4–6, Public Rec-ord Office; Davies, ed., *Documents*, 17:233, 269, 21:122; C.O. 5/82:287–88, 343, P.R.O.

[28] *Remembrancer*, 1779, pt. 2, pp. 273–74, 1780, pt. 1, pp. 152–58; Freder-ick Cook, ed., *Journals of the Military Expedition of Major General John Sullivan against the Six Nations* (Auburn, N.Y., 1887); Fitzpatrick, ed., *Writings of Wash-ington*, 16:478, 480, 492–93. On Daniel Brodhead, see Draper Mss., 1AA39; Louise Phelps Kellogg, ed., *Frontier Retreat on the Upper Ohio, 1779–1781* (Madison, Wis., 1917), pp. 56–62; *Pennsylvania Archives*, 1st ser. 12:155–58; Craig, ed., *Olden Time*, 2:308–17.

back and sustained minimal casualties, but an Onondaga chief later claimed that when the Americans attacked his town, "they put to death all the Women and Children, excepting some of the Young Women, whom they carried away for the use of their Soldiers & were afterwards put to death in a more shameful manner."[29]

Deprived of food and shelter, Iroquois women and children faced starvation as one of the coldest winters on record gripped North America. Refugees fled to British posts for support, and thousands of Indian men, women, and children huddled in miserable shelters around Fort Niagara.[30] Fearing retaliation from their relatives, many Oneidas abandoned their villages and placed themselves under American protection near Schenectady where, living in wretched refugee camps, they endured the prejudice of the American garrison.[31]

Thomas Jefferson wanted the Shawnees exterminated or driven from their lands, and American invasions of Shawnee country became a regular feature of the war. In 1779 Col. John Bowman attacked the town of Chillicothe on the Little Miami River. In 1780 the Shawnees burned Chillicothe as George Rogers Clark approached and fought a major engagement at Piqua. Clark returned two years later, burning Shawnee villages and orchards. The pattern continued in 1786 when Kentucky militia attacked Maquachake villages—murdering Molunthy as the old chief clutched an American flag and a copy of the treaty he had signed with the Americans just months before—and with Gen. Josiah Harmar's expedition in 1790. Chillicothe was destroyed four times in this period, but the Shawnees rebuilt it each time in different locations.[32]

[29] Haldimand Papers, 21762:238.

[30] Ibid., 21760:220, 244, 21765:140–41, 21770:242–46; *Collections by the Michigan Pioneer and Historical Society*, 19:461.

[31] Graymont, *Iroquois in the American Revolution*, pp. 242–44.

[32] Calloway, "'We Have Always Been the Frontier,'" pp. 43–44; William Albert Galloway, *Old Chillicothe: Shawnee and Pioneer History* (Xenia, Ohio, 1934); J. Martin West, comp. and ed., *Clark's Shawnee Campaign of 1780* (Springfield, Ohio, 1975); Draper Mss., 8J136–40, 210–12, 265–66, 320–22, 9J61–

American soldiers were impressed by the cornucopia they destroyed in Indian fields and villages; by eighteenth-century frontier standards, Indian communities were rich in agricultural foodstuffs when not disrupted by the ravages of war. Moreover, many Indian towns provided material comforts that were the envy of frontier whites. The Oneidas later submitted to Congress claims for compensation for their losses that included sheep, horses, hogs, turkeys, agricultural implements, wheat, oats, corn, sugar, linen, calico, kettles, frying pans, pewter plates, "10 tea-cups & sawcers," "6 punch bowls," tablespoons, wampum, candlesticks, silver dollars, harness, sleighs, plows, "a very large framed house [with a] chimney at each end [and] painted windows," a teapot, ivory combs, white flannel breeches, silk handkerchiefs, mirrors, and scissors.[33] The wealth they found in Indian country gave Americans an economic incentive to go on campaigns and made them eager to seize fertile Indian lands once the war was over.

Even when the war was not fought on the Indians' home ground, it produced disruption and misery in Indian communities. Men who fell in battle were not only warriors. They were "part-time soldiers" who were also husbands, fathers and sons, providers and hunters. Warriors who were out on campaign could not hunt or clear fields; women who were forced to flee when invasion threatened could not plant and harvest. Indians still tried to wage war with the seasons: warriors preferred to wait until their corn was ripe before they took up the hatchet, and according to one observer "quit going to war" when hunting season came.[34] But war now dominated the activities of the community and placed tremendous demands on the people's energy at the expense of normal economic and social practices. Even before Sullivan's campaign, there were food shortages in Iroquois longhouses as "the Young Men were already either out at War, or ready to go," and many Mohawks became sick from

---

70, 11J24, 26J3–5, 49J89–90; Haldimand Papers, 21781:76–77, 21756:91, 21760:147–48.

[33] Timothy Pickering Papers, 62:157–74, Massachusetts Historical Society, Boston.

[34] Draper Mss., 2AA70; Thwaites and Kellogg, eds., *Revolution on the Upper Ohio*, p. 190.

eating nothing but salt meat. At a time when the need for food increased greatly, Indians could not cultivate the usual quantities of corn and vegetables, and what they did grow was often destroyed before it could be harvested.[35] Crops also suffered from natural causes in time of war. The late 1770s marked the beginning of a period of "sporadically poor crops" among southeastern tribes. Partial failure of the Creek corn crop in 1776 produced near famine at a time when the influx of Cherokee refugees placed additional demands on food supplies. Choctaw crops failed in 1782, increasing the people's reliance on deer hunting.[36] Hunting became vital to group survival, but fewer hunters were available, and hunting territories could be perilous places in time of war.

As a result, Indian communities became increasingly dependent on British, American, or Spanish allies to provide them with food, clothing, and trade. Rival powers waged economic warfare to compel Indian allegiance, and harsh economic realities increasingly curtailed the tribes' freedom of action and governed their decisions.[37] Dependency on outside supplies of food and clothing rendered the end of the war all the more catastrophic, when allies deserted and supplies dried up.

Those tribes who supported the Americans or remained neutral suffered as much as those who fought with the British. In the spring of 1782, those Cherokees who remained friendly to the Americans were "in a deplorable situation, being naked & defenceless for want of goods and ammunition," besides being caught between loyalists and patriots who assumed they were hostile.[38] In December a group of Cherokees en route to Richmond elicited the sympathy of William Christian, one of the

[35] Haldimand Papers, 21765:34–35, 21774:7, 115–16; Peter C. Mancall, "The Revolutionary War and the Indians of the Upper Susquehanna Valley," *American Indian Culture and Research Journal* 12 (1988):39–57.

[36] Davies, ed., *Documents*, 17:233; Martha Condray Searcy, *The Georgia-Florida Contest in the American Revolution, 1776–1778* (University, Ala., 1985), p. 110; Richard White, *The Roots of Dependency: Subsistence, Environment, and Social Change among the Choctaws, Pawnees, and Navajos* (Lincoln, Nebr., 1983), pp. 28–29, 98.

[37] Davies, ed., *Documents*, 15:67.

[38] Draper Mss., 11S77–83.

generals who had carried devastation to their towns in the summer of 1776: "The miseries of those people from what I see and hear seem to exceed description; here are men, women & children almost naked; I see very little to cover either sex but some old bear skins, and we are told that the bulk of the nation are in the same naked situation." To make matters worse, Cherokee crops that year had been "worse than ever was known."[39] The next month the Cherokee chief Oconastota begged Col. Joseph Martin for trade at low prices, adding: "All the old warriors are dead. There are now none left to take care of the Cherokees, but you & myself, & for my part I am become very old."[40]

Disease took an additional toll. Smallpox raged at Onondaga in the winter of 1776–77, among the Creeks and Cherokees in the fall of 1779, and among the Chickamaugas and Georgia Indians in the spring of 1780. It struck the Oneida refugees at Schenectady in December 1780 and hit the Genesee Senecas in the winter of 1781–82. Cold and disease killed 300 Indians in the refugee camps at Niagara in the winter of 1779–80.[41]

The Revolutionary era intensified political changes in Indian communities. War chiefs, who traditionally exercised limited and temporary authority, took advantage of endemic warfare and outside support to elevate their status over village chiefs whose counsel held sway in normal circumstances. The abnormal was now normal, and war captains like Pipe and White Eyes of the Delawares spoke with an increasingly loud voice in their nation's councils. Tenhoghskweaghta, an Onondaga chief, explained: "Times are altered with us Indians. Formerly the Warriors were governed by the wisdom of their uncles the Sachems but now they take their own way & dispose of themselves without consulting their uncles the Sachems—while we wish for peace and they for war." Oneida chiefs agreed: "We Sachems have nothing to say to the Warriors. We have given them up for

---

[39] Ibid., 11S10.

[40] Ibid., 12S10.

[41] Papers of the Continental Congress, roll 73, item 153, vol. 3, pp. 59–60, roll 173:551–54; Anthony F. C. Wallace, *The Death and Rebirth of the Seneca* (New York, 1970), p. 195; Brown, *Old Frontiers*, p. 182n; Kellogg, ed., *Frontier Retreat*, p. 189.

the field. They must act as they think wise."[42] New leaders like Pluggy, Joseph Brant, and Dragging Canoe attracted followings that cut across village, tribal, and kinship ties. Older chiefs complained increasingly that they could not control their young men — or as was often the case in the polyglot communities created by the Revolution, control somebody else's young men.

The interference of outsiders further complicated tribal politics and undermined traditional patterns of leadership. The British elevated Mohawk Joseph Brant, protégé of Sir William Johnson and friend of the Prince of Wales, to a position in which he exerted tremendous influence in Indian councils during and after the Revolution.[43] The Americans granted a commission to Joseph Louis Gill of the St. Francis Abenakis, and the British offered to make him head chief of his village, even though Gill pointed out that his son had more right to the position.[44] The Americans appear to have interfered to disrupt traditional succession among the Delawares in favor of pro-American individuals and exerted their influence in the choice of a successor to White Eyes.[45] Among the Creeks, Alexander McGillivray's growing power owed as much to British connections as to his membership in the Wind clan.[46] British, Americans, and Spaniards cultivated client chiefs, and the practice of handing out commissions was so common that it became standard practice to identify Choctaw and Chickasaw leaders as "great medal," "small medal," and "gorget" chiefs. Access to guns and gifts was a key to securing the voluntary obedience

[42] Weslager, *Delaware Indians*, pp. 291–92; Speech of Tenhoghskweaghta at the Johnstown Conference, Mar. 10, 1778, Schuyler Papers, roll 7, box 14; *Papers of Gates*, 6:191.

[43] Haldimand Papers, 21717:39–40. On Joseph Brant see Isabel Thompson Kelsay, *Joseph Brant, 1743–1807: Man of Two Worlds* (Syracuse, N.Y., 1984).

[44] *Journals of the Continental Congress*, 15:1263, 16:334; Fitzpatrick, ed., *Writings of Washington*, 17:68–69; Haldimand Papers, 21772:2–4.

[45] Weslager, *Delaware Indians*, pp. 298, 324 n. 21; Kellogg, ed., *Frontier Retreat*, pp. 419–20n, 376; Kellogg, ed., *Frontier Advance*, p. 194.

[46] Michael D. Green, "Alexander McGillivray," in R. David Edmunds, ed., *American Indian Leaders: Studies in Diversity* (Lincoln, Nebr., 1980), pp. 41–63; John Walton Caughey, *McGillivray of the Creeks* (Norman, Okla., 1938).

that underlay so much of Indian political relations. Daniel Brodhead complained that the Indian chiefs appointed by the British commander at Detroit were "clothed in the most elegant manner," while chiefs appointed by Congress went naked and were scorned by the Indians. A Seneca chief warned the British he could not exert any authority over his warriors unless they provided him with goods to distribute to them.[47]

In addition, at a time when non-Indians in London and Philadelphia, Detroit and Fort Pitt, St. Augustine and Pensacola were making decisions that reverberated through Indian country, non-Indians who lived in Indian country played a growing role in Indian councils. Men like Simon Girty, Matthew Elliott, and Alexander McKee among the Ohio tribes, Alexander Cameron among the Cherokees, and James Colbert among the Chickasaws lived in Indian communities but maintained connections elsewhere and functioned as influential intermediaries, interpreters, leaders of expeditions, and conduits of supply and support.[48] White officers often accompanied and sometimes replaced Indian war chiefs on campaign. The end of the war did not end the presence or the influence of British trader agents, and in the South British companies continued their lucrative Indian trade with the grudging blessing of the Spanish authorities.[49]

The Revolution dislocated thousands of Indian people. Mobility was a fundamental feature of Indian life, but seasonal migration for social or subsistence purposes now gave way to flight from the horrors of war. Indian villages relocated to escape American assault; communities splintered and reassembled,

[47] C.O. 5/81:111, P.R.O.; Davies, ed., *Documents*, 15:153–57; Draper Mss., 3H52; Haldimand Papers, 21783:276–79. For information on Choctaw "medal chiefs," see White, *Roots of Dependency*, chaps. 2–3, and idem, *Middle Ground*, esp. pp. 322, 403–6.

[48] Reginald Horsman, *Matthew Elliott: British Indian Agent* (Detroit, 1964); Colin G. Calloway, "Simon Girty: Interpreter and Intermediary," in James A. Clifton, ed., *Being and Becoming Indian: Biographical Studies of North American Frontiers* (Chicago, 1989), pp. 38–58; C.O. 5/82:114, P.R.O.; Papers of the Continental Congress, roll 104, item 78, vol. 24, pp. 435, 440–43.

[49] William S. Coker and Thomas D. Watson, *Indian Traders of the Southeastern Spanish Borderlands: Panton, Leslie and Company, and John Forbes and Company, 1783–1847* (Pensacola, Fla., 1986).

sometimes amalgamating with other communities. Many
Shawnees migrated from Ohio to Missouri where they took up
lands under the auspices of the Spanish government. By the
end of the Revolution, those Shawnees who remained in Ohio
were crowded into the northwestern reaches of their territory,
and in time they joined other Indians in creating a multitribal,
multivillage community centered on the Auglaize.[50] Indian refugees flooded into Niagara and Schenectady, Detroit and St.
Louis, St. Augustine and Pensacola; Iroquois loyalists relocated
to new homes on the Grand River in Ontario.[51] Stockbridge Indians, unable to secure relief from their former allies after the
Revolution, joined other Christian Indians from New England
in moving to lands set aside for them by the Oneidas. By 1787
"there was a vast concourse of People of many Nations" at New
Stockbridge.[52] Hundreds of refugee Indians drifted west of the
Mississippi and requested permission to settle in Spanish territory. Abenaki Indians, dispersed by previous wars from northern New England into the Ohio Valley, turned up in Arkansas
after the Revolution.[53] Nor were Indian people the only mi-
grants in Indian country. Micmacs in Nova Scotia suffered from
the inroads of Loyalist settlers fleeing the Revolution to the
south; English refugees fleeing Spanish reprisals following the
Natchez rebellion took refuge in Chickasaw country.[54]

Escalating warfare and concomitant economic dislocation
reached even into ritual and ceremonial life. Eastern woodland

[50] Davies, ed., *Documents*, 12:199–203, 214; Galloway, *Old Chillicothe*,
pp. 40–42; Draper Mss., 5D12; Thomas L. McKenney and James Hall, *History
of the Indian Tribes of North America*, 3 vols. (Philadelphia, 1836–44), 1:18;
Calloway, "'We Have Always Been the Frontier,'" pp. 44–45; Helen Hornbeck
Tanner, "The Glaize in 1792: A Composite Indian Community," *Ethnohistory*
25 (1978):15–39.

[51] *Carleton Papers*, roll 17, no. 6742:18, roll 23, no. 6476:3; Charles M.
Johnston, ed., *Valley of the Six Nations: A Collection of Documents on the Indian
Lands of the Grand River* (Toronto, 1964).

[52] Harold Blodgett, *Samson Occom* (Hanover, N.H., 1935), p. 195.

[53] Kinnaird, "Spain in the Mississippi Valley," 3:186, 203–8, 255.

[54] Ruth Holmes Whitehead, ed., *The Old Man Told Us: Excerpts from Micmac
History, 1500–1900* (Halifax, Nova Scotia, 1991), p. 77; Kinnaird, ed., "Spain
in the Mississippi Valley," 3:xi–xii, 15, 32–33, 60.

Indians tried to maintain their social and ceremonial calendar tied to the rhythm of the seasons: in 1778 the Creeks frustrated the British by refusing to take the warpath until after the Green Corn Ceremony.[55] But the endemic warfare of the Revolution threw many traditional religious practices and sacred observances into disarray. Not only did the ancient unity of the Iroquois league crumble but many of the ceremonial forms that expressed that unity were lost. Preparatory war rituals were neglected or imperfectly performed, and the Cayuga leader Kingageghta lamented in 1789 that a "Great Part of our ancient Customs & Ceremonies have, thro' the Loss of Many of our principal men during the War, been neglected & forgotten, so that we cannot go through the whole with our ancient Propriety."[56] The traditional Cherokee year was divided into two seasons, with the winter reserved for war, and returning warriors underwent ritual purification before reentering normal village life. Now war was a year-round activity and Chickamauga communities existed on a permanent war footing. In addition, the Cherokees' six major religious festivals of the year became telescoped into one—the Green Corn festival. Many Cherokees remembered the 1780s as marking the end of the old ways.[57] The loss of sacred power threatened the Indians' struggle for independence, and, according to historian Gregory Evans Dowd, Indian resistance movements of the Revolutionary and post-Revolutionary era drew strength from the recognition that they "could and must take hold of their destiny by regaining sacred power." Indians in the new republic sought to recover through ritual, as well as through war and politics, some of what they had lost.[58] New religious practices also suffered in the Revolution.

[55] Davies, ed., *Documents*, 15:180.

[56] Graymont, *Iroquois in the American Revolution*, p. 224; Kingageghta to Col. Guy Johnson, Jan. 25, 1780, quoted in Dorothy V. Jones, *License for Empire: Colonialism by Treaty in Early America* (Chicago, 1982), p. 131.

[57] Gearing, "Priests and Warriors," pp. 47, 49, 74, 104; compare Dowd, *Spirited Resistance*, p. 10: "The warlike state of man [was] an unnatural state that had been ritually prepared."

[58] Dowd, *Spirited Resistance*, p. 27. Compare Joel W. Martin, *Sacred Revolt: The Muskogees' Struggle for a New World* (Boston, 1991).

Missionary work was disrupted and Christian Mohawks devoted less time to their observances because war occupied their attention. Delaware Moravian communities endured forced relocation at the hands of the British and destruction at the hands of Americans.[59]

For all the devastation they suffered, Indians remained a force to be reckoned with during and after the Revolution. Most survived the destruction of their villages and cornfields. The Shawnees, for example, sustained minimal casualties when the Americans invaded their country, withdrew before the invaders, then returned and rebuilt their villages when the enemy retreated. Untouched food sources beyond the enemy's reach and support from the British at Detroit sustained the Shawnee war effort in the face of repeated assaults. George Rogers Clark recognized the limitations of the American search-and-destroy strategy so long as the Indians could resort to the British supplies at Detroit.[60] Sullivan's campaign too was more effective in burning houses and crops than in killing Iroquois: as one American officer noted, "The nests are destroyed but the birds are still on the wing."[61]

The real disaster of the American Revolution for Indian people lay in its outcome. The Indians were "thunderstruck" when they heard that the British and Americans had signed the Treaty of Paris, without so much as a mention of the tribes. Little Turkey of the Overhill Cherokees concluded, "The peacemakers and our Enemies have talked away our Lands at a Rum Drinking." Alexander McGillivray protested that the Indians had done nothing to permit the king to give away their lands, "unless . . . Spilling our blood in the Service of his Nation can

[59] Papers of the Continental Congress, roll 54, vol. 3, p. 137; Annual Report of the Society for the Propagation of the Gospel (1781), p. 41. On the Moravian experience see, for example, Earl P. Olmstead, *Blackcoats among the Delaware: David Zeisberger on the Ohio Frontier* (Kent, Ohio, 1991), chap. 2.

[60] Calloway, "'We Have Always Been the Frontier,'" p. 47; Draper Mss., 26J27–28; James Alton James, ed., *George Rogers Clark Papers, 1771–1781* (Springfield, Ill., 1912), p. 383.

[61] Cook, ed., *Journals of Sullivan*, p. 101.

be deemed so."[62] Americans gloated to the Shawnees: "Your Fathers the English have made Peace with us for themselves, but forgot you their Children, who fought with them, and neglected you like Bastards."[63]

The Treaty of Paris brought Indians no peace. Some wanted to evacuate along with the redcoats. Others fled their homelands rather than come to terms with their former enemies. Most stayed and adjusted to the new situation.[64] Catawbas derived maximum mileage from their Revolutionary services, but they were an exception.[65] While other Revolutionary veterans were granted land bounties, Indian veterans lost land. Mashpee lost its right of self-government in 1788 when Massachusetts established an all-white board of overseers. Samson Occom and other Indian missionaries at New Stockbridge lamented that "the late unhappy wars have Stript us almost Naked . . . we are truly like the man that fell among Thieves, that was Stript, wounded and left for dead in the high way."[66] Penobscots found their hunting territories invaded by their former allies, and Massachusetts deprived the tribe of most of its land in a series of post-Revolution treaties.[67] The Oneidas, who suffered mightily in the American cause during the war, fared little better than their Cayuga and Seneca relatives in the post-Revolutionary

[62] Colin G. Calloway, "Suspicion and Self-Interest: British-Indian Relations and the Peace of Paris," *Historian* 48 (1985):41–60; idem, *Crown and Calumet: British-Indian Relations, 1783–1815* (Norman, Okla., 1987), pp. 3–23; Haldimand Papers, 21717:146–47; C.O. 5/82:446–47, P.R.O.; Caughey, *McGillivray of the Creeks*, p. 92.

[63] Haldimand Papers, 21779:117.

[64] C.O. 5/82:372–73, P.R.O.; Peter Marshall, "First Americans and Last Loyalists: An Indian Dilemma in War and Peace," in Esmond Wright, ed., *Red, White, and True Blue: The Loyalists in the Revolution* (New York, 1976), pp. 37–38.

[65] Merrell, *Indians' New World*, pp. 215–22.

[66] Calloway, "New England Algonkians"; William De Loss Love, *Samson Occom and the Christian Indians of New England* (Boston, 1899), p. 276.

[67] Papers of the Continental Congress, roll 71, item 58, pp. 59–63, 67–68, 75–79; Colin G. Calloway, ed., *Dawnland Encounters: Indians and Europeans in Northern New England* (Hanover, N.H., 1991), pp. 128–31.

land-grabbing conducted by the federal government, New York state, and individual land companies.[68]

The end of the Revolution opened the gate for a renewed invasion of Indian lands by a flood of backcountry settlers, who broke arrangements of coexistence that had been built up over generations and knocked the heart out of federal attempts to regulate the frontier.[69] Many were Scotch-Irish immigrants coming from a borderlands heritage of their own, where violence had been a way of life for centuries. They had their own experiences of dispossession and their own understanding of clan and kinship, blood feud, and custom, which they applied with grim determination in their new world.[70] American policymakers were no more capable of controlling such citizens than were Indian chiefs of controlling their young men.

A delegation of 260 Iroquois, Shawnee, Cherokee, Chickasaw, Choctaw, and "Loup" Indians visiting St. Louis in the summer of 1784 told the Spanish governor that the Revolution was "the greatest blow that could have been dealt us, unless it had been our total destruction. The Americans, a great deal more ambitious and numerous than the English, put us out of our lands, forming therein great settlements, extending themselves like a plague of locusts in the territories of the Ohio River which we inhabit. They treat us as their cruelest enemies are treated, so that today hunger and the impetuous torrent of war which they impose upon us with other terrible calamities, have brought our villages to a struggle with death."[71]

---

[68] J. David Lehman, "The End of the Iroquois Mystique: The Oneida Land Cession Treaties of the 1780s," *William and Mary Quarterly*, 3d ser. 48 (1990):524–47.

[69] White, *Middle Ground*, chaps. 9–11.

[70] Denys Hays, "England, Scotland, and Europe: The Problem of the Frontier," *Transactions of the Royal Historical Society*, 5th ser. 25 (1975):77–91; David Hackett Fischer, *Albion's Seed: Four British Folkways in America* (New York, 1989); Bernard Bailyn, *Voyagers to the West: A Passage in the Peopling of America on the Eve of the Revolution* (New York, 1986); Forrest McDonald and Ellen Shapiro McDonald, "The Ethnic Origins of the American People, 1790," *William and Mary Quarterly*, 3d ser. 37 (1980):179–99.

[71] Kinnaird, ed., "Spain in the Mississippi Valley," 3:117.

American commissioners demanded lands from the Iroquois at Fort Stanwix in 1784; from the Delawares, Wyandots, and their neighbors at Fort McIntosh in 1785, and from the Shawnees at Fort Finney in 1786, in arrogant confidence that the lands were theirs for the taking by right of conquest. The Treaties of Hopewell, with the Cherokees (1785) and the Choctaws and Chickasaws (1786), confirmed tribal boundaries but did little to preserve them. Cherokee chiefs Corn Tassel and Hanging Maw told Virginian Joseph Martin that "we find your people Settle much Faster on our Lands after A Treaty than Before." Meanwhile, a handful of compliant Creek chiefs made land cessions to Georgia.[72] Confronted with renewed pressures and aggressions, many of the tribes renewed their confederacies. Led by capable chiefs like Brant, Little Turtle, Buckongahelas, Dragging Canoe, and McGillivray, they continued the wars for their lands and cultures into the 1790s and exposed the American theory of conquest for the fiction it was.[73]

In the new world created by the Revolution, new communities emerged, new power blocs developed, and new players called different tunes. Americans in the new republic, like their British and Spanish rivals, were often hard pressed to keep up with it all. Chickamauga Cherokees and militant Shawnees joined hands in common cause even as older chiefs apologized for their behavior. Chickasaws on the Mississippi River had responded to American threats of invasion during the Revolution by offering to meet them halfway: "Take care that we don't serve you as we have served the French before with all their Indians, Send you back without your Heads."[74] Come the end of the Revolution, they sent out very different, and very mixed, signals. By October 1782 Chickasaw headmen were blaming the

[72] All the treaties are reprinted in Colin G. Calloway, ed., *Revolution and Confederation*, Early American Indian Documents: Treaties and Laws, vol. 18 (Frederick, Md., 1993); the Cherokee speech is in Papers of the Continental Congress, roll 69, item 56, p. 417.

[73] Dowd, *Spirited Resistance*, chap. 5, provides details on the post-Revolution confederacy.

[74] Papers of the Continental Congress, reel 65, item 51, vol. 2, pp. 41–42; C.O. 5/81:139–41, P.R.O.

British for putting "the Bloody Tomahawk" into their hands. In July 1783 they sent word that they were being courted on all sides but would wait to hear from Congress "as it is our earnest desire to remain in peace and friendship with our Br[others] the Americans for ever."[75]

Economic realities dictated political and diplomatic choices. The shutting-off of British trade and supplies had to be made up somewhere, especially as the Chickasaws became embroiled in hostilities with the neighboring Kickapoos. The United States represented one source of trade and protection, but only one: Chickasaw delegates from six villages attended the Mobile Congress in 1784, placing themselves under Spanish protection and promising to trade exclusively with Spanish-licensed traders. Two years later Chickasaws promised the Americans the same trade monopoly at the Treaty of Hopewell.[76] But the appearance of a unified and duplicitous Chickasaw foreign policy obscures more complex realities of division and disunity that both limited and expanded diplomatic choices. Chickasaw "factions" crystallized in the early republic: the pro-British group shifted their allegiance to the United States and remained anti-Spanish; the old French party in the nation consorted with Spain; others were ambivalent.[77] The United States was adept at exploiting factionalism within Indian societies, implementing divide-and-rule strategies, but factionalism could prove an asset in frontier diplomacy. Different parties cultivating good relations with different powers prevented domination by any one outside force.[78] The United States had to cut through multiple and shifting Chickasaw foreign policies; the Chickasaws had to deal with shrinking foreign policy options as the United States

[75] Papers of the Continental Congress, roll 104, item 78, vol 24, pp. 445–49; Palmer, ed., *Calendar of Virginia State Papers*, 3:357, 515–17.

[76] Papers of the Continental Congress, roll 69, item 56, p. 113. The Chickasaw villages represented at Mobile are listed in Kinnaird, ed., "Spain in the Mississippi Valley," 3:102.

[77] Arrell M. Gibson, *The Chickasaws* (Norman, Okla., 1971), 75; Caughey, *McGillivray of the Creeks*, pp. 238–40, 265–67, 336–38, 343, 348–49, 351.

[78] White, *Roots of Dependency*, p. 64.

emerged as their only "available" foreign power in the postwar geopolitical contest for the lower Mississippi Valley.

The emergence of the independent United States as the ultimate victor from a long contest of imperial powers reduced Indians to further dependence and pushed them into one of the darkest ages in their history. War, invasion, economic dislocation, political factionalism and fragmentation, disruption of ancient traditions, hunger, disease, and betrayal into the hands of their enemies continued to wreak havoc in Indian country. Seneca communities, in the words of anthropologist Anthony F. C. Wallace, became "slums in the wilderness," wracked by poverty, loss of confidence in traditional certainties, social pathology, violence, alcoholism, witch fear, and disunity.[79]

And yet, in the kaleidoscopic, "all-change" world of the Revolutionary era, there were exceptions and variations. The upheaval generated by the Revolution offered opportunity as well as oppression. Seminole warriors, wearing scarlet coats and British medals, armed with British guns, and executing British strategies, appeared to be dependent on outsiders and vulnerable to a transfer of that dependence to new masters. But the Seminoles fought for their own reasons[80] and maintained their independence against both Spain and the United States. Despite new colors on the map of Florida, political change in Seminole country reflected not new dependence on a foreign power so much as increasing *independence* from the parent Creek confederacy. While Alexander McGillivray continued traditional Creek "play-off" policies with considerable skill, the Seminoles emerged by the new century as a new player and an unknown quantity in the Indian and international diplomacy of the Southeast.[81] Moreover, the American Revolution added to the changing ethnic

[79] Wallace, *Death and Rebirth of the Seneca.*

[80] 80 C.O. 5/79:37, P.R.O.

[81] William C. Sturtevant, "Creek into Seminole," in Eleanor Burke Leacock and Nancy Oestreich Lurie, eds., *North American Indians in Historical Perspective* (New York, 1971), pp. 92–128; Charles H. Fairbanks, "The Ethno-Archaeology of the Florida Seminoles," in Jerald Milanich and Samuel Proctor, eds., *Tacachale: Essays on the Indians of Florida and Southeastern Georgia during the Historic Period* (Gainesville, Fla., 1978), pp. 170–71; Richard Sattler, "*Simi-*

composition of Seminole and Creek communities as African slaves who had fled to the British lines found refuge in Indian country after Yorktown.[82] Many Indian communities succumbed and some disappeared in the new world produced during the Revolution, but others were in process of formation, asserting their separate identity, and doing some nation-building of their own.

The Revolutionary war destroyed many Indian communities—in Iroquoia, the upper Susquehanna Valley, the Smoky Mountains—but new communities—at Grand River, Chickamauga, and the Auglaize—grew out of the turmoil and played a leading role in the Indian history of the new republic. The black years following the Revolution saw powerful forces of social and religious rejuvenation in Handsome Lake's Longhouse religion among the Iroquois, political movements like the northwestern Indian confederacy of the 1780s and 1790s, and multitribal unity under the leadership of Tecumseh and the Shawnee Prophet in the early years of the new century.[83] By the end of the eighteenth century, Indian peoples already had plenty of experience suffering and surviving disasters. They responded to the American Revolution as they had to previous cataclysms: they set about rebuilding their world.

In the long run, however, almost as devastating as the burned towns and crops, the murdered chiefs, the divided councils, the shattered lives, and the towns and forts choked with refugees was the legacy that the war produced in the minds of non-Indians. As Kenneth M. Morrison has pointed out, "For many

---

noli Italwa: Socio-Political Change among the Oklahoma Seminoles between Removal and Allotment, 1836–1905," Ph.D. diss., University of Oklahoma, 1987, pp. 64–84; Brent Richards Weisman, *Like Beads on a String: A Culture History of the Seminole Indians in North Peninsular Florida* (Tuscaloosa, Ala., 1989), pp. 8–10, 80–81.

[82] J. Leitch Wright, Jr., *Creeks and Seminoles: The Destruction and Regeneration of the Muscogulge People* (Lincoln, Nebr., 1986), pp. 84–90.

[83] Wallace, *Death and Rebirth of the Seneca*; Dowd, *Spirited Resistance*; R. David Edmunds, *The Shawnee Prophet* (Lincoln, Nebr., 1983).

Americans, the story of who they are winds back to the Revolution."[84] It is equally true that for many Americans the story of who the Indians are winds back to that time.

Americans at different times have always invented versions of Indians to suit their particular policies and purposes,[85] but the Revolution had particularly enduring influence. Embodied in the document that marked the nation's birth, the image of Indians as vicious enemies of liberty became entrenched in the minds of generations of white Americans. Siding with the redcoats meant opposing the very principles on which the new nation was founded: having fought to prevent American independence, Indians could not expect to share in the society that independence created.

Looking back from nineteenth- and twentieth-century vantage points, their view obscured by chronicles of border warfare, racist writings of Francis Parkman and Theodore Roosevelt, and romanticized depictions of conflict in paintings like John Vanderlyn's *Death of Jane McCrea* (1804) or Carl Wimar's *Abduction of Daniel Boone's Daughter* (1853), Americans telescoped the Revolution and the colonial wars into one long chronicle of bloody frontier conflict. Periods of peace and patterns of interdependence were ignored as racial war took a dominant place in the national mythology. Responsibility for the brutality and destruction of the Revolutionary War on the frontier was placed squarely on the shoulders of the Indians and their British backers. In American eyes, the Gnadenhutten massacre and reports of American atrocities at Onondaga and Piqua paled in comparison with descriptions of white "Women and Children strip'd, scalped, and suffered to welter in their gore," whole families "destroyed, without regard to Age or Sex," infants "torn from their mothers Arms & their Brains dashed

---

[84] Kenneth M. Morrison, "Native Americans and the American Revolution: Historic Stories and Shifting Frontier Conflict," in Frederick E. Hoxie, ed., *Indians in American History* (Arlington Heights, Ill., 1988), p. 95.

[85] Roy Harvey Pearce, *Savagism and Civilization: A Study of the Indian and the American Mind*, rev. ed. (Baltimore, 1965); Robert F. Berkhofer, Jr., *The White Man's Indian: Images of the American Indian from Columbus to the Present* (New York, 1978).

out against Trees."[86] The well-worn story of William Crawford's capture and torture by Delaware warriors in 1782 featured prominently in narratives of border warfare;[87] the more typical peacekeeping efforts and shuttle diplomacy of Cornstalk, White Eyes, and Kayashuta tended to be forgotten. After the war, lurid accounts tended to increase rather than diminish, and the growing popularity of narratives of Indian captivity fueled popular stereotypes. Powerful images and long memories of Indian violence primed subsequent generations for trouble with new Indian groups encountered farther west.[88]

The fiction that all Indians had fought for the British in the Revolution justified massive dispossession of Native Americans in the early republic, whatever their role in the war. As historian Gary B. Nash has pointed out, most Americans were no more willing to extend the Revolution's principles to Indian people than they were to fulfill the Revolutionary ideal of abolishing slavery. Indian land, like African slave labor, was a vital resource for the new republic, and the new republic would not and could not forego its exploitation.[89] A century and a half earlier, Pequot William Apess bitterly understood the extent to which the Revolution excluded African Americans and Native Americans from the republican principles on which it was based. Referring to the guardian system reinstituted by Massachusetts after the war, he wrote, "The whites were no sooner free themselves, than

[86] *Virginia Magazine of History and Biography* 27 (1919): 316; Palmer, ed., *Calendar of Virginia State Papers*, 2:48.

[87] Archibald Loudon, ed., *A Selection of Some of the Most Interesting Narratives, of Outrages Committed by the Indians, in Their Wars with the White People* . . . (1808; reprint ed., New York, 1971).

[88] Compare Peter C. Mancall, *Economic Culture along the Upper Susquehanna, 1700–1800* (Ithaca, N.Y., 1991), pp. 158–59. Russell Bourne's *The Red King's Rebellion: Racial Politics in New England, 1675–1678* (New York, 1990), sees a similar phenomenon in New England after King Philip's War. John D. Unruh, Jr., *The Plains Across: The Overland Emigrants and the Trans-Mississippi West, 1840–1860* (Urbana, Ill., 1979), chap. 5, esp. pp. 120–21, 136.

[89] Gary B. Nash, "The Forgotten Experience: Indians, Blacks, and the American Revolution," reprinted in Richard D. Brown, ed., *Major Problems in the Era of the American Revolution* (Lexington, Mass., 1992), pp. 277–83.

they enslaved the poor Indians."[90] Other groups in American society—women and industrial laborers as well as African slaves—found that the victory in the War for Independence for them meant continued, if not increased, dependence.[91] But most Native Americans found that, as their land became the key to national, state, and individual wealth, the new republic was less interested in their dependence than in their absence.

Having fought against the republic at its birth, Indians continued to fight against the very civilization on which the republic prided itself. Outright military resistance gave way to more subtle forms of cultural resistance, but that only reinforced the inherited view that Indians fought against civilized people and civilized ways. As Bernard W. Sheehan has pointed out, the so-called philanthropists of the new nation were almost more deadly than Indian-hating and land-hungry frontiersmen, since they demanded that Indians commit cultural suicide: "Philanthropy had in mind the disappearance of an entire race."[92] If Indian country were to continue to exist, it must do so beyond the Mississippi. Artistic depictions of Indian people showed them retreating westward, suffused in the heavy imagery of setting suns, as they faded from history.[93]

Confronting the question of where Indian people fit in the new republic, Americans looked back to the Revolution and found their answer to be explicitly negative. Indians belonged to the past, and it was a violent past.[94] A future of peace and prosperity held no place for them. Indian people survived the

[90] Barry O'Connell, ed., *On Our Own Ground: The Complete Writings of William Pess, a Pequot* (Amherst, Mass., 1992), pp. lxix, lxxiii, 239–40.

[91] For example, Elaine F. Crane, "Dependence in the Era of Independence: The Role of Women in a Republican Society," in Jack P. Greene, ed., *The American Revolution: Its Character and Limits* (New York, 1987), pp. 253–75.

[92] Bernard W. Sheehan, *Seeds of Extinction: Jeffersonian Philanthropy and the American Indian* (1973; reprint ed., New York, 1974), pp. 277–78.

[93] For example, Rick Stewart, Joseph D. Ketner II, and Angela L. Miller, *Carl Wimar: Chronicler of the Missouri River Frontier* (Fort Worth, Tex., 1991), plates 1–2, 4–15; Brian W. Dippie, *Catlin and His Contemporaries: The Politics of Patronage* (Lincoln, Nebr., 1990), plate 12.

[94] Pearce, *Savagism and Civilization*, pp. 154, 160.

Revolution and, as they had in the past, proceeded to build new worlds on the ruins of old worlds. But in American eyes their continuing struggles to survive as Indians guaranteed their exclusion from the new nation. The United States looked forward increasingly to a new world without Indians.

I

Patterns of Interaction

REGINALD HORSMAN

The Indian Policy of an "Empire for Liberty"

AMERICAN INDIAN POLICY in the years immediately following the Revolution lacked both practicality and a sense of principle. Congress, by taking the position that in aiding the British the Indians had lost any right to lands within American territory, ignored colonial precedent in failing to acknowledge any Indian right of soil and ignored the reality that most Indians westward to the Mississippi River had played no part in the Revolution. The Indian policy shaped by congressional committees between 1783 and 1786 was intended both to provide land for the settlers advancing beyond the Appalachians and to help solve the nation's financial problems by the sale of western lands. The main federal interest was northwest of the Ohio, because the pattern of state land cessions meant that a federal domain was being created in the Old Northwest while the land south of the Ohio remained in the possession of the individual states. It was hoped that Indian cessions north of the river would provide the lands that would provide a source of income for the new federal government.

The treaties that were signed between 1784 and 1786 to obtain land northwest of the Ohio conceded no remaining Indian right of soil in the land east of the Mississippi River. Indians at these treaties were told that the British had ceded this land to the United States and that as the Indians had been allied with the British in the Revolution, they could now be expelled from American territory if the United States so desired. Shocked Indian leaders signed the treaties, but returned to their villages to ignore them and to prepare for war. The British still controlled the land on the southern fringe of the Great Lakes, and British Indian agents and traders denied the contention that the British grant of sovereignty had also meant the grant of the

Indian right of soil. The impoverished, ill-armed United States did not have the means to carry out the policy of force that it had adopted.[1]

While the federal government acted irrationally in the North, southerners pressed forward both in the backwoods and in their state legislatures. Georgia and North Carolina had not ceded their western claims, and, like the federal government, they acted as though they could ignore Indian desires. In the years after the war Georgia avoided the strong general Creek aversion to further land cessions by signing treaties with the few chiefs who were willing to cede land. North Carolina issued land warrants with no regard for Indian land claims.[2]

In the mid-1780s warfare swept the western borders of the new nation. With only one regular regiment under arms and no money to raise any others, the government of the Confederation did not have the means to carry out the policy of naked force that dominated Indian relations. The Indian policy that had been shaped in the two years after the end of the war provoked Indian hostility, disappointed the states and their settlers, and failed to achieve its objectives of providing land for settlement while easing the financial problems of the federal government.

The nature of postwar Indian policy stemmed from the hatreds generated by Indian warfare during the Revolution, an overconfidence produced by victory over the British, and from the arrogance with which the congressional committees shaped policy. Benjamin Lincoln, who had been appointed to the newly created position of secretary at war in 1781, had done little to shape Indian policy. After his resignation in October 1783, Congress took almost a year and a half to name his successor.[3] Confederation Indian policy was under the direction of a weak Congress and its committees, both of which were constantly fluctuating in membership.

[1] See Reginald Horsman, *Expansion and American Indian Policy, 1783–1812* (East Lansing, Mich., 1967), pp. 3–31; also Dorothy V. Jones, *License for Empire: Colonialism by Treaty in Early America* (Chicago, 1982), pp. 120–56.

[2] Horsman, *Expansion and American Indian Policy*, pp. 24–28.

[3] See Harry M. Ward, *The Department of War, 1781–1795* (Pittsburgh, 1962), pp. 7–8, 40–41, 50–54.

A turning point in post-Revolutionary Indian policy came with the appointment of Henry Knox as secretary at war in March 1785. In the waning years of the Confederation, Knox took the lead in outlining an Indian policy for the new nation, and from 1789, while serving as secretary of war under Washington, he used the new powers given to the central government by the Constitution to shape the policies that guided governmental relationships with the Indians until the 1820's. Substantial aspects of his policies shaped formal relationships with the Indians throughout the nineteenth century.

Knox had no doubt that American settlers would continue their advance across the Mississippi Valley, but he hoped that this advance could be pursued without excessive cost, without general warfare, and in a manner that would reflect credit on the government. By the time he left office at the end of 1794, his policies were in the process of being adopted. They achieved their fullest and best-known expression in the presidency of Thomas Jefferson. Their ultimate failure is revealing of the eighteenth-century beliefs that produced them, of the desire for land that characterized the actions of Europeans in America and throughout the world, and of the ethnocentrism with which Europeans approached all other peoples.

Knox had an unlikely background for a framer of early American Indian policy. Born in Massachusetts, he had been obliged to make his own way from an early age. He earned his living in bookselling, first working in a bookstore and later owning one. He read widely, often on military matters, but it is clear from his later pronouncements on Indian affairs that he also imbibed an Enlightenment philosophy of human progress. Knox left his bookstore to plunge into the military actions of the Revolution, and though he had later acted as an Indian commissioner for Massachusetts, he was chosen as secretary at war because of his first-class military credentials, not because of any special knowledge of the American Indian. But he made use of the office to change the course of American Indian policy.[4]

---

[4] For Henry Knox's early life, see North Callahan, *Henry Knox: General Washington's General* (New York, 1958). His career as secretary of war is discussed in Ward, *Department of War*. There is a discussion of Knox and Indian policy in

Knox quickly demonstrated a willingness to acknowledge the realities of the situation in the transappalachian West. He also exhibited a desire to rise above pragmatic considerations to frame policies that he thought would better represent the ideals of the young republic. It became quite obvious in 1786 and 1787 that postwar Indian policies were a complete failure. Indian tribes resisted the advance of the frontier throughout the West, and the Confederation government did not have the means to impose a military solution. The United States fully intended to advance its settlements across the eastern half of the Mississippi Valley—the Northwest Ordinance of July 1787 made that quite clear—but the existing policies toward the Indians were doing little to achieve that objective.

In the summer of 1787, while the delegates in Philadelphia shaped a constitution that would ensure a far more centralized control of Indian affairs, Henry Knox began to suggest a revised approach to Indian relations and expansion. He warned Congress that the country did not have the money to provide the troops necessary to protect the frontiers from Indian attacks. He was perturbed at the growth of an Indian confederacy in the Northwest, and he argued that the United States should abandon its position that the land westward to the Mississippi already belonged to the United States and return to the pre-Revolutionary practice of buying the Indian right of soil.[5]

In January 1789 this recommendation was followed at the treaties of Fort Harmar. The land in the Old Northwest that in the earlier postwar treaties had been demanded from the Indians by right of conquest was now purchased. This nominal purchase did little to quell Indian resistance, for the tribes of the Old Northwest were now determined to block American expansion at the Ohio River and were encouraged by the lack of effective American military action in the 1780s.[6]

John Harder, "The Indian Policy of Henry Knox, 1785–1794," M.A. thesis, University of Wisconsin, Milwaukee, 1964.

[5] Knox to Congress, July 10, 20, 1787, *Journals of the Continental Congress, 1774–1789*, 34 vols. (Washington, D.C., 1904–37), 32:327–32, 33:388–91.

[6] Horsman, *Expansion and American Indian Policy*, pp. 42–49. See also Randolph C. Downes, *Council Fires on the Upper Ohio: A Narrative of Indian Affairs in the Upper Ohio Valley until 1795* (Pittsburgh, 1940), pp. 305–24.

In the spring of 1789, with the beginning of the government under the Constitution, Knox felt that he could now take stronger steps to redirect American Indian policy along lines he believed to be more practical and more honorable. In May, in reporting on treaties with the northwestern Indians, he observed that the Indians were "greatly tenacious of their lands, and generally do not relinquish their right, excepting on the principle of a specific consideration expressly given for the purchase of the same." To violate colonial and English precedents in this regard, he argued, would merely mean "an expense greatly exceeding the value of the object."[7]

Knox, unlike most of those actually engaged in the westward advance, showed a willingness to recognize that Indian hostility was often stimulated by white actions. Writing of the chronic warfare between the Kentuckians and the Wabash tribes since 1783, he commented in June 1789 that the "injuries and murders have been so reciprocal, that it would be a point of critical investigation to know on which side they have been the greatest." During the past year, he wrote, the Kentuckians had killed "a number of peaceful Piankeshaws, who prided themselves in their attachment to the United States."[8]

Knox warned Washington and Congress that unless prompt action was taken there would be general war among the northwestern Indians. He saw two alternatives for action. The United States could act by raising an army and "extirpating the refractory tribes entirely," or treaties of peace could establish boundaries by which Indian rights would be clearly defined and by which provision would be made for punishing whites who violated these rights. Knox addressed the first alternative—that of the use of force—on both moral and pragmatic grounds. It could be questioned, Knox wrote, whether the United States had "a clear right, consistently with the principles of justice and the laws of nature, to proceed to the destruction or expulsion of the savages, on the Wabash," even if the force were easily

[7] Knox to George Washington, May 23, 1789, *Annals of Congress*, 1st Cong., 1st sess., pp. 40–41.

[8] The material in this and the following four paragraphs is from Knox to Washington, June 15, 1789, *American State Papers: Indian Affairs*, 2 vols. (Washington, D.C., 1832–34), 1:12–14.

attainable. Any nation "solicitous of establishing its character on the broad basis of justice" should reject propositions to benefit itself by injuring a neighboring community, "however contemptible and weak it might be, either with respect to its manners or power." His conclusion was that the Indians, "being the prior occupants, possess the right of the soil. It cannot be taken from them unless by their free consent, or by the right of conquest in case of a just war. To dispossess them on any other principle, would be a gross violation of the fundamental laws of nature, and of that distributive justice which is the glory of a nation."

Having expressed moral objections to a policy of naked force, Knox observed that such a policy was in any case financially impossible. He estimated that the United States would need 2,500 regulars to wage war on the Wabash Indians. There were less than 600 regulars on the frontier; to raise and equip another 1,900 would cost $200,000. This he thought was not possible given the variety of demands on the new government.

Knox admitted that if the government were to listen only to the frontiersmen, then an expedition would be essential regardless of the cost. He said that the frontiersmen, from the killing of their relatives, had the strongest prejudice against the Indians. But from a wider view, Knox argued, the nation had to be influenced "by reason, and the nature of things, not by its resentments." Both "policy and justice" dictated an attempt at negotiation. Knox argued that henceforth "the dignity and interest of the nation" would be advanced by making "the Indian right to the lands they possess" the basis of future relations with them.

Yet though Knox was concerned for what he conceived of as justice as well as practicality, his suggestions were not intended as a means of permanent tribal ownership of any of the lands on which the Indians lived but rather as a means by which he believed the United States could more honorably and cheaply remove them. Knox estimated that the Indian population in the eastern half of the Mississippi Valley south of the Great Lakes was some 76,000. He thought that with a policy of conciliation rather than force the average annual cost of managing relations with the Indians over the next fifty years would be $15,000. A policy of "coercion and oppression," he argued, would probably cost much more, and "the blood and injustice which would stain the character of the nation, would be beyond all pecuniary calculation." Conciliation would be more honorable, it would be cheaper, and it would also lead to acquisition of Indian lands. Knox, repeating an argument used by future Secretary of War Timothy Pickering in the mid-1780s,[9] said that as whites approached the boundaries made by treaties, the game would be diminished, and as the land was valuable to the Indians only as hunting grounds, they would be willing to sell additional land "for small considerations." When fifty years had passed, Knox argued, the Indians, "by the invariable operation of the causes" that had always existed in their relations with the whites, would be reduced to a very small number. Knox was soon to decide that this also was discreditable to a new republic and was to suggest policies to escape what he viewed as otherwise inevitable.

A month after Knox had used his report on the Wabash Indians to suggest a revised approach to American Indian policy, he continued to urge his policy of cheap and honorable land acquisition in reporting on the Creeks. As in discussing the Wabash Indians, Knox advanced the alternatives of force or negotiation and reached the same conclusion as he had about the northern Indians. War would be both costly and dishonorable. In this report on the southern Indians, he also strongly emphasized the necessity of centralizing Indian affairs under the federal government. The United States, he argued, should assert that the Indians possessed the right of soil of their own lands and could not be divested of it unless in treaties under the authority of the federal government. The independent tribes of Indians should be regarded as foreign nations, not as subjects of any particular state. Each state should retain the right of preemption for land within its limits, but the federal government should have the sole right to make treaties on which depended peace or war. Knox argued that federal troops should police Indian boundaries that southern pioneers had so often violated in the 1780s. The westward movement of settlers could not be prevented, but Knox believed that it could be restrained and regu-

[9] Timothy Pickering to Rufus King, June 1, 1785, Charles R. King, ed., *The Life and Correspondence of Rufus King*, 6 vols. (New York, 1894–1900), 1:104–5.

lated by postponing new purchases of territory and by preventing intrusions on Indian lands.[10]

Since reporting on the Wabash Indians, Knox had clearly given additional thought to the somber conclusion he had drawn about the inevitability of Indian disappearance, for in this report on the Creeks he now suggested what he regarded as a far more moral alternative. The Indians, he argued, could be saved by the process of civilization. In the most settled states in America the Indians had become extinct. Unless changes were made, he wrote, the same fate would befall all the Indians east of the Mississippi. "How different would be the sensation of a philosophic mind to reflect," wrote Knox, "that, instead of exterminating a part of the human race by our modes of population, we had persevered, through all difficulties, and at last had imparted our knowledge of cultivation and the arts to the aboriginals of the country, by which the source of future life and happiness had been preserved and extended."

Knox argued that previously it had been considered impracticable to civilize the Indians of North America, but he considered this opinion "more convenient than just." Although the civilization of the Indians would be difficult and require patience, wrote Knox, it was possible; to deny that would be "to suppose the human character under the influence of such stubborn habits as to be incapable of melioration or change—a supposition entirely contradicted by the progress of society, from the barbarous ages to its present degree of perfection." Here Knox was writing in the full Enlightenment tradition of faith in progress, as well as in the equally strong ethnocentric tradition that dominated European and American thought until the end of the nineteenth century.

To begin the process of civilization, Knox suggested that, at first, presents of sheep or other domestic animals could be made to chiefs or their wives, and they should be sent individuals to teach the use of them. At the same time, to help attach the Indians to the United States, the British practice of presenting chiefs with medals and uniforms should be followed.

[10] The material in this and the following three paragraphs is in Knox to Washington, July 7, 1789, *American State Papers: Indian Affairs*, 1 : 52–54.

Missionaries, well-supplied with implements of husbandry and livestock, should be sent to reside among the tribes. These missionaries should not trade or buy lands from the Indians— "they should be their friends and fathers." Even if this did not fully civilize the Indians, it would probably have the effect of attaching them to the United States. Such policies, Knox argued, would be highly economical compared to a policy of coercion.

In the first three months of the new government under the Constitution, Knox had proposed a new framework for American Indian policy. Land acquisition was to be centralized under the federal government, the Indian right of soil was to be acknowledged and purchased, boundary lines were to be enforced by federal troops, and pioneers prevented from illegally entering Indian territory.

To Knox, much of this represented a return to colonial practice, but he had gone further by emphasizing that the new republic had an additional responsibility. Colonial settlement had largely resulted in Indian extinction in the eastern states. Knox believed that a new republic inspired by Enlightenment ideals should attempt to reverse what had previously been the inevitable accompaniment of the frontier advance. With an Enlightenment faith in progress, and in the advance of society from savagery to civilization, combined with an ethnocentric view of non-European peoples that was an integral part of Enlightenment thought, Knox wanted to justify American expansion over Indian lands by conferring what he believed were the inestimable advantages of the American version of European civilization. The Indians would give up tribalism and their existing way of life and adopt private property and the lifestyle of American pioneer farmers.

Knox served as secretary of war until the end of 1794, and during that time he continued to express his faith in the policies he had outlined after inheriting the chaos of post-Revolutionary Indian policy. In a message to the northwestern Indians in April 1792 he told them that the United States wanted the opportunity of giving "all the blessings of civilized life, of teaching you to cultivate the earth, and raise corn; to raise oxen, sheep, and other domestic animals; to build comfortable houses, and to educate your children, so as ever to dwell upon the land."[11] In the same year he suggested to his friend the Rev. David McClure that he favored a bounty to encourage young men to marry Indian women. He also favored a plan for young women who had "strayed from virtuous paths" in the large cities, but had now repented, to marry Indian men. His object was to encourage the Indians to become farmers.[12] Like all framers of American Indian policy in these years, he chose to discuss the eastern Indians as hunters, ignoring the extensive agriculture among the woodland tribes.

In advocating his new Indian policy, Knox often indicated that it was not simply its supposed greater economy and convenience that inspired him. Like so many other leaders of the Revolutionary generation, he exhibited a belief in the uniqueness of the American republican experiment and the hope that it would help to shape a better world. Knox wanted the United States to expand, but he also wanted it to be respected as a nation inspired by what was right as well as by what was successful. Like Jefferson, Knox hoped that the United States would not be a traditional European-style nation-state, conducting its affairs in the tradition of Realpolitik.

Even after Josiah Harmar's failure in 1790, and Arthur St. Clair's disastrous defeat of 1791, Knox retained his hope for a new direction in Indian relations. Writing to Anthony Wayne in January 1793, he complained that "if our modes of population and War destroy the tribes the disinterested part of mankind and posterity will be apt to class the effects of our Conduct and that of the Spaniards in Mexico and Peru together."[13] He echoed this fear when he had already submitted his letter of resignation. "It is a melancholy reflection," he wrote to President Washington in December 1794, "that our modes of population have been more destructive to the Indian natives than the conduct of the conquerors of Mexico and Peru. The evidence of

[11] Knox to the Northwestern Indians, Apr. 4, 1792, ibid., 1:230.

[12] See Callahan, *Knox*, p. 322.

[13] Knox to Anthony Wayne, Jan. 5, 1793, Richard C. Knopf, ed., *Anthony Wayne, a Name in Arms: Soldier, Diplomat, Defender of Expansion Westward of a Nation* (Pittsburgh, 1960), p. 165.

this is the utter extirpation of nearly all the Indians in most populous parts of the Union. A future historian may mark the causes of this destruction of the human race in sable colors." His remedy for this bleak future was a steady persistence in the civilization policy, combined with restraint on the excesses of the frontier settlers. His final recommendations were for a line of military posts on the frontier within Indian territory (with Indian permission) to try to keep Indians and hostile frontiersmen apart. He wanted the posts to be in Indian territory so that they would be outside state jurisdiction. He also wanted the implementation of plans for government trade with the Indians and the appointment of agents to reside in the principal Indian towns. He expressed the hope that the experiment of "a system of justice and humanity" would continue and that this would bring "honorable" tranquillity to America's frontiers.[14]

Knox did not obtain honorable tranquillity for the American frontier, either while he was serving as secretary of war or in the future. While he still served under Washington, hostilities were almost continuous. In both the Northwest and the Southwest, Indian tribes were disgusted at the intrusion of settlers into the rich lands of the Mississippi Valley and at the total disregard for Indian rights that had been shown after the Revolution. They also resented and resisted the continuous pressure for land cessions by both the state and federal governments. Only after Wayne's victory at Fallen Timbers in 1794 was there to be a temporary peace in the Old Northwest. In the South peace came as the population increases in Kentucky and Tennessee made Indian attacks increasingly difficult.

Yet in spite of the chronic fighting of the first half of the 1790s, Knox's suggestions for a new Indian policy were largely implemented in the two Washington administrations. In dealing with the Mississippi Valley frontier, the federal government began to achieve success in asserting its authority over the states and over the settlers themselves. The Indian right of soil was

[14] Knox to Washington, Dec. 29, 1794, *American State Papers: Indian Affairs*, 1:543–44. He submitted his letter of resignation on December 28. See Ward, *Department of War*, p. 183.

recognized, and the government began to curb the worst violations of boundary lines. In the Trade and Intercourse Acts of 1790, 1793, and 1796 the violation of Indian territory was forbidden, provision was made for the punishment of crimes committed in Indian country, and licences for trade were required. Provision was also made in the 1793 act for the distribution of useful articles to the Indians and for the appointment of agents to help in promoting the civilization policy.

The civilization policy had been introduced early in the first Washington administration. Beginning with the Creek treaty of August 1790, the promotion of agriculture was provided for in Indian treaties. Attempts at civilization now became an established part of American policy. Also, after Knox left office, Congress provided for trade measures that he had advocated. It was hoped that the factory system of trading posts established in April 1796 would win the allegiance of the Indians by fair trading practices. These posts would also further land acquisition and civilization policies by cultivating tastes that it was hoped the Indians would satisfy by the cession of lands and the adoption of private property.[15]

Knox's dream of simultaneously satisfying the national desire for land and the republican desire for virtue was equally attractive to President Thomas Jefferson. Indeed, Bernard W. Sheehan has argued that Jeffersonian concepts of "the Indian and his relationship to civilization" dominated the entire period from the Revolution to Removal. Jefferson looked forward to a time when European Americans would spread throughout the American continent and believed that such expansion was desirable both for the United States and the rest of the world. He also believed that his "empire for liberty" would ensure the success of the American republican experiment by providing the land for a nation of yeoman farmers.[16] Yet Jefferson was also far

[15] For a full discussion of the trade and intercourse acts and efforts to bring rationality to Indian affairs, see Francis Paul Prucha, *American Indian Policy in the Formative Years: The Indian Trade and Intercourse Acts, 1790–1834* (Cambridge, Mass., 1962).

[16] See Thomas Jefferson to James Madison, Apr. 27, 1809, Andrew A. Lipscomb and Albert Ellery Bergh, eds., *The Writings of Thomas Jefferson*, 20 vols. (Washington, D.C., 1903–4), 12:277.

more a man of the Enlightenment than Knox. He believed that the advance of the human race from savagery to civilization was about to achieve its perfection in the United States. His doubts about the capabilities of the slaves who surrounded him at Monticello were not present when he wrote of distant Indians. In the 1780s he had stated that the "proofs of genius given by the Indians of N. America, place them on a level with Whites in the same uncultivated state."[17]

At the beginning of his second term as president, after he had initiated a process of the rapid acquisition of remaining Indian lands east of the Mississippi, Jefferson still wrote of the Indians in Enlightenment terms as endowed "with the faculties and the rights of men, breathing an ardent love of liberty and independence." As the Indians were now being overwhelmed "and reduced within limits too narrow for the hunter's state," Jefferson wrote, "humanity enjoins us to teach them agriculture and the domestic arts." This would encourage the Indians "to that industry which would enable them to maintain their place in existence and to prepare them in time for that state of society which to bodily comfort adds the improvement of the mind and morals."[18] Immersed in Enlightenment optimism and ethnocentrism, Jefferson envisioned Indians willingly accepting a different way of life as white expansion confined them on smaller and smaller areas of land.

Henry Dearborn, Jefferson's secretary of war, fully accepted Jefferson's Enlightenment vision of a total absorption of Indians within a "higher" culture. In 1803, after hearing of Creek adoption of some white ways, he argued that it showed that all the differences between "what are called Savages and civilized people" could be erased.[19] He had earlier told an agent sent into the

---

[17] See Jefferson to Chastellux, June 7, 1785, Julian P. Boyd et al., eds., *The Papers of Thomas Jefferson*, 28 vols. to date (Princeton, 1950–), 8:185; Bernard W. Sheehan, *Seeds of Extinction: Jeffersonian Philanthropy and the American Indian* (Chapel Hill, N.C., 1973), p. 6.

[18] James D. Richardson, ed., *A Compilation of the Messages and Papers of the Presidents*, 20 vols. (New York, 1897–1917), 1:368 (Mar. 4, 1805).

[19] Henry Dearborn to Benjamin Hawkins, May 24, 1803, Record Group 75, War Department, Letters Sent, Indian Affairs, A, 349–51, National Archives, Washington, D.C.

Old Northwest that by introducing useful arts among the Indians, the government wanted "to prepare them for the enjoyment of a higher degree of happiness than any of which they could be susceptible of if left to themselves."[20] Jefferson and Dearborn were able to convince themselves that the acquisition of Indian land was an essential step in bringing the Indians to adopt what they considered a better and happier way of life.

Jefferson took any evidence of changes in the Indian way of life in these years to mean that a process of general assimilation was about to take place. In his first annual message, he wrote of Indians becoming more and more aware of the advantages of farming and household skills over hunting and fishing,[21] and in spite of ample empirical evidence to the contrary, he continued to express such beliefs to the end of his presidency. From time to time he also echoed the earlier suggestion of Knox that intermarriage would complete the transformation from an Indian to a European way of life. This theme was in his mind at the very end of his presidency, at a time when Indian resistance to his policies was reaching a peak. In December 1808 he told a delegation of Delawares, Mohicans, and Munsees to give up hunting and to take up farming. "You will unite yourselves with us, and we shall all be Americans. You will mix with us by marriage. Your blood will run in our veins and will spread with us over this great island." A month later he told another Indian delegation: "In time you will be as we are: you will become one people with us; your blood will mix with ours."[22]

The reality of expansion was nothing like the mutually beneficial transfer of lands envisioned by Knox, Jefferson, and Dearborn. In spite of the new policies, the advance of the American frontier in these first years under the new Constitution brought extensive Indian suffering and widespread Indian resistance. Some Indians began to adapt to the ways of the white invaders, but more strove desperately to retain their lands and their way of life. Faced by resistance, Jefferson was prepared to ride roughshod over Indian desires. Convinced that future American po-

[20] Dearborn to William Lyman, July 14, 1801, ibid., A, 91–97.

[21] Richardson, ed., *Messages and Papers*, 1:314 (Dec. 8, 1801).

[22] War Department, Letters Sent, Indian Affairs, B, 395–96, 412–13.

litical stability and safety required the rapid acquisition of lands westward to the Mississippi, he urged his agents to find all possible means to hasten the transfer of Indian land. Veiled or overt threats, bribery, and relentless negotiation brought huge Indian cessions of land both north and south of the Ohio. In a famous letter to Gov. William Henry Harrison of the Indiana Territory, Jefferson urged him to make use of government trading houses to encourage influential Indians to contract debts more than they could pay. These debts could then be satisfied by land cessions.[23]

Jefferson told Benjamin Hawkins in February 1803 that the furtherance of agriculture and household industries among the Creeks would enable them to live on much smaller portions of land, making more land available for the Americans who needed it. To Jefferson, this transaction was of mutual benefit and should be encouraged by all interested in the best interests of the Indians. "I feel it consistent with pure morality," he wrote, "to lead them towards it, to familiarize them to the idea that it is for their interest to cede lands at times to the US, and for us thus to procure gratifications to our citizens, from time to time, by new acquisitions of land."[24]

By 1806 southern Indians were refusing to cede any more land. The Creeks, Cherokees, Choctaws, and Chickasaws were still powerful enough to put up a powerful resistance to American expansion, and though the northern tribes continued cessions until 1809, Tecumseh and the Prophet were directly challenging both the land acquisition and civilization policies of the United States government. While Tecumseh reacted to federal efforts to stress individual land ownership by arguing that even single tribes had no right to sell lands that belonged to all the Indians, the Prophet asked his followers to cast off all aspects of white civilization. While Jefferson ignored evidence of the Indian rejection of basic federal policies, Governor Harrison simply blamed northwestern Indian resistance on the machina-

[23] Jefferson to William Henry Harrison, Feb. 27, 1803, Logan Esarey, ed., *Messages and Letters of William Henry Harrison*, 2 vols. (Indianapolis, 1922), 1:69–73.

[24] Jefferson to Hawkins, Feb. 18, 1803, Paul Leicester Ford, ed., *The Works of Thomas Jefferson*, 12 vols. (New York, 1904–5), 9:446–48.

tions of British agents. The British were taking advantage of Indian discontent, but the fundamental cause of this discontent was American expansion, not British intrigue.[25]

Knox and Jefferson attempted to bring rationality to American Indian policy. They also hoped to bring justice, morality, and a way in which the pioneer advance would not result in the destruction and disappearance of the Indians. But though the Indians were not to disappear, they were to be decimated by the frontier advance, and most of the survivors of those Indians east of the Mississippi that Knox and Jefferson hoped to save were eventually removed west of the Mississippi. In spite of Knox's hopes, contemporary observers of nineteenth-century Indian policy and future historians were to condemn the destruction brought upon the Indians by the westward advance of the American nation. The rhetoric, and some of the objectives, were humane, the reality was not.

Although both Knox and Jefferson wanted American Indian policy to assume new standards of morality and justice, they were thwarted by the complete ethnocentrism of the Enlightenment view of human progress, by the frontiersmens' desire for land, by the phenomenal rate of population and economic growth in the young United States, and by the desire of most Indians to preserve their lands and their own way of life.

The American belief that their new republic embodied the essence of Enlightenment progress and that the continued advance of human society depended upon the success of the American experiment made continued American growth far more basic to American policy than the attempted transformation of the American Indians. Knox, Jefferson, and others like them wanted a good conscience in regard to the Indians, but they believed that future westward expansion was inevitable and would ultimately justify any short-term suffering. Expansion might be controlled or temporarily checked, but it could not be stopped.

---

[25] After 1805 the correspondence in Esarey, ed., *Messages and Letters of Harrison*, constantly reveals Harrison's determination to blame the British for all aspects of Indian resistance. For the nature of British action among the Indians in these years, see Reginald Horsman, *Matthew Elliott: British Indian Agent* (Detroit, 1964), pp. 157–91.

Those leaders of post-Revolutionary America who wanted morality and justice in Indian relations knew that Indian treaties expressed less than the truth when they said that the Indians had the full right in the future to sell or to refuse to sell the land they retained on their side of the established boundary lines. Even in the early 1790s, when the United States desperately wanted to establish peace with the Indians, negotiators insisted that the government right of preemption should be in every treaty. Those who shaped Indian policy were quite confident that this preemption right could be used when the advance of settlers made it necessary. Either Indians decimated by the white advance would always, as in the past, sell for a small consideration, or, if the new policies of civilization succeeded, it was assumed that the Indians who gave up their tribalism for private property and white mores would give up the extensive hunting lands they no longer required.

A fundamental problem for those who believed that justice and humanity would be served by civilizing the Indians as the frontier advanced was that they grossly underestimated the magnitude of the task of persuading the Indians to give up their own way of life. They were trapped in the assumption that the world exhibited a natural progress from savagery to civilization, that the latter was obviously the preferable state, and that all peoples, if given the opportunity, would be ready and eager to pursue a European-style way of life. This was less pessimistic than the later view that the Indians were doomed to destruction as an inferior race, but it completely misjudged the magnitude of the proposed task. Only small sums were appropriated to further the complex task of assimilation. Confined within the limits of their assumptions, American leaders could not understand the tenacity with which the Indians resisted giving up the way of life they had known.

The American government found that the policies framed after 1789 brought more orderliness to the frontier advance, but these policies did not prevent periodic warfare, nor did they preserve any sizable numbers of transformed Indians as individual farmers on their lands. Time after time, when Indians learned that strict, protected boundaries were only temporary, younger warriors attempted to resist by war the inevitable government demands for more land. The policies formulated in the first two decades of the new nation facilitated rather than curbed American expansion.

Another fundamental problem with the policies first shaped and implemented by Knox and Jefferson in the years before the War of 1812 was that their policies could not effectively curb the anti-Indian attitudes generated among frontiersmen by the Indian-white struggle for land. The American federal system was a system created for expansion. The territorial system set up in the 1780s was adopted by the new government. Those frontiersmen who fought, and often came to hate, the Indians soon had their senators and representatives in Washington.

In the thirty years after the adoption of the Constitution the nation was still dominated by politicians from states with few Indians left within their boundaries. The transatlantic ideas of the European Enlightenment could flourish east of the Appalachians in areas where Indians no longer held sizable areas of land or presented any threat. Of the states along the eastern seaboard, only Georgia still had most of its lands in the possession of the Indians, and in that state frontier, not Enlightenment, attitudes dominated the arguments of its politicians. Henry Knox and Thomas Jefferson had no constituents anxious to advance onto Indian lands, and in their states the hatreds generated by earlier fights for land had faded.

The politicians from the new states of the trans-Mississippi West, like the politicians from the still largely Indian state of Georgia, spoke for those who were still struggling for Indian land and who had immediate memories of the bloodshed that had accompanied white expansion. From the 1740s to the 1790s, warfare had swept the outer edge of the American frontier. As the westerners achieved statehood and developed greater political power, the politicians from older states, who wished to shape a policy that would help Indians as well as whites, found themselves under increasing attack.[26]

---

[26] For a discussion of the shaping of frontier attitudes, see Reginald Horsman, "The Image of the Indian in the Age of the American Revolution," in Francis P. Jennings, ed., *The American Indian and the American Revolution* (Chicago, 1983), pp. 1–11.

The years of conflict from 1809 to 1815 served to confirm the frontiersmen and their representatives in their hatred of the Indians and in their belief that the policies developed by Knox and Jefferson were wrong because they envisioned a future in which transformed Indians would retain land desired by frontier settlers. Frontiersmen did not want Indians, assimilated or not, to remain on the lands they coveted. They were not prepared to separate Indians who were in the process of being assimilated within white society from those who were determined to defend tribal lands and Indian ways of life. When Andrew Jackson retaliated against those Creeks who had attacked white settlers during the War of 1812, he made no distinction between those who were peacefully trying to enter white society and those who were resisting. The treaty of Fort Jackson wrenched huge territories from friend and foe alike.[27]

In the years between 1815 and 1829 the Enlightenment dream that transformed Indians would remain on lands east of the Mississippi by adopting white ways was gradually abandoned. Even Jefferson himself had realized that the all-encompassing demands of the American frontiersmen would be impossible to resist. At the time of the Louisiana Purchase, when he drafted a constitutional amendment that he thought was needed to legitimize the purchase, he included the suggestion that the new domain west of the Mississippi could be used as the place to which the Indians east of the Mississippi could be persuaded to move.[28] The plan was abandoned, along with the proposed constitutional amendment, but it reemerged rapidly after the War of 1812.

Ultimately, removal was defended by American politicians on the grounds that it had become necessary to save eastern Indians shattered and demoralized by prolonged warfare and by the overwhelming advance of white settlers. By this argument, the process of civilization again would become possible in isolated

---

[27] See Robert V. Remini, *Andrew Jackson and the Course of American Empire, 1767–1821* (New York, 1977), pp. 224–33.

[28] See Annie Heloise Abel, "The History of Events Resulting in Indian Consolidation West of the Mississippi," in *Annual Report of the American Historical Association for the Year 1906*, 2 vols. (Washington, D.C., 1908), 1:241–59.

areas beyond the Mississippi. The rhetoric was similar, but the heart had gone out of the Indian policy of Knox and Jefferson.

If the United States government had been dealing only with the region north of the Ohio River, then the argument that removal was necessary to save the Indians might have been valid. The Indians immediately south of the Great Lakes had been decimated and disorganized by the prolonged warfare and by the tide of settlers that had engulfed them. Even friends of the Indian, who had hoped that the Indians could remain on the land as European-style farmers, believed that removal might be in their interest.[29]

But the main political battles surrounding removal were about southern, not northern, Indians. Southern states east of the Mississippi were determined that the Indians in the path of the expanding cotton kingdom should be removed. What particularly disturbed the politicians of these states was that among a sizable minority of Cherokees, the Knox-Jefferson aim of perpetuating Indians on the land by transforming them into white farmers was clearly working. Even though the Creeks had suffered massively as a result of Jackson's campaign in the War of 1812, the main southern tribes were not as demoralized as those in Ohio, Indiana, and Illinois. There were divisions between those who wanted to adapt to white ways and those who wished to reject them, but if the federal government honored its promises there seemed good reason to suppose that many southern Indians could survive successfully on their existing lands. These were not totally demoralized tribes unable to provide for themselves in their present state, nor were they attacking advancing American settlers. Among them were communities able to compete agriculturally with their white neighbors.

In July 1817, when federal commissioners tried to persuade Cherokees to move to lands west of the Mississippi, the Indians told them: "Our choice is to remain on our lands, and follow the pursuits of agriculture and civilization, as all the Presidents, our fathers, have recommended and advised us to do." If allowed to stay, they said, they hoped that, in time, "our white brothers will

---

[29] See George A. Schultz, *An Indian Canaan: Isaac McCoy and the Vision of an Indian State* (Norman, Okla., 1972), pp. 59–140.

not blush to own us as brothers."[30] Seven years later, when the cabinet discussed intense Georgia pressure for the Indian removal, Secretary of State John C. Calhoun pointed out that the "great difficulty arises from the progress of the Cherokees in civilization. They are now, within the limits of Georgia, about fifteen thousand, and increasing in equal proportion with the whites; all cultivators, with a representative government, judicial courts, Lancaster schools, and permanent property."[31] This represented a success for the policies of Knox and Jefferson, but it was unacceptable to southerners who wanted the Indian lands and to the politicians who represented them.

For ten years after 1815 the executive attempted to deflect the intense southern pressure for the removal of the Indians, but Tennessee and Georgia, the states that took the lead in pressing the federal government, were able to get considerable support from congressional committees dealing with Indian affairs. Generally, Congress was willing to allow the southern states that wanted to remove the Indians to dominate the committees that dealt with Indian affairs.[32]

William H. Crawford, who served as secretary of war under President James Madison, still hoped that assimilation would be possible, though he was disappointed by the extent of Indian resistance to the idea.[33] Crawford came under most pressure from the state of Tennessee. In the years immediately after the War of 1812, Gov. Joseph McMinn and Andrew Jackson urged the federal government to take action to reduce Indian landholdings in Tennessee. Jackson argued that the government was so anxious to avoid injustice to the Indians "as even to be unjust to themselves." Governor McMinn believed that the solution

---

[30]*American State Papers: Indian Affairs*, 2:142–43.

[31] Charles F. Adams, ed., *Memoirs of John Quincy Adams*, 12 vols. (Philadelphia, 1874–77), 6:272 (Mar. 29, 1824).

[32] See Reginald Horsman, *The Origins of Indian Removal, 1815–1824*, Clarence M. Burton Memorial Lecture, 1969 (East Lansing, Mich., 1970), pp. 12–15.

[33] See *American State Papers: Indian Affairs*, 2:26–28 (report of Mar. 13, 1816).

was to persuade the Cherokee to remove to lands beyond the Mississippi.[34]

As secretary of war under President James Monroe, John C. Calhoun was convinced that the Indians would be better off beyond the Mississippi, but he opposed forcing the Indians to make such a move. Both Congress and the executive, however, moved ahead with plans to persuade Indians to exchange their lands in the East for lands west of the Mississippi. The government hoped to do this by assuring the Indians that if they ceded their tribal lands, individual Indians would be able to remain on privately owned farms, but it soon became apparent that states east of the Mississippi were reluctant to give rights of permanent occupancy to any Indians.[35]

The government had some minor success in persuading Indians to move beyond the Mississippi, but most would not move, and in the 1820s Georgia took the lead in pressing for Indian Removal, with strong backing from Tennessee, Mississippi, and Alabama. Georgia politicians felt that they had a particularly strong case for demanding federal action because on the cession of Georgian land claims in 1802 the federal government had promised to extinguish Indian land claims within the state.[36] This promise had helped to get a Georgia cession, but, as Georgia interpreted it, it directly contradicted the contemporary Jeffersonian promises to perpetuate the Indians upon the land as they adopted white civilization. In the 1820s the federal government was bitterly assailed by Georgia politicians. It was made quite clear that Georgia wanted no Indians within the state, whether or not they had agreed to adopt the ways of white society.[37]

In this period between 1815 and 1829, as the Indian policy of Knox and Jefferson was challenged, there were definite signs that the Enlightenment belief that Indians, as fellow members

[34] Andrew Jackson to William H. Crawford, June 10, 1816, and Joseph McMinn to Crawford, Oct. 25, 1816, ibid., 2:110–11, 115.

[35] See Horsman, *Origins of Indian Removal*, pp. 8–9, 11–13.

[36] Clarence Edwin Carter et al., comps. and eds., *The Territorial Papers of the United States*, 28 vols. (Washington, D.C., 1934–75), 5:142–46.

[37] See Horsman, *Origins of Indian Removal*, pp. 11–15.

of the human race, could be transformed in ways that would enable them to meld equally within American society was about to be challenged. This view had always inspired eastern political leadership, not frontiersmen, but political leaders from the states anxious to remove Indians were beginning to show a willingness to state openly what had previously often been unstated frontier assumptions.

When in 1816 Gov. Joseph McMinn suggested that if the Cherokees agreed to remove to lands west of the Mississippi, individuals who wished to stay could have individual plots of land, he argued that those who remained could have "all the rights of a free citizen of color of the United States."[38] In a slave state, or in any other American state in the 1820s, this was a long way removed from Jefferson's rhetoric of intermarriage and a mingling of the two peoples. In reality McMinn was suggesting this partial concession to earlier policies to facilitate the rapid removal of Indians from the state, not in any effort to further the assimilation of individual Indians.

In 1824 Gov. George Troup of Georgia, who was intent on removing all Indians from his state, argued that it was clearly in the interests of the Indians to leave. If they stayed, they would not be accepted within white society. "The utmost of rights and privileges which public opinion would concede to Indians," wrote Troup, "would fix them in a middle station, between the negro and the white man." He argued that as they could not possibly reach "the elevation" of the latter, they would sink to the condition of the former.[39]

In the following year Henry Clay demonstrated in a cabinet meeting that the Enlightenment beliefs of the first generation of Revolutionary leaders were beginning to give way to the racialism of the mid-nineteenth century. Clay argued that "it was impossible to civilize Indians. . . . It was not in their nature." They were, he argued, "essentially inferior to the Anglo-Saxon race," and "they were not an improvable breed." He said that he believed the Indians "were destined to extinction," and "he

[38] McMinn to Crawford, Oct. 25, 1816, *American State Papers: Indian Affairs*, 2:115.

[39] George Troup to John C. Calhoun, Feb. 28, 1824, ibid., 2:475–76.

did not think them, as a race, worth preserving."[40] Knox and Jefferson had thought of Indians as human beings like themselves, but in a different stage of society; Troup and Clay thought of them as essentially different and inferior.

Knox and Jefferson had attempted to reconcile expansion over Indian lands with republican idealism by adopting policies that they hoped would move the Indians from what they believed to be a "lower" to a "higher" stage of society. They had an Enlightenment faith in the progress of the human race and in innate human capacity. Their policies, if successful, would transform the Indian way of life and for this reason were unacceptable to most Indians, but such policies would, they hoped, lead to the acceptance of individual Indians within American society on an equal basis. These policies were in the process of rejection between 1815 and 1829. Indian Removal of the 1830s paid lip-service to the ideal of Indian assimilation, but, beginning with the Monroe-Calhoun plan of removal presented to Congress in January 1825, the federal government yielded to southern and frontier political pressure and accepted the argument that Indians were not to be allowed to share equally in what were viewed as the infinite benefits of republican society. The groundwork for Jackson's policy of removal was firmly laid before 1830.[41]

Secretary of War James Barbour, who served under President John Quincy Adams, was a Virginian still inspired by the Enlightenment ideals that were fast disappearing. He wrote in 1826 that the Indians who had been urged to settle down, farm, and accept white civilization, were now being told to move. "They see our professions are insincere," he wrote, "that our promises have been broken; that the happiness of the Indi-

[40] Adams, ed., *Memoirs of Adams*, 7:90 (Dec. 22, 1825). The abandonment of Enlightenment beliefs and the growth of a new racialism are discussed in Reginald Horsman, *Race and Manifest Destiny: The Origins of American Racial Anglo-Saxonism* (Cambridge, Mass., 1981).

[41] Bernard Sheehan interprets removal not as a rejection of Jeffersonian policy but as its "fitting denouement." He sees a consistency in attitudes toward the Indian from the first policies during the Washington administration to removal. See Sheehan, *Seeds of Extinction*, pp. 3–5, 11. For the Monroe-Calhoun removal plan, see *American State Papers: Indian Affairs*, 2:541–47.

ans is a cheap sacrifice to the acquisition of new lands."[42] He knew that removal had become essential, not because Indians could only be civilized if placed in more distant areas beyond the Mississippi, but because the southern states would not let them stay.[43]

The policies of Knox and Jefferson were unacceptable to most Indians because they required the abandonment of an existing way of life. Ultimately, they were also unacceptable to most Americans because they envisaged Indians as individuals retaining lands desire by whites and blending equally within white society. The federal policy of early national America stemmed from eighteenth-century patterns of thought and from an earnest desire to make expansion of benefit to others as well as to those who were expanding. By the 1830s that necessity was not central to the shaping of American Indian policy because increasingly it was believed that expansion meant the disappearance or subordination of other peoples, not their acceptance as equal participants in a republican society.

[42] See *American State Papers: Indian Affairs*, 2:647–49 (Feb. 3, 1826).

[43] See Ebenezer C. Tracy, *Memoir of the Life of Jeremiah Evarts* (Boston, 1845), p. 271.

RICHARD WHITE

The Fictions of
Patriarchy
Indians and Whites
in the Early Republic

THE CENTERPIECE OF Mark Twain's essay "Fenimore Cooper's Literary Offenses" describes how six of Cooper's Indians, lying in wait for a settler's scow in a sapling above a stream, miss the boat. The boat is ninety feet long; it is wide enough to be nearly scraping the banks. The Indians could, Twain points out, simply have stepped onto it from the borders of the stream, but they insist on dropping to the deck from the tree. It takes more than a minute for the boat to pass underneath the tree. The first Indian, carefully timing his jump, bangs his head and knocks himself unconscious. The next five, leaping one after another, miss the vessel entirely. Each drops farther astern than the last. They are typical Cooper Indians. "There was," Twain notes, "seldom a sane one among them."[1]

Cooper's idiot Indians were one variety of the Indians of American romanticism. They were the inversion of Cooper's noble savages, Uncas and Chingachgook ("pronounced Chicago" Twain suggested). They were inventions, products of "a sublime burst of invention," as Twain sarcastically put it.

Twain, the American realist, was, of course, rather squarely in the inventing business himself. He ridiculed Cooper's Indians not because they were imagined but because there was no "real

[1] Samuel Langhorne Clemens, "Fenimore Cooper's Literary Offenses," *Literary Essays, by Mark Twain* (New York, 1918), pp. 68–69.

invention" in them. These fictions were implausible; they could not persuade; they had an "air of fictitiousness and general improbability over" them. Cooper's Indians poised over the scow, like Cooper himself, missed the obvious. They, according to Twain, "never notice anything." In "the matter of intellect, the difference between a Cooper Indian and the Indian that stands in front of the cigar shop is not spacious."[2]

The example of Cooper's Indians holds up for examination the possibility of failed fictions, of implausible or impossible inventions. Twain's interest in discriminating among fictions was literary. But fictionalizing—creating plausible versions of the Other and sketching out possible plots involving them—extends beyond authors of novels and stories. Fictionalizing provides a key to relations between Indians and whites in the early republic. And this inventing was not necessarily bad. Fictions, by definition, are not reality; they describe possible worlds. But all fictions are not equal. To work in history, fictions must be plausible or else they fail. Like Cooper's Indians, failed fictions result from the author's or inventor's "inadequacy as an observer." Twain doesn't demand that Cooper describe actual Indians; he demands only that such Indians be plausible within the world we know or have known.

Invention of the Other is hardly a new theme, but it can profitably be reintroduced in this context for two reasons. The first is that invention has largely remained the domain of whites. As Bernard W. Sheehan put it in *Seeds of Extinction*, "The Indian became a victim of the white man's proclivity for conceptualization and idealization." By implication, the conceptualizations and idealizations by Indians—and their fictions—lacked equal importance, if such things existed at all. Secondly, there is a tendency to denigrate fictions in comparison to a supposedly distinct reality. The invented Indians, and the equally invented whites, at issue here differ from the invented Indians of Robert F. Berkhofer. Berkhofer posits a sharp distinction between invented Indians and real Native Americans (at least until the late twentieth century), but it is a distinction that cannot hold. The Indian peoples that are the subjects of this essay—mostly

[2] Ibid.

63

those of the Old Northwest but also the Cherokees—had already experienced a century to a century and a half of contact with Europeans at the birth of the republic. They were already deeply involved in a common history with Europeans and Africans. Part of that history was the stories these various peoples invented about each other. Both sides had no choice but to respond to the versions of themselves the other side invented, and in responding they blurred the line between invention and actuality, between the people who existed in the minds of others and those who acted on their own behalf, between objects and subjects.[3]

William G. McLoughlin in his remarkable series of histories of the Cherokees has acutely argued that as Americans first invented themselves as republicans and then as romantic nationalists, they invented corresponding versions of Indian peoples. Cooper's Indians and the various theatrical Indians, of whom Metamora was the most famous, formed the last stage of this process in the early republic. But Indians were not just objects of white invention. They were also subjects, inventors themselves. The Cherokees matched invention with invention, transformation with transformation, and emerged with a romantic nationalism of their own. They became, in Mary Elizabeth Young's telling phrase, a mirror of the republic. As McLoughlin emphasizes, the ultimate removal of most of the Indian peoples from east of the Mississippi, the culmination of early American Indian policy, was not "simply an incident in this cultural transformation; it was an integral part of it. The changing attitude toward the Indian's place in the new nation was essentially a redefinition of what it meant to be an American." Twain found Cooper's romantic Indians implausible; Indian peoples found them life-threatening. With romantic Indians, the choices narrowed to resistance or disappearance. The stage Indians of American romanticism could bless or curse the encroaching whites, but they could not share a world with them. Yet at the

[3] Bernard W. Sheehan, *Seeds of Extinction: Jeffersonian Philanthropy and the American Indian* (New York, 1973), p. 8; Robert F. Berkhofer, Jr., *The White Man's Indian: Images of the American Indian from Columbus to the Present* (New York, 1978), pp. xv–xvi, 3.

beginning some white Americans and some Indian peoples imagined other choices.[4]

At the birth of the republic, the most powerful Indian peoples that the new Americans confronted—the Six Nations, the various peoples of the Old Northwest, the Cherokees, Creeks, and Choctaws—had long shared a world with whites. And in the Old Northwest in particular, the result of more than a century of mutual invention was a middle ground.[5]

The middle ground depended on deficiencies of power and surpluses of need and desire. It existed in the Old Northwest because the various Indian peoples of the area (who, for convenience, will be referred to as Algonquians) and first the French, then the English, and finally the Americans, needed and desired each other as trading partners, allies, and sexual partners but lacked the power to force each other to act in desired ways. All sides had to arrive at some common conception of appropriate action.[6]

The process of creating the middle ground passed through various stages. Its initial stage, in which Europeans saw Indians as exotic and virtually nonhuman, and Indian peoples saw Europeans as other-than-human persons, is at once the most noticed and, in terms of actual relations, the least important. These were fictions that could not be maintained under the

[4] William G. McLoughlin, *Cherokee Renascence in the New Republic* (Princeton, 1986), pp. xvi–xix, quotation p. xvi; Werner Sollors, *Beyond Ethnicity: Consent and Descent in American Culture* (New York, 1986), pp. 119–45; Kenneth M. Morrison, "Native Americans and the American Revolution: Historic Stories and Shifting Frontier Conflict," in Frederick E. Hoxie, ed., *Indians in American History* (Arlington Heights, Ill., 1988), pp. 95–115; Mary Elizabeth Young, "The Cherokee Nation: Mirror of the Republic," *American Quarterly* 33 (1981): 502–24.

[5] For a much fuller account of many of the arguments that I make here, see Richard White, *The Middle Ground: Indians, Empires, and Republics in the Great Lakes Region, 1650–1815* (Cambridge, 1991), pp. 50–93.

[6] The impossibility of considering any society in isolation is one of the major themes of Eric Wolf, *Europe and the People without History* (Berkeley, Calif., 1982), pp. 3–23, 385. It is also a position taken by Anthony Giddens, *A Contemporary Critique of Historical Materialism* (Berkeley, Calif., 1981), pp. 23–24.

close observation of daily life that Twain represented as the arbiter of fictions. Because the French were literate, however, these fictions could survive as potent cultural relics among those who never dealt with actual Indians.[7]

The middle ground, as it survived in history, was thus a creation of peoples in direct contact. It was not a creation of European savants or distant imperial administrators. The middle ground that Americans inherited and participated in was the result of a century or more of creative misunderstandings. Because neither side could gain their ends through force, Europeans and Indians had to attempt to understand the world and the reasoning of others and to assimilate enough of that reasoning to put it to their own purposes. Particularly in diplomatic councils, the middle ground was a realm of constant invention that once agreed upon by both sides, became convention.

The central and defining aspect of the middle ground was a willingness, born of necessity, for one set of people to justify their actions in terms of what they perceived to be their partners' cultural premises. In seeking to persuade others to act, they sought out congruences, either perceived or actual, between the two cultures. The congruences arrived at often seemed—and, indeed, were—results of misunderstandings or accidents. Indeed, the explanations offered by members of one society for the practices of the other often were ludicrous. This, however, did not matter. Any congruence, no matter how tenuous, could be put to work and take on a life of its own as long as it was accepted by both sides.

The governing fiction of the middle ground for over a century was the agreement by Algonquians and Europeans to act as if Europeans were fathers and Algonquians were children. This, of course, left undetermined what it meant to act as a father and as a child. A century of history in the region can be seen as giving content to that metaphor. This content was always contested, always open to renegotiation, but the basic metaphor of European fathers and Indian children held, and both the fur trade and the alliance of the Algonquians with first the French

[7] See, for example, Cornelius Jaenen, "Les Sauvages Ameriquians: Persistence into the Eighteenth Century of Traditional French Concepts and Constructs for Comprehending Amerindians," *Ethnohistory* 29 (1982):43–56.

and then the English were in a sense its products. The result was an odd imperialism where mediation succeeded and force failed, where colonizers gave gifts to the colonized and patriarchal metaphors were the heart of politics.

The fathers and children of this history are not the *Fathers and Children* of Michael Paul Rogin's book title. For Rogin the metaphor is entirely European; patriarchy is identical the world over, and its meaning appears most clearly through psychoanalytic theory.

> Indian dispossession, as experienced by the whites who justified it and carried it out, belongs to the pathology of human development. Indians remained in the white fantasy, in the earliest period of childhood, unseparated from "the exuberant bosom of the common mother." They were at once symbols of a lost childhood bliss and, as bad children, repositories of murderous, negative fantasies. . . . Projecting primitive rage onto Indians, independent adult whites revenged themselves for their own early loss.[8]

In the actual history of the colonial period and early republic, however, Indians refused to remain in white fantasy. The patriarchal metaphor was their own; they contested its meaning with whites. Rogin rightly argued that the "uniformly familial language" Americans employed in speaking of Indians be taken seriously, but he was as deaf to the uses Indians made of this language as the historians he attacked were to the uses whites made of it. In the early republic Indians were subjects as well as objects of white policies and fantasies. The reversion to patriarchal metaphors came after an attempt to try others. In their early dealings with the American Revolutionaries, both they and the Americans, for different reasons, were willing to discard it in favor of fraternal metaphors.[9]

[8] Michael Paul Rogin, *Fathers and Children: Andrew Jackson and the Subjugation of the American Indian* (New York, 1975), p. 9; also see p. 15.

[9] Ibid., p. 12. Rogin's actual use of the metaphors can be quite selective. Although recognizing the Indians' use of paternal metaphors, and the white adoption of them, he writes: "The savages' connection to nature and freedom from paternal governmental authority seemed to excite white imaginations most" (p. 115). Similarly, either ignoring or ignorant of the common maternal metaphor discussed below, he makes the mother-child metaphor nearly exclusive to Indians.

The American Revolution, of course, represented a challenge to patriarchal metaphors in general. George III had become in Thomas Paine's *Common Sense* a "wretch . . . with the pretended title of FATHER OF HIS PEOPLE." And it is no accident that the initial metaphorical phrasing of American republicans and American Indians was as brothers, children of a common mother. In June 1776 the Shawnee leader Cornstalk, who would be murdered by Americans, tried out a version of a common, fraternal past in a meeting with George Morgan, who was the representative of Congress to the Indians of the Ohio: "Our white Brethren who have grown out this same Ground with ourselves—this Big Island being our common Mother, we & they are like one Flesh and Blood." It was a fiction that the American Commissioners of Indian Affairs along the Ohio quickly seized on and elaborated. "We are sprung from one common Mother, we were all born in this big Island; we earnestly wish to repose under the same Tree of Peace with you; we request to live in Friendship with all the Indians in the Woods We call God to Witness, that we desire nothing more ardently than that the white & red Inhabitants of this big Island should cultivate the most Brotherly affection, & be united in the firmest bonds of Love & friendship." [10]

Unless they were observers on the level of Cooper's Indians, neither Cornstalk nor the commissioners could have thought that these proclamations of fraternity described actual relations along the Ohio River. They were instead fictions; they were versions of possible identities that carried with them possible plots: union in "the firmest bonds of Love & friendship." The question was, of course, whether such formulations were plausible.

It is important to note here that the fictional identity of brothers was accepted by both sides, but the meaning of that identity, "the firmest bonds of Love & friendship," was an American,

[10] Thomas Paine, *Common Sense*, quoted in Winthrop D. Jordan, "Familial Politics, Thomas Paine, and the Killing of the King," *Journal of American History* 40 (1973): 299. First extended quotation, Cornstalk, Morgan Diary, June 1, 1776; second quotation, American Commissioners for Indian Affairs to Delawares, Senecas, Munsees, and Mingos, Pittsburgh, 1776, George Morgan Letterbook, Carnegie Library, Pittsburgh, copy in Great Lakes Ethnohistorical Archives, Indiana University, Bloomington.

not Algonquian, construction. Algonquians attached a different meaning to fraternal relations, and the best indication of this is that they continued to address the Americans as brothers long after the truce between the peoples broke down and they were busily slaughtering each other.

For the Algonquians, fraternity was a more neutral relation than paternity. The Americans as a whole stood as brothers to both the western confederacy and the Six Nations until the mid-1790s. These fraternal relations were relations of equality, but of all the kinship terms of Indian diplomacy, brother seems, except for cousin, the one least fraught with mutual obligation. Brothers shared opinions and sentiments. Older brothers took precedence over younger brothers, but one brother did not follow the commands or advice of the other. Brothers did not necessarily share warm feelings. Brothers could be less than friends. The Ottawa chief Aguishiway meant to elevate the Americans in standing when he told Anthony Wayne that he did not consider him a brother but rather a friend. Even as the Americans and confederated Indians killed each other, they addressed each other as brothers.[11]

American diplomacy at its most successful formulated a set of fictions that meshed with fraternal equality. Such equality was largely devoid of love, but it did capitalize on common resentments against fathers. The most successful creator of such fictions was a man who hated Indians: George Rogers Clark. Clark told the captured British governor of Detroit, Henry Hamilton, that he expected to see the whole Indian race extirpated, and "for his part he would never spare Man woman or child of them on whom he could lay his hands." But in dealing with Indians, Clark emulated the French, and in doing so he compromised his Indian hating.[12]

---

[11] Actions of brothers, Council, Treaty of Greenville, Speech of Little Turtle, July 28, 1795, *American State Papers: Indian Affairs*, 2 vols. (Washington, D.C., 1832–34), 1:575; Friend, ibid.; Speech of Au-goosh-a-way, July 23, 1795, ibid., p. 572.

[12] Henry Hamilton Journal, Feb. 25, 1779, John D. Barnhart, ed., *Henry Hamilton and George Rogers Clark in the American Revolution, with the Unpublished Journal of Lieutenant Governor Henry Hamilton* (Crawfordsville, Ind., 1951),

To defeat the British, Clark needed the very Indians that he hated, and so he stressed their similarities with the backcountry whites: the Big Knives. "The Big Knife are very much like the Red people they don't know well how to make Blanket powder and cloath &c they buy from the English (whom they formerly desended from) and live chiefly by making corn Hunting and Trade as you and the French your Neighbours do."

According to Clark, the response of the Wabash Indians to this message was that the "Indians had as great a right to fight the English (their old fathers) as they (the Virginians) did." Whether Clark was sincere or not and whether Virginians and Indians actually shared a common way of living and a common relation to the British was less important historically than that they agreed, for a time, to act as if they did. And in common resentments and common action they found equality if not love.[13]

This attainment of equal standing within the metaphorical relation of brothers proved short-lived. At the end of the Revolution the Americans abandoned pretensions of equality and put forth a fiction of conquest. This was fiction that Arthur St. Clair and Josiah Harmar tried to test against a rather recalcitrant reality. They, and the fiction, failed.[14]

---

p. 189. For Clark's strategy, see George Rogers Clark's Memoir, James Alton James, ed., *George Rogers Clark Papers, 1771–1781* (Springfield, Ill., 1912), pp. 23, 224. George Rogers Clark to Mason, Nov. 19, 1779, ibid., pp. 122–23; Clark to Chief of the Winnebago, Aug. 22, 1778, ibid., p. 65. Clark's Proclamation to the Fox Indians, Aug. 28, 1778, ibid., p. 66; and Clark to Mason, Nov. 19, 1799, ibid., p. 124.

[13] Clark's Memoir, James, ed., *Clark Papers*, pp. 242–44; for response, see Clark to Mason, Nov. 19, 1779, ibid., p. 124.

[14] The confederation continued to address the Americans as brothers: Speech of the United Indian Nations at Their Confederate Council . . . 28 November and 13th Dec. 1786, *American State Papers: Indian Affairs*, 1 : 3. The Iroquois and the Americans continued to address each other as brothers into the early republic. See, for example, No. 49, The Six Nations and Others, Communicated to Congress, May 21, 1794, ibid., pp. 477–82. Indeed, *brothers* was also the form of address in the South. See, for example, To the Head-men, Chiefs, and Warriors of the Cherokee Nation, June 7, 1789, and In a Meeting of the Lower Creeks in the Cussetahs, July 27, 1787, ibid., pp. 33–34. Al-

The defeats of St. Clair and Harmar demonstrated the weakness of the new republic; the victories of the Indians demonstrated, ironically, their dependence on the British, who most Algonquians felt had betrayed them in the peace that ended the Revolution. Both the Indian confederacy north of the Ohio and the Americans needed peace, but neither side wanted it at any price. Such a combination of desire and the inability to fulfill that desire without cooperation from another had previously supported the middle ground. Yet in 1794, when the new republic both sent negotiators to the Confederation and prepared another army under Anthony Wayne, a political middle ground failed to emerge. The reasons have partially to do with invention.

The practical issues dividing the Americans and the Algonquians were the terms of peace: boundaries, payments for lands, and the legal status of the Indian confederation and individual villages. But *direct* negotiations over these issues never took place in any conventional diplomatic forum. Instead of specific negotiations regarding agreed upon differences, the diplomatic conversation was a struggle over images, and it took place within rather than between groups.[15]

This was a diplomacy of mirrors, and image-making became the real basis of negotiations. It was as if neither side could effectively negotiate until they had determined the identity of those they negotiated with. For the middle ground to succeed, each side had to agree on its metaphorical identity, on the fictions that would govern negotiations. Once established, images became part of larger reality and certain images of the Other demanded certain responses regardless of what the Other actually said or what concessions the Other offered. What the confederation was to do about the Americans, for example, ultimately depended on who the Americans were—what their true nature

---

though here kinship terms could be mixed as when the Lower Creeks referred to "you our fathers, friends, and brothers," in A Talk from the Chiefs, Headmen and Warriors, of the Lower Creek Nation, June 1, 1789, ibid., p. 34.

[15] For the American summary of the unsuccessful attempt to negotiate with the confederacy, see Benjamin Lincoln to Henry Knox, Aug. 21, 1793, ibid., pp. 359–60.

was. In the same way, what the Americans would do about the Indians, and their allies the British, depended on who the Indians were. Interpreting the actions of the Other and deciding what those actions meant were critical activities on both sides.

Images of the Other were fictions, but they remained fictions that had to be constantly tested against the world of action and alternate images. This process was not new, but what complicated it immensely was that it largely ceased to be face to face. Federal officials knew little about northwestern Indians. Backcountry whites and Indians knew each other largely as murderers and victims. The popular, and quite murderous, beginning of what Reginald Horsman has called "racialism" and what Herman Melville examined as the metaphysics of Indian hating had already flowered among backcountry whites. On the older middle grounds of English and French metaphors of kinship, bonds of kinship had often emerged. But this older common world of the region yielded by the 1790s to a frontier over which people crossed only to shed blood.[16]

As the fiction of conquest failed, the Americans struggled to find a more plausible relation with Indians, one that conformed to their own republican ideals and the defeat of their armies. In the early 1790s Congress and the nation were badly divided over a thus far expensive and futile war. "Indian war," as Secretary of War Henry Knox wrote, "was destructive to the interest of humanity and an event from which neither dignity or profit can be reaped." In a nation of self-created republicans such a war was both financially and ideologically embarrassing. According to Secretary of State Thomas Jefferson, the war's unpopularity forced the government to attempt negotiations if only "to prove to all our citizens that peace was unattainable on terms which any of them would accept." At stake for Americans was their republican virtue, for to many of its own citizens and to many Europeans the new republic seemed a greedy aggressor.[17]

---

[16] Reginald Horsman, *Race and Manifest Destiny: The Origins of American Racial Anglo-Saxonism* (Cambridge, Mass., 1981), pp. 4–5.

[17] Reginald Horsman, *Expansion and American Indian Policy, 1783–1812* (East Lansing, Mich., 1967), pp. 90–96. For Jefferson quotation, see idem, "The British Indian Department and the Abortive Treaty of Lower Sandusky,"

The federal government had no intention of giving up the Indian lands that it had obtained in rump treaties on the Ohio, but it was ready to give up the fiction that it had conquered the Indians. They admitted that they did not have title to their lands by right of conquest and that Great Britain had no right to cede, and had not ceded, the Indian's land. By giving up its role as conqueror, the United States could and did pose as an injured party. It only sought the land that had been "freely" ceded in the postwar treaties. The lands unceded by earlier treaties were the Algonquians to keep or to sell to the United States as they chose.

This new position had several advantages. Tactically, such a stance served to split the Indian alliance. The lands ceded in the rump treaties following the Revolution threatened only the Shawnees, refugee Cherokees, Delawares, Wyandots, Mingoes, and various fragments of more recent immigrants from the East such as the Munsees. As the American negotiator Rufus Putnam explained, the Indian confederation gained much greater strength by using the American claims of conquest and demands for new cessions to persuade other Indians that the Americans "are after your lands they mean to take them from you and to drive you out of the country . . . they will never rest until they got the whole." By renouncing their claims to conquest and abstaining from immediate requests for more land, American negotiators hoped to isolate those people with a direct stake in the cessions. Obtaining all the lands north of the Ohio still remained the ultimate goal of American policy. If the Indians made peace, federal officials believed, cessions would come as a matter of course, as American settlers killed game and encroached on Indian lands. If the Indians refused peace, then the negotiations would at least gain time for Anthony

---

Ohio Historical Quarterly 70 (1961):195. Henry Knox had been particularly conscious of the damage done to the "dignity and interest" of the nation by the claims to Indian land since 1789. See Knox to President [George Washington], June 15, 1789, *American State Papers: Indian Affairs*, 1:12–13. He was already advocating a policy close to that eventually pursued by Jefferson. For treaty instructions, see Instructions to Rufus Putnam, May 22, 1792, Rowena Buell, ed., *Memoirs of Rufus Putnam and Certain Official Papers and Correspondence* (Boston, 1903), pp. 258–67, Knox quotation, p. 267.

Wayne, who was raising and training a new army, and would perhaps split the confederacy, making military victory easier.[18]

But the American position was not totally cynical. They presented themselves as a people seeking peace, and they constructed an explanation as to why Indians might refuse their sincere and generous offers of friendship. To explain the Indian stance, the Americans retreated to a version of savagery that, ironically, actually deprived Indian peoples of any real agency. They attributed native actions to ignorance and naïveté. In the words of Henry Knox, Indian threats resulted more from "the misrepresentations of bad people, than any hardened malignity of the human heart." They were, in other words, a simple people, easily led. (Interestingly, this view was later extended to African Americans when whites were asked to account for slave rebellions.)

Others assumed a more deep-seated form of Indian savagery. Anthony Wayne, eager to fight the Indians, spoke for this more cynical group when he called the Ohio tribes a "victorious, haughty and insidious enemy,—stimulated by British emissaries to a continuance of war." All Americans agreed, however, on a common rhetorical and diplomatic goal: the transformation of republican virtue from an impediment to conquest to a rationale for combat.[19]

These images of the Other were forms of fiction; they functioned typologically, and they called to mind stories and plots. In 1793 Benjamin Lincoln, one of the American commissioners sent to negotiate a treaty with the confederation, kept a journal while he waited for a conference that would never take place. A New Englander who had served with distinction during the Revolution and crushed Shays's Rebellion afterward, Lincoln had virtually no experience with Indians. He did not know of the vast corn fields and the herds of cattle, horses, and pigs surrounding many of the villages of the *pays d'en haut*. He did not know that the Indians of the *pays d'en haut* were prob-

[18] For the ideology of expansion, see Horsman, *Race and Manifest Destiny*, pp. 103–7.

[19] Instructions to Putnam from Knox, May 22, 1792, Buell, ed., *Memoirs of Putnam*, pp. 262, 267; for Wayne quotation, see Wayne to James Wilkinson, Aug. 5, 1792, p. 331.

ably increasing in numbers in the late eighteenth century. He drew his Indians not from experience but from an old and powerful story in western culture: the story of Abraham and Ishmael. Lincoln recognized the Indians as children of Ishmael, and once he had established the proper typology, he knew the fate of the Indians: they must yield or disappear.[20]

For Lincoln the Indians were the children of Ishmael; the Americans were the children of Abraham. As the typological descendants of Ishmael, Indians were hunters and savages. At best they were backward, ignorant, and misled; at worse, they were irretrievably savage. These were the alternative images of American policy recast in biblical terms. The Bible had a plot as well as characters, and Lincoln used the plot to spell out Indian possibilities. God had foreordained the earth to be fully populated, and "no men will be suffered to live by hunting on lands capable of improvement." Thus, "if the savages cannot be civilized and quit their present pursuits they will in consequence of their stubbornness, dwindle and moulder away."[21]

The Indians had brought their fate upon themselves. His logic foreshadowed the conventional nineteenth-century logic of the vanishing Indian. But there is a second interesting aspect to Lincoln's typology, for he chose the story of Abraham and Ishmael over the more common typology of Esau and Jacob. Esau and Jacob were brothers. Abraham was Ishmael's father. The Americans, about to become the fathers of Indians, were already preparing to disinherit them. This was the beauty of metaphorical thinking. In becoming fathers the Americans switched the actual pattern of property exchange. Instead of receiving the continent from the Indians, the Americans possessed it and could bestow it, or fail to bestow it, on their deserving or undeserving metaphorical children.

Lincoln's implicit movement toward patriarchy was not an individual quirk. Americans continued to follow the Indian ex-

[20] Benjamin Lincoln, Journal of a Treaty, *Collections of the Massachusetts Historical Society*, 3d ser. 5 (1836):139. For increase in population, see Jeanne Kay, "The Fur Trade and Native American Population Growth," *Ethnohistory* 31 (1984):265–87.

[21] Kay, "Fur Trade"; for a discussion of Jacob and Esau, see Rogin, *Fathers and Children*, pp. 126–27.

ample and use fraternal forms of address in dealing with the Iroquois and the confederation, but they tried to make an exception of George Washington. They inserted him into the diplomatic discourse as a common father of Indians and whites. In council with the Six Nations at Buffalo Creek in February 1794, for example, the American emissary, General Chapin, addressed the Iroquois as brothers and was so addressed by them, but Chapin also referred to Washington as "your Father General Washington," thus giving the president an equal status with the British King "your father." The Iroquois pointedly, however, refrained from referring to Washington as their father; he was "your President."[22]

This drift toward patriarchy was met with a second kind of metaphorical discourse. Americans equated metaphorical paternity with metaphorical seniority, and this the Indians challenged. As Joseph Brant told the Americans, "We as the Ancient inhabitants of this Country and sovereigns of the soil, say that we are equally as free as you, or any nation, or nations, under the sun." Similarly, the western nations informed the Americans that "they wish it to be considered that they were the first people the Great Spirit seated on this island, for which reason we look on the Americans as children, to call them our younger brethren." As younger brothers to the Indians, the Americans would answer summons to council and speak after their elders.[23]

[22] Proceedings of a Council of the Six Nation Indians &c Held at Buffaloe Creek on the Seventh Day of February 1794, *Collections and Researches Made by the Michigan Pioneer and Historical Society*, 40 vols. (Lansing, Mich., 1874–1929), 24:633–42. Reply of the Six Nations . . . the 21st April, 1794 to a Speech from General Knox, E. A. Cruikshank, ed., *The Correspondence of Lieutenant Governor John Graves Simcoe*, 5 vols. (Toronto, 1923–31), 2:214–16. Wayne repeated this brother-father form. See Wayne to the Indians of Sandusky, Jan. 1, 1795, Cruikshank, ed., *Correspondence of Simcoe*, 3:252–53.

[23] Speech of the Cornplanter and New Arrow to Major General Wayne, Dec. 8, 1792, *American State Papers: Indian Affairs*, 1:337. This message was delivered to Red Jacket by the Shawnee chiefs in council in October 1792. Knox to President [Washington], Dec. 6, 1792, ibid., p. 322. See Speeches of the Western Indians to the Six Nations, Nov. 16, 1792, ibid., p. 323. Reply of the Six Nations, Cruikshank, ed., *Correspondence of Simcoe*, 2:214–16.

In these rhetorical sparrings, Indians did not just counter America fictions. They offered fictions of their own. Benjamin Lincoln was not the only emissary to keep a journal in the early 1790s, and the Americans were not the only ones to resort to typologies. The Indians of the confederacy debated the proper stance to take toward the Americans, and, like Lincoln, they created identities for their enemies that would dictate and justify their own action. In the case of the confederacy in 1792, there was already a pressing action to justify and interpret. Warriors, acting on their own, had murdered two American envoys, Maj. Alexander Trueman and Col. John Hardin, and most of their parties before they even reached the headquarters of the Indian confederacy at the Auglaize. The meaning of these killings, rather than the peace proposals the emissaries brought, became the pressing diplomatic issue. For the Indians the legitimacy of the killings depended on the metaphorical identity of the murdered men. The struggle they waged over the image of the Americans, and thus the proper interpretation of the killings, becomes most apparent in the journal kept by Hendrick Aupaumut at the villages on the Auglaize in 1792.[24]

The sometimes shrewd, sometimes bewildered Aupaumut was a Stockbridge Indian, one of a group of Connecticut Mohicans, Hudson River Indians, and Long Island Indians, who had sought refuge from white encroachments among the Oneidas. He was Christian and literate, and he acted as an American emissary in the western councils. Like other Stockbridges, he believed that farming, Christianity, and the adoption of American gender roles would allow the Indians to incorporate themselves peacefully into American society. Aupaumut would for the next twenty years urge such accommodation, but he never secured it for the Stockbridges, who had to move repeatedly to avoid conflict with the whites and other Indians.[25]

[24] For murder of American emissaries by Indians, see An Account of the Fate of Col. Hardin, Major Trueman, and Several Other Persons, Draper Manuscripts, Frontier Wars, 5U28, State Historical Society of Wisconsin, Madison.

[25] For Stockbridges, see Bruce Trigger, ed., *Northeast*, Handbook of North American Indians, vol. 15 (Washington, D.C., 1978), pp. 181, 209–11; for Aupaumut, see "A Narrative of an Embassy to the Western Indian, from the

Aupaumut recorded and participated in the Algonquian debate over image while he delivered an American message urging a negotiated peace. The message itself contained the contending images of Americans, for it distinguished between the United States, which in the metonymic imagery became the fifteen fires or George Washington, and the Big Knives, which now included most, but not all, frontier whites. Aupaumut persuaded several significant Delaware leaders—Pipe, Big Cat, and Buckongahelas—to become proponents of the image of the Americans as George Washington. The Shawnees, the Miamis, and some of the Hurons and Wyandots held out the counter-image of the Americans as Big Knives. The course of future actions and negotiations depended on whether the Indians were dealing with Big Knives, whose forts were "blood," or George Washington—a potential father—and his "good message." Neither Aupaumut nor his rivals sought to convert each other as much as they wanted to convince the "back nations"—the Ottawas, Chippewas, Potawatomis, Sauks, Fox, and Wabash villages who provided the bulk of the confederation's potential strength.[26]

Aupaumut, who at the end of the narrative summarized his own and his opponents' arguments, clearly recognized that the central issue was who the Americans were. The Americans were, the Shawnees argued, inevitably "deceitful in their dealings with us, the Indians." Their promises of benevolence were their most potent weapons. They missionized Indians "to gain their attention, and then they would (have) killed them, and have killed of such 96 in one day at Coshuhkeck, few years ago." They had promised the Shawnee chief Molunthy that their flag would always protect him, but when he hoisted his flag "Big knives did not regard it, but killed the chief and numbers of his friends." The Big Knives "know how to speak good, but would not do good

---

Original Manuscript of Hendrick Aupaumut," *Memoirs of Historical Society of Pennsylvania* 2 (1827).

[26] "Narrative of an Embassy to the Western Indian," pp. 92–110, 121, 124. For Buckongahelas, see Account of Fate of Harden, Trueman, Draper Mss., Frontier Wars, 5U28.

towards the Indians." What Big Knives said could not and did not matter.[27]

Aupaumut countered by distinguishing the Big Knives from the United Sachems or George Washington. If all Americans were Big Knives, he and his people "would have been long ago annihilated," but the Americans sought to lift them up that "we may stand up and walk ourselves, because we the Indians, hitherto have lay flat as it were on the ground, by which we could not see great way." The United Sachems, chosen from all Americans, "must be very honest and wise, and they will do Justice to all people." The Big Knives were "thieves and robbers and murderers" who had run away to escape the laws. They were no different from the Cherokee renegades among the Shawnees. In expanding, the United States was subduing the Big Knives. The "law now binds them."[28]

The Shawnees and Miamis won the argument. The warriors justified the murders of Trueman and Hardin by using the Big Knife argument: they had already been deceived by the Americans and had no intention of being deceived again. Having killed the peace emissaries, and continuing to raid themselves, the warriors then denounced the actions of American soldiers during the summer and fall of 1792 as the actions of Big Knives. The Americans talked peace, but their preparations were for war. The Big Knives killed some Delawares even as Aupaumut praised the Americans' peaceful intent. The Delaware chiefs Big Cat and Captain Pipe could not carry the council and make peace, but they sent a message to Washington telling him that

[27] "Narrative of an Embassy to the Western Indian," pp. 122–31, quotations pp. 126–27.

[28] Ibid., p. 113. Although Joseph Brant, like Aupaumut, sought peace, he attempted to buttress his own fading credibility at Aupaumut's expense. Brant feared that his own earlier visit to Philadelphia at the invitation of the Americans might be taken as a betrayal of the confederation, and he sought to establish his own credibility by sending word to the council that neither Washington nor Aupaumut was to be trusted. There were rivalries even among the accommodationists. Aupaumut had to remind the Algonquians that Brant was a Mohawk, and the "Mauquas have deceived you repeatly [*sic*]" (ibid.). For Brant's visits to Philadelphia and his position, see Isabel Thompson Kelsay, *Joseph Brant, 1743–1807: Man of Two Worlds* (Syracuse, N.Y., 1984), pp. 458–82.

if he demonstrated that he could "govern the hostile Big Knife" by withdrawing them from "the forts which stands on our land," then they could secure peace, for the "war party will be speechless." The Indians treated Washington as a civil chief unable to control or persuade his young men.[29] They imposed their metaphor on the situation, demonstrating the fragility of government-sponsored images in areas beyond its control.

The defeat of the Indians at Fallen Timbers necessitated what was to be the final fiction of the early republic: The Algonquians had, under the most inauspicious of circumstances, to imagine the Americans as fathers, and the Americans had to accept the Indians as children. As a mere linguistic turn, the creation was not difficult. This was a familiar ritual language. But to be effective, as it had been for more than a century, the language had to call into being such a powerful fiction of kinship that each side would conform to it. The familial metaphors were not simply a transference of some universal and transparent kinship but instead a language developed on the middle ground.[30]

Patriarchal language as the idiom of Indian relations long antedated the early republic, but the meaning of patriarchal metaphors had always been contested. And it was a contest in which Indian peoples had a significant say in the imposition of meaning. The Canadian governor Charles de la Boische de Beauharnois and the Intendant Gilles Hocquart had to explain to the French court in 1730, accustomed to its own patriarchal

---

[29] For justification, see Wayne to Putnam, Aug. 6, 1792, Buell, ed., *Memoirs of Putnam*, p. 312. For peace messages, see Speech of Knox to Indians, Apr. 4, 1792, *Collections by the Michigan Pioneer and Historical Society*, 24:394–96. The Delawares agreed with the Shawnees and Miamis in the spring, but then wavered. See extract from the Speech of the Shawanoes, Delawares, and Miamis, Apr. 15, 1792, Wayne Papers, William L. Clements Library, University of Michigan, Ann Arbor. For triumph of warriors, see Proceedings of a General Council of Indian Nations, 30 Sept. 1792 . . . until the 9th day of Oct., *Collections by the Michigan Pioneer and Historical Society*, 24:483–91.

[30] For *father*, see Minutes of Treaty, 10 June . . . 10 Aug. 1795, *American State Papers: Indian Affairs*, 1:581–82; for Washington as father, see Washington to Chiefs and Warriors . . . of Wiandots, etc., Nov. 9, 1796, Wayne Papers.

assumptions, the meaning of political patriarchy to the Algonquians: "You know Monseigneur, that all the nations of Canada regard the governor as their father, which in consequence, following their ideas, he ought at all times to give them what they need to feed themselves, clothe themselves and to hunt."[31]

The Algonquians had to invent the Americans as fathers and persuade the Americans to accept the fiction. Their attempts to do so can be traced in two different sets of negotiations. The first followed from Rufus Putnam's successful attempt to detach the Wabash and Illinois villages from the confederation in the spring of 1792. The second were the negotiations of the confederation itself with Anthony Wayne at Greenville. In the first set of negotiations, the Wabash chiefs had an advantage, for they had not yet suffered significant military defeat by the Americans.

The Eel River and Wea chiefs were the first to address the Americans as father. In using the word they moved into an arena already partially occupied by American use of ritual language, for the Americans had referred to Washington as their father. When the Illinois chief, John Baptiste de Coigne, acting as speaker for the Wabash and Illinois, addressed Washington as father, however, he tried to move him toward an Algonquian paternity.[32]

In their speeches Baptiste de Coigne and the Wabash chiefs laid out the expectations of Washington's fatherhood, implicitly distinguishing it from Anglo-American paternity. They, for example, differentiated between the white children of Washington, whom he should *order* to do what was right, and his red children, whom he should protect. The distinction grew from a long history of Algonquian perceptions of whites being a

[31] Charles de la Boische de Beauharnois et Gilles Hocquart au Ministre, Oct. 15, 1730, C11A, v. 51, fols. 33–36, Archives Nationales, Paris.

[32] For Indian use of *father*, see, for example, Hamtramck to Secretary of War [Knox], Mar. 31, 1792, Clarence Edwin Carter et al., comps. and eds., *The Territorial Papers of the United States*, 28 vols. (Washington, D.C., 1934–75), 1: 380–81. For American references to Washington as their father, see Wilkinson to Wyandot and Ottawa . . . , May 1792, *Collections by the Michigan Pioneer and Historical Society*, 24:413–14.

people of law and Indians a people of custom. Washington, in effect, was to act like an Anglo-American patriarch toward his American children and as an Algonquian father toward his Algonquian children. An Algonquian father was a "friend" who took care of his children. A father should, in the key Algonquian phrase, take pity on his children. Pity was what the supplicant sought; pity was what the Indians asked from their manitous. To pity was to be beneficent and grant wishes. Although treated differently, having a common father made the Indians and Americans "one people" who would "hunt and play, and laugh together." Their American father was "rich"; he had all things at his command; he wanted for nothing. De Coigne commended "our women and children to [his] care."[33]

At the Treaty of Greenville, the main body of the confederation similarly hoped to move the Americans toward this older view of patriarchy, but they operated under the significant disadvantage of defeat. The metaphors of patriarchy had come to have such power because neither side could control them; both sides had understood them as a compromise and had acted within them. But patriarchy now increasingly became a metaphor over which Indians were losing control.

At Greenville the confederated Indians accepted the Americans as George Washington and made George Washington their father. During most of the negotiations, each side addressed the other as brother. The bestowal of the title of father came at the end of the negotiations, when both sides had agreed on the terms of peace. Tarhe, the chief of the Wyandots, the uncle of the Delawares and Shawnees, the keeper of the council fire at Brownstown, told his "brother Indians" that they now acknowledged "the fifteen United States of America to be our father, and . . . you must call them brothers no more." As children, they were to be "obedient to our father; ever listen to him when he speaks to you, and follow his advice."

[33] The quotations are taken from Thomas Jefferson's recording of the French translation of the chiefs' speeches. Washington at the time listened to an English translation that, according to Jefferson, "varied much from the other." See Speeches of John Baptist de Coigne, Chief of the Wabash and Illinois Indians, and Other Indian Chiefs, Feb. 1, 1793, H. A. Washington, ed., *The Writings of Thomas Jefferson*, 9 vols. (New York, 1859), 8:176–84.

Tarhe also sketched out the duties of a father in a patriarchal alliance. The Americans were to "take care of all your little ones . . . and do not suffer them to be imposed upon. Don't show favor to one, to the injury of any. An impartial father equally regards all his children, as well those who are ordinary as those who may be more handsome; therefore, should any of your children come to you crying and in distress, have pity on them, and relieve their wants."[34]

A father was not a stern patriarch; a father was a generous friend. When New Corn, a Potawatomi chief, spoke after Tarhe, he addressed the Americans as both father and friend. As other chiefs spoke, they commended themselves to their father's protection; they asked him for aid. They would, in the words of Masass, a Chippewa chief, "rejoice in having acquired a new, and so good, a father."[35]

The Americans heard the call for beneficence, and they were ready to grant it, but on their own terms. These were the terms of what Bernard Sheehan has called Jeffersonian philanthropy. Indians were not metaphorically but literally children. They were in the infancy of civilization. Indians were, as Thomas L. McKenney put it much later, "children and require to be nursed, and counselled, and directed as such." Indians had lost control of the language of patriarchy, of the fiction of patriarchy, and the price they would pay would be a terrible one.[36]

This was not to say that the struggle was over when Tarhe, in defeat, acknowledged the Americans as fathers. Chiefs like Black Hoof would struggle within an American alliance to turn the Americans into the older fathers of the middle ground. Tecumseh and Tenskwatawa would struggle to break out of the bonds of American benevolence. But both would fail. The truth was that the older language of patriarchy had not been born of defeat. The French alliance had developed in the face of a common cause against the Iroquois. The British alliance had grown

[34] Treaty of Greenville, Aug. 7, 1795, Speech of Tarhe, *American State Papers: Indian Affairs*, 1:580.

[35] Speeches, Aug. 8, Aug. 10, 1795, ibid., 1:580–82.

[36] Sheehan, *Seeds of Extinction*, p. 153.

from the standoff following Pontiac's Rebellion. The patriarchal alliance with the Americans was born in the defeat at Fallen Timbers.

The Americans would inherit a legacy of a different sort. As much as Cooper, American policymakers like McKenney created fictions. And like Cooper's fictions, they were powerful. They had incredible cultural staying power. By making Indians literally children, by denying them the power to be heard, they left only whites as the arbiters of their credibility. In the long run, like Cooper's Indians, these formulations were not credible. They were a failed fiction. But in the shorter run, they would shape a reality. They would do great damage.

THEDA PERDUE

Native Women in
the Early Republic

Old World Perceptions,

New World Realities

"How opposite is the savage" wrote Bernard Romans in *A Concise Natural History of East and West Florida*, published in 1775. Developing a theme common in eighteenth- and early nineteenth-century commentaries on Native Americans, Romans pointed out that unlike Europeans, North American Indians had "no idea of religion," that they were "incapable of bearing labour," and that "a savage man discharges his urine in a sitting posture, and a savage woman standing." He added, "I need not tell you how opposite this is to our common practice."[1] However startling and even offensive we may find Romans's observation today, it demonstrates a typical approach of eighteenth- and early nineteenth-century historians, travelers, philosophers, and social theorists. As part of the "natural" world, Native peoples received the same kind of scrutiny as flora, fauna, and land forms, and no aspect of their personal lives, however private, escaped commentary, if the observer had access to it. The context in which Euro-Americans tried to make sense of what they saw, of course, was their own culture, and, consequently, their analysis was usually a comparative one.[2] Unlike subsequent generations of historians and even anthropologists, however, these people

[1] Bernard Romans, *A Concise History of East and West Florida* (1775) (Gainesville, Fla., 1962), pp. 40–43.

[2] Among the many works that explore the creation of Euro-American images of Native peoples are Robert F. Berkhofer, Jr., *The White Man's Indian: Images of the American Indian from Columbus to the Present* (New York, 1978);

85

wrote about women as well as men.[3] Women do not receive as extensive commentary as men, probably because observers believed that men controlled Native governments and economies and led intrinsically more interesting lives. Furthermore, early observers were men, and gender conventions restricted their access to many of the activities and rituals of women. Nevertheless, they attempted to record as much detail as they could about women's physical appearance, work, and sexuality.

The result is a remarkably uniform assessment of Native women. Romans phrased it this way: "Their women are handsome, well made, only wanting the colour and cleanliness of our ladies, to make them appear lovely in every eye; their strength is great, and they labour hard, carrying very heavy burdens a great distance; they are lascivious, and have no idea of chastity in a girl, but in married women, incontinence is severely punished; a savage never forgives that crime."[4] According to Romans and hundreds of other writers whose works were read and even revered in the early years of the United States, Native American women did most of the work, and they had a rather casual attitude toward sexual intercourse. Modern recognition of the enormous variety of Native cultures and women's experiences makes it difficult to generalize about the validity of such conclusions, but most evidence suggests that within European definitions of labor and promiscuity, Romans was right. We have come to understand, however, that cultures define labor and promiscuity differently, and so it is important to look at European accounts of Native women in the context of Native cul-

---

Edward Dudley and Maximillian E. Novak, eds., *The Wild Man Within: An Image in Western Thought from the Renaissance to Romanticism* (Pittsburgh, 1972); Roy Harvey Pearce, *Savagism and Civilization: A Study of the Indian and the American Mind* (Berkeley, Calif., 1988); and Bernard W. Sheehan, *Seeds of Extinction: Jeffersonian Philanthropy and the American Indian* (Chapel Hill, N.C., 1973).

[3] For works on Native women, see Rayna D. Green, *Native American Women: A Contextual Bibliography* (Bloomington, Ind., 1983); Deborah Welch, "American Indian Women: Reaching beyond the Myth," in Colin G. Calloway, ed., *New Directions in American Indian History* (Norman, Okla., 1988); and the annotated bibliography in Gretchen M. Baitaille and Kathleen Mullen Sands, *American Indian Women: Telling Their Lives* (Lincoln, Nebr., 1984).

[4] Romans, *Concise History*, pp. 40–43.

tures, as we currently understand them. We also should examine the role of these accounts in shaping Anglo-American views of Indians in the early republic.

However inaccurate, observations and commentaries on Native peoples did not prove to be mere intellectual exercises. Although many of the accounts cited in this essay predated the American Revolution, they comprised a body of evidence that informed and molded early United States Indian policy.[5] One of the problems faced by the early republic was how to deal with the Native peoples who lived within its bounds. Experience taught that war was a costly way of regulating the behavior of Native peoples and obtaining their lands. Consequently, the United States looked for other ways to extinguish Native title and provide for the expansion of its own burgeoning population. The "civilization" program sought to make Native peoples assimilable by teaching them to farm, read and write, pray, and govern themselves like Euro-Americans.

Scarcely had the "civilization" program gotten off the ground before policymakers turned to an alternate and somewhat contradictory policy—removing eastern Indians west of the Mississippi where they could continue their "savage" life and adjust more slowly to "civilization." The "civilization" and removal policies emerged in response to the demands of United States citizens for land, but they developed in the intellectual context of travel accounts and natural histories. The authors of these works were the expert witnesses of the late eighteenth and early nineteenth centuries. We must, therefore, look beyond a mere critique of these sources. Why did European observers see what they did? Why did they choose to record particular aspects of Native women's lives? And finally, why did the early republic find these observations relevant, and how were they used to create a "new world" for Native women?

[5] For the development and implementation of policy, see Reginald Horsman, *Expansion and American Indian Policy, 1783–1812* (East Lansing, Mich., 1967); Francis Paul Prucha, *American Indian Policy in the Formative Years: The Indian Trade and Intercourse Acts, 1790–1834* (Cambridge, Mass., 1962); and Ronald N. Satz, *American Indian Policy in the Jacksonian Era* (Lincoln, Nebr., 1975).

The relationship between image and reality, in respect to Native peoples, is not a new line of inquiry, nor indeed is the impact of image on policy. What is missing in the study of Native Americans is the relationship between gender and policy. In part, this omission stems from the absence of women in the records that normally relate to policy—agency correspondence, treaty negotiations, and the like. However, feminist inquiry, particularly along the lines developed by Joan Wallach Scott, suggests that in addition to rewriting social and literary history to include women, "we must also be willing to rethink the history of politics and the politics of history."[6] Scott challenges historians to examine the ways in which "implicit understandings of gender are being invoked and reinscribed" so that they can find "new perspectives on old questions."[7] We not only need to read familiar documents in a new way, we also must look at the contemporary and long-term ramifications of the descriptions and accounts of women that these documents contain. An analysis of images of Native women in the early republic and the impact of those images on the development of United States Indian policy does indeed provide just such a new perspective. Since history as a discipline produces "cultural knowledge"[8] just as surely as two-hundred-year-old observations, a reevaluation of those images can restore women to a Native history long dominated by chiefs and warriors.

Eighteenth- and early nineteenth-century observers of Indians normally experienced Native cultures in a superficial way, but even the most cursory experience led to assumptions about fundamental values. Accounts of sexual promiscuity rested, in part, on just such a foundation. Euro-Americans, accustomed to the enveloping clothes of their women, looked askance at the remarkably little clothing of Native women.[9] Amerigo Vespucci

[6] Joan Wallach Scott, *Gender and the Politics of History* (New York, 1988), p. 11.

[7] Ibid., pp. 49–50.

[8] Ibid., p. 8.

[9] For examples, see Robert Beverley, *The History and Present State of Virginia* (1705), ed. Louis B. Wright (Chapel Hill, N.C., 1947), p. 166; Patrick Gass, *A*

certainly linked nudity and sexuality: "The women . . . go about naked and are very libidinous."[10] Three hundred years later, the explorer William Clark followed his comments on how "litely" Native women on the Northwest Coast dressed with a further observation that "The *Chin-nook* womin are lude and carry on sport publickly."[11] Although clothing differed dramatically from one Native society to another, it tended to be comfortable and utilitarian. Women often wore loose skirts and blouses or cloaks that enabled them to move with ease. Many Europeans found these quite fetching, particularly when the wind blew, as Stephen Long phrased it, "exposing a well formed thigh."[12] According to Patrick Gass, a member of the Lewis and Clark expedition, ornamentation combined with inclement weather could also provide a cheap thrill for Europeans: "These tassels or fringe [skirts] are of some use as a covering, while the ladies are standing erect and the weather calm; but in any other position, or when the wind blows, their charms have a precarious defence."[13] In summer, Europeans did not need to wait for a breeze: women simply took off their blouses "without any sense of indelicacy" when the weather was hot.[14] While Native clothing appealed to the prurient interests of most commentators, the reformer Dr. Benjamin Rush saw great advantages to sartorial sensibility. He found Native clothing superior to that of

---

Journal of the Voyages and Travels of a Corps of Discovery (Minneapolis, 1958), p. 229; Milo M. Quaife, ed., *The Journals of Captain Meriwether Lewis and Sergeant John Ordway, Kept on the Expedition of Western Exploration, 1803–1806* (Madison, Wis., 1916), pp. 319, 334; idem, ed., *Alexander Mackenzie's Voyage to the Pacific Ocean in 1793* (Chicago, 1931), p. 340; Reuben Gold Thwaites, ed., *Original Journals of the Lewis and Clark Expedition, 1804–1806*, 8 vols. (New York, 1904–5), 3:126.

[10] Quotation in Berkhofer, *White Man's Indian*, pp. 7–9.

[11] Thwaites, ed., *Journals of Lewis and Clark*, 3:294.

[12] Maxine Benson, *From Pittsburgh to the Rocky Mountains: Major Stephen Long's Expedition, 1819–1820* (Golden, Colo., 1988), p. 331.

[13] Gass, *Voyages and Travels*, p. 200.

[14] Benson, *Long's Expedition*, pp. 280, 331.

European women whose tight garments in hot weather compromised their health.[15]

Breasts might be exposed frequently, particularly in warm weather, but pudenda were likely to be kept covered. When women did bare all, Europeans had another shock in store. Native women in many societies plucked their pubic hair.[16] Thomas Jefferson attempted to explain the practice: "With them it is disgraceful to be hairy in the body. They say it likens them to hogs. They therefore pluck the hair as fast as it appears. But the traders who marry their women, and prevail on them to discontinue this practice say, that nature is the same with them as with whites."[17] However comfortable Euro-American men may have been with visible penises, depilation left female genitalia far more exposed than most could bear. It seemed to be a flaunting of female sexuality.

Another cultural modification to the female physique also provoked comment. Among many Native peoples, women as well as men wore tattoos.[18] While some Euro-Americans became so enamored of the practice that they adopted it,[19] others regarded tattooing in the same light as makeup applied to make one more physically attractive. Benjamin Rush, for example, compared the body markings of Native peoples to cosmetics used by the French, a people whom he described as "strangers to what is called delicacy in the intercourse of the sexes with

[15] Benjamin Rush, "Medicine among the Indians of North America," Dagobert D. Runes, ed., *The Selected Writings of Benjamin Rush* (New York, 1947), p. 271.

[16] Beverley, *History and Present State of Virginia*, p. 159; Benson, *Long's Expedition*, p. 230; Quaife, ed., *Mackenzie's Voyage*, p. 42; Samuel Stanhope Smith, *An Essay on the Causes of the Variety of Complexion and Figure in the Human Species* (1810), ed. Winthrop D. Jordan (Cambridge, Mass., 1965), p. 112.

[17] Paul Leicester Ford, ed., *The Writings of Thomas Jefferson*, 10 vols. (New York: 1892–99), 3:154–55.

[18] Benson, *Long's Expedition*, p. 93.

[19] Adolph B. Benson, ed., *Peter Kalm's Travels in North America: The English Version of 1770* (Mineola, N.Y., 1987), pp. 577–78.

each other."[20] Unnatural markings on the body, to Europeans, signaled an enhanced sexuality.

The reputation of the French as sexually uninhibited extends back at least to the eighteenth century, and here too Rush found common ground: "A similar want of delicacy appears in the intercourse of the sexes with each other among the Indians."[21] Rush observed that among both peoples, "their women seldom conceal those wants and necessities to which their sex has subjected them, from the knowledge of men." In a remarkably modern interpretation of the effect of repressed sexuality, Rush cited medical research that demonstrated that the "following of nature must be favourable to the health among the female sex."[22] Other observers, perhaps less well informed, were more disapproving of what seemed to be rampant sexual misconduct.

Native people were often quite open about sexual matters. Meriwether Lewis found that conversation with Native men along the Northwest Coast often turned to women about whom they spoke "without reserve in their presents, of their every part, and of the most familiar connection."[23] The fur trader Pierre Antoine Tabeau claimed that although Arikara men were "absolutely nude, . . . no notice is taken of it. The women and the young girls mingle with the men and laugh, inconsequently, at the most obscene things."[24] People seemed to accept genitalia as respectable organs and sex as a normal part of life.

[20] George W. Corner, ed., *The Autobiography of Benjamin Rush: His "Travels through Life," Together with His Commonplace Book for 1789–1813* (Princeton, 1948), p. 71.

[21] Ibid. Others used the French analogy. Louis-Philippe, who visited the Cherokees on his American tour in the late eighteenth century, insisted that "no Frenchwoman could teach them a thing." And Patrick Gass reported that "the severe and loathsome effects *of certain French principles* are not uncommon among them" (Louis-Philippe, *Diary of My Travels in America*, trans. Stephen Becker [New York, 1977], p. 84; Gass, *Voyages and Travels*, pp. 87–88).

[22] Rush, "Medicine among the Indians," p. 271.

[23] Thwaites, ed., *Journals of Lewis and Clark*, 3:315.

[24] Annie Heloise Abel, ed., *Tabeau's Narrative of Loisel's Expedition to the Upper Missouri* (Norman, Okla., 1939), p. 181.

Domestic space probably contributed to this open attitude, as well as to the image of Native peoples as sexually promiscuous. Samuel Stanhope Smith admitted that Indians were unjustly "represented as licentious because they are seen to lie promiscuously in the same wigwam."[25] Several generations, as well as visitors, usually slept in the same lodge. Nevertheless, few Natives allowed the lack of privacy in their homes to become a barrier to sexual fulfillment or sexual tiffs.[26] When Patrick Campbell was traveling in western New York in the late eighteenth century, he spent a memorable night with an Iroquois woman and her family: "She and her husband slept in the far end of the house. An old squaw slept in a bed near the fire, where I and my servant were stretched on the bare floor, with our soles to the fire. After we had lain down to rest, a drunken Indian came in, made a hideous noise, leaping and capering about, which made me fear he would fall down or trample on my head. After continuing a while in this way, he sprung into bed with the old squaw, who did not seem to feel so well as he did. She made a noise, got out of bed, and sat by us at the fireside. Her gallant soon followed; on which she returned to bed, where he still pursued her; and in this way the farce was kept up for some time, alternately leaping in and out of bed, until the Indian in the other end of the house got up and turned him out of the house, and freed us all of this disagreeable guest."[27]

Openness about sexuality manifested itself in the humor of Native women, which some Europeans found terribly bawdy. Most women enjoyed teasing and joking with those to whom it was socially acceptable. Pranks and jokes with sexual overtones were not necessarily taboo. While visiting a Gros Ventre village, for example, the botanist John Bradbury encountered a group of young women while attempting to cross a river by canoe. They stripped off their clothes and began to play "a number of mischievous tricks" such as splashing the occupants of the canoe, grabbing the paddle, and pulling the canoe off course.

[25] Smith, *Variety of Complexion and Figure*, p. 128.

[26] Frances Latham Harris, *John Lawson's History of North Carolina* (Richmond, 1937), pp. 37–38.

[27] Patrick Campbell, *A Journey through the Genesee Country, Finger Lakes Region, and Mohawk Valley* (1793) (Rochester, N.Y., 1978).

Bradbury's party ultimately recovered its composure and joined in the fun—they hid the young women's clothes—but they remained quite astounded at their brazenness.[28] One Native woman even managed to shock a Frenchman. Louis-Philippe made a tour of the American West at the end of the eighteenth century, and during his visit to the Cherokees his guide made sexual advances to several women. "They were so little embarrassed," wrote the future French king, "that one of them who was lying on a bed put her hand on his trousers before my very eyes and said scornfully, *Ah sick.*"[29]

Directness characterized courtship as well as rejection. While Tabeau recognized the many cultural differences between the Sioux and Arikaras, he observed that the women in both groups were "generally hostile to ceremony and, to avoid the embarrassment of an intrigue, they ordinarily make the first advances in a less equivocal manner and it is here where one truly takes romance by the tail."[30] Thomas Jefferson, in his classic defense of the Native libido, explained why Indian men seemed to exhibit "frigidity": "A celebrated warrior is oftener courted by the females, than he has occasion to court: and this is a point of honor which the men aim at. . . . Custom and manners reconcile them to modes of acting, which, judged by Europeans would be deemed inconsistent with the rules of female decorum and propriety."[31]

While a few observers offered testimony to the virtue of Native women,[32] most agreed that they were "of an amorous temperature" and "of a more lusty make than the other sex."[33]

---

[28] John Bradbury, *Travels in the Interior of America in the Years 1809, 1810, and 1811* (Lincoln, Nebr., 1986), pp. 164–65.

[29] Louis-Philippe, *Diary of Travels*, pp. 84–85.

[30] Abel, ed., *Tabeau's Narrative*, p. 178.

[31] Thomas Jefferson, *Notes on the State of Virginia* (1787), 2d Am. ed. (Philadelphia, 1794), p. 299.

[32] Gass, *Voyages and Travels*, p. 229; Quaife, ed., *Mackenzie's Voyage*, p. 42; Benson, *Long's Expedition*, p. 43.

[33] Quaife, ed., *Mackenzie's Voyage*, p. 117; Jonathan Carver, *Travels in Wisconsin* (1779), 3d London ed. (New York, 1838), p. 160. Carver's *Travels* was probably the work of Dr. John Coakley Lettson.

Women often openly solicited sex from Euro-Americans. Sometimes sexual relations were a matter of survival: Tabeau related how Bois Brules women offered "their favors" for a few mouthfuls of dried meat or soup.[34] Among other peoples, sex gave women an opportunity to participate in the emerging market economy. Unlike men who exchanged deerskins, beaver pelts, and buffalo hides to Europeans for manufactured goods, women often had to rely on "the soft passion" to obtain clothing, kettles, knives, hoes, and trinkets. This sort of sexual encounter, Euro-Americans understood. Patrick Gass noted: "An old Bawd with her punks, may also be found in some of the villages on the Missouri, as well as in the large cities of polished nations."[35] Among some peoples a kind of specialization developed. Natural historian John Lawson claimed that coastal Carolina peoples designated "trading girls," and Gass described a Chinook woman who kept nine girls and "frequently visited our quarters."[36] Sometimes prostitution was more widespread. Louis-Philippe insisted that "all Cherokee women are public women in the full meaning of the phrase: dollars never fail to melt their hearts."[37]

Selling sex was one thing; the apparent gift of women by their husbands and fathers was quite another. Sex was a kind of commodity to Europeans: they purchased it from prostitutes with money and from respectable women with marriage. An honorable man protected the chastity of his wife and daughters as he would other property. Native men in many societies, however, condoned or even encouraged sexual relations between Europeans and women "belonging" to them. Meriwether Lewis claimed that Native peoples in the Northwest would "prostitute their wives and daughters for a fishing hook or a strand of beads."[38] Even husbands who might object to "secret infidelities" sometimes offered their wives to visitors. An Arapaho whom Long encountered was particularly persistent: "After we

[34] Abel, ed., *Tabeau's Narrative*, p. 73.

[35] Gass, *Voyages and Travels*, pp. 87–88.

[36] Harris, *Lawson's History*, pp. 37–38; Gass, *Voyages and Travels*, p. 229.

[37] Louis-Philippe, *Diary of Travels*, p. 72.

[38] Thwaites, ed., *Journals of Lewis and Clark*, 3:315.

had retired to our tent at night, a brother of the grand chief, Bear's-tooth, continued to interrupt our repose, with solicitations in favor of a squaw he had brought with him, until he was peremptorily directed to begone, and the centinel was ordered to prevent his further intrusion."[39]

Most amazing of all sexual encounters was the one experienced by the Lewis and Clark expedition and reported by the fur trader Pierre Antoine Tabeau. The Mandans with whom the explorers had wintered in 1803 invited their guests to participate in a ceremony intended to "draw the cow near the village," that is, to encourage a buffalo herd to come within easy range. In this ceremony, old men stripped naked, and young men offered their wives to them. The old men, according to Tabeau, began to "touch them, bellow, roar, paw the earth, strike it with their heads and make dust fly." The women then took the old men outside the lodge where the ceremony had begun and engaged in sexual intercourse with them on the prairie. When the old men reentered the lodge, "the husbands thank them very humbly, and the ceremony continues all night, the actors only changing partners at each scene." Normally it took ten to fifteen nights of repeating the ceremony before the buffalo came close enough, but according to Tabeau, the ceremony in which the Lewis and Clark expedition participated lasted only two or three nights: "This early success the Mandans attributed to the captains' people, who were untiringly zealous in attracting the cow."[40]

Blatant disregard of marital vows was shocking enough, but many Native peoples exhibited little concern for the chastity of their daughters. Jean-Bernard Bossu reported that "when an unmarried brave passes through a village, he hires a girl for a night or two, as he pleases, and her parents find nothing wrong with this. They are not at all worried about their daughter and explain that her body is hers to do with as she wishes."[41] Gass ex-

---

[39] Benson, *Long's Expedition*, pp. 333–34; Abel, ed., *Tabeau's Narrative*, p. 178; Carver, *Travels*, p. 229.

[40] Abel, ed., *Tabeau's Narrative*, pp. 196–97.

[41] Seymour Feiler, ed., *Jean-Bernard Bossu's Travels in the Interior of North America, 1751–1762* (Norman, Okla., 1962), pp. 131–32.

pressed dismay that "for an old tobacco box, one of our men was granted the honour of passing the night with the daughter of the headchief of the Mandan nation."[42] Such wanton abandon did not seem to diminish the reputation of young women among many Native peoples. Jonathan Carver maintained that women "before they are married are not the less esteemed for the indulgence of their passions."[43]

According to these accounts, Native women clearly *were* lascivious. Some evidence, however, suggests that Native women were not as amenable to sexual encounters as Europeans suggest. Louis-Philippe's anecdote reveals a woman, however bold and uninhibited, rejecting a sexual advance. When women did engage in sexual activity, many of them probably succumbed to pressure or force rather than charm. European culture at this time countenanced considerable violence against women.[44] William Byrd's confidential account of surveying the boundary line between North Carolina and Virginia, for example, describes several episodes of sexual aggression. One young woman, he wrote, "wou'd certainly have been ravish't, if her timely consent had not prevented the violence."[45] This cavalier attitude toward women's right to refuse sex characterized much interaction between Native women and Europeans. Race, in fact, probably exacerbated the situation. The records of the South Carolina Indian trade are replete with Native complaints of sexual abuse. One trader "took a young Indian against her Will for his Wife," another severely beat three women including his pregnant wife whom he killed, and a third provided

[42] Gass, *Voyages and Travels*, pp. 87–88.

[43] Carver, *Travels*, p. 160.

[44] So did some Native cultures, at least in the late nineteenth century. A Cheyenne woman told Truman Michelson that a young man had torn the sleeve of her dress in the process of courtship and that her mother went to extraordinary lengths to protect her virtue "against the attacks of an over anxious young man" (Truman Michelson, "Narrative of a Southern Cheyenne Woman," *Smithsonian Miscellaneous Collections* 87, pt. 5 [1932]:3–4).

[45] William K. Boyd, ed., *William Byrd's Histories of the Dividing Line betwixt Virginia and North Carolina* (Raleigh, 1929), pp. 147–48; also see pp. 53, 57, 67, 91.

enough rum to a woman to get her drunk and then "used her ill."[46] Certainly the women in these incidents were not the ones who were lascivious. Some Native peoples came to regard sexual misbehavior as the most distinguishing feature of European culture. The Cherokee Booger Dance, in which participants imitated various peoples, portrayed Europeans as sexually aggressive, and the men playing that role chased screaming young women around the dance ground.[47]

Even when women engaged willingly in sexual relationships, they were not as free of restraints as most whites thought. Europeans failed to realize that Native Americans did have rules regulating marriage and sexual intercourse, although the rules were sometimes quite different from those that Europeans espoused. The Arapaho, Cheyenne, and Fox women whom Truman Michelson interviewed in the early twentieth century about their lives in the nineteenth, underwent instruction in the rules of courtship at menarche, and their mothers constantly reminded them about proper observance.[48] The Cheyenne woman told Michelson that her mother even tied rawhide "around my hips and pudendum" in order "to preserve my virtue." In the Southeast, unmarried people could engage freely in sex, but many factors other than marital state regulated and limited sexuality. A warrior preparing for or returning from battle (sometimes much of the summer), a ball player getting

[46] William L. McDowell, ed., *Journals of the Commissioners of the Indian Trade, Sept. 20, 1710–Aug. 29, 1718* (Columbia, S.C., 1955), pp. 4, 37; idem, *Documents Relating to Indian Affairs, 1754–1765* (Columbia, S.C., 1970), p. 231.

[47] Frank G. Speck and Leonard Broom, *Cherokee Dance and Drama* (Berkeley, Calif., 1951).

[48] Truman Michelson, "Narrative of an Arapaho Woman," *American Anthropologist* 35 (1933):601; idem, "Cheyenne Woman," pp. 4–5; idem, "The Autobiography of a Fox Woman," *Fortieth Annual Report of the Bureau of American Anthropology* (1925):305–7. These accounts are, of course, from the twentieth century. I have used them for two reasons. First, Native women left few accounts of their own, particularly from the nineteenth century. In fact, the farther back one reaches, the less there is. Virtually nothing survives from the early republic. Secondly, and more significantly, I think that these women relate practices that are very old and most likely existed in the period this essay addresses.

ready for a game, a man on the winter hunt (three to four months in the winter), a pregnant woman, or a woman during her menstrual period abstained from sex.[49] The Arapaho woman interviewed by Michelson was taught to refuse intercourse while she nursed an infant, and Arapaho women usually weaned their children at the age of two.[50] In other words, many Native peoples had to forego sexual intercourse for a far greater percentage of their lives than Europeans.

Furthermore, there were inappropriate venues for sex. While a Native couple might engage in sex in a room occupied by others, there were places, such as fields, where amorous encounters were forbidden. Violation of this rule could have serious consequences. The Cherokees blamed a devastating smallpox epidemic in 1738, according to the trader James Adair, on "the adulterous intercourses of their young married people, who the past year, had in a most notorious manner, violated their ancient laws of marriage in every thicket, and broke down and polluted many of the honest neighbours bean-plots, by their heinous crimes, which would cost a great deal of trouble to purify again."[51] For many Native peoples, therefore, a "toss in the hay" would have been a very serious offense.

Native peoples often imbued sex with different meaning from Europeans, who copulated for pleasure and procreation. The ceremony for attracting the buffalo, engaged in by members of the Lewis and Clark expedition, was not an orgy in Native eyes. Instead, the old men transferred their spiritual power, which had manifested itself in a lifetime of successful hunts, to the younger men through sexual intercourse with the young hunters' wives. In another example, the wife of an Arapaho man who sponsored a Sun Dance, had intercourse twice with the previous sponsor so that she could convey the power to con-

[49] Harris, *Lawson's History*, p. 197; Samuel Cole Williams, ed., *Adair's History of the American Indians* (Johnson City, Tenn., 1930), pp. 130, 171, 244; Frans M. Olbrechts, "Cherokee Belief and Practice with Regard to Childbirth," *Anthropos* 26 (1931): 17–33.

[50] Michelson, "Arapho Woman," p. 606.

[51] Williams, *Adair's History*, p. 244.

duct the ceremony to her husband. Sex, in these societies, could be a spiritual experience rather than a physical one.[52]

While the sexual freedom of women troubled Europeans who did not understand the Native rules regulating it, they found familial relationships even more alarming. In particular, they tended to regard polygamy as rendering women "contemptible in men's eyes."[53] Many Native peoples practiced polygamy.[54] Tabeau claimed that the Arikaras sought several wives because "the more women a Ricara has, the more opulent is his lodge."[55] Certainly, additional women in the household contributed to subsistence and eased the workload. Many societies encouraged sororal polygamy in which a man married sisters. Pretty-Shield, for example, a Crow woman who was interviewed in the early twentieth century, married her older sister's husband when she was sixteen. The same man also married her younger sister.[56] Europeans, however, considered such unions to be incestuous. Jedidiah Morse, in his *Universal Geography*, wrote: "When a man loves his wife, it is considered his duty to marry her sister, if she has one. Incest and bestiality are common among them."[57]

Native peoples had rules against incest, but they did not define incest in the same way as Morse and other Euro-Americans. Intercourse or marriage with a member of a person's own clan, for example, usually was prohibited, and the penalty could be

[52] Alice B. Kehoe, "The Function of Ceremonial Sexual Intercourse among the Northern Plains Indian," *Plains Anthropologist* 15 (1970):99–103.

[53] "Reflections on the Institutions of the Cherokee Indians," *Analectic Magazine* 45 (1818):36.

[54] For example, see Abel, ed., *Tabeau's Narrative*, pp. 148–49; Quaife, ed., *Mackenzie's Voyage*, pp. 38–39; Alexander Longe, "A Small Postscript on the Ways and Manners of the Indians Called Cherokees," ed. David H. Cockran, *Southern Indian Studies* 21 (1969):30.

[55] Abel, ed., *Tabeau's Narrative*, pp. 148–49.

[56] Frank Linderman, *Pretty-Shield, Medicine Woman of the Crows* (1932) (Lincoln, Nebr., 1972), pp. 131–32.

[57] Jedidiah Morse, *The American Universal Geography; or, A View of the Present State of All the Kingdoms, States, and Colonies in the Known World* (Boston, 1812), p. 105.

death. Clan membership, that is, all those people who traced their ancestry back to a remote ancestor, often ran into the thousands and included many people whom Europeans would not have regarded as relatives. Consequently, the number of forbidden partners was far greater than under the European definition of incest. The Cherokees, for example, had seven clans. No one could marry into their own clan, nor was father's clan an acceptable marriage pool. The result was that almost one-third of all Cherokees were off-limits as sexual partners.[58] Each Native people had particular rules regarding marriage and incest. When those rules permitted polygamy, the effect was not necessarily the devaluation of women. Some cultural anthropologists suggest, in fact, that sororal polygamy correlates positively with high female status.[59]

Polygamous or not, in the estimation of many Euro-Americans, Native marriage meant little. Although adultery usually carried a stiff penalty, marriages could be dissolved easily. Tabeau reported that Arikara marriages sometimes lasted no longer than an hour.[60] Mary Jemison, a captive child whom the Senecas adopted, revealed in her early nineteenth-century autobiography that "divorces are frequent. If a difficulty of importance arises between a married couple, they agree to separate."[61] Other narratives of Native women who lived later in the nineteenth century often mention divorce, usually at the instigation of the wife.[62] Lawson described the ease with which the Native peoples of coastal Carolina altered their marital status: "The marriages of these Indians are no further binding than

[58] John Phillip Reid, *A Law of Blood: Primitive Law of the Cherokee Nation* (New York, 1970); Alexander Spoehr, *Changing Kinship Systems: A Study in the Acculturation of the Creeks, Cherokee, and Choctaw* (Chicago, 1947).

[59] Alice Schlegel, *Male Dominance and Female Autonomy: Domestic Authority in Matrilineal Societies* (New Haven, 1972), pp. 87–99.

[60] Abel, ed., *Tabeau's Narrative*, p. 181.

[61] James Everett Seaver, *A Narrative of the Life of Mary Jemison* (1824) (New York, 1949), p. 171.

[62] Linderman, *Pretty-Shield*, p. 34; Michelson, "Fox Woman," p. 325; Michelson, "Arapaho Woman," p. 606.

the man and woman agree together. Either of them has the liberty to leave the other upon any frivolous excuse they can make."[63] The Illinois, according to Bossu, "merely separate when they are no longer happy together, claiming that marriage is a matter of love and mutual assistance."[64] A Cherokee priest explained to the trader Alexander Longe his people's lax attitude toward marriage: "They had better be asunder than together if they do not love one another but live for strife and confusion."[65]

When husband and wife parted, children usually remained with their mothers. That is because many Native peoples east of the Rockies—among them, the Iroquois of the Northeast, all southeastern peoples, and the Mandans, Hidatsas, and Arikaras of the upper Missouri—were matrilineal: they traced kinship through women.[66] John Lawson attributed what seemed to him to be a very odd way of reckoning kin to "fear of Impostors; the Savages knowing well, how much Frailty possesses *Indian* women, betwixt the Garters and the Girdle."[67] While paternity might be questioned, maternity could not be. However logical such a system seemed, Europeans had both intellectual and practical objections. Matrilineality was, in Colden's words, "according to the natural course of all animals."[68] "Civilized" man, of course, had moved beyond this "natural course" and had adopted laws, civil and religious, that bound fathers to children and husbands to wives. But when Euro-American men married Native women and then separated, it became "impossible for

---

[63] Harris, *Lawson's History*, pp. 197–98.

[64] Feiler, ed., *Bossu's Travels*, p. 77.

[65] Longe, "Postscript," p. 30.

[66] Morse, *American Universal Geography*, pp. 575–76; Cadwallader Colden, *History of the Five Indian Nations of Canada which are Dependent on the Provinces of New York* (1747), 2 vols. (New York, 1922), 1:xxxii; Albert Gallatin, "Synopsis of the Indian Tribes within the United States East of the Rocky Mountains," in *Archaeologia Americana: Transactions and Collections of the American Antiquarian Society* 2 (1836):112–13.

[67] Harris, *Lawson's History*, pp. 37–38.

[68] Colden, *Five Indian Nations*, 1:xxxiii.

the Christians to get their children."[69] In these matrilineal societies, men had no proprietary interest in their offspring.
Thomas Nairne wrote of the Creeks: "A Girles Father has not
the least hand or concern in matching her." Nor did children
benefit from whatever distinctions their fathers enjoyed: "Sons
never enjoy their fathers place and dignity."[70]

Yet familial bonds held most Native societies together. In
his justification for removing eastern Indians, Andrew Jackson's
secretary of war, Lewis Cass, wrote: "Government is unknown
among them; certainly, that government which prescribes general rules and enforces or vindicates them. The utter nakedness
of their society can be known only by personal observation. The
tribes seem to be held together by a kind of family ligament;
by the ties of blood, which in the infancy of society are stronger
as other associations are weaker." Euro-Americans might employ familial imagery and pay homage to the "father of his
country," but family could not substitute for government among
a "civilized" people. Terrible abominations resulted when responsibility for law and order rested with families, in particular "retaliation on the next of kin . . . for the accidental killing of one of their own tribe." Reliance on family meant that
Native peoples failed to establish the fundamental institutions of "civilization." According to Cass, "They have no criminal code, no courts, no offices, no punishments. They have
no relative duties to enforce, no debts to collect, no property to
restore."[71]

Even those kinship bonds that served as government seemed
weak because clans frequently adopted prisoners of war to replace deceased members. How could family affection be strong
if clans so willingly took in captives, particularly captives from
the same tribe responsible for the deaths of kinsmen? How

[69] John H. Logan, *A History of the Upper Country of South Carolina, from the
Earliest Periods, to the Close of the War of Independence*, 2 vols. (Charleston, S.C.,
1859), 1:288.

[70] Alexander Moore, ed., *Nairne's Muskogean Journals: The 1708 Expedition to
the Mississippi River* (Jackson, Miss., 1988), pp. 33, 45.

[71] Lewis Cass, "Removal of the Indians," *North American Review* 30 (1830):
73–74, 91.

could the captives so easily transfer allegiance to former enemies? Was this not unpatriotic or even treasonous? Samuel
Stanhope Smith posed these questions in his *Essay on the Causes
of the Variety of Complexion and Figure in the Human Species.*[72] He
found many "circumstances . . . which render the relinquishing
of his native region a much less sacrifice to the savage, than to
the citizen," among them, the fact that the citizen "is attached
to his country by property, . . . [and] by a long dependence
upon parents." On the contrary, Smith contended, "a savage
can hardly be said to have a country." Property and family
helped create citizens. Many Euro-Americans contended that
Native peoples did not have a fully developed concept of either.[73] In his account of the Lewis and Clark expedition, Patrick
Gass reported that "these Indians on the coast have no horses,
and very little property of any kind, except their canoes. The
women are much given to venery, and like those on the Missouri are sold to prostitution at an easy rate."[74] In his journal,
Gass linked the absence of property and the looseness of
women. So devoid were these people of any notion of property
that men did not even have an exclusive proprietary interest in
their wives, nor were they certain of the paternity of their wives'
offspring. The absence of property and proprietary rights was at
the very heart of Native "barbarism."[75]

The organization and governance of families seemed particularly significant for citizens of the early republic. Not only
did political ideology and rhetoric employ familial imagery,
family polity, republicans believed, had enormous influence on
government. An unregulated family life could not be expected

[72] Smith, *Variety of Complexion and Figure*, pp. 235–41.

[73] Carver observed that "the Indians in the common state are stranger to
all distinctions of property" (*Travels*, p. 21). The Lewis and Clark expedition,
on the other hand, carefully noted the lands specific Native nations claimed.
Nevertheless, they used phrases such as "They claim the country in which they
rove," which hardly implied absolute ownership (Thwaites, *Journals of Lewis
and Clark*, 6:83–95).

[74] Gass, *Voyages and Travels*, p. 229.

[75] James Hall, *Sketches of History, Life, and Manners in the West*, 2 vols. (Philadelphia, 1835), 1:128.

to produce civic virtue.[76] The concept of republican mother-hood placed considerable responsibility for inculcating republican values on women and linked female private virtue, defined as purity and piety, to the male civic virtues of independence, reason, moderation, and productivity. According to Linda K. Kerber, "Responsibility for maintaining public virtue was channeled into domestic life."[77] What Euro-Americans perceived as blatant disregard of marriage vows and willful abrogation of parental authority by Native peoples, therefore, had significance far beyond the individuals involved. Such behavior bespoke an absence of rules. Divorce occurred frequently among the Illinois, according to Bossu, because they were "not bound by civil contract."[78] Sexual freedom had political ramifications: James Adair described the Cherokees' lack of laws against adultery as "petticoat-government."[79] Freedom within the family translated into anarchy within the state. "The Indians, as individuals," wrote the Jeffersonian Albert Gallatin, "have preserved a much greater independence than is compatible with a more advanced state of civilization. They will hardly submit to any restraints."[80] Furthermore, the affection shared by family members seemed to be absent. How could a doting father prostitute his daughter? How could a loving husband surrender his wife to another man? How could a respectable wife and mother engage in sex outside the marriage bed? Sexual freedom, according to Europeans, degraded women, jeopardized civic order, and subverted republican values. On the other hand, sexual purity liberated women in the same way as political independence and economic autonomy liberated men.

[76] In *From Colonies to Commonwealth: Familial Ideology and the Beginnings of the American Republic* (Baltimore, 1985), Melvin Yazawa charts the demise of familial ideology in the early republic. Although citizens of the United States may no longer have viewed themselves as members of a patriarchal national family, they certainly understood other societies in terms of this familial ideology. See also Linda K. Kerber, *Women of the Republic: Intellect and Ideology in Revolutionary America* (Chapel Hill, N.C., 1980).

[77] Kerber, *Women of the Republic*, p. 287.

[78] Feiler, ed., *Bossu's Travels*, p. 77.

[79] Williams, ed., *Adair's History*, p. 153.

[80] Gallatin, "Synopsis of the Indian Tribes," p. 108.

Early republicans found the economic productivity of women equally threatening to post-Revolutionary adaptations of Revolutionary ideology. Carroll Smith-Rosenberg has described the way in which essayists rendered middle-class white women sexually powerless and economically unproductive: the early republic depicted women as consumers, not producers.[81] Yet Native women not only farmed, but the sexual division of labor in most Native societies, unlike plantation slavery or yeomen agriculture, assigned farming *primarily* to women and exempted men from many of the most arduous tasks, such as hoeing. The most appropriate analogy for such an arrangement, in which women performed most of the labor and men enjoyed the fruits of that labor, was slavery. For republicans, slavery was the very antithesis of liberty. They had employed the imagery effectively in articulating the Revolutionary cause: the British king, they charged, had attempted to enslave them, to deprive them of their property. And yet many in the early republic held slaves.[82] This tension between slavery and freedom characterized early American history and provided a vocabulary to describe the status of Native women. Therefore, it is not surprising that Gallatin, in his "Synopsis of the Indian Tribes," should adopt the imagery: "Women are everywhere slaves and beasts of burden."[83]

The characterization of Native women as drudges is common in the travel literature and natural histories of the eighteenth and early nineteenth centuries. This image is not surprising because the array of tasks performed by women was daunting. They procured much of the food: they grew vegetables, gath-

---

[81] Carroll Smith-Rosenberg, "Dis-Covering the Subject of the 'Great Constitutional Discussion,' 1786–1789," *Journal of American History* 79 (1992): 841–73.

[82] Edmund S. Morgan, *American Slavery, American Freedom: The Ordeal of Colonial Virginia* (New York, 1975); Kenneth S. Greenberg, *Masters and Statesmen: The Political Culture of American Slavery* (Baltimore, 1985); William J. Cooper, *Liberty and Slavery: Southern Politics to 1860* (New York, 1983).

[83] Gallatin, "Synopsis of the Indian Tribes," p. 151. Gallatin, like Jefferson, was very well read in accounts of American Indians including those of Lawson, Colden, Jesuits, Beverley, Romans, DeSoto, Long, Mackenzie, Carver, and Lewis and Clark.

ered berries and nuts, dug roots, made sugar and salt, and caught fish. They cooked this produce or preserved it for later use. They also prepared the meat men provided. Women cut firewood, carried water, and made shoes and clothing. Among many peoples, they erected their houses and furnished them with couches, mats, blankets, pottery, baskets, and other house-hold goods.[84] When they traveled with their families, the re-sponsibility of transporting belongings usually fell to them. "It is not uncommon," Alexander MacKenzie wrote of the Beavers, "while the men carry nothing but a gun, that their wives and daughters follow with such weighty burdens, that if they lay them down they cannot replace them."[85]

As Mackenzie reveals, the division of labor, as much as the labor itself, troubled Euro-Americans. Men seemed to do very little to contribute to the support and comfort of their families. "The sole occupation of an Indian [man's] life," wrote Lieuten-ant Timberlake about the Cherokees, "are hunting and warring abroad, and lazying at home."[86] Cadwallader Colden went fur-ther in his description of the Iroquois: "At times, when it is not proper to hunt, one finds the old Men in Companies, in Con-versation; the young Men at their Exercises, shooting at Marks, throwing the Hatchet, Wrestling, or Running, and the Women all busy at Labour in the Fields."[87] In other words, women worked while men played.

The refusal of men to assist women in their tasks further con-firmed the view that women were slaves. "War and the chase,"

[84] Feiler, ed., *Bossu's Travels*, pp. 131–32; Colden, *Five Indian Nations*, 1: xxxii; Benson, *Long's Expedition*, p. 93; Quaife, ed., *Journals of Lewis and Ord-way*, p. 359; Bradbury, *Travels in the Interior of America*, p. 175; Samuel Cole Williams, *Lieut. Henry Timberlake's Memoirs, 1756–65* (Johnson City, Tenn., 1927), p. 68; Williams, ed., *Adair's History*, pp. 434–41, 447, 453–56; Louis-Phillippe, *Diary of Travels*, p. 78; *Letters of Benjamin Hawkins, 1796–1806* (Sa-vannah, 1916), p. 24; William Bartram, "Observations on the Creek and Cherokee Indians, 1789," *Transactions of the American Ethnological Society* 3, pt. 1 (1853):31, 82; Harris, *Lawson's History*, p. 194.

[85] Colden, *Five Indian Nations*, 1:xxxii; Benson, *Long's Expedition*; Quaife, ed., *Mackenzie's Voyage*, p. 39.

[86] Williams, *Timberlake's Memoirs*, p. 99.

[87] Colden, *Five Indian Nations*, 1:xxxii.

Gallatin wrote, "are the only pursuits the men do not think beneath their dignity."[88] William Clark observed among the Shoshones that "women doe all the drudgery except fishing and takeing care of the horses, which the men apr. to take upon themselves."[89] Stephen Long watched an Omaha man depart a trading post with his Sioux wife "to whom he appears to be much attached": she bore "a heavy load, consisting of the goods which her husband had received in exchange for his beaver, on her back, whilst he carried only a keg of whiskey over his shoulders, and his gun and hunting apparatus."[90] Mackenzie was appalled that Beaver "men will not deign" even to assist women in lifting their packs to their backs.[91] The reformer Dr. Benjamin Rush and Secretary of War Lewis Cass, two men with quite different perspectives and concerns, agreed that Indian men "despise labor."[92] Tabeau grudgingly acknowledged that Arikara men helped their wives build forts to protect them from their enemies, but added, "What cannot panic terror do!"[93]

The contrast between male and female occupations led many Europeans to assume that women were indeed slaves of men. Tabeau was perhaps the most outraged. Women were, he claimed, "in the fullest sense slaves." The female sex had been "reduced to the most humiliating slavery by tyrants, who enjoy all the fruits of its labors."[94] Mackenzie also referred to their "abject state of slavery."[95] Both men were traders who had spurned a life of agricultural or industrial toil. They associated the strenuous yet menial tasks that women performed with slave labor and doubted that anyone would willingly do such work. But women's bondage also derived from the theft of their prop-

[88] Gallatin, "Synopsis of the Indian Tribes," p. 151.

[89] Thwaites, ed., *Journals of Lewis and Clark*, 3:10.

[90] Benson, *Long's Expedition*, p. 127.

[91] Quaife, ed., *Mackenzie's Voyage*, p. 39.

[92] Corner, ed., *Autobiography of Rush*, p. 303; "Removal of the Indians," pp. 73–74.

[93] Abel, ed., *Tabeau's Narrative*, p. 204.

[94] Ibid., pp. 148–49, 182.

[95] Quaife, ed., *Mackenzie's Voyage*, p. 40.

erty, that is, the goods they produced and the services they provided. "They endure alone, all the labor of farming," Tabeau railed, "a resource without which the men would probably not be able to live; because of their sloth and laziness; for it is only by its means that the women procure their food and the clothes that the men buy from strange nations. . . . all that they obtain by their work is employed for the use and for the dissipation of these idle barbarians and they cannot even procure the iron tools necessary for their work."[96] Women performed back-breaking work and then surrendered the fruits of their labor. Surely this was slavery.

Much to the astonishment of many observers, Native women did not seem to object to doing most of the work.[97] Thomas Say, a member of Stephen Long's expedition, chronicled women's tasks among the Kansas and then added: "These duties, as far as we could observe, they not only willingly performed as a matter of duty, but they exhibited in their deportment a degree of pride and ambition to acquit themselves well; in this respect resembling a good housewife amongst the civilized fair."[98] Daniel Butrick, a missionary to the Cherokees, came to a similar conclusion: "Though custom attached the heaviest part of the labour to the women, yet they were cheerful and voluntary in performing it. What others have discovered among the Indians I cannot tell, but though I have been about nineteen years among the Cherokees, I have perceived nothing of that slavish, servile fear, on the part of women, so often spoke of."[99] The testimony of Native women, both in the early republic and in later years, suggests the same attitude toward labor. Mary Jemison fondly recalled a community of women working together: "Our labor was not severe. . . . In the summer season, we planted, tended and harvested our corn, and generally had no master to oversee or drive us, so that we could work as leisurely as we

[96] Abel, ed., *Tabeau's Narrative*, pp. 148–49.

[97] The most negative response Tabeau got from his women neighbors was that "if enough whites come, the Ricaras would have no women" (ibid., p. 149).

[98] Benson, *Long's Expedition*, p. 93.

[99] John Howard Payne Papers, 4:27, Newberry Library, Chicago.

pleased." Seneca women did not have "that endless variety that is to be observed in the common labor of the white people." Cooking utensils and household articles were few and needed little care. Spinning, weaving, and knitting were unknown, and so women dressed simply. In fact, Jemison, who chose to remain with the Senecas, believed that "their task is probably not harder than that of white women . . . and their cares certainly are not half as numerous, nor as great."[100]

Why did women work so willingly? First of all, most Native peoples defined gender in terms other than merely biological ones. Women were women not only because they could bear children but also because they had responsibility for certain tasks, and men who did those tasks came to be regarded as women in other respects: they dressed in women's clothes, associated with women, and performed sexually as women.[101] Farming, in particular, was linked to women's identity, sexuality, and procreative role. Among the Cherokees, Selu, the first woman, gave birth to the human race as well as to corn, and she was the corn spirit.[102] Each generation of women, in turn, became the progenitor of corn. Waheenee, Buffalo-Bird woman, interviewed in the twentieth century, recalled her childhood in a traditional Hidatsa town: "We cared for our corn in those days, as we would care for children. We thought that the corn plants had souls, and that the growing corn liked to hear us sing, as children like to hear their mothers sing."[103] In the Native

---

[100] Seaver, *Life of Mary Jemison*, pp. 46–48. Although she was genetically white, culturally Jemison was comfortable as a Seneca. Consequently, she can give us a relatively good view of how Seneca women regarded their lives.

[101] For typical descriptions of berdache, see Benson, *Long's Expedition*, p. 93; "The Mississippi Voyage of Jolliet and Marquette, 1673," in Louis Phelps Kellogg, ed., *Early Narratives of the Northwest, 1634–1699* (1917; reprint ed., New York, 1967), p. 244. Also see Raymond DeMallie, "Male and Female in Traditional Lakota Culture," in Patricia Albers and Beatrice Medicine, eds., *The Hidden Half: Studies of Plains Indian Women* (Lanham, Md., 1983), pp. 237–68; Walter L. Williams, *The Spirit and the Flesh: Sexual Diversity in American Indian Culture* (Boston, 1986).

[102] James Mooney, "Myths of the Cherokee," *Nineteenth Annual Report of the Bureau of American Ethnology* (1900), pp. 242–52.

[103] Gilbert Wilson, ed., "Waheenee: An Indian Girl's Story, Told by Herself," *North Dakota History* 38 (1971):94. Waheenee was Wilson's chief informant for

Southeast, women ritually presented the new crop at the Green Corn Ceremony, which repaired social relations as well as commemorated the harvest.[104] A spirituality, therefore, permeated the sexual division of labor in Native societies and made even the most difficult of menial tasks metaphysical. To fulfill one's task not only assured economic prosperity, it reaffirmed cosmic order.

Work also brought social rewards. Native women usually labored as a community. Pretty-Shield, a Crow woman interviewed in the twentieth century, recalled the days when her people followed the buffalo: "It was good hard work to get things packed up, and moving; and it was hard, fast work to get them in shape again, after we camped. But in between these times we rested our traveling horses. Yes, and we women visited while we traveled."[105] Waheenee remembered that her mothers' friends "came in to [the lodge to] sit and chat; and they often joined my mothers at whatever task they might be doing." Girls looked forward to their admission into this community of women: "I could hardly wait to eat my breakfast the next morning," Waheenee recalled, "for my mothers had promised to take me with them to gather wood, [a task that signaled her transition to adulthood]."[106] Men as well as women socialized girls into their adult roles. The interviews Michelson conducted with Cheyenne and Arapaho women reveal men praising their daughters for completion of small tasks such as making a pair of moccasins or preparing a meal. The appreciative response of these fathers suggests that women knew that men as well as other women valued their work.[107]

The notion that women lost all proprietary interest in what they produced is not supported by the evidence. European notions of ownership do not translate well into Native terms, par-

---

his *Agriculture of the Hidatsa Indians: An Indian Interpretation* (Minneapolis, 1917).

[104] Williams, ed., *Adair's History*, pp. 105–17.

[105] Linderman, *Pretty-Shield*, p. 22.

[106] Wilson, ed., "Waheenee," pp. 51, 85.

[107] Michelson, "Cheyenne Woman," pp. 1–13; idem, "Arapaho Woman," pp. 595–610.

ticularly among societies (such as those in the Southeast) that had redistributive economies, but it is clear that women had control over the product of their labor.[108] The naturalist William Bartram observed that among the Creeks and Cherokees, "marriage gives no right to the husband over the property of his wife."[109] The "property" included agricultural produce, household and personal goods, and their dwelling, which belonged to the wife's lineage. Eighteenth-century travelers in the Southeast normally purchased corn from women instead of men, and in the 1750s the British garrison at Fort Loudoun actually employed a female purchasing agent to procure corn.[110] On the upper Missouri, where agricultural produce was a central component of the complex system of Native trade, the Mandan and Arikara women who cultivated the crops seem to have participated in their exchange.[111] According to the accounts of Waheenee and Pretty-Shield, women as culturally different as the agricultural Hidatsa and nomadic Crow owned the lodges they constructed.[112] At the western extreme of the American republic, women exercised even more control over property, perhaps because status on the Northwest Coast derived from the accumulation (and dispersal) of goods. Tlingit women often vetoed deals struck by men, and Haida women reportedly beat their husbands if they made a bad bargain.[113] These were not powerless women, deprived of their labor and its product.

No discussion of the outrage Europeans expressed over the status of women would be complete without a comment on their actions. Apparently subscribing to the adage "When in

[108] Mark Van Doren, ed., *The Travels of William Bartram* (New York, 1928), p. 401.

[109] Bartram, "Observation," p. 66.

[110] McDowell, ed., *Documents Relating to Indian Affairs*, p. 303; Williams, *Timberlake's Memoirs*, pp. 89–90; Hawkins, *Letters*, p. 110.

[111] Quaife, ed., *Journals of Lewis and Ordway*, pp. 149, 160; Thwaites, ed., *Journals of Lewis and Clark*, 1:97, Gass, *Voyages and Travels*, p. 77.

[112] Wilson, ed., "Waheenee," p. 16; Linderman, *Pretty-Shield*, p. 27.

[113] Erna Gunther, *Indian Life on the Northwest Coast of North America as Seen by the Early Explorers and Fur Traders during the Last Decades of the Eighteenth Century* (Chicago, 1972), pp. 121, 164.

Rome . . . ," most non-Native men quickly adopted the Native division of labor. John Lawson pointed out that "the English traders are seldom without an Indian female for his bedfellow." The reason may have been as much survival as romance because, according to Lawson, "the Indian miss's ever securing her white friend provisions whilst he stays with them."[114] And Native women certainly eased western travel. Father Jacques Marquette recorded very matter-of-factly in his journal, "The Illinois women complete our portage in the morning."[115]

If women did all the work, then what did Native men do? They, of course, hunted. Colden maintained that Iroquois men "employ themselves alone in hunting, as the only proper Business for soldiers," and Gallatin insisted that "war and the chase are the only pursuits which the men do not think beneath their dignity."[116] Thomas L. McKenney, a key figure in United States Indian affairs in the Monroe, Adams, and Jackson administrations, wrote disapprovingly of Native men's "passion for the chase . . . [and] the preference he cherishes for sport and pastimes."[117] Hunting, according to most Europeans, could hardly be considered labor in such a land of plenty. Benjamin Franklin wrote that "almost all their wants are supplied by the Spontaneous Productions of Nature, with the additions of very little Labour, if Hunting and Fishing may indeed be called Labour when Game is so plenty."[118]

While women did what Europeans considered to be work—they farmed—men pursued the sport of kings.[119] Benjamin

[114] Harris, *Lawson's History*, p. 25.

[115] "Marquette's Last Voyage, 1674–1675," in Kellogg, ed., *Early Narratives*, p. 263.

[116] Colden, *Five Indian Nations*, 1:xxxii; Gallatin, "Synopsis of the Indian Tribes," p. 151.

[117] Thomas L. McKenney, *Memoirs Official and Personal; with Sketches of Travels among the Northern and Southern Indians*, 2 vols. (New York, 1846), 1:232–33.

[118] A. O. Aldridge, "Franklin's Letter on Indians and Germans," *Proceedings of the American Philosophical Society* 94 (1950):391–95.

[119] Most Native peoples within the boundaries of the United States farmed, but there are obvious exceptions. People on the northwest coast lived well

Rush, who believed that "the highest degrees of civilization" (in his estimation the French) "border upon the savage life," conceded the economic necessity of Native hunting, but nevertheless put that activity in a European context: "The people of rank and fortune among the French are very fond of fishing and hunting. These employments are the sources of pleasure only, but with the Indian they are the means of pleasure and subsistence."[120] Men abandoned the household chores to their wives while they frolicked in the forests, and they whiled away their hours in recreation while women worked. Such indolence, most Euro-Americans believed, characterized Native men.

Native peoples, however, did not regard hunting or the male character in quite the same way as Euro-Americans. Hunting, they knew, was a strenuous and even dangerous job. Maj. John Norton, a Mohawk who visited Cherokee relatives in the early nineteenth century, observed: "The Chace was the field of industry for man. . . . Throughout the hunting, it may be asserted with confidence, that there are no symptoms of laziness, or an indolent disposition."[121] Women also apparently appreciated the difficulty of men's lives. Pretty-Shield described the economic contributions of Crow men: "War, killing meat, and bringing it into camp, horse-stealing and taking care of horses, gave our men plenty of hard work."[122] Native peoples and Euro-Americans simply had different cultural definitions of labor.

---

without farming, Great Basin and plateau peoples hunted, gathered, and traded for subsistence, and some Great Lake peoples exploited wild rice resources. Another exception is the northern plains, where the highly specialized trading economy freed peoples such as the Sioux from the necessity of farming. The Sioux exchanged European goods to agricultural peoples, such as the Arikaras and Mandans, for corn and horses. See James P. Ronda, *Lewis and Clark among the Indians* (Lincoln, Nebr., 1984); John C. Ewers, "The Indian Trade of the Upper Missouri before Lewis and Clark," *Bulletin of the Missouri Historical Society* 10 (1954):429–46; and Colin G. Calloway, "The Inter-Tribal Balance of Power on the Great Plains, 1760–1850," *Journal of American Studies* 16 (1982):25–47.

[120] Corner, ed., *Autobiography of Rush*, p. 73.

[121] Carl F. Klinck and James J. Talman, eds., *The Journal of Major John Norton, 1816* (Toronto, 1970), p. 126.

[122] Linderman, *Pretty-Shield*, p. 134.

These contrary definitions of labor might have remained nothing more than a curiosity if agrarianism had not been such a major component of republican ideology in the early years of the United States.[123] Rush divided all mankind into three groups: "The savage lives by fishing and hunting, the barbarian by pasturage, and the civilized man by agriculture." Agriculture, he believed, was "the true basis of national health, riches and populousness."[124] At the same time, ideology was beginning to define quite distinct roles for men and women in American society. The cult of domesticity arose from industrialization and the separation of home and industry, and it made the home and domestic virtues the province of women while men came to be associated with the capitalistic values of the new industrial order.[125] Societies in which women worked outside the home became suspect: Jefferson, for example, suggested that heavy labor by women indicated extreme poverty.[126] McKenney applied the concept of domesticity to Native women and bemoaned her degraded state: "The woman, having no field for the exercise of the virtues peculiar to her sex, never appears in her true character, nor is invested with the tender, healthful, the ennobling influences which renders her, in her proper sphere, the friend and adviser of man."[127] Others attached even more profound meaning to the Native division of labor in which women seemed to be the primary source of support. "There can be no hesitation in asserting," Gallatin wrote in his long discourse on Native peoples, "that the labor necessary to support a man's family is,

[123] A. Whitney Griswold, "The Agrarian Democracy of Thomas Jefferson," *American Political Science Review* 40 (1946): 657–81; also see Joyce O. Appleby, "Commercial Farming and the 'Agrarian Myth' in the Early Republic," *Journal of American History* 68 (1982): 833–49.

[124] Corner, ed., *Autobiography of Rush*, p. 71; Rush, "Medicine among the Indians," p. 290.

[125] Glenna Matthews, *Just a Housewife: The Rise and Fall of Domesticity in America* (New York, 1987).

[126] Julian P. Boyd et al., eds., *The Papers of Thomas Jefferson*, 28 vols. to date (Princeton, 1950–), 11:415.

[127] Thomas L. McKenney and James Hall, *History of the Indian Tribes of North America*, 3 vols. (Philadelphia, 1836–44), 3:249.

on the part of the man, a moral duty; and that to impose on woman that portion, which can be properly performed only by man, is a deviation from the laws of nature."[128] The real problem with Native societies, according to Gallatin, was that women instead of men did the farming.[129]

The specter of women farming was, to many Euro-American writers, contrary to the laws of nature. Their interpretation was shaped to some extent by the writings of the Scottish social theorists who provided a framework for understanding Native peoples. Native peoples were "savages" whose cultures were less complex than "civilized" ones. "Savage" peoples lived off the bounty of the land without investing their labor while "civilized" peoples were busy, as Robert F. Berkhofer has phrased it, "transforming nature into property."[130] "Savage" peoples, according to the learned academicians revered by the early republic, did not farm. But the evidence still pointed to the agricultural base of most Native economies within the boundaries of the United States. The Lewis and Clark expedition provides a good index to the extent of agriculture. In his instructions to the explorers, Jefferson requested specific information on the Native peoples they encountered including "whether they cultivate or not." Until Lewis and Clark met the Sioux on the northern plains, they noted "cultivates Corn, Beans &c. &c." for all the nations they described. And even one band of Sioux grew some corn. They remarked that along the Platte River, Native peoples re-

[128] Gallatin, "Synopsis of the Indian Tribes," p. 158.

[129] Observers, in fact, often attributed a relatively high status to women in nonagricultural societies. Willlam Clark wrote of the Shoshones: "The women are held more sacred among them than any nation we have seen"; and of women on the northwest coast: "Men take more of the drudgery off the women than is common with Indians." Among neither group did women farm. See Thwaites, ed., *Journals of Lewis and Clark*, 3:10, 183; and Gunther, *Indian Life*, pp. 121, 164. The nonagricultural Sioux are an exception to this characterization, but that can probably be attributed to the extreme prejudice against the Sioux of Lewis and Clark, Tableau, and others, who believed that the Sioux oppressed the Mandans and Arikaras, whom they admired. For an example, see Bradbury, *Travels in the Interior of America*, p. 109. Also see Marla N. Powers, *Oglala Women: Myth, Ritual, and Reality* (Chicago, 1986).

[130] Pearce, *Savagism and Civilization*, pp. 66, 83–90; Berkhofer, *White Man's Indian*, p. 138.

turned to their villages from buffalo hunting to get corn.[131] Others commented on the culinary implications of agriculturally based Native societies. DeSoto complained of a steady diet of corn with little meat in the sixteenth century, while in the eighteenth century, Romans ate meat only about once a month during his stay with the Choctaws.[132] How could Euro-Americans reconcile what they saw with what they were supposed to see?

Many responded to this unnatural arrangement by adjusting the facts to fit. Commentators, even those who had observed Native cultures or had read extensively in first-hand accounts, ignored the economic role of women and the importance of agriculture to Native subsistence.[133] Lieutenant Timberlake, who purchased corn from Native women, described the Cherokees in his *Memoirs* as hunters.[134] James Hall, McKenney's co-author who certainly knew that women farmed, wrote in his history of the West, "The Indians subsist entirely by hunting," and Samuel Stanhope Smith described hunting as "the necessary means of their subsistence."[135] Others simply belittled the economic importance of agriculture or blurred the distinction between gathering wild foods and farming. Robert Beverley described "the natural Production of that Country, which the Native *Indians* enjoy'd, without the Curse of Industry, their Diversion alone, and not the Labour, supplying their Necessities. . . . But none of the Toils of Husbandry were exercised by this happy

---

[131] Thwaites, ed., *Journals of Lewis and Clark*, 1 : 89; 6 : 80–94.

[132] The absence of meat in the diet of southeastern peoples may be attributed to the season in which DeSoto and Romans visited. Summer was the time for agriculture; winter was for hunting (Gallatin, "Synopsis of the Indian Tribes," p. 108).

[133] Native peoples such as Iowas, Saukees, and Foxes who had been farmers for centuries must have been somewhat perplexed over treaty provisions "to aid them in their agriculture." Creek and Cherokee treaties contained promises of assistance in their transition to "herdsmen and cultivators, instead of remaining in the hunter state" (*American State Papers: Indian Affairs*, 2 vols. [Washington, D.C., 1832–34], 1 : 82, 125; 2 : 525).

[134] Williams, *Timberlake's Memoirs*, p. 99.

[135] Hall, *Sketches of History, Life, and Manners*, 1 : 92; Smith, *Variety of Complexion and Figure*, p. 216.

People; except the bare planting a little Corn, and Melons, which took up only a few Days in the Summer, the rest being wholly spent in the Pursuit of their Pleasures."[136] In *Notes on the State of Virginia*, Thomas Jefferson wrote: "All the nations of Indians in North America lived in the hunter state and depended for subsistence on hunting, fishing, and the spontaneous fruits of the earth, and a kind of grain which was planted and gathered by the women, and is now known by the name Indian corn."[137] Few Euro-Americans ever fully appreciated the contradiction embodied in their depictions of Native peoples as primarily hunters while they themselves cultivated Native crops using Native techniques.[138] Racism may well have led whites to denigrate Native crops in general, but the sex of the farmers prompted them to minimize the relative importance of agriculture in Native societies. The fact that women, rather than men, farmed, permitted Euro-Americans to shape their view of Native culture to conform to their own cultural presuppositions.

In addition to adapting Native cultures to the theoretical constructs in vogue in the late eighteenth and early nineteenth centuries, the dismissal of agriculture as an important component of Native economies served far more concrete purposes. Europeans recognized a limited right of Native peoples to territory. They could occupy land, but ultimate ownership vested in the European "discoverer" who put it to proper use. These discoverers legitimately acquired title through just wars or treaties.[139] In the financially strapped early republic, war seemed out of the question, but opportunities existed to acquire the Native title by treaty and, at the same time, save the "savage." Thus emerged the "civilization" program designed by Washington's secretary of war, Henry Knox.[140]

[136] Beverley, *History and Present State of Virginia*, p. 156.

[137] Jefferson, *Notes on the State of Virginia*, p. 302.

[138] G. Melvin Herndon, "Indian Agriculture in the Southern Colonies," *North Carolina Historical Review* 44 (1967):283–97.

[139] For Jefferson's explication of the principle, see his "Opinion on Georgia Land Grants," May 3, 1790, Ford, ed., *Writings of Jefferson*, 5:166.

[140] Henry Knox to George Washington, July 7, 1789, *American State Papers: Indian Affairs*, 1:53.

Policymakers considered economic change to be at the heart of the "civilization" program. They must transform hunters into farmers who would no longer need "surplus & waste lands."[141] When he became president in 1801, Thomas Jefferson endorsed the program because he believed that its success would bring land cessions: "The extensive forests necessary in the hunting life will then become useless, and they will see advantage in exchanging them for the means of improving their farms and increasing their domestic comforts." What Jefferson and others regarded as an economic change, however, involved a far more profound transformation in Native societies: men must replace women as farmers.[142] Such a change called into question fundamental values and beliefs.

Not surprisingly, many Native peoples resisted "civilization." Gallatin complained that "although the men may to some extent have assisted the women in the cultivation of the ground, the greater part of the labors still fell upon the latter."[143] He did concede that the Cherokees had, in a limited way, "become an agricultural nation, meaning thereby that state of society, in which the men themselves do actually perform agricultural labor." But even among the Cherokees, he estimated, only one-third of the men farmed. Furthermore, he regarded the growth

[141] Thomas Jefferson to the Senate and House of Representatives, Jan. 18, 1803, James D. Richardson, ed., *A Compilation of the Messages and Papers of the Presidents*, 20 vols. (New York, 1897–1917), 1:340; Draft of Jefferson's Fifth Annual Message, Ford, ed., *Writings of Jefferson*, 8:394. Actually, a dual policy developed in Jefferson's administration that promoted hunting west of the Mississippi and commerce with United States traders. See Jefferson to Congress, Jan. 18, 1803, *American State Papers: Indian Affairs*, 1:684–85. The impact of this policy on women, particularly those who lived on the upper Missouri, was substantial. United States control of the trade disrupted long-established patterns of exchange and forced people who had not hunted commercially to do so. A more nomadic life disrupted villages and agricultural production.

[142] Albert Gallatin was one of the few people who explicitly stated that Native men must farm. Most others simply assumed that the plows sent under the auspices of the "civilization" program would be taken up by men while women used their new spinning wheels and looms (Gallatin, "Synopsis of the Indian Tribes," pp. 152–53).

[143] Ibid., p. 108.

of African-American slavery in the Cherokee Nation as an attempt by men to avoid farming.[144] By the election of Andrew Jackson in 1828, many lamented the failure of the "civilization" program and the suffering of Native peoples who refused to save themselves from destruction. Yet Lewis Cass, a key figure in Jackson's administration, concluded, "Distress could not teach them providence, nor want industry."[145]

The proclaimed failure of the "civilization" program came at a convenient time. The southern states in the 1820s had become insistent that the Native peoples within their bounds be removed west of the Mississippi. Long recognized as a solution to the "Indian problem," removal hinged on acquisition of Native title to remaining lands in the East.[146] Basing their argument on the widely accepted jurisprudence of sixteenth-century theoretist Emmerich de Vattel, politicians maintained that no people had a right to land they did not farm. The needs of farmers took precedence over those of hunters.[147] Georgia Governor Wilson Lumpkin summarized the position of those who demanded immediate removal: "I believe the earth was formed especially for the cultivation of the ground, and none

---

[144] Ibid., p. 157. Cass concurred ("Removal of the Indians," p. 71).

[145] Cass, "Removal of the Indians," p. 67.

[146] Jefferson wrote John C. Breckinridge, Aug. 12, 1803, concerning the Louisiana Purchase: "The best use we can make of the country for some time, will be to give establishments in it to the Indians on the East side of the Mississippi, in exchange for their present country." Jefferson also mentioned this use in a draft of a constitutional amendment providing for territorial acquisition (Ford, ed., *Writings of Jefferson*, 8:243–45).

[147] In his *Handbook of Federal Indian Law* (Charlottesville, Va., 1982), Felix Cohen supports the contention of Francisco de Victoria that "the aborigines in question were true owners, before the Spaniards came among them, both from the public and private point of view" (p. 50). He maintains that this recognition of Native title forms the basis of modern Indian law. While this may be true, late eighteenth- and early nineteenth-century writers subscribed to Vattel's opposing view that Natives had only limited rights, and failure to cultivate the soil was a major cultural feature restricting their absolute ownership. For example, Cass referred to Vattel by name in his formal justification of Indian removal ("Removal of the Indians," p. 95). Also see, Berkhofer, *White Man's Indian*, pp. 120–26, 129–32; and Pearce, *Savagism and Civilization*, pp. 70–71.

but civilized men will cultivate the earth to any great extent, or advantage. Therefore, I do not believe a savage race of heathens, found in the occupancy of a large and fertile domain of country, have any exclusive right to the same, from merely having seen it in the chase, or having viewed it from the mountain top."[148] Far more moderate minds agreed with the extremist Lumpkin on this point. John Quincy Adams, for example, contended that Native peoples enjoyed "mere occupancy for the purpose of hunting. It is not like our tenures; they have no idea of a title to the soil itself. It is overrun by them, rather than inhabited."[149] In the Indian policy of the early republic, therefore, even opponents concurred on what constituted legitimate ownership of land: cultivation of the soil. Minimal farming by mere women clearly did not qualify.[150]

Native peoples dependent on hunting also had no right to claim political independence. James Hall wrote: "We cannot believe that the mere fact, that a wandering horde of savages are in the habit of traversing a particular tract of country in pursuit of game, gives to them the ownership and jurisdiction of the soil, as sovereign nations."[151] The solution, of course, was to bring Native peoples under the jurisdiction of the United States. Those who remained in the states should be subject to the laws of those states. Those who removed should submit to the "paternal authority" of the United States.[152] Under United States

[148] Wilson Lumpkin, *The Removal of the Cherokee Indians from Georgia*, 2 vols. (New York, 1907), 2:150.

[149] John Quincy Adams made this argument in his appearance before the Supreme Court in *Fletcher* v. *Peck* (1810) (Cass, "Removal of the Indians," p. 80).

[150] Andrew Jackson's Second Annual Message, Richardson, ed., *Messages and Papers*, 2:1083; Cass, "Removal of the Indians," pp. 72–73. Men were not quite sure that their agricultural labor counted either, or at least that their farming would enable them to keep their land. Cornplanter announced at a council in Philadelphia that the Seneca men intended to become farmers, "but before we speak to you concerning this, we must know from you whether you mean to leave us and our children any land to till" (*American State Papers: Indian Affairs*, 1:141–42).

[151] Hall, *Sketches of History, Life, and Manners*, 1:118.

[152] Cass, "Removal of the Indians," pp. 91–92, 121.

tutelage, they could learn the civic values, nurtured at home and embodied in institutions, that Euro-Americans considered appropriate to good government.

Political domination became a means of cultural transformation in the Jacksonian years. A conception of what Indians were and what they must become justified and shaped that policy. The domination of the Jacksonian era carried with it a model of womanhood that was to be imposed on Native societies. Accounts of Native life had described wanton, oppressed women, a far cry from the chaste, orderly housewife caring for hearth and home that had become the ideal in Euro-American society. The goal of missionaries, philanthropists, and the United States government, therefore, was clear: the Indian man was to become a farmer so that the Indian woman could "rise into her high distinction and shine out in all her loveliness, heaven's best gift to man." [153] The Rev. Jedidiah Morse, like many advocates of this policy, believed that reformers should focus their efforts specifically on women: "It is essential to the success of the project of the Government, that the female among our native tribes, be raised from its present degraded state, to its proper rank and influence. This should be a *primary* object with the instructors of the Indians." [154] And so the United States government went about implementing an Indian policy born of land hunger but conceived in the literature of the age. The model of womanhood incorporated into this policy created a reality that Native peoples would have to inhabit for decades and established the terms for an ongoing debate over women and their role in Native society.

After the republic had entered its second century, Waheenee talked about the changes that the policy had brought to the Hidatsa and to her own family: "My little son grew up in the white man's school. He can read books, and he owns cattle and has a

[153] McKenny, *Memoirs Official and Personal*, 1:236.

[154] Jedidiah Morse, *A Report to the Secretary of War of the United States on Indian Affairs* (1822; reprint ed., New York, 1970), p. 74. For one example of the application of this policy, see Mary Elizabeth Young, "Women, Civilization, and the Indian Question," in Mabel E. Deutrich and Elizabeth C. Purdy, eds., *Clio Was a Woman: Studies in the History of American Women* (Washington, D.C., 1980).

farm. . . . My son's wife cooks by a stove. But for me, I cannot forget our old ways. Often in summer I rise at daybreak and steal out to the cornfields; and as I hoe the corn I sing to it, as we did when I was young. No one cares for our corn songs now. Sometimes at evening I sit, looking out on the big Missouri. The sun sets, and dusk steals over the water. In the shadows I seem again to see our Indian village, with smoke curling upward from the earth lodges; and in the river's roar I hear the yells of warriors, the laughter of little children as of old. It is but an old woman's dream. Again I see but shadows and hear only the roar of the river; and tears come into my eyes. Our Indian life, I know, is gone forever."[155] The perceptions of Euro-American travelers and writers often had had a limited basis in the realities of Native life, but those perceptions had helped create a new reality for Native women.

[155] Wilson, ed., "Waheenee," pp. 175–76.

II

Native Communities
and the New Nation

DANIEL K. RICHTER

Onas, the Long Knife
Pennsylvanians and Indians,
1783–1794

IN APRIL 1792 the war chief Red Jacket led a delegation of
Seneca Iroquois to the federal capital at Philadelphia. Their
main business was with the president and Congress, but the Native leaders also paid a courtesy call on Pennsylvania governor
Thomas Mifflin. Standing beneath a portrait of William Penn in
the statehouse council chamber, Red Jacket addressed his host
as "Brother Onas Governor." *Onas*, as everyone present knew,
was an Iroquoian word meaning "quill" and thus was a translation of the Pennsylvania founder's surname; throughout most
of the eighteenth century, Indian diplomats had used the term
to refer to successive governors and governments of the province and state. The sight of Onas's portrait, Red Jacket declared,
"brought fresh to our minds the freindly [*sic*] conferences that
used to be held between the former governor of Pennsylvania and our tribes and the love which your forefathers had of
Peace." It was, the Seneca leader told Mifflin, "still our wish, as
well as yours to preserve peace between our tribes and you and
it would be well if the same Spirit [prevailed] among the Indians to the Westward and thro' every part of the United States."[1]

A little over a year later, the fragility of such hopes for
peace on the frontiers of the United States became apparent
in another encounter between Indians and Pennsylvanians;

[1] Executive Minutes of Thomas Mifflin, Apr. 2, 1792, *Pennsylvania Archives*,
9th ser., 10 vols. (Harrisburg, Pa., 1931–35), 1:pt. 1, pp. 345–46. On the
council title *Onas* (its Algonquian language equivalent was *Miquon*), see
Francis P. Jennings et al., eds., *The History and Culture of Iroquois Diplomacy: An
Interdisciplinary Guide to the Treaties of the Six Nations and Their League* (Syracuse,
N.Y., 1985), p. 246.

then a quite different name was used to describe William Penn's successors. On what started as a pleasant afternoon stroll near the British post at Detroit, Philadelphia Quakers William Hartshorne and John Parrish heartily greeted a half-dozen young Ojibwas who had recently arrived from Michilimackinac. Perhaps amused at the Pennsylvanians' awkward attempt at saying "How do you do?" in trade pidgin, the Indians initially returned the salutation, but when Parrish and Hartshorne extended their arms, they "drew back and refused to shake hands, and said 'Shemockteman Boston.'" The word that Parrish rendered *Shemockteman* meant, he explained, "'Long knives,' a name . . . given to the Virginians, as a warlike people, which is now spread throughout the whole country[;] as the States unite in one they are all looked upon to be 'Shemocktemen.'" Seeking to set the record straight, the Quakers—true children of Onas if ever there were any—protested that they were "from Philadelphia," but the Indians would hear nothing of it.[2] The Ojibwas "soon grew furious," Hartshorne recalled, "calling us in their way, long knife, and with furious countenances, and violent gestures." The Quakers believed themselves lucky to escape the conversation alive.[3]

[2] John Parrish, "Trip to Lower Sandusky, 1793" (1882 manuscript copy by Richard Eddy), pp. 118–21, Historical Society Pennsylvania, Philadelphia.

[3] William Hartshorne, "Journal of a Journey to Detroit, 1793" (typescript copy), June 14, 1793, Friends Historical Library, Swarthmore College, Swarthmore, Pa. The Ojibwas' simultaneous use of *Shemockteman* (Virginian) and *Boston* may not have been unusual and perhaps epitomizes the degree to which they conflated all residents of the United States. In the mid-1780s Native diplomats in the Great Lakes region and Ohio country often applied phrases interpreters translated as "Bostonians" to the United States as a whole; for examples see Speech of Joseph Brant, May 21, 1783, John Deserundyon to Daniel Claus, July 7, 1783, Papers of Sir Frederick Haldimand, Add. Mss. 21,756, fol. 140v, 21,774, fol. 322r, British Museum, London; and Richard Butler to William Butler, Sept. 11, 1786, *Iroquois Indians: A Documentary History* (Woodbridge, Conn., 1985, microfilm), roll 38. For similar uses of "Big Knives" or "Virginians" as names for people and leaders of the United States during the same period, see Treaty minutes, June 30, Sept. 8, and Oct. 6, 1783, Haldimand Papers, Add. Mss. 21,799, fols. 1134, 138v, 144v–45r. On the origin of the term in the colonial period (its Iroquoian version, *Assaryquoa* had been used at least since Virginia governor Lord Howard of Effingham presented a cutlass to headmen of the Five Nations Iroquois at a treaty coun-

The names and imageries applied to Pennsylvanians in these two encounters—*Onas* the just founder and *Shemockteman* the treacherous killer—could not contrast more starkly. Clearly, in the early 1790s some disagreement existed between Pennsylvanians who wrapped themselves in the mantle of Onas and Indians who insisted they were Long Knives. But Red Jacket's invocation of the memory of William Penn also suggests a more profound contest between Pennsylvania officials and Indian leaders and among Native peoples themselves over the very meaning of the title *Onas*. During the decade after the close of the American War for Independence, Indians seeking some way to live, hunt, and trade on lands claimed by Pennsylvania repeatedly attempted to call the commonwealth back to the supposed ideals of its founder. Despite their efforts, however, and despite Pennsylvania officials' preference for the pen to the knife in deeds as well as rhetoric, little distinguished the state's basic policies from those of the Confederation and federal governments. Thus, in the view of many Native people, Onas took his place among the other Long Knives of the new republic.

Not surprisingly, most Pennsylvanians who wielded political power or cultural influence in the 1780s and 1790s liked to think that they remained true to the spirit of Onas. "We hope," Mifflin told a delegation of Muskogee (Creek) leaders visiting Philadelphia in 1790, "the conduct of Pennsylvania, from the landing of William Penn to this day, has unequivocally proved *her* love of justice, *her* disposition for peace, and *her* respect for the rights and happiness of her neighbors."[4] Yet citizens of the commonwealth, then as now, were a diverse lot, and one suspects that the reputation of Long Knife was embraced proudly by such western frontierfolk as those who, in 1787, found quaint "an old law of the Provence of Pennsylvania, which prohibited any person from shooting at an Indian until

---

cil in 1684), see Jennings et al., eds., *History and Culture*, p. 230. Today, Great Lakes Native peoples still sometimes refer to Euro-Americans as *Chomokomon* (see R. David Edmunds, personal communication, Mar. 4, 1992).

[4]*Minutes of the Supreme Executive Council of Pennsylvania, from Its Organization to the Termination of the Revolution, Colonial Records of Pennsylvania*, 16 vols. (Harrisburg, Pa., 1851–53), 16:404.

the Indian should first shoot at him"—not to mention by those who participated in such atrocities as the massacre of dozens of Christian Delawares at the Moravian community of Gnadenhutten in 1782.[5] Understandably, then, on the Native side of the frontier, the Ojibwas at Detroit were not alone in their contemptuous refusal to distinguish among Pennsylvanians, Virginians, and Bostonians. As Detroit trader Isaac Williams told Parrish, "The Indians had in time past had confidence in the People of Pennsylvania, but since the different governments centered in one, as the thirteen United fires, they now look upon them all under the denomination of Virginians, and called the whole, Bigknives."[6]

The shift in terminology was not trivial. To Native people, it mattered a great deal whether Pennsylvanians were called "Brother Onas" or lumped together with backcountry Virginians as "Long Knives," with whom Indians had no familial ties. Such words were part of a rich eighteenth-century vocabulary of intercultural diplomacy in eastern North America in which the names leaders used for each other—known as "council titles"—were key symbols in a discourse about who peoples were and the nature and history of their relationships. Typically, council titles consisted of two parts. The first expressed a fictive kinship relationship that established terms of authority, deference, and intimacy. Traditionally, for instance, the Senecas and others of the Six Nations Iroquois had been "brothers" of Pennsylvania and other English colonies, but "children" of their "father," the governor of New France. Other Indian nations might

---

[5] David Redick to Jonathan Hoge, May 14, 1787, *Pennsylvania Archives*, 1st ser., 12 vols. (Philadelphia, 1852–56), 11:148 (quotation); Thomas P. Slaughter, *The Whiskey Rebellion: Frontier Epilogue to the American Revolution* (New York, 1986), pp. 75–77.

[6] Parrish, "Trip to Lower Sandusky," pp. 57–59. Moravian minister John Heckewelder confirmed that the Wyandots, too, called "all the People of the United States . . . Brothers the big Knifes," and as early as 1786 a Seneca headman had addressed a land surveyor from Pennsylvania in similar terms (John Heckewelder, "Journey with the Commissioners to the Indian Treaty," Apr. 8 and Sept. 25, 1793, Ferdinand Julius Dreer Collection, fol. 24v [second pagination], Hist. Soc. of Pa., Philadelphia; James Dickinson to John Lukens, Jan. 24, 1786, *Pennsylvania Archives*, 1st ser., 10:740–41).

be either "brothers," "nephews," or "children," of their Iroquois "brothers," "uncles," or "fathers" and assume a corresponding status as either "children" or "brothers" of the English in turn. The matrilineal kinship systems of many Native societies gave such terms meanings that patrilineal Euro-Americans seldom fathomed. In a society in which descent was traced through the female line and divorce was frequent, brothers, uncles (mothers' brothers), and nephews—as members of the same lineage—were closer and more deeply obligated kin than were fathers and children. Thus, an uncle commanded far greater obedience from the younger generation than did a father, who should be respected for his age and wisdom and could be a source of advice and protection in times of trouble, but was not due unquestioned allegiance.[7]

The second element of a council title was often the name of a historical personage who, like "Brother Onas," was believed to have established the relationship between two peoples on its proper footing. Such a name served two functions: it embodied an ideal standard of behavior that tended to be elaborated through time as positive aspects were stressed and negative ones suppressed, and it gave a relationship historical depth and continuity, for the title was applied from generation to generation almost regardless of the personal qualities of current office-holders.[8] In the Pennsylvania case, as Red Jacket's speech shows,

[7] "Names by Which the Different Indian Nations Address Each Other in Public Conferences," *Iroquois Indians*, roll 1; William N. Fenton, "Structure, Continuity, and Change in the Process of Iroquois Treaty Making," in Jennings et al., eds., *History and Culture*, pp. 10–14, 21–22; Richard White, *The Middle Ground: Indians, Empires, and Republics in the Great Lakes Region, 1650–1815* (Cambridge, 1991), pp. 84–85.

[8] Two prominent examples are the council titles for the governors of New France and New York, used widely in the intercultural diplomacy of the northeastern quarter of the continent. *Onontio* ("Great Mountain") was an Iroquoian translation of the surname of an early governor of New France, Charles Huault de Montmagny. *Corlaer*, an alternate spelling of the name of Arent van Curler (a prominent figure in early relations between Dutch colonists and Native peoples of the Hudson and Mohawk River valleys), was applied to English governors of New York beginning in the late 1670s (Jennings et al., eds., *History and Culture*, pp. 235, 240, 247; Daniel K. Richter, *The*

Brother Onas evoked an idealized memory of honest treaties among equals in which Euro-Americans scrupulously paid Native owners a fair price for the lands they occupied. That memory—whatever the accuracy of its original historical referent—assumed particular relevance in light of the perversion of the treaty process by which William Penn's sons and their agent James Logan defrauded the Delawares of most of their northeastern Pennsylvania lands during the mid-eighteenth century.[9]

Such historical experiences ensured that the meanings of council titles could be highly contested. To a certain degree, the fact that they *were* contested actually contributed to the stability of intercultural relationships; shared fictions and deliberate misunderstandings allowed Natives and Euro-Americans to believe what they wanted about each other.[10] But the *open* contest over titles that occurred at Detroit in 1793 suggests that shared fictions were breaking down, that the image one group constructed of itself could no longer be reconciled to the image current in the discourse of the other. To avert such a crisis, a diplomat could, as Red Jacket did in Philadelphia in 1792, try to use a traditional council title to *educate* the other side—to outline its responsibilities and call it back to the historical principles the name evoked. "You particularly expressed that . . . your disposition is that for which the ancient Onas Governor[s] were remarkable," the Seneca leader thus reminded Governor Mifflin.[11]

In the 1780s lessons about William Penn, about treaties among equals, and about fair purchase prices assumed far more than antiquarian interest as Pennsylvania officials used the treaty process to acquire legal title to a massive tract of land in the northwestern third of what became the modern state. The

Ordeal of the Longhouse: The Peoples of the Iroquois League in the Era of European Colonization (Chapel Hill, N.C., 1992), pp. 93–95, 131–32, 140–41).

[9] Francis P. Jennings, *The Ambiguous Iroquois Empire: The Covenant Chain Confederation of Indian Tribes with English Colonies from Its Beginnings to the Lancaster Treaty of 1744* (New York, 1984), pp. 309–46.

[10] White, *Middle Ground*, pp. 52–53.

[11] Executive Minutes of Mifflin, Apr. 2, 1792, *Pennsylvania Archives*, 9th ser., 1:pt. 1, p. 346.

territory lay beyond the boundary line between Natives and colonists that British and Iroquois diplomats had agreed upon at the first Treaty of Fort Stanwix in 1768. By the time Great Britain acknowledged the independence of the United States in the Treaty of Paris of 1783, most of these lands were devoid of Indian inhabitants, although the Penn of memory would not have approved of the way that situation came about. Some of the most brutal fighting of the War for Independence had destroyed the many ethnically mixed Indian villages of the upper Susquehanna watershed and the Wyoming Valley; there the real jurisdictional struggle in the 1780s was not between Euro- and Native Americans but between armed groups of whites who claimed competing patents under Connecticut and Pennsylvania. Similarly, the Ohio and Big Beaver valleys near Pittsburgh had long swarmed with immigrants from Pennsylvania and Virginia, although governments of the Keystone State and the Old Dominion vigorously competed with the squatters and each other for title to the real estate there.[12]

Only in the Allegheny River and French and Conewango creek watersheds of the extreme northwestern corner of the tract Pennsylvania claimed did any substantial communities of Natives remain. Indian populations were in great flux as refugee communities resettled after the War for Independence, but in the mid-1780s the core residents of that area and the neighboring portion of what became New York state consisted of about five hundred Seneca Iroquois and a small number of

---

[12] Peter C. Mancall, "The Revolutionary War and the Indians of the Upper Susquehanna Valley," *American Indian Culture and Research Journal* 12 (1988): 39–57; Solon J. Buck and Elizabeth Hawthorn Buck, *The Planting of Civilization in Western Pennsylvania* (Pittsburgh, 1939), pp. 135–203. The violent struggle between Connecticut and Pennsylvania claimants for control of the Wyoming Valley may be followed in *Minutes of Executive Council*, vols. 12–15, and *Pennsylvania Archives*, 1st ser., vol. 10. For brief overviews of Pennsylvania's boundary disputes see Buck and Buck, *Planting of Civilization*, pp. 156–74; and Peter S. Onuf, *The Origins of the Federal Republic: Jurisdictional Controversies in the United States, 1775–1787* (Philadelphia, 1983), pp. 49–73. Among the state governments involved, the border with Virginia was finally resolved in 1785 and that with New York in 1787; Pennsylvania's western boundary line was surveyed and marked in 1786 (*Minutes of Executive Council*, 14:360, 15:116–18, 340).

Munsee Delawares led by the Seneca war chiefs Guyasuta (Great Cross), Half-Town (Hachuwoot), Great Tree (Keandochgowa or Karontowanen), and, most prominently, Cornplanter (John O'Bail, Kayentwahkeh). Like nearly all members of their nation, these "Cornplanter" or "Allegany" Senecas had fought in the War for Independence beside the British, or perhaps more accurately against the United States.[13]

After the signing of the Treaty of Paris, however, a variety of geographical and historical factors inclined these Senecas southward toward Pennsylvania rather than northward toward the British posts of Niagara and Detroit that kept many other Senecas in the British orbit. Since before the era of European contact, the western Seneca communities in the Allegheny and Genesee river watersheds had been socially and politically distinct from eastern members of their nation whose prewar homes clustered around Seneca Lake.[14] After Continental troops commanded by John Sullivan and James Clinton destroyed their towns in 1779, most eastern Senecas—of whom Red Jacket was the leader best known to whites—lived for nearly two years as refugees at Niagara, almost entirely dependent on that post's storehouses for food, clothing, and weapons. By 1781 many were resettling nearby in new villages along Cattaraugus and Buffalo creeks, where they maintained close economic and political links with the British military.[15]

All of the major western Seneca towns had also been razed by the Sullivan-Clinton campaign and a simultaneous inva-

[13] George P. Donehoo, *A History of the Indian Villages and Place Names in Pennsylvania, with Numerous Historical Notes and References* (Harrisburg, Pa., 1928), pp. 39–40; Anthony F. C. Wallace, *The Death and Rebirth of the Seneca* (New York, 1969), pp. 168–69; Donald H. Kent, *Iroquois Indians I: History of Pennsylvania Purchases from the Indians* (New York, 1974), pp. 224–28.

[14] Charles F. Wray and Harry L. Schoff, "A Preliminary Report on the Seneca Sequence in Western New York, 1550–1687," *Pennsylvania Archaeologist* 23 (1953):53–63; Richter, *Ordeal of the Longhouse*, p. 256.

[15] Guy Johnson to Frederick Haldimand, Apr. 23 and May 19, 1781, and Jan. 11, 1783, Haldimand Papers, Add. Mss. 21,767, fols. 175–76, 181–84; 21,768, fols. 129–32; Barbara Graymont, *The Iroquois in the American Revolution* (Syracuse, N.Y., 1972), pp. 192–222.

sion of the Allegheny country by the Pennsylvania troops of Daniel Brodhead. As a consequence, many of their residents also fled temporarily to Niagara. Two Allegheny villages, however, escaped destruction to provide an alternative locus of re settlement in a region that contained many of the traditional hunting territories, cemeteries, and ceremonial centers of the western Senecas. Yet even on this familiar ground, the Allegany Senecas depended on trade with Euro-Americans. At least a hundred miles and a ridge of cliffs separated them from Niagara. By contrast, a comparatively easy river route to Pittsburgh offered it an attractive alternative to the clientage facing the many Cattaraugus and Buffalo Creek men and women who still drew military provisions from the redcoats. So the Allegany Senecas pinned their hopes for survival and independence on ties to Pennsylvania.[16]

But Onas's descendants had other ideas about rights to lands within what they called, in a nicely passive-voiced phrase, "the acknowledged limits of this State."[17] In their view, Native land claims had to be extinguished rapidly and in a way that left no questions about legal ownership of title to the real estate. In part, their need stemmed from Pennsylvania's boundary disputes with neighboring states. Other factors were schemes to dominate trade between the Atlantic coast and the Great Lakes and the influence of "land jobbers" eager to profit from western speculations.[18] Yet the primary motive for quickly acquiring legal title to Indian lands stemmed from the commonwealth's

[16] Allan Maclean to Ephraim Douglass, July 16, 1783, Haldimand Papers, Add. Mss. 21,763, fol. 192; Wallace, *Death and Rebirth of the Seneca*, pp. 163–72, 195.

[17] *Minutes of Executive Council*, 14:40; see also pp. 45–46; and Promissory Note and Deed, Oct. 23, 25, 1784, *Pennsylvania Archives*, 1st ser., 11:507–9.

[18] William Bradford to Elias Boudinot, July 24, [1794], Wallace Papers, II, fol. 95, John Williams Wallace Collection, Hist. Soc. of Pa., Philadelphia (quotation); Carl B. Lechner, "The Erie Triangle: The Final Link between Philadelphia and the Great Lakes," *Pennsylvania Magazine of History and Biography* 116 (1992):59–85. Lechner discounts the role of land speculation, but Norman Wilkinson makes a strong case for its role in the state's actions ("Land Policy and Speculation in Pennsylvania, 1779–1800: A Test of the New Democracy," Ph.D. diss., University of Pennsylvania, 1958, esp. pp. 61–63).

financial situation. Strapped for cash, in 1780 the Pennsylvania legislature had voted to fulfill many monetary obligations to its troops with promises of land: a "donation" of acreage would serve in lieu of an enlistment bounty, and "depreciation certificates" redeemable at the state land office were to compensate officers and men for the lost purchasing power of their paper-money pay. By war's end, the depreciation certificates comprised an enormous portion of the state's debt: entries in the Supreme Executive Council minutes between 1783 and 1785 approve interest payments alone of at least £37,487 ($116,585), and as late as 1790 the outstanding principal was calculated at nearly $1.5 million, roughly three-quarters of the remaining obligations incurred by the state on its own, rather than the Continental government's, behalf.[19]

The beauty of the depreciation certificate plan was that redemption of this substantial liability would cost the commonwealth and its taxpayers next to nothing, provided sufficient "free" real estate were available. As one historian puts it, for Pennsylvanians, "land" promised to be "the path to solvency."[20] Depreciation certificates could be used to purchase any unpatented acreage, and a significant portion of them paid for newly platted city lots in Philadelphia. But it seemed clear that, given the size of the financial obligation the certificates represented and the overwhelmingly agricultural nature of the late eighteenth-century economy, much larger and more ru-

---

[19] Buck and Buck, *Planting of Civilization*, pp. 203–7; Wilkinson, "Land Policy," pp. 19–44. Statistics calculated from *Minutes of Executive Council*, vols. 13–14, 16:264–66. The exact recorded total of payments authorized in 1783–85 for interest due as of April 1782 and April 1784 was £37,486.10.9. That this was only a fraction of the total actually due (claimants apparently had to apply for payment) is indicated by a comparison of the $1,500,000 total principal cited for 1790 and the amounts of principal due listed with the interest payments: £147,704 ($459,359) in 1783; £235,642 ($732,847) in 1784; and £241,317 ($750,496) in 1785 (inferring from the interest rate of 6 percent, figures rounded to the nearest pound or dollar). Thanks to JoAnna McDonald for her assistance in compiling these figures.

[20] *Minutes of Executive Council*, 14:271–74 (quotations); Message from General Assembly to Council, Dec. 24, 1794, *Pennsylvania Archives*, 1st ser., 10:379–84; Wilkinson, "Land Policy," p. 19 (quotation).

ral tracts would be necessary. Accordingly, in March 1783 the Pennsylvania legislature declared most of the southern half of the territory west of the Allegheny River to be "Depreciation Lands" set aside for redemption of the certificates and instructed surveying parties to lay out lots for sale. Meanwhile, plans were being drafted to set aside the northern half of the region as "Donation Lands" for war veterans.[21] As a mutiny by unpaid Pennsylvania soldiers rocked the capital in June of that year and as squatters pouring across the Allegheny and Ohio threatened to overrun the region before it could be distributed to law-abiding citizens who would help to cancel the commonwealth's liabilities, the rapid—and cheap—acquisition of legal title to the remaining Indian lands within "the acknowledged limits of this state" assumed vital importance.[22]

[21] *Minutes of Executive Council*, 13:477, 596; Dickinson to Surveyor General, [June?] 1783, *Pennsylvania Archives*, 1st ser., 10:53–54. On patents for Philadelphia city lots, see *Minutes of Executive Council*, vols. 13–15. The Donation Lands were formally set aside in March 1785; surveys began the following summer, and distributions in late 1786 (*Minutes of Executive Council*, 14: 386; 15:71; William Irvine to Dickinson, Aug. 17, 1785, *Pennsylvania Archives*, 1st ser., 11:513–20).

[22] Daniel Brodhead to Joseph Reed, Nov. 2, 1780, Daniel Brodhead Letterbook, 1780–81, Hist. Soc. of Pa., Philadelphia; *Minutes of Executive Council*, 13:425–26, 617, 644–45; 14:16; Treaty minutes, Aug. 31, 1783, Alexander McKee to John Johnson, Sept. 9, 1783, Haldimand Papers, Add. Mss. 21,779, fols. 132, 141; Frederick Muhlenberg to Pennsylvania Delegates, Sept. 12, 1783, *Iroquois Indians*, roll 37; Josiah Harmar to Dickinson, May 1, 1785, *Pennsylvania Archives*, 1st ser., 10:448; Robert L. Brunhouse, *The Counter-Revolution in Pennsylvania, 1776–1790* (Harrisburg, Pa., 1942), pp. 135–40. Most of the depreciation certificates and rights to Donation Lands were gobbled up at heavy discount by speculators who sat on them in hopes of nice profits. As a result, not only were dreams of a republic of happy, debt-free yeoman thwarted, the patenting of the Donation and Depreciation Lands—like all western Pennsylvania acreage—moved very slowly until early in the nineteenth century. The state liquidated its debt instead through sales of lands farther east, through taxation, through statutes of limitation, and, finally, through the Federal Funding and Assumption Plan of 1790 (Thomas Henry, "Depreciation Lands—Pennsylvania Population Company," in Joseph H. Bausman, *History of Beaver County, Pennsylvania, and Its Centennial Celebration*, 2 vols. (New York, 1904), 2:1227–33; Buck and Buck, *Planting of Civilization*, pp. 206–14; Wilkinson, "Land Policy," pp. 27–44, 126–36). Yet it matters little that the scheme for erasing the state's debt through creative real estate marketing came to

Yet none of the territory beyond the 1768 treaty line had yet been purchased from Native owners. Indeed, peace had not even been made between the United States and the Senecas or any other Native peoples, and raids and counterraids between Indians and frontier whites threatened to reignite full-scale warfare at any moment. Some forty Pennsylvanians reportedly lost their lives in early 1783 alone. "The particular Circumstances of this state render an attention to Indian affairs indispensably necessary," John Dickinson, president of the commonwealth's Supreme Executive Council, thus concluded in a letter to his state's congressional delegation in April of that year. The council, he said, "earnestly desire[d] that" Congress would "adopt without Loss of Time, the most effectual measures, for making Peace with all the Indian nations."[23]

Later that month Dickinson clarified to the delegates a vision of a peace imposed on defeated enemies rather than negotiated with independent powers: Congress should notify the Indians "that Peace has been made with Great Britain . . . ; that the Back Country with all the Forts is thereby ceded to us; that they must now depend upon us for their Preservation and, that unless they immediately cease from their outrages . . . we will instantly turn upon them our armies that have conquered the king of Great Britain . . . and extirpate them from the Land where they were born and now live." This "conquest theory," of which Dickinson was one of the earliest articulators, rested upon a peculiar interpretation of the fact that the Treaty of Paris, in declaring all lands south of the Great Lakes and east of the Mississippi to be within the boundaries of the United States, failed to mention Britain's Indian allies at all, much less any rights they may have had to the lands in question.[24]

---

naught. The important point is that, as state officials approached their earliest postwar Indian treaties, the scheme stood foremost in their minds.

[23] Dickinson to Delegates, Apr. 4, 1783, *Pennsylvania Archives*, 1st ser. 10:25.

[24] *Journals of the Continental Congress, 1774–1789*, 34 vols. (Washington, D.C., 1904–37), 23:516–17; Dickinson to Delegates in Congress, Apr. 29, 1783, *Pennsylvania Archives*, 1st ser., 10:45 (quotation); Treaty minutes, July 2, 1783, Haldimand Papers, Add. Mss. 21,779, fols. 115–16; Reginald Horsman, "American Indian Policy in the Old Northwest, 1783–1812," *William and Mary*

Native leaders, of course, utterly rejected the conquest theory. "They never could believe," a British Indian agent explained, "that our King could pretend to Cede to america What was not his own to give, or that the americains Would accept from him What he had no right to grant."[25] Nonetheless, Pennsylvania's position was clear. "If any Indians converse with you on this Business," Dickinson informed his surveyor general, "you may assure them that those Lands are within the Boundary of Pennsylvania . . . , and we have full power to maintain our title by force of arms." "Yet," Dickinson added, "we sincerely intend to treat them, as our ancestors treated their Forefathers, and to deal friendly with them, if they will suffer us to do so." Like Dickinson's two sentences, the Pennsylvanian as Long Knife and the Pennsylvanian as Onas stood uneasily together.[26]

Pennsylvania's attempts to "deal friendly with" the Indians under the auspices of the Continental government moved at a glacial pace. Congress almost immediately adopted verbatim Dickinson's articulation of the conquest theory, but the membership took six months to resolve "that a convention be held with the Indians . . . who have taken up arms against the United States, for the purpose of receiving them into the favour and protection of the United States and of establish[ing] boundary lines of property for separating and dividing the settlements of the Citizens from the Indian Villages and hunting grounds." The resolution invited Pennsylvania to send its own representatives to make "a treaty for the purchase of the Indian Claim to lands within the jurisdiction of that State," and in February 1784 the Supreme Executive Council appointed Samuel J.

Quarterly, 3d ser. 18 (1961):35–40; Dorothy V. Jones, *License for Empire: Colonialism by Treaty in Early America* (Chicago, 1982), pp. 139–56.

[25] Maclean to Haldimand, May 18, 1783, Haldimand Papers, Add. Mss. 21,763, fol. 118.

[26] Dickinson to Surveyor General, [June?] 1783, *Pennsylvania Archives*, 1st ser., 10:54. The same rhetorical juxtaposition occurs in Dickinson's Apr. 19, 1783, letter to the state's congressional delegation, in which the phrase "extirpate them from the Land where they were born and now live" is followed immediately by "But, that if they behave as they ought to do, they shall be treated not only justly, but friendly" (ibid., p. 45).

Atlee, William Maclay, and Francis Johnston to perform the chore.[27] Reflecting the state's priorities, the legislation authorizing the appointments placed them in the context of preparations for "laying off and surveying the lands appropriated for the redemption of the military depreciation certificates." According to state House of Representatives Speaker Frederick Muhlenberg, "The custom of Pennsylvania has always been, to purchase the right of possession, from the Indian nations, as being more consonant to Justice and less expensive, than force," yet neither the Indians' asking price nor even their willingness to sell entered a picture framed by the conquest theory. In August the assembly appropriated slightly less than $10,500 "worth of such goods, merchandize and trinkets as are known to be very acceptable among the Indians" as the amount to be paid "for the purpose of finally purchasing the said territory agreeable to ancient usage"; the only recorded debate was over a proposal to raise the payment to £9,000 ($27,990).[28]

After many additional delays that led Pennsylvania officials seriously to consider proceeding apart from the Confederation government, congressional commissioners Richard Butler, Arthur Lee, and Oliver Wolcott finally met over six hundred Six Nations Iroquois men, women, and children at Fort Stanwix (present-day Rome, N.Y.), in October 1784. Atlee, Maclay, and Johnston amicably observed the proceedings and waited their turn "in perfect harmony with the Continental Commission-

[27] Minutes of Congress, May 1 and 15, and Oct. 30, 1783, Instructions to Samuel J. Atlee, William Maclay, and Francis Johnston, Aug. 31, 1784, *Pennsylvania Archives*, 1st ser., 10:46, 119–25 (quotation), 320–21; *Minutes of Executive Council*, 14:40.

[28] Muhlenberg to Delegates, Sept. 12, 1783, *Iroquois Indians*, roll 37 (first quotation); Reports and Resolutions of General Assembly, Sept. 25, 1783, and Aug. 25, 1784; "List of Goods Necessary towards Effecting the Purchase of the Unpurchased Territory within the State of Pennsylvania," Aug. 28, 1784, *Pennsylvania Archives*, 1st ser., 10:111 (second quotation), 316–17 (third quotation), 318–19; *Minutes of Executive Council*, 14:186–87. An additional £1000 ($3,110) was allocated for the commissioners' expenses. The 1784–85 exchange rate of £1 = $3.11 (conversely, $1.00 =£0.32) is based on "State of the Accounts of the Pennsylvania Indian Commissioners," *Pennsylvania Archives*, 3d ser., 30 vols. (Harrisburg, Pa., 1894–99), 7:483.

ers," who extolled them as an example of the commonwealth's "Wisdom and Confederal Policy." In this, the Pennsylvanians stood in stark contrast with their counterparts from New York, whose unilateral negotiations with the Iroquois led Butler, Lee, and Wolcott to post armed guards to exclude the Empire State's agents from the grounds.[29]

When the treaty council opened, the congressional commissioners informed the Iroquois that they were "ready on their part if desired to give peace . . . upon just and reasonable terms and to receive them into the friendship favour and protection of the United States." As a mark of that friendship, the Iroquois should propose a mutually satisfactory boundary between their territory and that of the Euro-Americans.[30] Mohawk Iroquois leader Joseph Brant—whose comprehension of spoken English was excellent—reported a few days later that the commissioners assured the Indians that the United States did "not claim any part of" Iroquois lands falling within the boundaries described by the Treaty of Paris. "We wanted," the commissioners said according to Brant's account, "to have a part of your lands to pay

[29] "List of Indians at Fort Stanwix (dated) October 22d 1784," *Iroquois Indians*, roll 38; Atlee, Maclay, and Johnston to Dickinson, Oct. 4, 1784, *Pennsylvania Archives*, 1st ser., 10:346 (first quotation); Arthur Lee and Richard Butler to George Clinton, Aug. 19, 1784, in "Proceedings of the Commissioners Appointed to Hold Treaties with the Indians in the State of New York," *Iroquois Indians*, roll 37 (second quotation); U.S. Commissioners Minutes, Oct. 12, 1784, Neville B. Craig, ed., *The Olden Time*, 2 vols. (1848; reprint ed., Cincinnati, 1876), 2:415; Hallock F. Raup, ed., "Journal of Griffith Evans, 1784–1785," *Pennsylvania Magazine of History and Biography* 65 (1941): 208–9. On Pennsylvania's plans to proceed alone, see Resolutions of Assembly, Sept. 25, 1783; Minutes of Congress, Oct. 30, 1783; Dickinson to Delegates, Dec. 16, 1783; and Reports and Resolutions of General Assembly, Aug. 25, 1784, *Pennsylvania Archives*, 1st ser., 10:111, 124–25, 152, 317; *Minutes of Executive Council*, 14:45–46. Only the fact that "a separate treaty must be attended with a very great expence" prevented the Pennsylvanians from following the example of their New York neighbors, who did conduct independent negotiations (*Minutes of Executive Council*, 14:46).

[30] "Extracts from the Journal of the Commissioners of Indian Affairs, for the Northern and Middle Departments—Commencing in 1784; and Ending 8th February 1786," Indian Treaties, 1778–95, pp. 27r–31r, quotation from p. 30r, Anthony Wayne Papers, Hist. Soc. of Pa., Philadelphia.

our troops with, which we owe to them and mean to pay you for it, if you let us have it."[31]

Yet when Cornplanter took the commissioners at their word and suggested a modification of the 1768 treaty line that would have yielded much of the area bounded by the present-day Pennsylvania–New York border and the Allegheny River, the offer was privately derided as, in the words of one Pennsylvanian, "a mere farce upon the design, attempting to cede great [part] of the State of Pennsylvania long ago purchased." After considerable debate among themselves, Butler, Lee, and Wolcott dropped their conciliatory facade in favor of a blunt explication of the conquest theory. "You are mistaken in supposing that having been excluded from the treaty between the United States and the King of England you are become a free and independent nation and may make what terms you please," Lee declared in what one observer called "a most spirited grand speech." Indians who allied themselves with the British in the War for Independence were, the commissioner said, "a subdued people," and any patches of ground the United States chose to give to them would belong to them not by right but through the "magnanimity and mercy" of the conquerors. Ignoring the Iroquois headmen's protestations that they had no authority from their peoples to cede additional lands, the commissioners then dictated a boundary that deprived the Six Nations of the western tip of New York state and any pretensions to territory beyond the western boundary of Pennsylvania.[32]

---

[31] "Captain Brants Account of . . . the Treaty in October 1784," *Iroquois Indians*, roll 38. See also David Hill to his brother-in-law [Daniel Claus], Nov. 6, 1784, ibid.

[32] [Richard Butler], Notes on Meeting of Commissioners, Oct. 18–20, 1784, *Iroquois Indians*, roll 38; Raup, ed., "Journal of Evans," pp. 212, 214 (first and third quotations, brackets in original); "Extracts from Journal of Commissioners," Indian Treaties, pp. 31r–42v (remaining quotations from p. 37v); Commissioners Minutes, Craig, ed., *Olden Time*, 2:422–23; Randolph C. Downes, *Council Fires on the Upper Ohio: A Narrative of Indian Affairs in the Upper Ohio Valley until 1795* (Pittsburgh, 1968), pp. 277–92; Graymont, *Iroquois in the American Revolution*, pp. 266–83; Kent, *Iroquois Indians*, pp. 40–71. Because of confusion over Indian place-names, the commissioners may not have understood the extent of Cornplanter's offer to revise the 1768 treaty line. Even so, Cornplanter seemed to be overstepping his authority. When the Iro-

The conquest theory propounded at Fort Stanwix dominated the dealings of the United States with Native peoples throughout the Confederation's existence and guided the treaties forced upon a group of Wyandots, Delawares, Ottawas, Chippewas, and Potawatomis at Fort McIntosh on the Ohio in 1785 and upon some Shawnee leaders at Fort Finney at the mouth of the Great Miami River in 1786. It was no coincidence that all these negotiations—if the term is even appropriate to describe them— took place under the guns of United States military posts and that Congress took pains to raise substantial troops in preparation for them.[33] The treaties of Forts Stanwix and McIntosh in particular were among the most notoriously fraudulent in the sordid history of such affairs. White traders kept the Native participants drunk much of the time, while the congressional commissioners practiced various forms of psychological and military intimidation during the headmen's sober moments. As a University of Pennsylvania professor understated during a visit to Fort McIntosh a few months after the treaty was signed there, "It was the 'general' opinion of the American officers, who were at the treaty, that the proceedings of the whites were unfair, and, indeed, that the Indians were, in a manner, 'compelled' to sign the articles."[34]

---

quois leaders agreed to attend the Fort Stanwix council, they stated explicitly that they were "not impowered to conclude a final Peace with the United States" and were only "to settle some Points necessary to be arranged previous to a more general Meeting which is intended to be held, to establish an everlasting Peace and Friendship between all the Nations and the Unites States" (Brant to Henry Glen, Aug. 11, 1784, *Iroquois Indians*, roll 37).

[33] "Extracts from Journal of Commissioners," Indian Treaties, pp. 44r–55v, 63v–64v, 72r–94r; "Articles of a Treaty Concluded at Fort McIntosh," Jan. 21, 1785; and "Articles of a Treaty Concluded at the Mouth of the Great Miami," Jan. 31, 1786, Wayne Papers, 19, fols. 47, 50; *Minutes of Executive Council*, 14:143; Lee and Richard Butler to Dickinson, Sept. 11, 1784; Harmar to Dickinson, Sept. 1, 1785; and Atlee and Johnston to Dickinson, Dec. 11, 1783, *Pennsylvania Archives*, 1st ser., 508–9; 11:510.

[34] Benjamin Smith Barton, Journal (Pa.—Indian Visits), n.d. [1785], s.v. "Fort McIntosh, Indian Treaty," Hist. Soc. of Pa., Philadelphia (quotation); Christopher Hayes to Dickinson, June 14, 1784, *Pennsylvania Archives*, 1st ser., 10:279; "Extracts from Journal of Commissioners," Indian Treaties, pp. 42v–44r, 64v–66r, 90r–91v; "Speech of the United Indian Nations, at

The Pennsylvania commissioners who followed the congressional delegation from Fort Stanwix to Fort McIntosh made no recorded protests against the tactics and can hardly have escaped the prevailing climate of sleaze. One wonders whether moral, more than physical, exhaustion undergirded Atlee's complaint that the Fort Stanwix experience was "the most fateaguing piece of Business" he "ever undertook" and that his "Western Duty" at Fort McIntosh promised to "be much more disagreeable than the former."[35] Whatever the case, he and his colleagues secured at Fort Stanwix a deed—signed by two Mohawks, three Oneidas, two Onondagas, one Cayuga, three Senecas, and two Tuscaroras on Oct. 23, 1784—that surrendered to Pennsylvania "all that part of the said Commonwealth not yet purchased of the Indians within the acknowledged Limits of the same." In return for a stated payment of $5,000 in goods, the Six Nations were to renounce "any Right Title Interest or property of . . . the said Tract," from which they were to "be forever ban[ned] and excluded."[36] Six years later, Cornplanter (who was present and signed the congressional treaty but not the Pennsylvania deed) asserted that the Pennsylvanians only offered $4,000, and the commissioners' minutes confirm his statement. Whatever the figure—even when added to the approximately $2,000 given to Wyandot and Delaware leaders for the same lands several weeks later at Fort McIntosh—it was well

---

Their Confederate Council, Held Near the Mouth of the Detroit River, the 28th November and 18th December, 1786," *New American State Papers: Indian Affairs*, 13 vols. (Wilmington, Del., 1972), 4:17–18; Wallace, *Death and Rebirth of the Seneca*, pp. 150–54; Wiley Sword, *President Washington's Indian War: The Struggle for the Old Northwest, 1790–1795* (Norman, Okla., 1985), pp. 23–30. Griffith Evans, secretary to the Pennsylvania commissioners, belittled the charges against liquor traders as politically motivated, but his journal recounts plenty of drinking and, on one occasion, notes with some surprise that the Native participants were "sober for want of an opportunity to get intoxicated" (Raup, ed., "Journal of Evans," pp. 208–14, quotation from p. 214).

[35] Atlee, Maclay, and Johnston to Dickinson, Nov. 15, 1784; and Atlee to Dickinson, Nov. 18, 1784, *Pennsylvania Archives*, 1st ser., 10:357, 360 (quotation).

[36] Copy of manuscript deed from Six Nations to Pennsylvania, Oct. 23, 1784 (brackets supplied from accompanying typescript), *Iroquois Indians*, roll 38.

under the legislative mandate of $10,500, of which the Natives were never informed.[37]

In striking their deal, the Pennsylvanians apparently replayed scenes previously acted out by the congressional commissioners. "I have the great pleasure," wrote Atlee, "of reporting that, that part of our mission that respected the Northern Tribes has been concluded to our utmost wish."[38] According to Cornplanter's later recollections, the Iroquois had refused to sell all the territory the Pennsylvanians claimed "for the use of their warriors" and instead offered "a part of it, which we pointed out to them in their map," probably repeating the proposal made to the congressional commissioners earlier. In response, Atlee, Maclay, and Johnston invoked the conquest theory to declare that "they must have the whole; that it was already ceded to them by the great king . . . and was *their own*." Yet the Pennsylvanians departed from the congressional script in evoking, as Dickinson had done earlier, the spirit of Onas: "they would not take advantage of" their conquest rights to the land "and were willing to pay . . . for it, after the manner of their ancestors." The intimidated Iroquois were, said Cornplanter, "unable to contend, at that time," and so several of them affixed their marks to the document.[39]

---

[37]*Minutes of Executive Council*, 16:501. According to the Pennsylvania commissioners' fiscal accounts, goods worth a total of £2104.5.7 (slightly over $6,544) were delivered to the Indian participants at Ft. Stanwix and Ft. McIntosh. The Ft. McIntosh Treaty stipulates a payment to the Wyandots and Delawares of "two thousand dollars, consisting of an excellent assortment of goods of the first quality, calculated in the best manner to supply your wants, which is a greater proportion than what we have given to your uncles, the Six Nations, and is certainly a very generous consideration" (Treaty minutes, Jan. 9–25, 1785, Bausman, *History of Beaver County*, 2:1203–10 [quotation from p. 1204]). If the Wyandots and Delawares indeed received $2,000 in goods, $4,544 would remain for the Iroquois at Ft. Stanwix. The commissioners had purchased an additional £732.13.1 ($2,280) worth of goods, which they did not see fit to distribute and resold after completing their work ("State of Accounts of Indian Commissioners," *Pennsylvania Archives*, 3d ser., 7:477–80; Raup, ed., "Journal of Evans," p. 232).

[38]Atlee to Dickinson, Nov. 18, 1784, *Pennsylvania Archives*, 1st ser., 10:360.

[39] "The speech of the Cornplanter, Half-Town, and the Great Tree," Dec. 1, 1790, *New American State Papers*, 4:24 (second and last quotations); *Minutes of*

Things were not that clear-cut, however. Two long days of bargaining had been necessary, the Pennsylvania delegation's secretary confessed, before "we brought them to accept of our offer," and "had our deed executed and our business concluded to our great satisfaction, [and] credit, and to the advantage of the state."[40] As a result, Atlee, Maclay, and Johnston left Fort Stanwix with, not one, but five documents, and the sheaf of papers allowed the Allegany Senecas some hope for the future. In his negotiations with the Pennsylvanians, Cornplanter recalled, "I begged of them to take pity on my nation and not buy [the land] . . . forever." The commissioners responded that "they would purchase it forever, but that they would give me further one thousand dollars in goods when the leaves were ready to fall"; thus the deed of cession was joined by a second document that pledged delivery of an additional payment the following October at Tioga on the New York state line. That paper secured Cornplanter's reluctant agreement to the bargain, but he recalled that he then further "requested, as they were determined to have the land[,] to permit my people to have the game and hunt upon the same, which request they complied with, and promised me to have it put upon record."[41] Accordingly, a third document explained "that it is not to be understood that the said Six Nations are by the same sale excluded from the privelege of hunting," which was "expressly reserved to them." Further caveats came from the Mohawk leader Aaron Hill (given up as a hostage to ensure compliance with the congressional treaty), who insisted upon a fourth text that detailed conditions for delivery of the additional payment and formalized an earlier offer from the Pennsylvanians to allow a Seneca leader to witness the survey of the Commonwealth's northern

---

Executive Council, 16:501–2 (remaining quotations); "Proceedings of the Treaties Held at Fort Stanwix and McIntosh," *Minutes of the First [through Third] Session[s] of the Ninth General Assembly of the Commonwealth of Pennsylvania* (Philadelphia, 1784[–85]), pp. 314–20.

[40] Raup, ed., "Journal of Evans," p. 214.

[41] *Minutes of Executive Council,* 16:501–2 (quotations); Treaty Document, Oct. 23, 1784, *Pennsylvania Archives,* 1st ser., 10:507; Thomas S. Abler, ed., *Chainbreaker: The Revolutionary War Memoirs of Governor Blacksnake, As Told to Benjamin Williams* (Lincoln, Nebr., 1989), pp. 163–68.

boundary. A final document pledged delivery to Cornplanter and Hill of "two good Rifles of neat workmanship . . . in consideration of their services."[42]

Seizing the small opening that these concessions afforded, during the next several years Cornplanter and his fellow Allegany Seneca leaders cultivated ties to Pennsylvania in order to secure a place for their people within a North American landscape dominated by the new republic. Their persistent goals were to retain possession of their village sites, to secure Native hunting rights in northwestern Pennsylvania, and to establish trading privileges at Pittsburgh. "I think Brother," Cornplanter had explained to the congressional commissioners at Fort Stanwix, "that we Warriors should have a large Country to range in, as our subsistence will depend on our having much hunting ground—and as it will also bring in money to you, it will tend to our mutual advantage."[43] In a message to Congress in May 1785, the Allegany Seneca leader announced that he and his political allies had "published the Articles of peace made between you and us, to Our Chiefs and Warriors, And we have all agreed to become the fourteenth State, and keep you by the Hand as Brothers if you mean [to abide] by the Agreement the Commissioners made at Fort Stanwix." For himself, he "intend[ed] settling on one of the Branches of the Allegany, to prevent (if possible) all Mischief that may accidentally arise" between Pennsylvanians and Senecas. "I wish," he continued, "my Friend General Butler with a Deputy from Virginia could meet me at Fort Pit[t] with all speed to settle a peace, that we may again Hunt and Trade with Our Ancient Friends without Molestation" and complete the work begun with the Pennsylvania commissioners at Fort Stanwix.[44]

[42] "Answer of the Six Nations to the Commissioners," Oct. 23, 1784, "Proceedings of Treaties at Fort Stanwix and McIntosh," *Minutes of the Ninth General Assembly*, pp. 317–18 (second quotation); Treaty Document, Oct. 25, 1784, *Pennsylvania Archives*, 1st ser., 10:508–9 (first and third quotations); Brant to Peter Schuyler, Mar. 23, 1785, *Iroquois Indians*, roll 37; Kent, *Iroquois Indians*, pp. 59–69.

[43] "Extracts from Journal of Commissioners," Indian Treaties, fol. 35v.

[44] Memorial from Cornplanter, May 20, 1785, *Iroquois Indians*, roll 38. Although his language seemed to include all of the Six Nations, Cornplanter set

Indeed much work remained to be done, and the Allegany Seneca leaders faced substantial criticism in their own and other Seneca communities. In July, Cornplanter and Guyasuta arrived at Fort Pitt in the company of a fellow Seneca named Hockushakwego (All Face). "It is hard with me," Cornplanter admitted to Col. Josiah Harmar, who, as commander of the Continental troops in the region, received the delegation in the absence of Butler. "I was a chief man at Fort Stanwix and my people blame me much, for the English have told our people that the great king never sold our lands to the thirteen fires." Hockushakwego brandished a copy of the Treaty of Fort Stanwix and protested the inadequate Native representation both there and at Fort McIntosh. Nonetheless, he blamed "the great king our father" for the sad state of relations between the Six Nations and the United States. "Now we take no advice from him and wish to sit in council with the Americans as we formerly did," he announced. "You told us we should live in peace on the lands you allowed us[;] Now brother we wish everything that was done at those councils to be strictly attended to." What the Allegany Senecas needed most was peace and trade on the western Pennsylvania frontier, and, for that, regularized channels of communication to Pittsburgh were crucial. "The council fire was always kindled here," Guyasuta recalled. "I was the man who had the fire removed from Fort Pitt[;] now I wish it brought back."[45]

Yet on the issue of trade at Pittsburgh or Tioga, as on many other matters, Pennsylvanians did little to fulfill the Allegany Senecas' hopes. Of the five Fort Stanwix documents, only the deed of absolute cession ever made its way into the legislative journals or land office books in Philadelphia. Although the state assembly initially acknowledged the right of a Seneca to witness the marking of the commonwealth's northern bound-

---

the Allegany communities apart from other Iroquois—even other Senecas— who protested the treaties. "We count Ourselves a people Capable of Speaking and Acting for Ourselves, and the Lands granted were Ours and not theirs," the Allegany leader said in answer to his Indian critics.

[45] Treaty Minutes, July 12, 1785 (enclosed in Harmar to Henry Knox, July 16, 1785), and Treaty Minutes, Mar. 27, 1786, *Iroquois Indians*, roll 38 (quotations from July 12, 1785).

ary and the Indians were allegedly "in a perfect good humour"
at the prospect, Pennsylvania and New York surveyors worked
for three summers to complete the chore, "without sending for
that man" (who nonetheless did join part of the second year's
activities on his own initiative). Moreover, Cornplanter later
complained, the line the surveyors marked ran several miles
north of the location to which the Iroquois thought they had
agreed.[46] Meanwhile, the "elegant rifles" promised Cornplanter
and Hill by April 1785 arrived in Iroquoia only in September,
after having been damaged en route. State officials neglected
the pledge to deliver the Six Nations an additional $1,000 in
goods until July, when Johnston prodded Dickinson to "a strict
and punctual observance of every promise made to the Savage
Nations."[47]

In the fall, when the council president sent Maclay to Tioga
to fulfill the obligation, he made clear his government's very
limited interpretation of the hunting rights Cornplanter be-

[46] Resolution of General Assembly, Feb. 18, 1785; and Maclay to Dickinson,
Feb. 26, 1785, *Pennsylvania Archives*, 1st ser., 10:412–13, 418 (first quotation); Andrew Ellicott and Andrew Porter to President and Council, Aug. 29,
1787, ibid., 11:178; Cornplanter, Half-Town, and Great Tree to Mifflin,
Dec. 30, 1790, ibid., 12:322 (second quotation); "Proceedings of Treaties at
Fort Stanwix and McIntosh," pp. 320–22. On the activities of the surveyors, see
Minutes of Executive Council, 14:364, 399, 454, 539–40; 15:12, 16, 19, 38–39,
180, 190–91, 202, 204, 212, 220, 340. On the Seneca Tiowanies's observation of the survey from Conewango Creek to Lake Erie, see Merle H. Deardorff and Donald H. Kent, eds., "John Adlum on the Allegheny: Memoirs for
the Year 1794," *Pennsylvania Magazine of History and Biography* 82 (1960):318–
19n; and Kent, *Iroquois Indians*, pp. 104–5. Kent's evaluation of Seneca reactions to survey parties in general (pp. 85–128) sharply disagrees with the
interpretation offered here.

[47] "State of Accounts of Indian Commissioners," *Pennsylvania Archives*,
3d ser., 7:478–85 (first quotation from p. 485); and Johnston to Dickinson,
July 29, and Aug. 10, 1785, *Pennsylvania Archives*, 1st ser., 10:489–90 (second
quotation), p. 496; *Minutes of Executive Council*, 14:400, 507–8, 528. Surviving
records indicate even less of an effort to comply with the terms of the deed extracted from the Wyandots and Delawares at Ft. McIntosh in January 1785,
which pledged rifles for two of the chiefs who signed it. See Atlee and Johnston to Dickinson, Dec. 11, 1784, *Pennsylvania Archives*, 1st ser., 11:510; Atlee
and Johnston to Dickinson, Jan. 16, 1785, *Pennsylvania Archives*, 1st ser., 10:
395–96; *Minutes of Executive Council*, 14:365–67, 379; Executive Minutes of
Mifflin, Aug. 5, 1794, *Pennsylvania Archives*, 9th ser., 2:pt. 1, 820.

lieved he had extracted from the commissioners at Fort Stan-wix: "We wish you to avail yourself of the opportunity . . . of reading the Treaty to the Indians as it is entered on the public Journals of the General Assembly, of explaining the Expressions relating to the Privilege of hunting on the Lands *untill they are improved*, of demonstrating the absurdity of constructing those Expressions so as to overthrow the strong words of Conveyance in their Deeds." On Maclay's return, the Supreme Executive Council declared his dealings with the Iroquois at Tioga to be "another instance to the experience of Pennsylvania, that the friendship of Indians is only to be secured by treaties founded upon reciprocal advantage fairly conducted and strictly ad-hered to."[48]

Despite the self-congratulations of those who claimed the heritage of Onas, however, Seneca discontent with the com-monwealth's deceptions—and their leaders' acquiescence in them—mounted. Cornplanter "refused" to meet with a party of Pennsylvanians surveying the Donation Lands near Venango in January 1786, and Hockushakwego advised them to turn back if they valued their lives. "Brother of the Big Knife," he said to people he failed to call *Onas*, "many of our young Warriors are dissatisfied with . . . the Reward we received for the Lands Thinking it inadequate for so large a Body; it not being one pair of Mokosons a piece."[49] That spring, Cornplanter left his fam-ily at Pittsburgh and, fearing that his Seneca opponents might take his life, set off for New York City in an unsuccessful effort to seek relief from Butler and the Confederation Congress meet-ing there.[50]

While he was gone the situation deteriorated further. In late April Hockushakwego led nearly fifty Allegany Senecas from

[48] Dickinson to Maclay, Sept. 3, 1785, *Pennsylvania Archives*, 1st ser., 10:510 (first quotation; emphasis added); *Minutes of Executive Council*, 14:531, 536–37, 664 (second quotation).

[49] Dickinson to Lukens, Jan. 24, 1786, *Pennsylvania Archives*, 1st ser., 10:740–41.

[50] Richard Butler to President of Congress, Apr. 25, 1786; Speech of Cornplanter to Congress, May 2, 1786; and Speeches of Butler and Corn-planter, June 1, 1786, *Iroquois Indians*, roll 38; *Journals of the Continental Congress*, 30:234–36.

French Creek to Pittsburgh. After "several Days trading" and drinking, they "took away with them" Cornplanter's kin. When asked why, one "laughed, [and] said the Cornplanter was not coming back this way." As the party left Pittsburgh, Half-Town warned trader Thomas Gibson to leave his store at Slippery Rock because war was likely. Taking his own advice, the Seneca leader announced his intention to move with his family from French Creek to Cattaraugus until things settled down. "He parted with me in friendship," Gibson reported, "and said he might see me in friendship again and perhaps not."[51] Such warnings were well taken. On the Muskingum River a few weeks later, a party of Mingoes and Cherokees living in the Ohio country killed four employees of the Pittsburgh traders William Dawson and Charles McClain "because the[y] have had their Goods from the United States."[52] That attack was one of many that, in the years after the Fort Stanwix and Fort McIntosh treaties, demonstrated the utter failure of the conquest theory to bring about peace through force. The militancy of such raids reflected a stiffening resistance to the United States. A new western confederacy—in which the Mohawk leader Brant was a central figure—was attempting to turn this freelance resistance into a systematic defense of Indian lands against incursions from Kentucky, Virginia, and Pennsylvania.[53]

Resisting intense pressure to join the confederacy, the Allegany Senecas remained committed to their alliance with Pennsylvania and regularly reported to Butler and other state and Continental officials on the westerners' plans. Nevertheless, their hopes of using the alliance to foster economic ties with Pittsburgh were almost completely dashed as attacks on Indians by frontier whites joined attacks by Indians on white traders to

[51] Robert Galbraith et al. to Benjamin Franklin and Council, [Apr. 29, 1786], inclosing Deposition of Thomas Gibson, Apr. 28, 1786, *Pennsylvania Archives*, 1st ser., 12:300–302.

[52] Michael Huffnagle to John Armstrong, inclosing Deposition of John Leith, May 17, 1786, ibid., 1st ser., 10:763.

[53] Samuel H. Parsons to President of Continental Congress, Oct. 27, 1785, and "Speech of the United Indian Nations, at Their Confederate Council Held . . . Between the 28th November and 18th December 1786," *Iroquois Indians*, roll 38; White, *Middle Ground*, pp. 413–68.

stifle western Pennsylvania's sputtering Indian trade. Even if, as Butler claimed in the winter of 1786–87, Indians who reached Pittsburgh were "very civilly treated by the inhabitants," the roads to and from that market were anything but safe. A few miles outside town, for example, one of Cornplanter's kinsmen was reportedly murdered simply because "he had a very fine riding horse; . . . was richly drest, and had about him a good deal of silver; and . . . had with him a very fine rifle." In separate incidents in the same neighborhood at about the same time Half-Town and an Indian informer en route to report on western confederacy councils each lost two horses to local thieves.[54] No wonder Half-Town, along with Great Tree and many other Senecas, fled northward to Cattaraugus and other Iroquois communities with trading ties to Niagara or New York State. Cut off from Pittsburgh, the shrinking numbers of Senecas who remained on the Allegheny struggled to survive on the meager stock of trade goods available from a poorly supplied and understaffed United States military post called Fort Franklin, established on French Creek in 1787.[55]

But Cornplanter and his fellow leaders were not yet ready to abandon their hopes for hunting rights, trade, and secure homes in western Pennsylvania. In 1788 the commonwealth's desire for land once again provided an opportunity. As lawyers, politicians, and surveyors completed their messy work of determining the Keystone State's boundaries with New York and the Northwest Territory, it became apparent that only about four miles of Lake Erie shoreline fell within Pennsylvania. Worse still, that brief stretch contained nothing remotely resembling a harbor to serve as an entrepôt for trade with the Great Lakes

[54] Richard Butler to Knox, Dec. 13, 1786 (extract); and Treaty Minutes, Jan. 31 and Feb. 10, 19, 22–24, 1787, *Iroquois Indians*, rolls 38 (first quotation), 39; *Minutes of Executive Council*, 16:504–5 (second quotation).

[55] Jonathan Heart to Knox, Oct. 18, 23, 1787, *Iroquois Indians*, roll 39; Thomas Hughes to Anthony Wayne, Nov. 22, 1792, and Feb. 24, 1793, Wayne Papers, 13, fol. 41 (quotation); 25, fol. 50(2). On the establishment of Ft. Franklin see Harmar to Franklin, Apr. 24, 1788, and "Fort Franklin, Venango Co.," *Pennsylvania Archives*, 1st ser., 11:271; 12:361–62. Great Tree was evidently living on the Genesee in 1789 (Sharongyowanew et al. to Clinton, July 30, 1789; Great ["Big"] Tree and Sagoyadyastha to Clinton, Dec. 10, 1789, *Iroquois Indians*, roll 39).

and points west. The excellent port of Presque Isle, however, lay within a vaguely defined tract known as the Erie Triangle, which New York had ceded, along with its other western claims, to the Confederation in 1781. In 1788 Pennsylvania officials thus began intensive negotiations for its purchase and within a few months agreed upon a price of 75¢ in Continental securities per acre. Upon final survey in 1791 the total came to a little over $150,000.[56]

As the bargaining with Congress proceeded, the legislature also made plans for "the purchase of the Country from the Indians, agreeably to the Policy and Justice which have ever marked the Conduct of Pennsylvania in such Cases." The price ordered to be paid to the Iroquois was £375 worth of goods, then equal to about $1,000, or roughly one-half cent an acre.[57] With congressional commissioners again preparing to hold a land-cession treaty with the Western Indians—this time at Fort Harmar on the Ohio River—the assembly deemed it "proper and oeconomical to take advantage of this Circumstance" and avoid "the Expence and delay of a particular Treaty" to complete the purchase of Native claims. Butler and John Gibson received commissions to carry out the task.[58]

[56] *Minutes of Executive Council,* 15:116, 121, 382; Resolution of General Assembly, Nov. 12, 1787; Peter Muhlenberg to Delegates in Congress, Feb. 5, 1788; Porter to Franklin, Feb. 16, 1788; and William Armstrong to Council, Feb. 16, 1788, *Pennsylvania Archives,* 1st ser., 11:211, 237, 241–43; William A. Russ, Jr., *How Pennsylvania Acquired Its Present Boundaries* (University Park, Pa., 1966), pp. 61–65; Lechner, "Erie Triangle," pp. 59–68.

[57] Francis Johnston, Estimate of Costs, Feb. 21, 1788; Resolutions of General Assembly, Sept. 13, 1788, *Pennsylvania Archives,* 1st ser., 11:245, 395–96; *Minutes of Executive Council,* 15:530–32, 553–55; Executive Minutes of Mifflin, Nov. 9, 1791, *Pennsylvania Archives,* 9th ser., 1:pt. 1, 276. The 1788 exchange rate of $1.00 = £.375 (£1 = $2.67) comes from "An estimate of Expense of the Lake Erie Lands, of the Six Nations of Indians, 1788," *Pennsylvania Archives,* 1st ser., 11:390; the figure agrees with Wilkinson's equation of £5393.16.7 with $14,350 in a discussion of a settling of the treaty commissioners' accounts that occurred in 1791 ("Land Policy," pp. 25–27). The purchase agreement with the federal government calculated the area of the Triangle at 202,187 acres.

[58] Resolutions of General Assembly, Sept. 13, 1788, and Commission for Richard Butler and John Gibson, Oct. 3, 1788, *Pennsylvania Archives,* 1st ser., 11:395–96 (quotations), 405.

More than pious rhetoric, familiar personnel, and a tight purse made Fort Harmar a replay of the Fort Stanwix and Fort McIntosh treaties. Cornplanter and his Iroquois political allies again played a prominent and, in the eyes of many Native people, entirely too accommodating role in helping to get signatures on documents ratifying an Indian-white boundary line unilaterally proclaimed by the United States. Guyasuta, Great Tree, and Half-Town were among more than two hundred Allegany Senecas and other Iroquois who had traveled with Cornplanter to Fort Harmar under the protection of a United States army escort. The Allegany leaders strove mightily to thwart the efforts of the Mohawk Brant to prevent the sham negotiations, although territorial governor Arthur St. Clair, who conducted the proceedings on behalf of Congress, refused even such modest requests as their proposal that he release a few Delaware prisoners as a sign of good faith. The Fort Harmar "treaty was effected altogether by the Six Nations; who seduced some of our young men to attend it," the Miami Little Turtle recalled six years later.[59]

But to the Allegany Senecas the dealings with Pennsylvania seemed anything but a sham. As at Fort Stanwix, they believed they had extracted significant concessions from the state's commissioners in exchange for selling land the Long Knives were determined to have anyway. "For *and in behalf* of the State of Pennsylvania, (Onas)," Butler and Gibson joined twenty-four Indians—the vast majority of them from the Allegany villages—in affixing signatures and seals to a document stating that, "as they have no country to remove to from where they now live, the said chiefs do reserve for their own and their people's residence, hunting and fishing, all that part of

[59] "Minutes of the Treaty of Fort Harmar, Commencing 13th December 1788, and Ending 11th January 1789"; "Return of Indians of the Six Nations, Present at the Treaty at Fort Harmar," n.d.; "Appendix to the Minutes of the Treaty of Fort Harmar, 1789"; and "Minutes of a Treaty . . . Begun at Greene Ville on the 16th Day of June, and Ended on the 10th Day of August 1795," Indian Treaties, 99r–v, 105r–v, 111(a)r–15r, 129v–30r, 132r, 140v–41r, 271r (quotation); Sword, *President Washington's Indian War*, pp. 73–75; Isabel Thompson Kelsay, *Joseph Brant, 1743–1807: Man of Two Worlds* (Syracuse, N.Y., 1984), pp. 424–26.

the tract . . . passing from Allegany River along the middle of the Cononwago Creek, the Chadochque [Chautauqua] Lake and a meridian line from the North end of the said lake to Lake Erie." In addition to nearly complete rights to a tiny chunk of the land sold to the commonwealth at Fort Stanwix, the Allegany Senecas were to retain "full and peaceable liberty to hunt and fish within any part of the [Erie Triangle] . . . , they demeaning themselves peaceably towards the inhabitants."[60]

Having gained these significant concessions, Cornplanter rose on the final day of the Fort Harmar proceedings to paint a picture of interracial economic cooperation and harmony in which the weak would thrive under the protection of a stronger people they no longer addressed by the council title of *Brother*. "Father!" he said to St. Clair,

> We now the Six nations acquaint you that our opinion is, we are one people and we will live as such, and unite ourselves like children to a father.
>
> Father! Now that we are settled in the midst of you, you will have pity on us, and if we should want clothing you will supply us.
>
> Father! We shall see you upon our Lands, and they will be planted with corn, and we will be hunting about for Deer; we also shall plant corn, and we shall want our hoes and other articles mended, and for that purpose we shall want a blacksmith to settle amongst us upon the Land, that we have now agreed to live with our brothers upon.
>
> Father! You will remember that a few days ago, we gave you the Belt of Friendship, and desired you to hold it fast; we now remind you of what we said then, and hope that it will not be forgotten by either of us.[61]

Cornplanter's dream of protection by Father Onas quickly became a nightmare. Surveys soon revealed that almost none of the land that the Fort Harmar agreement reserved to the Sene-

---

[60] Treaty Document, Jan. 9, 1789, *Pennsylvania Archives*, 1st ser., 11:529–33; Deed, Gyatwache, *alias* the Cornplanter, et al. to the State of Pennsylvania, January 1789, Record Group 26, no. 47, Pennsylvania State Archives, Harrisburg; *Minutes of Executive Council*, 16:502–3.

[61] "Minutes of Fort Harmer," Jan. 11, 1789, Indian Treaties, 129v–30r.

cas actually lay within the Erie Triangle and that most of it was within the limits of New York, which was not bound by the acts of Pennsylvania's commissioners. Moreover, Gibson and Butler had repeated the multiple document strategy first used at Fort Stanwix; their guarantees of Allegany Seneca rights appeared in a paper separate from a deed of cession that contained far more absolute language. The codicil did not find its way into the commonwealth's files until 1794, long after surveyors, speculators, road builders, and squatters had made a mockery of the hunting rights it supposedly guaranteed.[62]

Before all this became apparent, more immediate problems arose. The Pennsylvania commissioners did not bring to Fort Harmar the goods they promised in payment, for the state coffers lacked the unfunded assembly allocation of $1,000 (not, as stated in the text of the deed, $2,000). When the Supreme Executive Council finally found sufficient funds, their agents could not locate suitable merchandise in Philadelphia warehouses; lacking both strowdwater cloth and match coats—long standard components of diplomatic presents to Indians—they voted to substitute "some blankets now at Pittsburgh, which are said to be suitable for Indians."[63] In the cold of January, then, some 170 Allegany Senecas had to trudge away from Fort Harmar without a guide or military escort "thro' the wilderness through heaps of briars" (as Cornplanter later put it) to collect their payment. At least three times along the way, whites robbed the nearly starving band of rifles and other of their meager possessions. When the travelers finally reached Pittsburgh, they found that "one hundred of the blankets were all moth eaton and good fornot'g." According to Cornplanter, no interpreter

---

[62] Treaty Document, Jan. 9, 1789, as attested May 30, 1792, and recorded June 19, 1794, and Jonathan Hart to John Adlum, July 14, 1789, *Pennsylvania Archives*, 1st ser., 11:529–33, 593–94; *Minutes of Executive Council*, 16:161–62, 169, 375, 547; Executive Minutes of Mifflin, Apr. 15, 19, 21, 1793; Mar. 1, 24, 28, and Apr. 2, 4, 7, 1794, 9th ser., 1:pt. 2, 555, 559–60, 731–33, 740, 743, 747, 749–50; Kent, *Iroquois Indians*. p. 173.

[63] Johnston, Estimate of Costs, Feb. 21, 1788, *Pennsylvania Archives*, 1st ser., 11:245; *Minutes of Executive Council*, 15:553–55, 605, 607, 609, 616 (quotation), 629.

was present, and the Senecas—who needed the blankets simply to keep warm—could find no one to listen to their protests against Gibson, whom they blamed for the fraud.[64]

When the Allegany Senecas finally reached their homes, their leaders dictated to a literate white (probably interpreter Joseph Nicholson) a letter of protest. On receipt of it, the Supreme Executive Council—its Onas self-image severely shaken—invited the headmen to come to Philadelphia and seek redress during the September 1790 legislative session. "It gives us pain to hear from you that some bad people have plundered your camps and taken your property," the councilors said. "Our laws do not permit one man to injure another." As if to mock that statement, while Cornplanter and his colleagues prepared for their trip, three Pennsylvanians murdered a pair of Allegany Senecas on Pine Creek in Northumberland County on the New York border. Despite a show of state and federal government activity, only one of the perpetrators was ever caught, and he evidently never stood trial.[65]

In this tense atmosphere, Cornplanter, Half-Town, Great Tree, Guyasuta, and two other Senecas arrived in Philadelphia in October 1790, armed with testimonials to their good faith and services to the commonwealth written by officials at Fort Franklin, Pittsburgh, Greensburg, and Shippensburg. The Seneca leaders stayed in the capital until early March 1791 and negotiated extensively with state and federal officials, prominent Quakers, and speculators in their lands. "In former days when you were young and weak I used to call you brother, but now I call you father," Cornplanter told the Supreme Executive Council in a reprise of his redefinition of the relationships at Fort Harmar. "Father, I hope you will take pity on your children,

---

[64]*Minutes of Executive Council*, 16:503–4 (quotations); Hugh Brackenridge to Mifflin, Oct. 4, 1790, *Pennsylvania Archives*, 1st ser., 11:732–33.

[65]Proceedings, May 5, 10, 1790; July 9, Sept. 1, 3, 4, 18, and Oct. 30, 1790, *Minutes of Executive Council*, 16:353, 357–58 (quotation), 396–99, 437–40, 442, 456–57, 508; John Robinson to Thomas Procter, Aug. 17, 1790; "Description of the Indian Murderers," n.d. 1790; William Wilson to Mifflin, Sept. 23, 29, 1790; and John Wilkins, Jr., to Mifflin, Oct. 14, 1790, *Pennsylvania Archives*, 1st ser., 11:719–20; 12:319–21.

for now I inform you that I'll die on your side."[66] Similar themes of allegiance in exchange for fatherly protection ran through a message of Guyasuta to the city's Quakers: "When I was young and strong our country was full of game . . . and the People of my Nation had enough to eat and always something to give to our friends when they entered our Cabins," he recalled. But now "the game is driven away by the white people, so that the young men must hunt all day long to find game for themselves to eat. . . . We are old and feeble and hungry and naked, & that we have no other friends than you, the children of our beloved Brother Onas."[67]

But governmental changes allowed the children of Onas to profess powerlessness. Cornplanter's delegation had arrived in Philadelphia after the dissolution of the last legislature elected under Pennsylvania's expired 1776 constitution. A new frame of government would not take effect until December, and in the interim the Supreme Executive Council could spend no money. Thus Cornplanter's reiterated plea "that a store be established at Fort Pitt for the accommodation of my people" received no response, and even his request for "a loan of one hundred and ninety dollars on account, to procure supplies," had to be denied. A promise Butler had made to Cornplanter shortly after the Fort Harmar Treaty regarding confirmation of the headman's personal title to three tracts of land totaling some 1,500 acres similarly lay in financial limbo, despite legislative approval a year and a half earlier.[68]

Once the new state constitution took effect, officials essentially tried to buy the Allegany Seneca leaders' silence. In

[66] J. Jeffers, "To the Good People between Here [Ft. Franklin] and Philadelphia," [September] 1790, and Wilkins to Mifflin, Oct. 14, 1790, *Pennsylvania Archives*, 1st ser., 12:86–87, 321; Brackenridge to Mifflin, Oct. 4, 1790; Robert Galbraith to Mifflin, Oct. 7, 1790; and Procter to Mifflin, Nov. 1, 1790, *Pennsylvania Archives*, 1st ser., 11:732–33, 741; *Minutes of Executive Council*, 16:497, 502 (quotation).

[67] "Speech of Guayshuta, 1790," Ayer Manuscripts, N.A. 317, Newberry Library, Chicago.

[68] *Minutes of Executive Council*, 16:36–37, 505, 507–8, 510–11; Richard Butler to Mifflin, Mar. 23, 1789; and Procter to Mifflin, Nov. 1, 1790, *Pennsylvania Archives*, 1st ser., 11:562–63, 741.

compensation for the additional land acquired through what Cornplanter alleged to be the erroneous survey of the New York–Pennsylvania boundary, the legislature and governor paid Cornplanter, Half-Town, and Great Tree $800 "in trust for the use of the whole Seneca Nation of Indians and in full Satisfaction of all claims and demands whatsoever . . . against this Commonwealth."[69] Additionally, Cornplanter received his long promised land patents, and Great Tree obtained a deed to the island in the Allegheny River on which he resided. These private tracts—rather than a reservation vested in the nation as a whole—would be the only territories to which the Allegany Senecas ever acquired clear title from the state.[70]

While the Native leaders waited for the Pennsylvanians to act, major governmental shifts were also underway on the continental level as the new federal Constitution went into effect. The Indian Trade and Intercourse Act, passed by Congress in August 1790, stripped the states of many powers they had previously claimed in dealing with the Natives. And, already at the Fort Harmar Treaty, United States officials had begun to abandon the conquest theory in favor of at least the pretext of negotiated land purchases. Thus what the Fort McIntosh Treaty had described merely as gifts "in pursuance of the humane and liberal views of Congress" became in the Fort Harmar Treaty "consideration" paid, in combination with additional, much larger amounts, for lands east of the boundary. Moreover, in contradiction of its earlier declarations of absolute territorial sovereignty, the United States "relinquish[ed] and quit claim" to Native country west of the line.[71] Then, in 1790 and 1791,

---

[69] Cornplanter, Half-Town, and Great Tree to Mifflin, Dec. 30, 1790, *Pennsylvania Archives*, 1st ser., 322; Executive Minutes of Mifflin, Feb. 1, 3, 1791, *Pennsylvania Archives*, 9th ser., 1:pt. 1, 25–26 (quotation).

[70] Thomas Mifflin, Message to Legislature, Jan. 22, 1791, *Pennsylvania Archives*, 1st ser., 12:83–86; Executive Minutes of Mifflin, Jan. 29, Feb. 3, and May 31, 1791, *Pennsylvania Archives*, 9th ser., 1:pt. 1, 23–24, 26, 120–21; Merle H. Deardorff, "The Cornplanter Grant in Warren County," *Western Pennsylvania Historical Magazine* 24 (1941):1–22.

[71] Instructions to Arthur St. Clair, Oct. 26, 1787, and July 2, 1788; and Knox to George Washington, May 23, 1789, *New American State Papers*, 4:16–18; "Articles of Treaty at Fort McIntosh," and "Articles of a Treaty Made at Fort

the western confederacy's successive defeats of federal armies led by Harmar and St. Clair forced a further moderation of federal policy, to the extent that minor modifications of the United States–Indian boundary lay on the table through the period of Anthony Wayne's defeat of the western confederacy at the Battle of Fallen Timbers in 1794 and his reaffirmation and extension of the 1784 Fort Stanwix line in the 1795 Treaty of Greenville.[72]

Yet despite the changes that were beginning to take place in federal policy during the Senecas' 1790–91 sojourn in Philadelphia, negotiations with President Washington and Secretary of War Henry Knox in December and January produced no dramatic breakthroughs. Even Cornplanter's suggestion that the trusted interpreter Joseph Nicholson be stationed at Pittsburgh, where Senecas still hoped to trade on a large scale, was rejected. Washington did, however, pledge to prevent future fraudulent land purchases, to open federal courts to Iroquois grievances, to station a government agent in the Senecas' country as "their friend and protector," and to provide educational and economic assistance. "Continue to be strong in your friendship for the United States, as the only rational ground of your future happiness," the president advised the Senecas, "and you may rely upon their kindness and protection."[73]

Nothing encouraged the Allegany Senecas to rely on the kindness and protection of the children of Onas. Cornplanter and his party left Philadelphia carrying an additional present from the commonwealth of a little over £65 (about $175); just

---

Harmar," Jan. 9, 1789, Wayne Papers, 19:fols. 47 (first quotation), 73 (remaining quotations).

[72] Instructions to Rufus Putnam, Apr. 3–4, 1792; "Extracts from Journal of Commissioners of United States"; and "Minutes of a Treaty . . . at Greene Ville," Indian Treaties, 211r–15v, 254r–61r, 262r–313r; Knox to Wayne, Jan. 5, 1792 [1793]; and Timothy Pickering to Wayne, Apr. 8, 1795, Wayne Papers, 24:fol. 381/2; 40:fol. 35.

[73] Speeches of Cornplanter, Half-Town, and Great Tree, Dec. 1, 1790, Jan. 10 and Feb. 7, 1791, with replies of Washington, Dec. 29, 1790, and Jan. 19, 1791; and of Knox, Feb. 8, 1791, New American State Papers, 4:24–29 (quotations from pp. 28, 27); Knox to Mifflin, Dec. 23, 1790, Pennsylvania Archives, 1st ser., 12:32.

north of Pittsburgh, militiamen from Virginia attacked the boat on which the party was traveling and stole all of the merchandise those funds had purchased. A few months earlier, another group of Virginians, who were never caught, had murdered four Senecas in the same neighborhood. On the upper Allegheny, meanwhile, Pennsylvania surveyors accompanied by armed militia were completing an exploration of waterways in preparation for the occupation of Presque Isle, and an agent for Philadelphia merchant Robert Morris was plotting in the Senecas' village to attempt a massive private land purchase in the area.[74]

By 1794 the rapid occupation of the Erie Triangle had so trampled the Allegany Senecas' hunting and fishing rights that even Cornplanter had lost his patience; early that year he expelled a Pennsylvania storekeeper from his town and reportedly sought British aid "to Clear French Creek, By killing the White people and taking the Posts." Some young Allegany Seneca men, meanwhile, moved from talk to action and took the lives of several white Pennsylvanians in the area.[75] All of this occurred just at the point when Wayne's campaign against the western confederacy and President Washington's efforts to quell the Whiskey Rebellion left the Federal government no troops to spare; nonetheless, it took a personal appeal from Washington to convince Mifflin to order a brief suspension of state-sponsored activities in the Triangle.[76]

[74] Executive Minutes of Mifflin, Feb. 7, Apr. 23, May 7, and July 18, 1791; and Feb. 9, 21, 1792, *Pennsylvania Archives*, 9th ser., 1:pt. 1, 28, 89, 98, 160–61, 325, 328; Speech of Cornplanter, Apr. 9, 1791; and Thomas Procter Diary, s.v. Apr. 27, 1791, *New American State Papers*, 4:52, 43–44; *Minutes of Executive Council*, 16:547.

[75] John O'Bail (Cornplanter) to John Polhemus, May 8, 1794; and Knox to Wayne, June 7, 1794, Wayne Papers, 34:fol. 103; 35:fol. 88; Ebenezer Denny to Commissioners for Survey of Presque Isle, Apr. 25, 1794; Denny to Mifflin, May 2, 30, 1794; Deposition of Daniel Ransom, June 11, 1794 (quotation); Polhemus to John Gibson, June 12, 1794; and Treaty minutes, June 26, 1794, Correspondence of Ebenezer Denny, Denny and O'Hara Papers, ser. 3, box 11, folder 2, Historical Society of Western Pennsylvania, Pittsburgh; Wilkinson, "Land Policy," pp. 107–25A.

[76] Executive Minutes of Mifflin, Mar. 1–July 22, 1794, *Pennsylvania Archives*, 9th ser., 1:pt. 2, 731–814. The intercultural controversy over the Erie

At the height of the tensions, Pennsylvania surveyor John Adlum traveled from Pittsburgh to Fort Franklin intending to survey a million-acre tract of Allegheny land to which Pennsylvanian James Wilson had recently acquired title. Escorted by Half-Town, Adlum's flotilla of canoes received a strained ceremonial reception at Cornplanter's village, during which the welcoming shots fired by Seneca young men whizzed suspiciously close to the surveyor's head. Shortly thereafter, in a crowded council house where Adlum sought permission to conduct his surveys, he attempted to read elaborately beribboned messages he carried from Secretary of War Knox and Governor Mifflin. His interpreter had barely finished the first paragraph of Knox's letter when "the young Indians" sitting in the rafters "saluted" Adlum with "an univer[sal] roar, *vulgarly called farting*" and the women seated below joined in with cries of *"shame, scandalous."* Cornplanter "reprimanded" the rude musicmakers, who, Adlum said, then "descended from their roosts, and sneaked off." Next morning, in a more decorous meeting, Adlum received begrudging permission to plat approximately half the territory he intended, but not before Cornplanter informed him "that all persons who encroached on their lands were their enemies."[77]

Onas, Long Knives, Enemies: three Indian names for Pennsylvanians. Despite the repeated attempts of Seneca leaders to hold up the first as a model of behavior for Pennsylvania government officials, the last two were the ones that stuck. In Native eyes, Onas's descendants were no different from all the other Long

---

Triangle would only be put to rest in the fall of 1794 at the Treaty of Canandaigua, where Iroquois leaders received from the United States an additional payment of $10,000 and pledges of a $4,500 annual annuity. Significantly, Governor Mifflin refused an invitation for state commissioners to participate in the federal negotiations. See Harry M. Tinkcom, "Presque Isle and Pennsylvania Politics, 1797," *Pennsylvania History* 16 (1949):96–121; Kent, *Iroquois Indians*, pp. 173–81; and Jack Campisi, "From Stanwix to Canandaigua: National Policy, States' Rights, and Indian Land," in Christopher Vecsey and William A. Starna, eds., *Iroquois Land Claims* (Syracuse, N.Y., 1988), pp. 60–64.

[77] Deardorff and Kent, "Adlum on the Allegheny," pp. 287–324, quotations from pp. 304, 306.

Knives of the new republic. Nearly a decade of dealing with Pennsylvania had secured the Allegany Senecas title to precisely 1,500 acres of land and one island; their hopes for hunting and fishing rights inside the state's borders and for a flourishing trade with Pittsburgh remained unfulfilled. And by the early nineteenth century only a handful of Senecas would remain within the commonwealth, the rest having joined their kin across the state line on the New York Allegany reservation.[78] Long before, Senecas had apparently given up their hopes that accommodation with the commonwealth's government might help them achieve their goals of a secure land base, hunting rights, and trading privileges. The legacy of the commonwealth's Indian policies lived on, however, as the federal government embraced techniques the commonwealth had perfected and applied them widely in the years of the early republic: legalistic adherence to treaty documents, forced purchases of Indian territory, resales of the land acquired to its own citizens to pay government debts, and rhetoric that wrapped the process in professions of philanthropic justice.[79] In more ways than one, Onas became the Long Knife.

[78] Wallace, *Death and Rebirth of the Seneca*, pp. 179–83; Henry Rowe Schoolcraft, *Information Respecting the History, Condition, and Prospects of the Indian Tribes of the United States* (Philadelphia, 1851–55), 3:439–524, 583–86, 590–98.

[79] Bernard W. Sheehan, *Seeds of Extinction: Jeffersonian Philanthropy and the American Indian* (Chapel Hill, 1973); Jones, *License for Empire*, pp. 165–86.

R. DAVID EDMUNDS

"A Watchful Safeguard to Our Habitations"

Black Hoof and the

Loyal Shawnees

FOR MOST HISTORIANS, the association of Indian people with the War of 1812 conjures up images of Native American resistance. From Tippecanoe to the Thames and from Fort Mims to Horseshoe Bend, historians have concentrated upon this last, futile attempt by Native American people to solicit foreign assistance in defending their homelands east of the Mississippi. Within the past decade scholars have focused upon the emergence of religious and cultural revitalization as the core of this resistance or have argued that Indian attempts to form a centralized confederacy during this period was just the final stage in a much larger and continued effort at political consolidation. In their focus upon the War of 1812, both scholars and the general public have concentrated their attention upon those Native American leaders who chose to oppose the onrushing Euro-Americans. Most Americans have continued to be fascinated by leaders who championed an armed resistance. Pontiac, Osceola, and Black Hawk are familiar figures in American history textbooks.[1]

[1] Both Joel W. Martin, *Sacred Revolt: The Muskogees' Struggle for a New World* (Boston, 1991), and R. David Edmunds, *The Shawnee Prophet* (Lincoln, Nebr., 1983), emphasize the role of religious revitalization in the emergence of Indian resistance before the war. Gregory Evans Dowd, *A Spirited Resistance: The North American Indian Struggle for Unity, 1745–1815* (Baltimore, 1992), also focuses upon Native American spirituality as a key factor in the resistance movements of the period but argues that such spirituality also permeated political leadership and asserts that secular and religious influence was interwoven. He

But other leaders tried a different tactic. They attempted to walk the white man's road and to accommodate the demands of their white neighbors. Because their courage and tenacity were not displayed on the battlefield, they have frequently been overlooked. Most have either been ignored or forgotten.[2]

The Shawnee Indians who resided in western Ohio and Indiana during the early nineteenth century offer an interesting case study of this dilemma. Unquestionably, the two Native American leaders most closely associated with the War of 1812 are the Shawnee war chief Tecumseh and his brother Tenskwatawa, the Shawnee Prophet. Scholars may disagree about which factors fostered the brothers' emergence during these years, but these Shawnees' doctrines and activities have been the focal point of considerable recent scholarship.[3] Yet when Tenskwatawa's followers fought with William Henry Harrison at the Tippecanoe or Tecumseh fell at the Battle of the Thames, most Shawnee warriors were not in attendance. By 1800 almost half the Shawnee people, approximately one thousand individuals, already were living peacefully with the Americans in Missouri. During the War of 1812 most of those who lived east of the Mississippi, about eight hundred Indians, remained neutral or supported the Americans. In October 1813 fewer than ten Shawnee warriors were killed at the Battle of the Thames, and following that encounter, the Prophet led only thirty Shawnee

---

asserts that Tecumseh exemplified the logical culmination of such leadership. Richard White, *The Middle Ground: Indians, Empires, and Republics in the Great Lakes Region, 1650–1815* (Cambridge, 1991), argues that tribal consolidation and political centralization emerged under French hegemony during the late seventeenth and early eighteenth centuries. White traces the growth of these phenomena into the early national period. Alvin M. Josephy, *The Patriot Chiefs: A Chronicle of American Indian Leadership* (New York, 1961), focuses upon those leaders who led military resistance movements.

[2] Reginald Horsman, *Expansion and American Indian Policy, 1783–1812* (East Lansing, Mich., 1967), illustrates that American Indian policy offered Native American people few opportunities for meaningful accommodation.

[3] In addition to the volumes mentioned in the previous notes, see Bil Gilbert, *God Gave Us This Country: Tekamthi and the First American Civil War* (New York, 1989), and R. David Edmunds, *Tecumseh and the Quest for Indian Leadership* (Boston, 1984).

men and ninety women and children east toward Burlington, Ontario.[4]

In contrast to the small number of Shawnees who followed the doctrines of Tenskwatawa and Tecumseh, many others spent the first years of the nineteenth century in support of the policies of accommodation championed by Black Hoof, Captain Lewis, Logan, and others friendly to the government. In the decade following the Treaty of Greenville, they became convinced that they could no longer live in the manner of their forefathers. They decided to establish villages along the headwaters of the Auglaize and Miami rivers in Ohio and to seek a closer association with the United States. In conjunction with neighboring Wyandots, Delawares, and Miamis and Potawatomis near Fort Wayne, they solicited assistance from the Quakers and the federal government in establishing small farms similar to those of their white neighbors. They also requested that federal agents erect saw- and gristmills in their villages.[5]

The Indians' request pleased federal officials who had promoted a policy of acculturation. In the 1790s Congress had initiated the Indian Intercourse Acts, partially designed to promote the acculturation of the Indian tribes, and in 1802 Thomas Jefferson assured the Indians that although "hunting may fail, and expose your women and children to the miseries of cold and hunger," agriculture would never disappoint them. Moreover, according to Jefferson, the government would furnish them "with implements for the most necessary arts, and

---

[4] Charles Callender, "Shawnee," in Bruce Trigger, ed., *Northeast*, Handbook of North American Indians, vol. 15 (Washington, D.C., 1978), p. 634; John Johnston to John Mason, Mar. 16, 1812, Letters Received by the Secretary of War, Main Series (microfilm M221), roll 47, 1704, Record Group 107, National Archives, Washington, D.C.; Lt. Gen. Sir Gordon Drummond to George Prevost, Apr. 13, 1814, British Military and Naval Records, C ser., vol. 683, 30–34, Record Group 8, Public Archives of Canada, Ottawa.

[5] Helen Hornbeck Tanner, ed., *Atlas of Great Lakes Indian History* (Norman, Okla., 1987), pp. 98–101; *Some Account of the Conduct of the Religious Society of Friends toward the Indian Tribes* (London, 1844), p. 120; "Minutes of a Conference Held with the Delaware and Shawanoe Deputation," Feb. 5–10, 1802, Shawnee File, Great Lakes–Ohio Valley Indian Archives, Glenn A. Black Laboratory of Archaeology, Indiana University, Bloomington.

with persons who will instruct how to make use of them." At first both the federal government and the missionaries concentrated their efforts upon the Wyandots near Sandusky and among the Miamis and Potawatomis, but in June 1807 William Kirk, a Quaker missionary who previously had quarreled with Indian agents at Fort Wayne, withdrew from Indiana and founded a mission among the Shawnees. Kirk was warmly received at Wapakoneta, Black Hoof's village on the Auglaize.[6]

Several factors contributed to Kirk's welcome. Black Hoof and other Shawnee leaders previously had pleaded for agricultural assistance, but overriding this concern was the impact of intratribal politics. Shawnee political structure was egalitarian. Traditionally the tribe was separated into five patrilineal descent groups, each concentrated in a separate town. These divisions had particular political or ritual obligations. The Chalagawetha (Chillicothe) and Thawegila divisions supplied political leadership for the tribe, sometimes competing for such prominence. The Piquas were responsible for maintaining tribal rituals and supposedly had a particular affinity for religious affairs. The Kispokothas supplied war chiefs, while the Maykujays (perhaps the least prestigious of the divisions) were specialists in medicine and health. Before the American Revolution the five divisions had maintained their separate towns, but amidst the turmoil engendered by two decades of border warfare (1774–95), the distinct physical separation and explicit responsibilities of the divisions had become blurred. In 1774 many of the Thawegila people left the Ohio Valley and joined with the Creeks in Alabama, and five years later almost one thousand Shawnees, mostly members of the Kispokotha and Piqua groups, emi-

---

[6] Thomas Jefferson to the Miamis, Potawatomis, and Weas, Jan. 7, 1802, Records of the Secretary of War Relating to Indian Affairs, Letters Sent (microfilm M15), roll 1, 142–43, Record Group 75, Natl. Arch.; William Kirk to Henry Dearborn, May 28, 1807, Letters Received by the Secretary of War, Main Series, roll 9, 2854–61; Kirk to Dearborn, July 20, 1807, ibid., 2874–78. For a discussion of Presbyterian missionary efforts among the Wyandots, see Joseph A. Badger, *A Memoir of Joseph Badger* (Hudson, Ohio, 1851); for a discussion of Kirk's unsuccessful missionary activity among the Miamis and Potawatomis, see R. David Edmunds, "Redefining Red Patriotism: Five Medals of the Potawatomis," *Red River Valley Historical Review* 5 (1980): 13–24.

grated from Ohio to Missouri. After their departure the remnants of these three divisions joined with the Chalagawetha and Maykujay people to form new villages. But since the membership of the Chalagawethas and Maykujays remained primarily in Ohio, these divisions dominated the villages and began to usurp the other divisions' functions. In response, the refugee Thawegilas, Kispokothas, and Piquas harbored growing resentments.[7]

Dissension also emerged over the changing role of war and peace chiefs. Traditionally, the Shawnees had maintained a bifurcated political leadership comprised of both peace and war chiefs. In theory, either the Chalagawethas or Thawegilas had supplied a hereditary peace chief with limited authority over the entire tribe, but in actuality, since various divisions maintained separate villages, the "tribal" chiefs exercised only minimal control over Shawnees not living within the town where the chief was in residence. By the late eighteenth century each division, and indeed each village, was led by a village or peace chief who served as the leader of the local population. These village chiefs, usually middle-aged or older men of broad experience and good judgement, mediated intravillage and inter-village disputes and also represented their followers in negotiations with the local white population.[8]

In contrast, war chiefs were younger men who had proved themselves as warriors and whose authority was limited to military matters. Traditionally, Kispokotha warriors had taken the leadership in military affairs but had acquiesced in the guidance of the Chalagawethas or Thawegilas or of local village chiefs when the conflict ended. But by 1800 the Shawnees who remained in Ohio had endured almost half a century of continued warfare, and the political power of the war chiefs had increased. Accordingly, younger war chiefs had become more deeply involved in the tribe's negotiations with the Americans, and, since they were admired because of their military prowess,

---

[7] Callender, "Shawnee," pp. 623–24; Edmunds, *Tecumseh*, pp. 46–47. Also see Vernon Kinietz and Erminie Wheeler-Voegelin, eds., *"Shawnese Traditions": C. C. Trowbridge's Account*, Occasional Contributions from the Museum of Anthropology of the University of Michigan, no. 9 (Ann Arbor, Mich., 1939), pp. xiii–xiv, 8.

[8] Callender, "Shawnee," pp. 623–24; Edmunds, *Tecumseh*, pp. 48–49.

some of them, such as Tecumseh, also were functioning as village chiefs.[9]

Black Hoof, an elderly Maykujay village chief, resented many of these changes. Born shortly after 1740, Black Hoof had fought against the Americans in both the American Revolution and during the border warfare of the 1790s, but following the Treaty of Greenville he had led a growing number of followers down the path toward acculturation. By 1800 he had emerged as the most influential of the Shawnee village chiefs still remaining in Ohio, and, although the Shawnees no longer recognized a paramount chief, federal Indian agents in Ohio and Indiana considered him the focal point for their contact with the tribe. At the same time, Black Hoof's adherence to acculturation engendered opposition from Tecumseh, and as other Shawnee traditionalists moved into Tecumseh's camp, Black Hoof envisioned the Kispokotha war chief as a potential rival.[10]

In 1805, after the emergence of the Shawnee Prophet, the rivalry between Black Hoof and Tecumseh and Tenskwatawa intensified. The Prophet's doctrine that the Americans were the spawn of the Great Serpent, and all Indians who emulated them were guilty of witchcraft, was particularly threatening to Black Hoof and other champions of accommodation, particularly after March 1806, when the Prophet's followers among the Delawares burned four of their kinsmen at the stake. Three months later Tenskwatawa's successful prediction of a solar eclipse brought an influx of new converts to the Shawnee brothers' village near Greenville, and the suspicion and animosity between the two factions of Shawnees increased. Since 1795 Black Hoof and the other Shawnee chiefs on the Auglaize had been the recipients of the Shawnee annuity payments, but the new village near Greenville was burgeoning with recently arrived western Indians, and Black Hoof feared that federal agents might distribute part of the money and goods to his rivals. More-

[9] Edmunds, *Tecumseh*, pp. 48–49.

[10] Thomas L. McKenney and James Hall, *History of the Indian Tribes of North America, with Biographical Sketches and Anecdotes of the Principal Chiefs*, 3 vols. (Philadelphia , 1848–50), 1:238–39; "Anthony Shane's Statement," Tecumseh Papers, Draper Manuscripts, 12YY44–67, State Historical Society of Wisconsin, Madison.

over, like most of the Shawnees in Ohio, Black Hoof, Captain Lewis, and other chiefs from the Auglaize still considered Tenskwatawa a charlatan. They remembered him as a heavy-set, alcoholic, ne'er-do-well intent only upon his personal aggrandizement. Consequently, from Black Hoof's perspective, the establishment of Kirk's mission at Wapakoneta would counterbalance the growing influence of the Prophet. In addition the mission would enhance Black Hoof's prestige among the loyal Shawnees and strengthen his ties with the government.[11]

Kirk arrived none too soon. In June 1807 two of Black Hoof's followers were killed in the forest, and the chief suspected that they had been murdered by disciples of the Prophet. Representatives from both Shawnee camps met in Wapakoneta where the Prophet's emissaries disclaimed any responsibility for the murders, but Black Hoof remained dissatisfied. Meanwhile several settlers were killed by Indians near Staunton, and, in response to a request by Gov. Edward Tiffin, Black Hoof and Tecumseh journeyed to Springfield to meet with state officials. The meeting almost erupted in violence. Both factions of Shawnees disclaimed any responsibility for the murders, but when asked if he knew who was responsible for the deaths, Tecumseh placed his hand on Black Hoof's shoulder and proclaimed "This is the man who killed your white brother." Black Hoof then denounced Tecumseh as a liar and both men seized their weapons. Fortunately, white officials intervened and no bloodshed resulted, but the confrontation only deepened the rift between the two Shawnee camps. Ironically, subsequent investigation indicated that the murders had been committed by some vagabond Potawatomis.[12]

[11] William Wells to Dearborn, Apr. 19, 1807, Letters Received by the Secretary of War, Main Series, roll 14, 4566; Wells to Dearborn, May 28, 1807, ibid., roll 9, 2854–64; Jefferson to the Chiefs of the Shawnee Nation, Feb. 19, 1807, Andrew A. Lipscomb and Albert Ellery Bergh, eds., *The Writings of Thomas Jefferson*, 20 vols. (Washington, D.C., 1903–4), 16:421–25. Also see Edmunds, *Shawnee Prophet*, pp. 28–57.

[12] Kirk to Dearborn, July 20, 1807, Letters Received by the Secretary of War, Main Series, roll 9, 2874–78; Kirk to Dearborn, Aug. 9, 1807, ibid., 2880; Joseph Vance to Benjamin Drake, n.d., Tecumseh Papers, 2YY108–117; Simon Kenton Papers, 9BB1, Draper Mss.

Although Kirk arrived at Wapakoneta too late to begin any spring planting, he assisted Black Hoof's people in clearing land, erecting split rail fences, and building log cabins. During the spring of 1808 Black Hoof wrote to Thomas Jefferson, thanking the government for sending "our friends, the Quakers, to help us, and we find they are good people and concerned for our welfare and have done a great deal for us in instructing our young men in a good way and how to use the tools we see in the hands of our white brothers." By June the Shawnees at Wapakoneta had cleared and planted over five hundred acres with traditional crops such as corn, beans, squash, and pumpkins, but they also planted turnips, cabbage, and potatoes. In addition, they nurtured several small orchards of apples and had acquired a herd of hogs, cattle, and two yokes of oxen. With Kirk's assistance, the Shawnees purchased farm implements and hired a blacksmith who established a forge in their village. Construction was begun on both a sawmill and a gristmill, and in the fall of 1808 Black Hoof and his people reaped a "bounteous harvest." Kirk was so encouraged by the Shawnees' "progress" that he planned additional missions among the neighboring Wyandots and Senecas.[13]

Other factors also seemed to strengthen Black Hoof's position. In the spring of 1808 Tecumseh and the Shawnee Prophet moved their village from Greenville to the juncture of the Tippecanoe and Wabash rivers in Indiana, decreasing their influence among those Indians remaining in Ohio. Meanwhile, Black Hoof drew copious praise from white Ohioans and other American travelers who passed through Wapakoneta. Federal officials received reports of the Shawnees' well-groomed fields and "comfortable houses of hewn logs with chimneys." Others commented upon the Shawnees' sobriety and temperance ("a matter of surprise to those that are acquainted with Indians") and praised the Indians for their hospitality to white travelers. During the fall of 1808, the War Department received a petition

[13] Black Hoof and others to the President [Jefferson], Spring 1808, Letters Received by the Secretary of War, Main Series, roll 17, 5258; Kirk to Dearborn, Apr. 12, 1808, ibid., roll 25, 8114–15; Shawnee Chiefs to the President, Dec. 1, 1808, ibid., 8148–50; Kirk to Dearborn, Dec. 10, 1808, ibid., 8143–44; Kirk to Dearborn, Feb. 12, 1809, ibid., 8157.

from white citizens near Dayton who praised the Shawnees as a bastion against hostile Indians, commenting that "we find them sober and civil . . . and look upon them as a watchful safeguard to our habitations."[14]

Unfortunately, the acculturation programs at Wapakoneta soon ran afoul of bureaucratic politics. Kirk's ardor "to spread the gospel and the articles of husbandry" overshadowed his concern for fiscal responsibility. Thoroughly involved in expanding his mission, he overspent the funds that the government had appropriated for his venture, then delayed in sending his financial report back to the War Department. In 1807 Secretary of War Henry Dearborn reluctantly covered Kirk's overdrafts, but when Kirk again overspent his budget in 1808, Dearborn demanded an explanation. Kirk admitted that his mission "may have cost the government more in the outset than at first contemplated," but both he and Black Hoof argued that the expended funds had been invested for the Shawnees' welfare and that the coming year would prove that the money had been well spent.[15]

Kirk's problems played into the hands of William Wells, the Indian agent at Fort Wayne, who was jealous of Kirk's success and wished to regain control of the Shawnee annuities. In 1807 Wells wrote to Dearborn that Kirk had misspent federal funds and that the Shawnees were dissatisfied with his efforts. In addition, friends of Wells spread rumors that Kirk had entered into sexual liasons with Shawnee women and had spread vene-

---

[14] Wells to Dearborn, Apr. 20, 1808, Clarence Edwin Carter et al., comps. and eds., *The Territorial Papers of the United States*, 28 vols. (Washington, D.C., 1934–75), 7:555–60; "Diary of an Exploratory Journey of the Brethren Lukenbach and Haven, in Company of the Indian Brother Andreas, along the St. Mary's River, the South Tributary of the Miami, Which Flows into Lake Erie," Aug. 26–Sept. 13, 1808, Box 157, folder 11, Moravian Archives, Bethlehem, Pa.; Citizens of Ohio to the War Department, Sept. 25, 1808, Letters Received by the Secretary of War, Main Series, roll 25, 8147; Francis Douchet to the President [Jefferson], Dec. 4, 1808, ibid., 8145.

[15] Kirk to Dearborn, Dec. 25, 1808, Letters Received by the Secretary of War, Main Series, roll 9, 2888–91; Kirk to Dearborn, Jan. 28, 1808, ibid., 2897; Kirk to Dearborn, Apr. 12, 1808, ibid., roll 25, 8115; Shawnee Chiefs to the President [Jefferson] and the Secretary of War [Dearborn], Dec. 1, 1808, ibid., 8148–50; Kirk to Dearborn, Dec. 10, 1808, ibid., 8115.

real disease at Wapakoneta. In December 1808 Wells journeyed to Washington, and while he was in the capital, Dearborn dismissed Kirk and instructed him to leave the mission.[16]

Kirk's dismissal brought a series of protests from the Shawnees, and in January 1809 Black Hoof visited the capital to plead for the Quaker's reinstatement. Black Hoof informed federal officials that since Kirk had arrived at Wapakoneta "our women and children have had plenty to eat, he has helped us to make fences . . . we have done very well by his assistance," but the Shawnee's pleas were ignored, and in February he returned to Wapakoneta empty-handed.[17]

During the following months Black Hoof's people attempted to continue Kirk's acculturation programs. On January 27, 1809, Wells was also dismissed from the Indian Service, and in April, John Johnston, his successor, met with Black Hoof and other Shawnee leaders at Wapakoneta. After escorting Johnston through their settlement and demonstrating that the construction of both their sawmill and their gristmill was almost completed, they pleaded with the agent to send another missionary or agent. In response the War Department sent John Shaw, previously an assistant Indian agent at Fort Wayne, to reside in the Shawnee village. Johnston also agreed to employ an agricultural laborer to assist the Shawnees during the following summer.[18]

---

[16] Wells to William Henry Harrison, June 1807, Logan Esarey, ed., *Messages and Letters of William Henry Harrison*, 2 vols. (Indianapolis, 1922), 1:218; Wells to Dearborn, Aug. 20, 1807, Carter et al., comps. and eds., *Territorial Papers*, 7:469–71; Wells to Dearborn, Letters Received by the Secretary of War, Main Series, roll 15, 4815–16; Douchouquet to Dearborn, Mar. 30, 1809, Records of the Office of the Secretary of War, Letters Received by the Secretary, Unregistered Series (microfilm M222), roll 4, 1634, Record Group 107, Natl. Arch., Dearborn to Kirk, Dec. 22, 1808, Shawnee File.

[17] Wells to Dearborn, Jan. 16, 1809, Letters Received by the Secretary of War, Main Series, roll 33, 1317; Citizens of Dayton to the President [Jefferson], Jan. 30, 1809, ibid., roll 27, 8933; Chiefs and Headmen of the Shawnees to the President [Madison], Apr. 10, 1809, ibid., roll 24, 8053–54; William Eustis to William Hull, Apr. 5, 1809, Records of the Secretary of War Relating to Indian Affairs, Letters Sent, roll 2, 433.

[18] Dearborn to Johnston, Jan. 27, 1809, Frank J. Jones Collection, Cincinnati Historical Society, Cincinnati; Johnston to the Secretary of War [Eustis], Apr. 15, 1809, Carter et al., comps. and eds., *Territorial Papers*, 7:647–49;

Black Hoof's people spent the summer of 1809 cultivating their crops and bringing both of their mills into production, but intratribal politics again intruded. During late June and early July, William Henry Harrison met with Tenskwatawa at Vincennes, and although Harrison was convinced of the Prophet's hostility, he also believed that his influence had declined. Under pressure from federal officials to acquire title to additional Indian lands in Indiana, Harrison met with representatives from the Potawatomis, Miamis, and Delawares at Fort Wayne in September and purchased over three million acres.[19]

The treaty had a profound impact upon both groups of Shawnees. Obviously taken by surprise, Tecumseh redoubled his efforts to recruit new allies among those Indians who were opposed to the treaty, and his endeavors placed Black Hoof on the defensive. Black Hoof and his followers had not participated in the treaty proceedings, but Tecumseh charged that the Shawnees, Wyandots, and Senecas living in Ohio had supported the pact. In the treaty's aftermath, both Tecumseh and the Prophet threatened to kill those chiefs who had cooperated with the government, and during the following spring Tecumseh arrived at Wapakoneta hoping to convince many of the Shawnees in the village to abandon Black Hoof and move to Prophetstown. Black Hoof and most of the more influential warriors in the village refused to meet with him, but a few of the younger men, accompanied by Stephen Ruddell, a former white captive among the Shawnees who had been repatriated and now served as a Baptist missionary to the tribe, met in council with the Shawnee war chief. After listening to Tecumseh's ar-

Johnston to P. E. Thomas, Apr. 15, 1809, Gayle Thornbrough, ed., *Letter Book of the Indian Agency at Fort Wayne, 1809–1815*, Indiana Historical Publications, vol. 21 (Indianapolis, 1961), pp. 37–43; Eustis to Johnston, Records of the Secretary of War Relating to Indian Affairs, Letters Sent, roll 2, 437; Eustis to Johnston, May 23, 1809, ibid., 440–41.

[19] Harrison to Johnston, July 8, 1809, Jones Collection; Eustis to Harrison, July 15, 1809, Letters Sent by the Secretary of War Relating to Military Affairs (microfilm M6), roll 4, 103–4, Record Group 107, Natl. Arch.; Harrison to the Secretary of War [Eustis], Aug. 29, 1809, Carter et al., comps. and eds., *Territorial Papers*, 7:670–71; "A Treaty between the United States and the Tribes of Indians . . . September 30, 1809," Charles E. Kappler, ed., *Indian Treaties, 1778–1883* (1904; reprint ed., New York, 1972), pp. 101–2.

guments, Ruddell interrupted the war chief to state that Black Hoof's people had no intention of leaving Wapakoneta. Holding a recent letter from Harrison, Ruddell indicated that the Shawnees in Ohio were loyal to the president and considered the Prophet to be a charlatan. Angered, Tecumseh seized the letter from Ruddell's hands and cast it into the fire, claiming that American promises were no more than ashes. Yet Black Hoof's and Ruddell's influence prevailed, and Tecumseh left the village accompanied by only a handful of new followers.[20]

While Tecumseh found few recruits among the Shawnees, other members of his entourage were more successful among the Wyandot villages along the Sandusky River. Relying upon the Wyandot fear of witchcraft, they denounced several of the more acculturated Wyandots as sorcerers, and in late June 1810 the Wyandots burned three of these individuals, including the village chief Leatherlips, as witches.[21] In response, federal officials called village chiefs from eastern Michigan, Ohio, and Indiana to conferences at Fort Wayne and Brownstown, a Wyandot village south of Detroit. Almost all the Indians who attended were followers of village chiefs loyal to the Americans, and although some harbored resentment over the loss of lands at the Treaty of Fort Wayne, they utilized the meetings to denounce Tecumseh and the Prophet. The small Shawnee delegation that attended the Michigan conference was led by George Bluejacket and Logan, and although they subscribed to the pro-American sentiments espoused at Brownstown, they did visit with British Indian agents at Amherstburg, across the Detroit River in Ontario.[22]

[20] Johnston to Harrison, June 24, 1810, Esarey, ed., *Messages and Letters of Harrison*, 1:430–32; Wyandots of Sandusky to Hull, June 27, 1810, Wyandot File, Great Lakes–Ohio Valley Indian Archives; Johnston to Eustis, July 3, 1810, Letters Received by the Secretary of War, Main Series, roll 38, 4614–15; Johnston to Eustis, July 25, 1810, ibid., 4621.

[21] Wyandots of Sandusky to Hull, June 27, 1810, Wyandot File; Badger, *Memoir*, p. 125; J. Wetherell to Thomas Palmer, Oct. 13, 1810, Thomas Nuttall, "Thomas Nuttall's Travels in the Old Northwest: An Unpublished 1810 Diary," *Chronica Botanica* 14 (1951):60–61.

[22] Hull to the Different Nations, Sept. 30, 1810, Lewis Cass Papers, William L. Clements Library, University of Michigan, Ann Arbor; Chiefs at the

In contrast, Black Hoof and over three hundred Shawnees from Wapakoneta traveled to Fort Wayne, where their annuities were distributed. The Ohio Shawnees remained committed to the United States, but Black Hoof was rankled that federal officials deducted part of his people's annuities to pay for depredations charged to Shawnees loyal to Tecumseh and the Prophet. Yet ties of kinship still remained strong. Winimac, a Potawatomi chief often employed by Harrison, proposed that the Indians at Fort Wayne raise a large war party and attack Prophetstown, but Black Hoof spoke against such a campaign. He obviously disliked Tecumseh and Tenskwatawa, but many of his followers had relatives living on the Tippecanoe, and he was reluctant to shed the blood of his kinsmen.[23]

Following the Fort Wayne conference, Black Hoof and his people returned to Ohio and spent most of the winter in peace. Still eager for acculturation, they again contacted the Quakers, asking for another missionary, and in the spring they planted increased acreages of corn and potatoes. Meanwhile, Captain Logan, a mixed-blood Shawnee trader who also served as a government interpreter, made plans to open a trading post at Wapakoneta. But in the spring rumors of Indian attacks in Illinois and Indiana alarmed settlers as far east as Ohio. In response, Harrison met with Tecumseh at Vincennes, attempting to convince the Shawnee war chief that he should use his authority to dissuade the attacks. Unfortunately, the two leaders continued to disagree, and following the meeting Tecumseh left Vincennes to champion his cause among the Creeks, Choctaws, and Chickasaws.[24]

Council at Brownstown to the President of the United States [Madison], [September 1810], Shawnee File; Hull to the Secretary of War [Eustis], Oct. 4, 1810, Shawnee File; Matthew Elliott to William Claus, Oct. 16, 1810, *Collections and Researches Made by the Michigan Pioneer and Historical Society*, 40 vols. (Lansing, Mich., 1874–1929), 25:272–73.

[23] "Account of the Number of Indians Attending the Council at Fort Wayne, October 1, 1810," Cass Papers; Entry for Oct. 2, 1810, Thornbrough, ed., *Letter Book of Fort Wayne*, p. 78; Johnston to Eustis, Oct. 20, 1810, Shawnee File.

[24] Johnston to Phillip Thomas, Feb. 12, 1811, Letters Received by the Secretary of War, Main Series, roll 40, 6875; Eustis to Johnston, Feb. 18, 1811, Records of the Secretary of War Relating to Indian Affairs, Letters Sent, roll 3,

In Ohio, Indian agents John Johnston and John Shaw assured local settlers that the Shawnees and Wyandots remained friendly. In August, Johnston assembled the Shawnees near Piqua, and after a short statement by Captain Lewis, Black Hoof rose, handed a lighted calumet to settlers who were attending the conference, and reaffirmed his friendship to the United States. He assured his audience that "your interest and ours is inseperable." According to Black Hoof, the Prophet was the "principal cause of all the mischief that has been done," but Black Hoof explained that the Ohio Shawnees "have no intercourse or connection with him." Moreover, according to the chief, his people had no interest in any alliance with the British, who, he complained, had "always left us in difficulties." He did admit that the Ohio Shawnees still visited Amherstburg to receive British presents, but if hostilities again emerged between the Redcoats and the Long Knives, the Shawnees wanted no part of it. They planned to remain neutral. They would, however, provide the Americans with "early information if we know of any mischief coming your way." Black Hoof also requested that the Quakers return to "assist us as soon as possible," so that Shawnee children could become educated, and both Indians and whites "will be more united until we all land in heaven together." Following the conference, Johnston reported that the "result is as satisfactory as could be wished," and he distributed copies of Black Hoof's speech to several frontier newspapers.[25]

Yet if tensions were eased in Ohio, they exploded on the Wabash, for, with Tecumseh in the south, Harrison marched on Prophetstown, and in early November 1811 the Battle of Tippecanoe ended in an uncertain, although highly lauded, American victory. The Ohio Shawnees were wary, if not frightened,

---

46; Eustis to Johnston, July 16, 1811, ibid., 88; James Rogers and Thomas Fish to the President [James Madison], Mar. 29, 1811, Records of the Secretary of War Relating to Indian Affairs, Letters Received (microfilm M271), roll 1, 550–51, Record Group 75, Natl. Arch. Also see Edmunds, *Tecumseh*, pp. 139–46.

[25] Johnston to Eustis, Aug. 27, 1811, Letters Received by the Secretary of War, Main Series, roll 38, 4726–27; Johnston to Eustis, Aug. 29, 1811, ibid., 4723–25.

non-participants. Prior to his march Harrison ordered Johnston to inform Black Hoof of his intentions and to warn him to keep his people from the Wabash so that "no part of the exemplary vengance which we shall inflict against these tribes who have the temerity to attack us shall fall upon their heads." Black Hoof readily complied, and following the battle he joined with other friendly chiefs at Fort Wayne where they disavowed any responsibility for the warfare. In early December, Black Hoof, the Wolf, and other loyal Shawnees again met with settlers on the Mad River in Ohio, and although the Americans initially were suspicious of the Indians, Black Hoof persuaded them that his people remained friendly. Johnston again wrote to several newspapers in Ohio describing the Shawnees as friends of the United States, and the "Indian alarm" temporarily diminished.[26]

Yet Harrison's victory at Tippecanoe produced some negative results. Before the dispersal of the Prophet's followers, most of these anti-American Indians had been concentrated at Prophetstown. Following the Battle of Tippecanoe they scattered in a broad arc from Chicago to Lake Erie, and roving bands began to commit depredations in northwestern Ohio. In January 1812 rumors spread across the Ohio frontier that the Prophet was returning to Greenville, and Gov. Return J. Meigs of Ohio was flooded with petitions asking that the militia be sent to several locations along the Sandusky and Auglaize rivers. In early April five settlers were killed along the Maumee and Sandusky rivers, and later in the month another man was murdered on Greenville Creek, in what is now Darke County.[27] In response, federal

---

[26] Harrison to Johnston, September 1811, Esarey, ed., *Messages and Letters of Harrison*, 1:583–84; Speech by Black Hoof, Nov. 18, 1811, Letters Received by the Secretary of War, Main Series, roll 46, 997; Shawnee, Delaware, Potawatomi, and Miami Speeches in Council at Fort Wayne, Nov. 22, 1811, ibid., 998–99; Deposition of James McElvain, Dec. 4, 1811, Tecumseh Papers, 5YY8; Letter by Johnston, Nov. 19, 1811, Shawnee File.

[27] Fish and Enos Terry to Return J. Meigs, Jan. 14, 1812, Shawnee File; Meigs to Thomas Worthington, Jan. 23, 1812, Return J. Meigs Papers, Ohio State Historical Society, Columbus; John Shaw to James Rhea, Mar. 1, 1812, Letters Received by the Secretary of War, Main Series, roll 48, 2772; Johnston to Eustis, May 1, 1812, ibid., roll 46, 1056.

officials established a new Indian agency at Piqua and appointed Johnston as the agent there. Meanwhile federal troops marched from Dayton to Fort Loramie, in modern Shelby County, where Capt. William Perry erected a blockhouse and asked Black Hoof and other Shawnee chiefs to assemble for a conference.[28]

Black Hoof readily accepted the American summons. During March and April, Johnston had been absent from Ohio soliciting assistance for the Shawnees from Quakers in Baltimore, and the growing American resentment over the depredations had placed the friendly Indians on the defensive. On May 2, 1812, in response to recent Indian depredations in the region, militia units from Greenville murdered two friendly Potawatomi hunters, stole all their property, and made prisoners of their wives and children. Fearful that his people might suffer similar injuries, Black Hoof met with Perry on May 5 and reassured the officer that his people had remained at peace. Repeating many of the same promises he had made the previous August at Piqua, Black Hoof disclaimed any responsibility for the depredations and again promised to send intelligence of hostile Indians. He also promised to furnish two young warriors to serve as scouts for American military units that planned to patrol the Greenville Treaty line, the official border between Indian and white lands in Ohio.[29]

Following the conference at Fort Loramie, Black Hoof and his advisors met with Johnston at Piqua, but tensions between Indians and whites in Ohio continued to increase. Rumors of impending Indian onslaughts still swept the Ohio frontier, and although the Shawnees repeatedly provided federal officials with intelligence regarding the arrival of "western Indians," many white settlers remained suspicious. During May the same militia units who had killed the Potawatomis captured a small

[28] Eustis to Johnston, Mar. 5, 1812, Records of the Secretary of War Relating to Indian Affairs, Letters Sent, roll 3, 118; Francis Duchoquet to Johnston, Apr. 30, 1812, Letters Received by the Secretary of War, Main Series, roll 46, 10161–62; William Perry to Meigs, Apr. 30, 1812, Meigs Papers.

[29] Perry to Meigs, May 7, 1812, Meigs Papers; Duncan McArthur to Worthington, May 7, 1812, Thomas Worthington Papers, Ohio St. Hist. Soc.; McArthur to Worthington, May 8, 1812, Worthington Papers.

party of Shawnees hunting along the headwaters of the Wabash, and although Johnston immediately interceded and obtained their release, he wrote to Secretary of War William Eustis warning that "in consequence of the late murders by the savages, armed parties of our people are out in all directions breathing destruction against the Indians indiscriminately. . . . I have great difficulty in preserving the lives of those who come to me for protection." Meanwhile, William Perry, the commander of the troops patrolling the Greenville Treaty line, became so fearful for the safety of his two Shawnee scouts that he "sent them home, not wishing them to be . . . killed by some of the Inhabitants."[30]

News that war had been declared against Great Britain reached Ohio late in June, but by that time both state and federal officials were preparing for the conflict. During the spring Gen. William Hull had assembled an army in Cincinnati, and in May he marched to Dayton where he rendezvoused with other forces, then proceeded on to Urbana. Meanwhile, Governor Meigs again called the friendly Indians into council, requesting that they assemble at Urbana to grant permission for Hull's army to cross their lands en route to Detroit. Meigs also believed that the American army would intimidate the Indians and further prevent them from joining with the British. Black Hoof, Captain Lewis, and several other chiefs represented the Shawnees, while Tarhe led a large delegation of Wyandots, and Mathame spoke for a small village of Senecas. Meigs assured the assembled Indians that if they remained peaceful, they would have nothing to fear, since Hull's army would "strike none but enemies."[31]

[30] Edmund Munger to Meigs, May 14, 1812, Meigs Papers; Citizens of Montgomery County to Meigs, May 15, 1812, ibid.; Johnston to Meigs, May 22, 1812, ibid.; Perry to Worthington, June 24, 1812, Worthington Papers; Johnston to Eustis, May 21, 1812, Letters Received by the Secretary of War, Main Series, roll 46, 1064–66.

[31] Alec Gilpin, *The War of 1812 in the Old Northwest* (East Lansing, Mich., 1958), pp. 23–40; "Proceedings of a Council Begun and Held near Urbana, . . . the 6th of June, 1812," Milo M. Quaife, ed., *War on the Detroit: The Chronicles of Thomas Vercheres de Boucheville and the Capitulation by an Ohio Volunteer* (Chicago, 1940), pp. 197–201.

Speaking for the Wyandots, Tarhe assured Meigs of their fidelity, then Black Hoof rose, reiterated Tarhe's protestations, and held up a belt of white wampum and a packet of past correspondence between the Shawnees and the president that he claimed were symbolic of Shawnee-American friendship. He was followed by Captain Lewis, who had just returned from Washington, and who declared that "although the Heavens should fall assunder and the earth open beneath I will not part from the Americans." The meeting adjourned until the following day when Hull arrived at Urbana, and in a series of subsequent meetings the Wyandots agreed to allow Hull's army to construct a road through their hunting lands to Detroit. In addition, although the region was north and west of the Greenville Treaty line, both the Shawnees and the Wyandots agreed to allow the Americans to erect blockhouses at strategic locations along the route. Finally, although they earlier had expressed a wish to remain neutral, several Wyandots and Shawnees, including Logan and Captain Lewis, agreed to serve as scouts and interpreters for Hull's army on its march to Michigan.[32]

While Hull's army was marching to Detroit, officials in Ohio and Indiana made plans for a major Indian conference at Piqua. First conceived in the spring of 1812, the conference had been planned as the major cornerstone of the government's effort to maintain the neutrality of those tribes who had not already enlisted with Tecumseh and the British. Federal officials believed that within the first few weeks after war was declared, all those Indians already committed to the British cause would flee to Canada but that the vast majority of tribes such as the Miamis, Potawatomis, Ottawas, and Wyandots, who might waver in their loyalties, could be kept neutral in the contest if the United States could demonstrate sufficient military and economic strength to overawe them. Supposedly Hull's march to Michigan and the reinforcement of the garrison at Detroit,

[32] "Proceedings of a Council, . . . 6th of June, 1812," Quaife, ed., *War on the Detroit*, pp. 201–6; "Copy of an Agreement with the Wyandot, Shawnee, and Mingo Chiefs Made by William Hull, June 8, 1812," Shawnee File; Hull to Eustis, June 9, 1812, ibid.; Hull to Eustis, June 11, 1812, ibid.; Hull to Eustis, June 18, 1812, ibid.

in preparation for an American invasion of Canada, would provide the military component of such a strategy, while the conference at Piqua, where the Indians would be wined, dined, and provided with presents, would demonstrate American munificence and diplomacy.[33]

Things did not go as planned. The conference originally was scheduled to begin on August 1, 1812, but Hull's procrastinated march through Ohio had so depleted local food stores that Johnston could not amass sufficient provisions to feed the expected three thousand Indians. Moreover, trade goods and other commodities planned as presents also were in short supply, and expected shipments of such merchandise failed to arrive on schedule. Consequently, Johnston was forced to postpone the conference from August 1 to August 15. Meanwhile, British agents circulated reports that the conference was an American "contrivance" designed to "lead all the men from home, then fall upon their women and children, and destroy them, and burn their towns."[34]

Yet rumors and logistical problems paled in comparison to military events in Michigan. Although Hull reached Detroit on July 6, 1812, and promptly invaded Canada, he failed to capture Amherstburg, the center for British military and Indian activity in southwestern Ontario. Meanwhile, throughout July, Tecumseh, also at Amherstburg, was joined by increasing numbers of hostile Indians. On July 28 Hull learned that Michilimackinac had fallen to the enemy, and in early August, in battles at Brownstown and Monguagon, British and Indian forces cut Hull's communication and supply lines to Ohio. Hull repeatedly appealed for assistance from Meigs and Harrison, but none

---

[33] Johnston to Eustis, Mar. 21, 1812, Letters Received by the Secretary of War, Main Series, roll 46, 1069–70; Worthington to Eustis, June 24, 1812, ibid., roll 49, 3921–23; Circular by the War Department, June 11, 1812, Records of the Secretary of War Relating to Indian Affairs, Letters Sent, roll 3, 79; Leonard U. Hill, *John Johnston and the Indians in the Land of the Three Miamis* (Piqua, Ohio, 1957), pp. 62–63.

[34] Johnston to Eustis, July 2, 1812, Shawnee File; Benjamin Stickney to Nathan Heald, July 6, 1812, Thornbrough, ed., *Letter Book of Fort Wayne*, pp. 152–53; Stickney to Johnston, July 7, 1812, ibid., pp. 156–57; Stickney to Eustis, July 19, 1812, ibid., pp. 161–65.

was forthcoming. Frightened by the prospect of a British and Indian frontal assault on his post, Hull surrendered Detroit to the British on August 16.[35]

Black Hoof, Captain Lewis, Logan, and the Wolf were eye-witnesses to some of these events. Captain Lewis, Logan, and the Wolf had scouted for Hull on his march to Detroit, and early in July, Black Hoof joined them in Michigan. Hull was eager to keep the Indians in Michigan neutral, so in mid-July he sponsored a conference of neighboring tribes at the Wyandot village near Brownstown, about twenty miles south of Detroit, across from Amherstburg. The council began in mid-July, while American fortunes were waxing, and it seemed to achieve some temporary success. The Shawnee chiefs "made great exertions to detach the Indians from the British standards." They argued that twice before, after the American Revolution and following the Battle of Fallen Timbers, the British had deserted their Indian allies and could not be trusted. The tribes should not become involved in the war but should let the Redcoats and the Long Knives fight their own battles. Their Great Father, the president, had promised them that he wanted no more of their land. If the Indians remained neutral, they could be assured that their Great Father would care for his children. The conference ended on July 20, with many of the Indians vowing that they would remain neutral, and the Shawnee chiefs hurriedly left Michigan to attend the conference at Piqua.[36]

When they returned to Ohio, Black Hoof and his companions found that the Piqua conference had been postponed until August 15, and in the three weeks before they assembled for the meeting, they learned of the American setbacks in

[35] Hull to Eustis, July 7, 1812, Richard C. Knopf, ed., *Document Transcriptions of the War of 1812 in the Old Northwest*, 6 vols. (Columbus, Ohio, 1959), 6:85; Hull to Eustis, July 29, 1812, ibid., pp. 139–40; Hull to Meigs, July 29, 1812, ibid., p. 141; Hull to Eustis, Aug. 4, 1812, ibid., pt. 2, pp. 8–9; Hull to Eustis, Aug. 8, 1812, ibid., p. 16; "Capitulation for the Surrender of Detroit," Aug. 16, 1812, *Collections by the Michigan Pioneer and Historical Society*, 25:332. Also see Edmunds, *Tecumseh*, pp. 169–81.

[36] Hull to Eustis, June 9, 1812, Shawnee File; Hull to Eustis, July 14, 1812, *Collections by the Michigan Pioneer and Historical Society*, 40:413–15; Hull to Eustis, Jan. 21, 1812, ibid., pp. 419–21.

Michigan. The British and Indian victories had a profound impact upon the conference. Many of the Indians who earlier had agreed to journey to Piqua now joined the British. On August 16, when the conference began, there were approximately 750 Indians in attendance; Johnston originally had planned for 3000! Not surprisingly, most of the Indians who assembled were from those tribes already committed to the federal government: the loyal Shawnees, Wyandots, Delawares, and a few Ottawas and Kickapoos. While the conference was in progress, both the Indians and the commissioners learned of the fall of Detroit and the attack upon the garrison at Fort Dearborn.[37]

Ironically, after reviewing the recent military disasters, Gov. Return J. Meigs, Thomas Worthington, and Jeremiah Morrow, the commissioners appointed to meet with the Indians, decided to keep them at Piqua as long as possible, hoping that some good news might arrive to strengthen the government's position. Because the number of Indians in attendance was considerably smaller than what had been anticipated, there were ample provisions for an extended period. Moreover, Tarhe and most of the friendly Wyandots sent a message informing the officials that they would not arrive until sometime in September. They were so frightened of attacks by hostile Indians they had decided to move their village away from Upper Sandusky and south into the white settlements. Once their families were secure, they would come to Piqua.[38]

The speeches delivered by the commissioners were predictable. After reminding the tribespeople that the British had

[37] Johnston to Eustis, Mar. 21, 1812, Letters Received by the Secretary of War, Main Series, roll 46, 1069–70; Elliott to Claus, Aug. 8, 1812, Administrative Records of the Imperial Government, Records of the Superintendent's Office, Correspondence; vol. 28, 16397–99, Record Group 10, Pub. Arch. of Canada; Henry Procter to Isaac Brock, Aug. 11, 1812, A. B. Farney Papers, Fort Malden National Historic Park, Amherstburg, Ontario; Rhea to Meigs, Aug. 19, 1812, Meigs Papers; Hill, *John Johnston*, p. 69.

[38] "List of Goods Delivered from the Merchandise Forwarded for the Indian Council at Piqua," Oct. 11, 1812, Shawnee File; Worthington and Jeremiah Morrow to Eustis, Letters Received by the Secretary of War, Main Series, roll 4, 2032; Tarhe's Speech, Aug. 13, 1812, Meigs Papers; Paul Butler to Meigs, Aug. 24, 1812, ibid.; Joseph Foos to Meigs, Sept. 1, 1812, ibid.

betrayed them in the past, the commissioners asserted that although the Americans had suffered some temporary reverses, they ultimately would prevail. If the Indians joined with the British, they "would bring inevitable destruction upon themselves," but if they remained neutral "their annuities should be paid . . . , their lands held sacred, and they should, whenever they required it, be protected against the enemies of the United States." In response, Black Hoof, whom Thomas Worthington described as having "gone out of his way to assure us of his fidelity," disclaimed any intention of joining the British and promised to adhere to the terms of the Treaty of Greenville. The British, Black Hoof asserted, were responsible for most of the recent trouble that had befallen the Indians and "viewed the Indians as they did their dogs. That when they told them to bite, they must bite," but the Shawnees were "men and would make their own decisions." He also thanked the commissioners for offers of protection, but declined, stating that at the present the Shawnees had no enemies "with whom they were not able to contend." The proceedings continued intermittently until September 2, when William Henry Harrison and a force of over two thousand regulars and Kentucky volunteers arrived in Piqua en route to Fort Wayne. Harrison paused for two days and spoke to the assembled Indians, promising them protection, but "assuring them in terrible language which struck terror to all hearts," that those Indians who opposed the United States would be destroyed, and even their names "should not long be known among us." Assuming that the Indians had been cowed by the show of force, the commissioners ended the conference on September 7.[39]

Black Hoof and the other loyal Shawnees welcomed Harrison's arrival. Although Black Hoof previously had claimed that his people had no enemies "with whom they could not contend," the recent British victories had placed his people in con-

[39] Thomas Worthington Diary, entry for Aug. 18, 1812, Worthington Papers; S. W. Culbertson to Mr. Chambers, September 1812, Esarey, ed., *Messages and Letters of Harrison*, 2:139–40; Meigs, Worthington, and Morrow to Eustis, Sept. 10, 1812, Letters Received by the Secretary of War, Main Series, roll 49, 4163–66; Worthington to Eustis, Sept. 11, 1812, ibid., 4105.

siderable jeopardy. Early in September, while the conference at Piqua had been in progress, the Potawatomis had besieged Fort Wayne, and on September 14, 1812, Tecumseh and Maj. Adam Muir had left Amherstburg with over one thousand British and Indians intent upon assisting the Potawatomis in the capture of the post. Harrison's army, however, tipped the military scales in the American favor, and as he marched to relieve Fort Wayne, Captain Lewis, Logan, Captain Johnny, Bright Horn, the Wolf, and a handful of other Shawnee warriors enlisted in his service as scouts and interpreters. Their arrival at Fort Wayne broke the Potawatomi siege and reasserted the American position in the region, causing the Miamis and a few dissident Delawares to sue for peace. After Harrison's army was reinforced by a small contingent of Kentucky militia under Brig.-Gen. James Winchester, Harrison withdrew to Ohio to organize logistical support for a campaign to recapture Detroit.[40]

The Shawnee scouts, however, proceeded up the Maumee Valley with Winchester where they found that Muir had learned of the American reinforcements and had retreated back toward Canada. In contrast, many of the pro-British Indians remained in the region, and as the Shawnees advanced in front of the American column they encountered some of these former friends—now enemies. On October 8 Captain Lewis, Logan, and a small number of scouts were attacked by a Potawatomi war party led by the infamous Mar Poc, but they escaped before suffering any injuries. During the next two months they ranged across northwestern Ohio, collecting information on British and Indian troop movements. It was a hazardous assignment. Not only were they at risk from the British and hostile Indians, they also were endangered by American militia who considered

---

[40] Report by Meigs, Worthington, and Morrow, Sept. 10, 1812, Letters Received by the Secretary of War, Main Series, roll 49, 4163–66; Harrison to the Secretary of War [Eustis], Oct. 13, 1812, Esarey, ed., *Messages and Letters of Harrison*, 2:173–76; Johnston to Harrison, Oct. 23, 1812, ibid., pp. 186–87; Edward Tupper to Meigs, Nov. 28, 1812, Meigs Papers; Benson Lossing, *The Pictorial Field-Book of the War of 1812* (New York, 1869), p. 345. Also see Gilpin, *War of 1812*, pp. 134–45. Logan and a small party of Shawnee warriors previously had escorted a party of American women and children from Fort Wayne to Piqua. See Statement by John Johnston, Tecumseh Papers, 11YY20.

any Indian to be fair game and routinely treated all Indians as pro-British.[41]

Such suspicions inadvertently contributed to the death of Logan. During the third week in November, Logan, Captain Johnny, Bright Horn, and several other Indian scouts proceeded up the Maumee to gather intelligence regarding the number of British and hostile Indians near the rapids. They were ambushed by an enemy war party and so closely pursued that they scattered through the river bottom in an attempt to elude their attackers. All of the Shawnee scouts escaped, but Logan, Captain Johnny, and Bright Horn were separated from the others and returned to the American lines on the following day, after spending the night hiding in the forest. Their late arrival back in the American camp engendered some accusations that they had been taken prisoners by their enemies and had secured their release only after providing the British with information about the Americans. Attempting to prove their loyalty, on November 22 the three Shawnee warriors proceeded on foot toward the British lines, hoping to bring in either a prisoner or scalps. Traveling on the north bank of the river, they encountered a mounted party of Potawatomis and Ottawas led by Winimac, a Potawatomi war chief who had participated in the siege of Fort Wayne, and Alexander Elliott, the oldest son of British Indian agent Matthew Elliott. Attempting to pass through their ranks, Logan asserted that they were a party of pro-British Shawnees trying to rejoin Tecumseh's party, but Winimac recognized Logan and suggested that the Potawatomis escort the Shawnees to the British camp. The Potawatomis did not disarm the three Shawnees, but they guarded them very closely. After proceeding for several miles toward the British position, Winimac suggested to Elliott that Logan and his comrades be disarmed and bound. Overhearing their captors' conversation, the Shawnees suddenly opened fire, killing Elliott, Winimac, and one of the Ottawas, and wounding another. But in the return fire Logan was shot in the abdomen, and Bright Horn was hit

---

[41] Edward DeWar to Colonel McDonnell, Oct. 19, 1812, British Military and Naval Records, C ser., vol. 676, 136–39; Tarhe to Meigs, Oct. 28, 1812, Meigs Papers; Tupper to Meigs, Nov. 28, 1812, ibid.

in the leg. Captain Johnny apparently was not wounded. The Shawnees then seized the dead men's horses and raced back to the American camp. Bright Horn recovered, but Logan's wound proved fatal, and he died on November 24. Before his death he requested that his children be taken to Kentucky and provided with a formal education.[42]

In December the surviving Shawnee scouts returned to their homes at Wapakoneta or Lewistown and were not present in January 1813 when Winchester made his ill-advised march to Frenchtown. Consequently they suffered no losses in the subsequent American defeat, but when news of the "massacre" of American prisoners reached Ohio, a new wave of anti-Indian hatred swept many of the settlements. Worthington earlier had warned that both the Kentucky and Ohio militia made little effort to discriminate between friendly and hostile Indians, and although the Shawnees had remained loyal to the government, their livestock was stolen, some of their homes were burned, and individual Indians were stopped and robbed of their property.[43]

To diffuse the hostility and illustrate his people's loyalty, in January 1813 Black Hoof and several other Shawnees joined an expedition destined to reinforce the American position in northern Ohio. The enlistment almost cost him his life. En route to the Maumee, Black Hoof and the other scouts passed through McArthur's Blockhouse, a small supply post on the south bank of the Scioto, near modern Kenton, Ohio. During the evening of January 25, while Black Hoof and Captain Lewis were conferring with Brig.-Gen. Edwin Tupper in his cabin, an unknown militiaman fired a pistol through a hole in the chinking between the logs of the cabin striking Black Hoof in the

[42] Johnston to Henry Brown, Dec. 2, 1812, John Johnston Papers, Cincinnati Hist. Soc.; Harrison to the Secretary of War [Eustis], Dec. 14, 1812, Esarey, ed., *Messages and Letters of Harrison*, 2:246–48; Robert Breckinridge McAfee, *History of the Late War in the Western Country* (1816; reprint ed., Ann Arbor, Mich., 1966), pp. 472–76. Also see Reginald Horsman, *Matthew Elliott: British Indian Agent* (Detroit, 1964), p. 202.

[43] Worthington to Eustis, Sept. 11, 1812, Letters Received by the Secretary of War, Main Series, roll 49, 4105; Stickney to John Armstrong, July 8, 1813, ibid., roll 57, 1201–6; Tupper to Meigs, Jan. 26, 1813, Meigs Papers.

face. The bullet rendered him unconscious, passing through his left cheek and lodging in his right zygomatic arch, or opposite cheekbone. Although the wound was not fatal, the old chief was forced to remain at the post while the other Shawnees continued on to join Harrison. After a partial recovery, he returned to Wapakoneta. Tupper was infuriated by the attack and attempted to ascertain the identity of the assailant, but he received no cooperation from the militia, and the perpetrator was never apprehended.[44]

While Black Hoof was recovering from his wound at Wapakoneta, the other Shawnee scouts continued on to the Maumee. In February the Americans began the construction of Fort Meigs (on the south bank of the Maumee, near modern Perrysburg), which Harrison hoped to use as a base for the recapture of Detroit and the invasion of Canada. Meanwhile, the Shawnees patrolled the region downstream toward Lake Erie, but Tecumseh and the Prophet had returned to the Tippecanoe to recruit additional warriors for a summer offensive, and the late winter brought little warfare to Ohio.[45]

Circumstances changed in April. Tecumseh and the Prophet returned from Indiana with a large party of western Indians, and Col. Henry Procter was eager to attack Harrison before Fort Meigs could receive reinforcements. On April 27 British transports landed Procter, several pieces of artillery, and almost one thousand troops at the mouth of the Maumee where they rendezvoused with Tecumseh and twelve hundred Indians. The combined force then proceeded up the river, surrounded the fort, and by May 1 the British artillery was firing on the Americans.[46]

The Shawnees who had served as scouts took refuge in the fort with Harrison, but other members of the tribe already were

[44] Tupper to Meigs, Jan. 26, 1813, Meigs Papers; Lossing, *Pictorial Field-Book*, pp. 345–46 n. 2.

[45] Harrison to the Secretary of War [Eustis], Feb. 11, 1813, Esarey, ed., *Messages and Letters of Harrison*, 2:356–60; Prevost to the earl of Bathurst, Feb. 27, 1813, British Colonial Records, Lower Canada, C.O. 42/150/90–92, Public Record Office.

[46] Edmunds, *Tecumseh*, pp. 189–91.

en route to the Maumee, accompanying Gen. Green Clay and a force of almost twelve hundred Kentucky militia. Black Hoof remained convalescent, and since most of the loyal Shawnees who previously had served as scouts were besieged at Fort Meigs, the handful of scouts who accompanied Clay were less eager for service. Led by Black Fish, the son of the Shawnee war chief who had led the attacks upon Kentucky during the American Revolution, these warriors had preferred to remain neutral and joined the Kentuckians only after considerable pressure from their Indian agent, John Johnston. Clay's army had constructed barges on the Auglaize and planned to float downstream to its juncture with the Maumee, then proceed on to Fort Meigs. On May 1 a scouting party comprised of Black Fish and three Kentuckians preceded the main force in a canoe and descended the river to within sight of Fort Meigs, where they encountered a part of hostile Potawatomis and fled back up the river. Two of the Kentuckians were captured in the encounter and the third was wounded, but the latter, accompanied by Black Fish, managed to escape.[47]

Other Shawnees were not so fortunate. On May 4, 1813, Clay's main force landed just upstream from Fort Meigs shortly before dawn, and waited for daylight before descending through the rapids to the stockade. Following orders from Harrison, Clay dispatched Lt. Col. William Dudley and almost eight hundred men to land opposite the fort, capture and spike the British artillery, then retreat across the river to the palisade. Dudley's force was accompanied by the other new Shawnee scouts who were instructed to proceed in the vanguard of the action and to report the arrival of any British or Indian reinforcements. The attack was initially successful, and the Americans captured and spiked the British cannons, but in their jubilation over their success Dudley's soldiers continued to pursue a small force of Indians through the forest. While the Americans procrastinated, the British and Indians mounted a counterattack. The Shawnees, who had been ordered to provide security on the

---

[47] Stickney to Jacob Fowler, May 3, 1813, Michigan Papers, Clements Library; Johnston to Armstrong, June 4, 1813, Shawnee File; Lossing, *Pictorial Field-Book*, pp. 480–81.

American flanks, immediately surrendered, and Dudley's command was forced back toward the river. Finally, some of the Americans scrambled into their boats and crossed the river, but of the eight hundred men who had originally formed Dudley's command, only one hundred and fifty reached Fort Meigs safely. Some of the American captives then were killed by the Indians.[48]

Ironically, many of the hostile Indians captured so much plunder at Dudley's defeat that they deserted the British camp and carried the goods back to their villages. In consequence, Procter was forced to abandon the siege and retreat to Canada, but in the aftermath of the battle the Americans harbored some doubts about the loyalty of Black Hoof's Shawnees. Obviously, Captain Lewis, Captain Johnny, the Wolf, and other Shawnee leaders could be trusted, but the warriors who had accompanied Clay and Dudley had surrendered after little resistance, and in an effort to ingratiate themselves with their captors, they assured the British that they had been coerced into service with the Americans. Indeed, they informed Procter that almost all their kinsmen in Ohio wanted to serve the British but were being held as prisoners in the villages at Wapakoneta and Lewistown. In response, Procter offered to exchange the prisoners he had taken at Fort Meigs if Harrison would allow the loyal Shawnees to remove to Canada.[49]

Such proposals by the British only rekindled American suspicions, and the Shawnees at Wapakoneta were again accused of pro-British sentiments. Warriors attempting to barter for merchandise at frontier trading posts were harassed by local citizens, and militia units arbitrarily cut down Shawnee cornfields, burned their cabins, and slaughtered their livestock. In July a

[48] McArthur to Worthington, May 22, 1813, Worthington Papers; Richard M. Johnson to Armstrong, June 4, 1813, Shawnee File; Leslie Combs to George McLaughlin, Oct. 18, 1863, Tecumseh Papers, 6YY2; Lossing, *Pictorial Field-Book*, pp. 485–86.

[49] McArthur to Worthington, May 22, 1813, Worthington Papers; Johnson to Armstrong, June 4, 1813, Letters Received by the Secretary of War, Main Series, roll 54, 8276; Report of an Indian Council, July 21, 1813, William Henry Harrison Papers, Draper's Notes, 26S114–16, Draper Mss.

small party of Black Hoof's people who were hunting in Darke County were attacked by militiamen who seized all their property and made them prisoners. Black Hoof protested to federal officials, and Johnston interceded, freed the captives, and recovered part of the contraband, but their horses already had been taken to Kentucky. In mid-July, after settlers near Fort Loramie shot a Shawnee hunter, his brother retaliated and killed one of the attackers, but Black Hoof immediately surrendered the warrior to white authorities, and the Shawnee was promptly tried and convicted. Reflecting the tension, on July 21 Harrison met with a delegation of chiefs from the Shawnees, Wyandots, Delawares, and Ohio Senecas at Franklintown, where he informed them that "the President wished no false friends, and that it is only in adversity that true friends could be distinguished." Although the government earlier had urged the tribesmen to remain neutral, they now "should take a decided stand either for us or against us." Their families should cross over to the American side of the Greenville Treaty line, and their warriors should fight with the Long Knives against the British. Intimidated by the threat, but also aware that the conflict recently had turned in the Americans' favor, all the chiefs promised to supply warriors for the planned invasion of Canada.[50]

Since they had returned to their homes during July, the loyal Shawnees did not participate in the second siege of Fort Meigs, but in August, when Harrison's reinforcements marched north along the Sandusky valley, they were accompanied by a mixed force of over two hundred Shawnees and Delawares. Black Hoof, still recovering from his wound, did not accompany the expedition, but on August 7, accompanied by Tarhe, the Snake, and Chief Anderson of the Delawares, he met with Meigs and

---

[50]Johnston to Armstrong, June 4, 1813, Shawnee File; Stickney to Armstrong, Letters Received by the Secretary of War, Main Series, roll 57, 1201–6; William Barbee to Worthington, July 21, 1813, Worthington Papers; Report of an Indian Council, July 21, 1813, ibid.; Report of an Indian Council, July 21, 1813, Harrison Papers, Draper's Notes, 26S114–16; Johnston to Drake, Sept. 24, 1840, Tecumseh Papers, 11YY22; Harrison to Armstrong, July 23, 1813, Esarey, ed., *Messages and Letters of Harrison*, 2:494–95. The convicted warrior's sentence eventually was commuted by federal officials.

assured him that the warriors could be trusted. On August 19 a small party of Shawnees and Delawares skirmished with some pro-British Potawatomis near the mouth of the Maumee River, where they rescued an American soldier who had been captured by their enemies. Meanwhile, in preparation for the invasion of Canada, a delegation of Wyandots from Tarhe's village met with pro-British members of their tribe at Brownstown and attempted to convince them to desert the British. The American Wyandots were sternly denounced by Tecumseh, Matthew Elliott, and by Roundhead, a Wyandot chief long allied to Tecumseh, but Walk-in-the-Water, the chief of the Wyandots at Brownstown, confidentially informed his pro-American kinsmen that if the Long Knives marched to Detroit, he would not oppose their passage through his village.[51]

Yet while Captain Lewis, the Wolf, and other Shawnee warriors prepared for the invasion of Canada, their families again came under fire from white Ohioans. In mid-August a small war party of pro-British Indians penetrated the Ohio frontier and killed five settlers in the Sandusky and Dayton regions. They retreated past Wapakoneta, and Black Hoof informed federal officials of their presence, but the raiders escaped and local settlers accused the loyal Shawnees of collaborating with the enemy. Enraged by the attacks, local militia units drove Captain Lewis's followers from their village in modern Logan County, burned their homes, and destroyed their cornfields. Other settlers so threatened the Delawares whom Harrison also had resettled in west-central Ohio that they fled to Wapakoneta for safety. Both Black Hoof and Johnston appealed for calm, but Benjamin Whiteman, the commanding officer of the local militia, replied that he was determined to force all the Indians north of the Greenville Treaty line, and if they would not go peacefully, "the people will rise enmasse and remove them." In-

---

[51] Johnston to the Secretary of War [Armstrong], Aug. 3, 1813, Esarey, ed., *Messages and Letters of Harrison*, 2:509; Harrison to the Secretary of War [Armstrong], Aug. 22, 1813, ibid., pp. 525–26; Harrison to the Secretary of War [Armstrong], Sept. 8, 1813, ibid., pp. 537–38; "Extract of a Letter from a Correspondent, August 22, 1813," Shawnee File; Report of an Indian Council, Aug. 23, 1813, *Collections by the Michigan Pioneer and Historical Society*, 15:358–59.

deed, he warned that he intended to assemble a force of one thousand militia to surround and capture the Shawnees and Delawares, and "to kill all those who would not consent" to be prisoners. Fortunately, cooler heads prevailed, but Harrison wrote to Meigs emphasizing that "the conduct of the Shawanes . . . ought to satisfy everyone" and that "the Delaware Indians who have been most strongly suspected, have lately proven their fidelity in an exemplary manner." Harrison urged Meigs "to take immediate steps to afford security to these people. They have thrown themselves upon us for protection. The faith of the country has been solemnly pledged that this protection shall be afforded them. Many of their warriors are now here rendering important service to the army. . . . Their fidelity to the United States is unquestionable."[52]

When Harrison invaded Canada in September 1813, that fidelity again was demonstrated. In early September, Black Hoof led a small party of Shawnee reinforcements to Fort Meigs, and when the Americans landed at Hartley's point, four miles south of Amherstburg, on September 27, the Shawnees came ashore attached to Lt. Col. James V. Ball's regiment of United States dragoons. Black Hoof's age and infirmities precluded him from taking an active role in the campaign, so he remained at Amherstburg while the Shawnees were led by Captain Lewis and Blacksnake. Since Procter did not oppose the landing and retreated up the Thames Valley toward Kingston (Toronto), part of the Shawnees again served the Americans as scouts and skirmishers, guarding the American advance against ambushes by hostile Indians. Others accompanied Gen. Duncan McArthur back across the river to assist in the reoccupation of Detroit. Early on the morning of October 5 scouts brought information to Harrison that Tecumseh and Procter had decided to stand and fight about two miles west of Moraviantown, a Delaware settlement on the Thames River. There the road followed the north bank of the Thames and passed between the river and a series of swampy thickets. Tecumseh and the British-allied Indians had taken positions in the thicket, while the British troops

---

[52] Johnston to Meigs, Aug. 21, 1813, Meigs Papers; Benjamin Whiteman to Meigs, Aug. 22, 1813, ibid.; Johnston to Meigs, Aug. 23, 1813, ibid.; Harrison to Meigs, Sept. 4, 1813, Esarey, ed., *Messages and Letters of Harrison*, 2:533–35.

were assembled in two lines across the road and were supported by two pieces of artillery.[53]

Harrison approached the British position in mid-afternoon and ordered his infantry to engage the hostile Indians in the thickets. He planned to lead his cavalry against the British center while the loyal Shawnees, led by Captain Lewis, were to accompany a small force of American regulars and to creep along the river bank, pass behind the British regulars, and open fire upon their rear. Harrison believed that if Ball and the Shawnees were successful, Procter would believe that some of the pro-British Indians had betrayed him, and he would be forced to pull some of his regulars from the lines facing the Americans.[54]

The Shawnees never fired a shot. Before they could infiltrate the British lines, Harrison's cavalry charged, and after firing two volleys the British turned and fled toward Moraviantown. The cavalry then attacked Tecumseh and the Indians in the thickets, and Ball ordered Captain Lewis and his warriors to remain along the riverbank, afraid that in the confusion of the fighting they might be mistaken for hostile Indians. After a hotly contested battle of about an hour Tecumseh was killed. The pro-British Indians then also disengaged and the Battle of the Thames ended.[55]

Following the Battle of the Thames, most of the Shawnees journeyed to Detroit where they met Black Hoof and those kinsmen who had accompanied McArthur, then returned to Ohio. Since the British and hostile Indians had been defeated, settlers in Ohio felt less threatened and in turn manifested less resentment toward the Indians at Wapakoneta and Lewistown. The Indians spent the winter in peace, and in February 1814 Black Hoof and other chiefs journeyed to Dayton, where they met

[53] Harrison to the Secretary of War [Armstrong], Sept. 27, 1813, Esarey, ed., *Messages and Letters of Harrison*, 2:550–51; Lossing, *Pictorial Field-Book*, pp. 545–46.

[54] Harrison to the Secretary of War [Armstrong], Oct. 9, 1813, Letters Received by the Secretary of War, Unregistered Series, roll 8, 3007–13; Lossing, *Pictorial Field-Book*, pp. 552, 554.

[55] Harrison to the Secretary of War [Armstrong], Oct. 9, 1813, Letters Received by the Secretary of War, Unregistered Series, roll 8, 3007–13; McAfee, *History of the Late War*, pp. 389–99.

with Governor Meigs and reaffirmed their friendship. Black Hoof also assured Johnston that warriors from his village would readily enlist in any new American campaigns against the British or hostile Indians.[56]

Instead, the government brought many of the formerly hostile warriors to Ohio. Intent upon signing a peace treaty with many of their former enemies, federal officials invited warriors from the Potawatomis, Ottawas, Kickapoos, Miamis, and Wyandots, as well as the friendly tribes, to assemble in July at Greenville. Black Hoof and the friendly Shawnees opposed the conference since they believed that many of these Indians might commit acts of violence. The conference began on July 8, and although the Shawnees attended, they left their women and children at Piqua. Although they were lavishly praised by Harrison, Lewis Cass, and John Shelby, the treaty commissioners, Black Hoof and his kinsmen did not speak at the proceedings. They listened as Tarhe was interrupted and insulted by the Potawatomis, and although they signed the treaty reaffirming their allegiance to the United States, the Shawnees doubted the sincerity of many of the formerly hostile warriors who also made their mark upon the document.[57]

Article two of the treaty required that the tribes signing the agreement should "give their aid to the United States in prosecuting the war against Great Britain and such of the Indian tribes as still continue hostile." During the conference the commissioners attempted to recruit warriors for an autumn campaign against hostile Potawatomis in western Michigan. Fol-

[56] Perry to Meigs, Nov. 29, 1813, Meigs Papers; Johnston to Armstrong, Dec. 1, 1813, Letters Received by the Secretary of War, Main Series, roll 54, 8337; Johnston to Armstrong, Mar. 25, 1814, ibid., 8399; Report of an Indian Council, Feb. 6, 1814, Tecumseh Papers, 3YY143; Harrison to Armstrong, Feb. 11, 1814, William Henry Harrison Miscellaneous Collection, Indiana Historical Society, Indianapolis.

[57] McArthur to Armstrong, June 29, 1814, Duncan McArthur Papers, vol. 11, Library of Congress; Journal of the Treaty Commissioners, July 1814, *American State Papers: Indian Affairs*, 2 vols. (Washington, D.C., 1832–34), 1:827–36; "A Treaty of Peace and Friendship between the United States and the Tribes of Indians . . . , July 22, 1814," Kappler, ed., *Indian Treaties*, pp. 105–7.

lowing the proceedings, almost all of the tribes refused to honor their commitments. The Potawatomis, Ottawas, and Miamis withdrew into northern Indiana or Michigan, where they clandestinely warned other Indians of the government's plans; the Delawares and Tarhe's Wyandots, angered that settlers had recently built cabins on their lands, declared that they would not participate in the expedition. In contrast, although they had not spoken publicly at the conference, the Shawnee chiefs supplied scouts for Lewis Cass when he returned to Michigan.[58]

At Detroit the Shawnees joined several other pro-American Indians and rode west through Michigan, obtaining intelligence of the hostile Indians in the region. They returned to Ohio through Fort Wayne but warned American officials that the Potawatomis along the St. Joseph, Iroquois, and Tippecanoe rivers were well armed, anticipated an attack, and could rely upon additional assistance from tribesmen in northern Michigan or Illinois. In response, Col. Duncan McArthur, who originally had planned to attack Potawatomi villages near modern South Bend, Indiana, marched to Detroit, then turned east and invaded Ontario. Tarhe and the Wyandots again refused any service in the American cause, but about sixty loyal Shawnees led by Captain Lewis, Anthony Shane, Black Fish, and Captain Johnny accompanied the expedition.[59]

On October 23 McArthur's expedition entered Canada, intending to attack Burlington and then join with American forces at Niagara. The British had expected him to proceed westward into Michigan and were unprepared for his advance. Riding with the Kentucky militia, the Shawnees ranged across the countryside, destroying mills and storehouses filled with the

[58] Stickney to Harrison, May 25, 1814, McArthur Papers, vol. 9; McArthur to the Secretary of War [Monroe], July 17, 1814, ibid., vol. 13; Stickney to McArthur, Oct. 3, 1814, ibid., vol. 17; Isaac Shelby to Armstrong, July 17, 1814, Letters Received by the Secretary of War, Main Series, roll 62, 5556–60; Lewis Cass to Armstrong, July 25, 1814, ibid., roll 60, 3902–5.

[59] Cass to Armstrong, Sept. 3, 1814, Lewis Cass Papers, Burton Historical Collections, Detroit Public Library; Cass to McArthur, Sept. 5, 1814, McArthur Papers, vol. 15; Johnston to McArthur, Sept. 8, 1814, ibid.; McArthur to Captain Lewis, Captain Wolf, Captain Johnny, and Anthony Shane, Feb. 13, 1815, ibid., vol. 23.

recent harvest. They reached Brantford, on the Grand River, on November 6, skirmished with a force of Canadian militia and British Iroquois, then retreated back to Detroit. Although McArthur suffered one killed and six wounded, the Shawnees returned unscathed.[60]

In late November the Shawnee scouts arrived back at Wapakoneta and Lewistown where they found their families suffering from a lack of provisions. Because many of the warriors had been absent serving with the government, they had not planted sufficient crops to provide for their families, and even the small fields that had been cultivated had been depredated by local whites and passing parties of militia. The federal government had promised to provide for the Indians, but by late 1814 federal officals had exhausted their resources, and as the threat of Shawnee disaffection had diminished, federal funds and supplies earlier promised to the Indians had been diverted to other theaters. Moreover, the Shawnees had yet to receive any wages for their government service. Although neither Johnston nor McArthur could pay them, Johnston did provide them with sufficient rations to feed their families. In response, Captain Lewis assured the agents that he would raise another war party in the spring, but in February 1815 both the Indians and the settlers learned that Great Britain and the United States had signed the Treaty of Ghent. The war was over.[61]

While federal officials prepared for a formal conference to make peace with all the tribes, the Shawnees attempted to rebuild their acculturation programs. At Chillicothe, Captain Lewis met with McArthur and formally requested that the government provide his people with schools and teachers. Meanwhile, Black Hoof and the chiefs from Wapakoneta petitioned

[60] McArthur to George Izard, Nov. 18, 1814, McArthur Papers, vol. 19; McArthur to Stickney, Jan. 30, 1815, ibid., vol. 22; John Brant to Claus, Nov. 16, 1814, Records of the Superintendent's Office, Correspondence, vol. 29, 1367–68.

[61] McArthur to Lewis, Wolf, Johnny, and Shane, Feb. 13, 1815, McArthur Papers, vol. 23; McArthur to James Monroe, Mar. 15, 1815, ibid., vol. 24; McArthur to the Acting Secretary of War, Mar. 15, 1815, *Collections by the Michigan Pioneer and Historical Society*, pp. 519–20; Hill, *John Johnston*, p. 83.

Johnston to allow them to travel to Washington and Baltimore to solicit agricultural aid from both the president and the Quakers. Throughout the war they had labored mightily to keep their gristmill functioning, but because they had "devoted so large a portion of their time to military pursuits," their "agricultural affairs are entirely deranged." They also requested a blacksmith to repair their farm implements so they could "live upon their own resources."[62]

Federal officials were devoting all their efforts to the peace conference scheduled at Spring Wells, near Detroit, in August, and although they agreed to provide the Shawnees with provisions until they could harvest a crop, they made no immediate plans to reinstitute the acculturation programs. Black Hoof also was concerned about the upcoming conference. Never at a loss for unmitigated gall, the Shawnee Prophet had requested to return to the United States immediately after a formal peace treaty had been signed, and Black Hoof's people resolutely opposed such repatriation. Indeed, the Prophet's religious movement had been based upon a rejection of acculturation programs that Black Hoof had embraced, and the Shawnee patriarch did not welcome a renewal of the power struggle that had so divided his people in the prewar period. Moreover, if the Prophet returned to the Wabash, he would establish himself as another village chief, and the division of the Shawnee annuities would be further depleted. Fortunately for Black Hoof, most American officials shared his apprehensions.[63]

The conference was scheduled to begin on August 22, but during the summer many of the tribes, including the Shawnees, suffered from an epidemic, and by late August even McArthur,

[62] McArthur to the Acting Secretary of War, Mar. 15, 1815, *Collections by the Michigan Pioneer and Historical Society*, 10:519–20; Shawnee Chiefs to Johnston, Apr. 27, 1815, Letters Received by the Secretary of War, Main Series, roll 63, 6471; Johnston to the Secretary of War [Crawford], May 4, 1815, ibid., 6469.

[63] Shawnee Chiefs to Johnston, Apr. 27, 1815, Letters Received by the Secretary of War, Main Series, roll 63, 6471; Johnston to the Secretary of War [Crawford], May 4, 1815, ibid., 6469; Cass to A. J. Dallas, July 23, 1815, Cass Papers, Burton Hist. Coll.; Speech by the Shawnee Prophet, Aug. 4, 1815, Records of the Superintendent's Office, Correspondence, vol. 31, 18267–71.

Harrison, and John Graham, the government commissioners, had contracted the malady. Consequently, the negotiations were postponed until August 31. Discouraged by the delays and exhausted from their illness, the commissioners seemed eager to conclude the meeting. Black Hoof, Captain Lewis, and the other Shawnee leaders attended the conference, but Tarhe spoke for the loyal Indians and urged all the Indians in attendance to forget their former differences and live together in peace. Several of the war chiefs who had opposed the United States also were present, as was the Shawnee Prophet, who seemed properly contrite until Harrison informed him that he could only return to the United States by placing himself under Black Hoof's authority. Still denouncing the old village chief as "that Maykujay," Tenskwatawa was infuriated by Harrison's suggestion. On September 5 he withdrew from the conference and returned to Amherstburg. Obviously relieved that Tenskwatawa would now be forced to remain in Canada, Black Hoof and the other Shawnees signed the formal peace agreement on September 8.[64]

In the years that followed the War of 1812, the Quakers established another mission at Wapakoneta, and Black Hoof and the Shawnees continued to walk a precarious path toward acculturation. Yet in the two decades after 1815 white settlement surged across the Old Northwest, and Americans eager for inexpensive land and economic opportunity soon forgot those Indians who had risked their lives and property in defense of the American cause. Indians who once had been threats, then allies, now become anachronisms. As demands mounted for their lands, Black Hoof and his people found themselves under growing pressure to remove from Ohio to the West. Devoid of political or military power, the Shawnees no longer possessed the means to defend their sole remaining economic asset: their reserva-

[64] Speech by the Shawnee Prophet, Sept. 1, 1815, Records of the Superintendent's Office, Correspondence, vol. 31, 1838; George Ironside to Claus, Oct. 23, 1815, ibid., 18578–80; "Journal of the Proceedings," August–September 1815, *American State Papers: Indian Affairs*, 2:17–25; Harrison and John Graham to William H. Crawford, Sept. 9, 1815, Harrison Papers. Also see "A Treaty between the United States and the . . . Indians, September 8, 1815," Kappler, ed., *Indian Treaties*, pp. 117–19.

tion. Meanwhile, those very members of their tribe whom they had labored so mightily to defeat were either lionized or at least given some legitimacy. By 1830 Tecumseh already had emerged as the quintessential noble savage, an American folk hero, while in an even more bizarre and ironic twist of fate, his brother, the Shawnee Prophet, was encouraged by Lewis Cass to return to the United States, where he cooperated with federal officials and worked for Indian removal. And so the Shawnees at Wapakoneta found themselves in the same predicament that most tribes have encountered through the years: stripped of military, political, or economic power, they were forced to rely upon the fidelity and goodwill of the federal government for protection. But since that government was much more amenable to pressure from the non-Indian majority, its fidelity was marketable.[65]

At least Black Hoof was not a party to this final humiliation. He refused to sign the treaty of August 8, 1830, by which the Shawnees at Wapakoneta ceded their lands in Ohio. He died in 1832, before his family could be forced west to Kansas.[66]

[65] An account of the renewed Quaker mission effort at Wapakoneta can be found in Henry Harvey, *History of the Shawnee Indians* (Cincinnati, 1855), pp. 161–314. Also see Hill, *John Johnston*, pp. 99–137; Edmunds, *Tecumseh*, pp. 212–25; and idem, *Shawnee Prophet*, pp. 165–83.

[66] "Treaty with the Shawnee, 1831," Kappler, ed., *Indian Treaties*, pp. 331–34; Hill, *John Johnston*, p. 113.

DANIEL H. USNER, JR.

Iroquois Livelihood and Jeffersonian Agrarianism
Reaching behind the Models
and Metaphors

IN A LETTER addressed to Handsome Lake on November 3, 1802, President Thomas Jefferson defended recent cessions of some Onondaga, Cayuga, and Oneida land by invoking the authority of natural law. For a society "going into a state of agriculture," the Virginia sage informed the Seneca prophet, it may be advantageous, "as it is to an individual, who has more land than he can improve, to sell a part, and lay out the money in stocks and implements of agriculture, for the better improvement of the residue." Congratulating Handsome Lake for "the great reformation you have undertaken" and offering "the aid and protection of the United States," Jefferson urged that he "persuade our red brethren then to be sober, and to cultivate their lands; and their women to spin and weave for their families."[1] Time and time again, Jefferson exhorted American Indian leaders to abandon a life of hunting for one of farming, thereby setting their people on a path toward peace and prosperity. This prescription for social change became known as the "civilization program" of Jeffersonian Indian policy-makers.

The early national period of United States Indian policy-making bequeathed an abundance of confusing and controversial utterances. Among the most disturbing legacies from that era is the idea disseminated by Jeffersonians that Indian societies of the eastern woodlands, such as the Iroquois, needed to

[1] H. A. Washington, ed., *The Writings of Thomas Jefferson*, 9 vols. (Philadelphia, 1869), 8:188–89.

become agricultural despite abundant evidence that agriculture had long been an integral part of their economic life. To anyone familiar with the importance of Indian farming, not only within their own societies but also for the survival of early colonists, Jeffersonian descriptions of Indian livelihood are especially perplexing.[2] How could a generation of men who had witnessed, even contributed to, the destruction of bountiful Iroquois and Cherokee fields and orchards during the American Revolution fail to recognize the agricultural tradition of eastern North American Indians? Were Jeffersonians inadequately informed about Indian livelihood, or did their definition of "agriculture" exclude the kinds of farming practiced by Indian societies?

Even more troubling than these questions is the fact that historians have failed to ask them. Why has the discrepancy between reality and imagery gone unnoticed for so long? Not too long ago, historians of Indian policy during the early national period continued to accept at face value the words used by Jeffersonians to characterize Indian life. Without any quotation marks, Francis Paul Prucha summarized Jefferson's program as follows: "The process of civilization was to be marked by— indeed it was to be brought about by—transition from the nomadic life of the hunter, who depended on the chase, to the settled life of the farmer, who depended on the surer sustenance provided by agriculture." Readers unfamiliar with the actual nature of Indian livelihood might assume that this point of view is accurate. "By any civilized criteria," Bernard W. Sheehan stated, "the woman was the drudge of native society. She performed all the menial functions that kept ordinary existence intact, and by cultivating the soil, she compensated for the sparse return from her husband's hunting."[3] Such generalizations

---

[2] This and other historiographical problems regarding Indian agriculture are raised in Thomas R. Wessel, "Agriculture, Indians, and American History," *Agricultural History* 50 (1976):9–20. Also see R. Douglas Hurt, *Indian Agriculture in America: Prehistory to the Present* (Lawrence, Kans., 1987), and David Rich Lewis, *Neither Wolf nor Dog: American Indians, Environment, and Agrarian Change* (New York, 1994).

[3] Francis Paul Prucha, *American Indian Policy in the Formative Years: The Indian Trade and Intercourse Acts, 1790–1834* (Cambridge, Mass., 1962), p. 214;

made by scholars simply reiterate misrepresentations of American Indian economies left by highly subjective observers.

The more general literature on economic life in early America is also implicated in this historiographical hall of mirrors. From the progressive school of Charles A. Beard and Carl L. Becker to the current debate over rural capitalism, historians have consistently excluded American Indians from their analyses of social and economic change. In the early scholarship, an assumption about the "backwardness" of Indians determined that they would only serve as a contrasting backdrop to discussions of white industry and toil. Over the years scholarly attention devoted to Indian societies focused mainly on cultural and political dimensions of their relations with colonial societies. The more widely noticed inquiry into socioeconomic changes and their ideological ramifications among England's North American colonies, meanwhile, ignored connections and comparisons with American Indian experiences.[4] Consequently, the everyday forms of economic adaptation and resistance practiced by Indian people in and around the colonies went unnoticed. American Indians' own ideological concerns, as well as the ideological uses Euro-Americans made of their lives are both neglected in the wider histories.

In order to begin restoring American Indians to their integral place in both ideological and socioeconomic developments during the early national period, we must ask why Jeffersonians insisted on characterizing Indian people as hunters and not farmers even though a substantial portion of their sustenance came from corn, beans, and other food crops. Perhaps they were just ignorant of the full range of activities employed by In-

---

Bernard W. Sheehan, *Seeds of Extinction: Jeffersonian Philanthropy and the American Indian* (Chapel Hill, N.C., 1973), p. 165.

[4] Notable exceptions in recent scholarship are William Cronon, *Changes in the Land: Indians, Colonists, and the Ecology of New England* (New York, 1983) and Peter C. Mancall, *Valley of Opportunity: Economic Culture along the Upper Susquehanna, 1700–1800* (Ithaca, N.Y., 1991). An important contribution to the study of class formation and capitalist transformation in rural America before 1840 is Allan Kulikoff, *The Agrarian Origins of American Capitalism* (Charlottesville, Va., 1992), which characteristically neglects the involvement of American Indians.

dians to procure food. Most Americans who wrote about Indians, including Thomas Jefferson, had minimal or no exposure to the seasonal cycle of farming, gathering, and hunting that constituted village life. Even close-up observers of Indian livelihood during the colonial period lacked the conceptual framework for seeing either the efficiency in Native methods of cultivation or the energy spent by men in hunting important food sources. They were better equipped to notice what was missing from the picture—plows and fences, livestock and manure, and familiar crops like wheat and barley.[5] Ethnocentric myopia, however, did not prevent colonial American leaders like John Smith and Miles Standish from seeing the surpluses of food crops produced by Indian villagers and from acquiring them by trade or plunder.[6] And certainly by the late eighteenth century, worldly thinkers like Benjamin Franklin and Thomas Jefferson were capable of appreciating the successful applicability of Indian subsistence patterns to their natural environments.

The minimization of Indian agricultural practices might have been nothing other than a well-tested means of justifying the expropriation of land from Indians.[7] God intended Virginia to be cultivated, argued Samuel Purchas in the early seventeenth century, and not left to "that unmanned wild Countrey, which they range rather than inhabite." Europeans wrote profusely about nomadic people living off the forest, contrary to the evidence of sedentary Indian farming, in order to rationalize conquest and colonization. John Winthrop declared that New England Indians "inclose noe Land, neither have any setled habytation, nor any tame Cattle to improve the Land by, and soe have noe other but a Naturall Right to those Countries."[8] The legal principle of *vacuum domicilium*, as Francis P. Jennings ob-

---

[5] Cronon, *Changes in the Land*, pp. 43–44, 51–52; James Axtell, *The Invasion Within: The Contest of Cultures in Colonial North America* (New York, 1985), pp. 148–67.

[6] Francis P. Jennings, *The Invasion of America: Indians, Colonialism, and the Cant of Conquest* (Chapel Hill, N.C., 1975), pp. 60–84.

[7] A strong case for this explanation is made in David D. Smits, "The 'Squaw Drudge': A Prime Index of Savagism," *Ethnohistory* 29 (1982):281–306.

[8] Samuel Purchas quotation in Jennings, *Invasion of America*, p. 80; John Winthrop quotation in Cronon, *Changes in the Land*, p. 56.

served, "held the magic of a strong incantation and the utility of a magician's smokescreen." In the mid-eighteenth century, Swiss jurist and diplomat Emmerich de Vattel formulated the illusion of Indians underusing their land into a principle of international law: "It is asked if a nation may lawfully take possession of a part of a vast country, in which there are found none but erratic nations, incapable by the smallness of their numbers, to people the whole? We have already observed in establishing the obligation to cultivate the earth, that these nations cannot exclusively appropriate to themselves more land than they have occasion for, and which they are unable to settle and cultivate."[9]

As president of the United States at the beginning of the nineteenth century, Thomas Jefferson seemed ready to turn this ideology of conquest into a policy of misrepresentation and manipulation. The promotion of agriculture and household manufacture among Indians, he confided to Benjamin Hawkins in 1803, "will enable them to live on much smaller portions of land, and indeed will render their vast forest useless but for the range of cattle; for which purpose, also, as they become better farmers, they will be found useless, and even disadvantageous. While they are learning to do better on less land, our increasing numbers will be calling for more land." In an ironic metaphor of hunting with traps, Jefferson declared that "the wisdom of the animal which amputates & abandons to the hunter the parts for which he is pursued should be theirs."[10] Although the ultimate goal was to assimilate American Indians through this process of social reform and land transfer, government agents in the Jeffersonian era manipulated information about Indian livelihood according to immediate objectives.

At the beginning of his commission in the Cherokee nation, Return J. Meigs enthusiastically promoted plow agriculture as a means of reducing Indian landholdings. But when urging the migration of lower Cherokee towns from the Tennessee Valley in 1808, he highlighted their preference for hunting and advo-

[9] Jennings, *Invasion of America*, p. 81; Emmerich de Vattel quotation in Prucha, *American Indian Policy*, p. 241.

[10] Paul Leicester Ford, ed., *The Writings of Thomas Jefferson*, 10 vols. (New York, 1892–99), 8:213–14.

cated removal across the Mississippi to preserve the hunt. Meigs changed his tune again in 1811, when he sought the extension of state jurisdiction over the Cherokees. Now in his opinion they were promising farmers and competent citizens. In 1816 he returned to a portrait of sluggish agricultural improvement in order to rationalize removal one more time.[11]

Without downplaying the role of naïveté and duplicity, I want to reach behind the Jeffersonian characterization of Indian economic life by deconstructing the constellation of ideas that went into its making. The great divide between a hunting society and a farming society that dominated thought during the formative years of United States Indian policy was much more than a propaganda campaign to erase Indian agriculture from the national consciousness, although it unfortunately had such an effect. If this generation of American intellectuals really believed that Indians lived in a hunter state, we must turn anthropological analysis loose on them—an exercise that should delight American Indians who have received exorbitant attention from anthropologists. A deeper textual analysis of Enlightenment ideas about Indian livelihood discloses the making of a theory of social change that became so pervasive and predominant that we still have difficulty seeing through it. Here lies at least part of the explanation for historians' unquestioning acceptance of Jeffersonian description, because the intellectual apparatus of social science as well as the dogma of popular myth has important origins in the theoretical models constructed during the early national period.[12] And American Indians found themselves caught in the thick of this intellectual construction, being convenient guinea pigs for testing hypotheses about human behavior and social development.

By the late eighteenth century, European and American philosophers reached a new consensus about how to explain dif-

[11] William G. McLoughlin, *Cherokee Renascence in the New Republic* (Princeton, 1986), pp. 92–99, 128–32, 164–65, 214.

[12] For two penetrating critiques of how theoretical models from this era have affected historians and social scientists, see Charles Tilly, *Big Structures, Large Processes, Huge Comparisons* (New York, 1984), and Andrew C. Janos, *Politics and Paradigms: Changing Theories of Change in Social Science* (Stanford, Calif., 1986).

ferences and similarities among human societies. Believing in a uniformity of human behavior, they traced cultural variation to different modes of subsistence. Means of livelihood were treated as responses to environmental stimuli and as causes of social development. How a society utilized natural resources determined the rates of growth in population and of movement up a ladder of evolution. In his *Spirit of Laws*, Charles Louis de Secondat, baron de Montesquieu, relied upon a theory of natural abundance to explain everything from demographic to political conditions among American Indians. They cultivated small plots of land and supplemented farming with hunting and fishing, argued the French philosopher, because the earth spontaneously produced "many fruits capable of affording them nourishment." Most of the land in America remained uncultivated, and therefore Native Americans occupied the continent in low numbers and formed small nations.[13] This law of environmental determinism, we now realize, defied the fact that the indigenous population of the western hemisphere had been reduced by epidemic viruses carried by Europeans and Africans across the Atlantic Ocean. It also cannot withstand current anthropological knowledge that hunting-gathering activities involve conscious and creative decision-making about how, when, and where to procure resources.[14]

But there was a highly specific empirical background behind the confidence with which theoreticians associated modes of subsistence with sizes of population. During the early colonial period it was common for writers to explain Indian depopulation and European colonization as manifestations of divine will. In the aftermath of the Pequot War, Philip Vincent predicted that the small population in New England would increase by immigration, but more by "a faculty that God hath given the British . . . to beget and bring forth more children than any other

[13] Gilbert Chinard, "Eighteenth-Century Theories on America as a Human Habitat," *Proceedings of the American Philosophical Society* 91 (1947):27–57, Montesquieu quotation p. 28; Sheehan, *Seeds of Extinction*, pp. 34–39.

[14] The seminal work in our new understanding of hunting-gathering societies is Marshall Sahlins, "The Original Affluent Society," in his *Stone Age Economics* (Chicago, 1972), pp. 1–39.

nation of the world."[15] With great pride in the fecundity of English colonists, eighteenth-century American authors proferred what they considered to be a more scientific explanation for rapid growth in the colonial population—an explanation that relegated Indians to an inferior hunter state and elevated whites to an ideal agrarian state. In a 1755 essay entitled "Observations concerning the Increase of Mankind," Benjamin Franklin rewrote history to account for the unprecedented rate of procreation occurring among English-Americans:

> Europe is generally full settled with Husbandmen, Manufacturers, &c. and therefore cannot now much increase in People: America is chiefly occupied by Indians, who subsist mostly by Hunting. But as the Hunter, of all Men, requires the greatest Quantity of Land from whence to draw his Subsistence, (the Husbandmen subsisting on much less, the Gardner on still less, and the Manufacturer requiring least of all), the Europeans found America as fully settled as it well could be by Hunters; yet these having large Tracks, were easily prevail'd on to part with Portions of Territory to the new Comers, who did not much interfere with the Natives in Hunting, and furnish'd them with many Things they wanted.
>
> Land being thus plenty in America, and so cheap as that a labouring Man, that understands Husbandry, can in a short Time save Money enough to purchase a Piece of new Land sufficient for a Plantation, whereon he may subsist a Family; such are not afraid to marry; for if they even look far enough forward to consider how their Children when grown up are to be provided for, they see that more Land is to be had at Rates equally easy, all Circumstances considered.[16]

Franklin somehow failed to recognize that American Indian agricultural methods, especially their success with corn, helped make the rapid growth of the colonial population possible.[17] Instead, a demographic imperialism rested on the syllogism that

[15] Richard Slotkin, *Regeneration through Violence: The Mythology of the American Frontier, 1600–1860* (Middletown, Conn., 1973), p. 73.

[16] Leonard W. Labaree, ed., *The Papers of Benjamin Franklin*, 30 vols. to date (New Haven, 1959–), 4:228.

[17] Alfred W. Crosby has recently developed the point ignored by Franklin and many subsequent American pundits in "Maize, Land, Demography,

"husbandmen" use land more productively, as evidenced by their increasing numbers, and that additional land would be needed to support the growing population of "husbandmen." From Paris in 1786 Thomas Jefferson wrote to Archibald Stuart, "Our confederacy must be viewed as the nest from which all America, North and South is to be peopled." He considered the Spaniards to be good temporary possessors of the southern countries, fearing only "that they are too feeble to hold them till our population can be sufficiently advanced to gain it from them piece by piece."[18] But before the United States would "advance" upon Latin American countries, there was the matter of North American Indians. In his Inaugural Address of 1805 Jefferson commiserated how "the stream of overflowing population from other regions" overwhelmed "the aboriginal inhabitants." "Now reduced within limits too narrow for the hunter's state," the president declared, "humanity enjoins us to teach them agriculture and the domestic arts; to encourage them to that industry which alone can enable them to maintain their place in existence, and to prepare them in time for that state of society, which to bodily comforts adds the improvement of the mind and morals."[19]

Humanitarian wishes to avert the fate predicted by environmental and demographic determinism, however, did not inhibit the United States government from pushing American Indians westward. Urging a group of Delawares in 1808 to abandon hunting, Jefferson instructed them that "whites, on the other hand, are in the habit of cultivating the earth, of raising stocks of cattle, hogs, and other domestic animals, in much greater numbers than they could kill of deer and buffalo. Having always a plenty of food and clothing they raise abundance of children, they double their numbers every twenty years, the new swarms are continually advancing upon the country like flocks

and the American Characters," *Revue Française d'Etudes Américaines* 16 (1991): 151–62.

[18] Julian P. Boyd et al., eds., *The Papers of Thomas Jefferson*, 28 vols. to date (Princeton, 1950–), 9:218.

[19] Ford, ed., *Writings of Jefferson*, 8:344–45.

of pigeons, and so they will continue to do." Before the New-York Historical Society in 1811, Gov. DeWitt Clinton declared, "A nation that derives its subsistence, principally, from the forest, cannot live in the vicinity of one that relies upon the products of the field. The clearing of the country drives off the wild beasts; and when the game fails, the hunter must starve, change his occupation, or retire from the approach of cultivation." President James Monroe reported to Congress in 1817, "The hunter state can exist only in the vast uncultivated desert. It yields to the more dense and compact form and greater force of civilized population; and, of right, it ought to yield, for the earth was given to mankind to support the greater number of which it is capable."[20]

Such ultimatums delivered to Indian hunters went even deeper than a hunger for the land that they supposedly underused. Many Enlightenment thinkers believed that the very forests containing wild animals were detrimental to people's health and that the consumption of wild meat deteriorated social behavior. In the 1789 American Philosophical Society *Transactions*, Hugh Williamson wrote that "while the face of this country was clad with woods, and every valley afforded a swamp or stagnant marsh, by a copious perspiration through the leaves of trees or plants, and a general exhalation from the surface of ponds and marshes, the air was constantly charged with a gross putrescent fluid." Clearing forests for cultivation, therefore, would "increase circulation of air and raise the temperature." The *Massachusetts Centinel* celebrated the rapid settlement of Vermont by reporting, "Large tracts of land which two or three years past were nothing more than an uncultivated wilderness now teem with vegetation, nurtured by the industrious hand of agriculture. The axe of the husbandmen has made bare the forest, and fields of grain supply the place of lofty trees. In short the face of nature throughout every part of that district has

---

[20] Washington, ed., *Writings of Jefferson*, 8:225–26; DeWitt Clinton, "A Discourse Delivered before the New-York Historical Society, at Their Anniversary Meeting, 6th December, 1811," *Collections of the New-York Historical Society* 2 (1814):85; *American State Papers: Indian Affairs*, 2 vols. (Washington, D.C., 1832–34), 2:496.

a much more pleasant appearance, and gives us an idea of the future greatness of this young but rising empire."[21]

To this way of thinking, the coexistence of fields and forests was unacceptable. The only good vegetation was a crop like wheat, and the only attractive landscape was one of rectangular-shaped farmsteads. Dread of the "wilderness" has been traced far back to its Judeo-Christian roots.[22] But throughout the colonial period and well into the nineteenth century, it also reflected the immediate concern among elites that proximity to Indians and their environment would make American settlers uncontrollable and rebellious. Behind the nascent model of economic development lay fears of underdevelopment, captured repeatedly in such phrases as "to live like Indians" and "want in the midst of abundance."[23] Groups with an interest in commercial production and land speculation in backcountry regions worried that settlers would prefer the economic independence permitted by hunting, fishing, and other subsistence activities. As Alan Taylor and Rachel N. Klein have demonstrated for two different late eighteenth-century frontier regions, promoters of hierarchy and control condemned those frontiersmen who resisted commercial agriculture for succumbing to the temptations of savagery.[24]

[21] Hugh Williamson quotation in Sheehan, *Seeds of Extinction*, p. 39; *Massachusetts Centinel*, Sept. 15, 1784; Joyce O. Appleby, *Capitalism and a New Social Order: The Republican Vision of the 1790s* (New York, 1984), pp. 44–45; Myra Jehlen, *American Incarnation: The Individual, the Nation, and the Continent* (Cambridge, Mass., 1986), pp. 72–73.

[22] Frederick W. Turner, *Beyond Geography: The Western Spirit against the Wilderness* (New York, 1980). For a study of Genesis 1:28, rejecting the argument, begun years ago by Hayden White, that this verse in the Bible originated Europe's destructive treatment of the environment, see Jeremy Cohen, *Be Fertile and Increase. Fill the Earth and Master It: The Ancient and Medieval Career of a Biblical Text* (Ithaca, N.Y., 1989).

[23] This point is made in Peter S. Onuf, *Statehood and Union: A History of the Northwest Ordinance* (Bloomington, Ind., 1987), pp. 5–19.

[24] Alan Taylor, *Liberty Men and Great Proprietors: The Revolutionary Settlement on the Maine Frontier, 1760–1820* (Chapel Hill, N.C., 1990), pp. 49–59; Rachel N. Klein, *Unification of a Slave State: The Rise of the Planter Class in the South Carolina Backcountry, 1760–1808* (Chapel Hill, N.C., 1990), pp. 51–64.

J. Hector St. John de Crèvecoeur clearly expressed anxiety over the deleterious effects of hunting when he described life "near the great woods" in his *Letters from an American Farmer:* "It is with men as it is with the plants and animals that grow and live in the forests. . . . By living in or near the woods, their actions are regulated by the wildness of the neighborhood. The deer often come to eat their grain, the wolves to destroy their sheep, the bears to kill their hogs, the foxes to catch their poultry. This surrounding hostility immediately puts the gun into their hands; they watch these animals, they kill some; and thus by defending their property, they soon become professed hunters; this is the progress; once hunters, farewell to the plough. The chase renders them ferocious, gloomy, and unsocial." Adhering strongly to the maxim "You are what you eat," Crèvecoeur stated that "eating of wild meat, whatever you may think, tends to alter their temper." "As long as we keep ourselves busy in tilling the earth," he insisted, "there is not fear of any of us becoming wild; it is the chase and food it procures that have this strange effect."[25]

From the backwoods of Enlightenment thought, so to speak, we now reach the more familiar terrain of what is called Jeffersonian agrarianism. Like so much of American history, this important ideological development has been studied with very little attention to its relationship to American Indians. And this is no less true for the latest debate over the meaning of Jefferson's agrarian ideal.[26] Some historians emphasize its continuity from the classical conceptualization of agriculture as the best means to prosperity, freedom, and morality. "Those who labor in the earth are the chosen people of God," wrote Jefferson in *Notes on Virginia.* "Corruption of morals in the mass of cultivators is a phenomenon of which no age nor nation has furnished

[25] J. Hector St. John de Crèvecoeur, *Letters from an American Farmer and Sketches of Eighteenth-Century America,* ed. Albert E. Stone (New York, 1981), pp. 76–78, 219–20.

[26] For historiographical background and a particular interpretation on Jeffersonian agrarianism, see Joyce O. Appleby, "Commercial Farming and the 'Agrarian Myth' in the Early Republic," *Journal of American History* 68 (1982): 833–49.

an example." In post-Revolutionary America this faith in the virtue of agriculture took an added urgency as early national leaders sought to avoid problems that were arising in Europe, such as poverty, class conflict, industrialization, and urbanization. A citizenry of independent farmers was the best prevention, according to Jefferson. "While we have land to labor then, let us never wish to see our citizens occupied at a workbench, or twirling a distaff. Carpenters, masons, smiths, are wanting in husbandry; but, for the general operations of manufacture, let our workshops remain in Europe."[27] In the Jeffersonian mind, then, agriculture constituted a safe middle ground, protecting American citizens from the dangers of both European and American Indian societies.[28]

But far from being nostalgic or anticommercial, Jeffersonian agrarianism was animated by an immediately promising economic development that had profound ramifications for eastern North American Indians. As Joyce O. Appleby has emphasized, Jefferson's commitment to an agrarian society rested on Europe's growing demand for American food crops after the 1780s. An exploding population and a series of wars in Europe created the opportunity for American farmers to produce more crops on more land for a growing food market. "It is better to carry provisions and materials to workmen there," Jefferson urged in his *Notes*, "than bring them to the provisions and materials, and with them their manners and principles."[29] While

[27] Adrienne Koch and William Peden, eds., *The Life and Selected Writings of Thomas Jefferson* (New York, 1944), pp. 280–81. The influence of classical thought on Jeffersonian agrarians is argued effectively in Andrew W. Foshee, "Jeffersonian Political Economy and the Classical Republican Tradition: Jefferson, Taylor, and the Agrarian Republic," *History of Political Economy* 17 (1985):523–50. A tension between antiquity and innovation operating within Jeffersonian thinking is exposed in Drew R. McCoy, *The Elusive Republic: Political Economy in Jeffersonian America* (Chapel Hill, N.C., 1980), pp. 76–104.

[28] This worry about modernization going too far animated many United States leaders throughout the nineteenth century, especially the Democratic expansionists of the 1840s. See Thomas R. Heitala, *Manifest Design: Anxious Aggrandizement in Late Jacksonian America* (Ithaca, N.Y., 1985), pp. 95–122.

[29] Koch and Peden, eds., *Life and Writings of Jefferson*, p. 280; Appleby, "Commercial Farming," and *Capitalism and a New Social Order*, pp. 88–95.

European agrarian reformers attempted to accelerate the enclosure of common land and to increase productivity in order to meet the continent's needs, their counterparts in the United States worked to expand agricultural production over additional acreage. With their economies and territories threatened by this expansion of commercial agriculture, American Indians faced nothing less than the "agricultural revolution" that was melting, in the words of Eric Hobsbawm, "the great frozen ice-cap of the world's traditional agrarian systems and rural social relations."[30]

American Indian communities in the late eighteenth and early nineteenth centuries, therefore, had to contend with a model of agricultural development that affected them adversely in several ways. The rapid commercialization of farming, in response to foreign demand, made Indian methods of farming seem more anachronistic than ever before. The agrarian escape valve, which was supposed to ameliorate social problems in the United States, depended upon the acquisition of more and more Indian land for redistribution to new generations of white farmers.[31] The livelihood of American Indians came under closer scrutiny just when pressures on their territory made life notably more difficult. Agricultural reform thus constituted a double-edged sword, compelling Indians to participate in the commercial market while severing more land from tribal control. Their resistance to this process was perceived in terms similar to those held by advocates of agricultural change toward European peasants, as wasteful and irrational behavior that needed to be liberated from traditional obligations and constraints.[32] Jefferson summarized in 1805 what he considered "powerful obstacles" to teaching agriculture to Indians: "The

[30] E. J. Hobsbawm, *The Age of Revolution, 1789–1848* (Cleveland, 1962), pp. 149–52. For insight into changing images of peasantry in European culture, see Liana Vardi, "Imagining the Harvest in Early Modern Europe," *American Historical Review* 101 (1996): 1357–97.

[31] John R. Nelson, Jr., *Liberty and Property: Political Economy and Policymaking in the New Nation, 1789–1812* (Baltimore, 1987), pp. 96–98.

[32] Marc Bloch, *French Rural History: An Essay on Its Basic Characteristics*, trans. Janet Sondheimer (Berkeley, Calif., 1966), pp. 219–20; E. P. Thompson, *The Making of the English Working Class* (New York, 1963), pp. 218–20.

habits of their bodies, prejudice of their minds, ignorance, pride, and the influence of interested and crafty individuals among them, who feel themselves something in the present order of things, and fear to become nothing in any other."[33]

No group of American Indians was more involved in the struggle against Jeffersonian agrarian ambitions than the Iroquois nations of western New York. By the time President Jefferson addressed Handsome Lake about "going into a state of agriculture," twenty years had passed since the American Revolution. Following their painful dislocation caused by the war, the Iroquois faced relentless pressures from state and federal governments, from speculators and settlers, for most of the territory west of Oneida Lake. Through it all, the polarized imagery of farming and hunting pervaded the rhetoric of diplomacy. As early as 1785 George Clinton, the governor of New York, advised Oneida and Tuscarora chiefs that they should sell that part of their land bordering the state of Pennsylvania, "which being contiguous to the Settlements of the White People, will soon be of little Value for hunting, and the Price of it would enable You to purchase Cattle and Utensils of Husbandry and improve your Lands at Home to greater Advantage." Both New York state and the United States tried to buy Iroquois hunting grounds by offering to compensate for the lost resources with cash annuities and technical assistance.[34]

Iroquois spokesmen were highly defensive about the preservation of hunting grounds, apparently emphasizing their importance over farmland. If read uncritically, the rhetorical responses of Indian leaders seem to reinforce Jeffersonian perceptions of Indian dependence upon forest animals. Petrus of the Oneidas told Clinton in 1785 that "we cannot part with so much of our Hunting Lands, which are very dear to Us; as from

---

[33] Ford, ed., *Writings of Jefferson*, 8:345. The wider target of Jefferson's stricture against Indian economic conservatism was recently detailed in Noble E. Cunningham, Jr., *In Pursuit of Reason: The Life of Thomas Jefferson* (Baton Rouge, La., 1987), pp. 276–77.

[34] Franklin B. Hough, ed., *Proceedings of the Commissioners of Indian Affairs, Appointed by Law for the Extinguishment of Indian Titles in the State of New York*, 2 vols. (Albany, 1861), 1:86; Dorothy V. Jones, *License for Empire: Colonialism by Treaty in Early America* (Chicago, 1982), pp. 179–85.

thence We derive the Rags which cover our Bodies."[35] In 1800 Red Jacket played up the difference between societies in a speech to the Rev. Elkanah Holmes: "Probably the Great Spirit has given to you white people the ways that you follow to serve him, and to get your living; and probably he has given to us Indians the customs that we follow to serve him (handed down to us by our forefathers) and our ways to get our living by hunting, and the Great Spirit is still good to us, to preserve game for us."[36] But the following year this same spokesman for the Buffalo Creek Senecas admitted that it was necessary "for us to quit the mode of Indian living and learn the manner of white peoples." "Instead of finding our game at our doors," he exclaimed, "we were obliged to go to a great distance for it, and their finde it but scarce compared to what it us'd to be." Consequently, the Senecas "are determined in all our villages to take to husbandry, and for this purpose we want to be helped to a number of pair of cattle."[37]

What meanings lay behind this council language used by Indian speakers? This is an especially difficult question since the records contain only English versions of Iroquois thoughts, which were not easily or accurately interpreted. But the vocabulary of Indian leaders, like that of United States officials, might warrant some decoding. The diplomatic voice of Iroquois orators played as active a role in the struggle to shape events as did that of Jeffersonian discourse. Gender roles in Iroquois society were integrally tied to subsistence activities, with women assuming ownership of the land as its principal cultivators. "Our Ancestors considered it a great Transgression to reject the Council of their Women," Oneida chief Domine Peter warned in 1789, because "who bring us forth, who cultivate our Lands,

---

[35] Hough, ed., *Proceedings of Commissioners of Indian Affairs*, 1:91.

[36] "Letters of the Reverend Elkanah Holmes from Fort Niagara in 1800," ed. Frank H. Severance, *Publications of the Buffalo Historical Society* 6 (1903):199.

[37] Proceedings of Councils Held at Geneseo River with Senecas, Onondagas, Cayugas, and Delawares, Nov. 12, 1801, O'Reilly Papers, New-York Historical Society, New York City; also in *Iroquois Indians: A Documentary History* (Woodbridge, Conn., 1985, microfilm), roll 44.

who kindles our Fires and boil our Pots, but the Women." He further reported that women of the Cayuga nation "think their Uncles had of late lost the Power of Thinking, and were about sinking their Territory."[38] But hunting was the men's sphere, so male diplomats might predictably underscore its importance— sometimes annoying their female relatives. Between formal speeches delivered at Buffalo Creek in April 1791, a group of women elders hastened to inform Colonel Proctor that "you ought to hear and listen to what we, women, shall speak, as well as to the sachems; for we are the owners of this land,—and it is our's. It is we that plant it for our and their use."[39]

Hunting grounds might have demanded special attention because they were also the most vulnerable kind of Indian land at the end of the eighteenth century, as game became harder to find and hunters encountered hostile settlers. "Turn our faces which way we will," Cornplanter complained to Washington in 1797, "we find the white people cultivating the ground which our forefathers hunted over, and the forests which furnish'd them with plenty now afford but a scanty subsistence for us, and our young men are not safe in pursuing it. If a few years have made such a change, what will be the situation of our children when those calamities increase?"[40] "The white people are scattered so thick over the Country," Red Jacket complained in 1801, "that the dear have almost fled from us." Nearly two decades later he cited a longer list of common threats: "Our venison is stolen from the trees where we have hung it to be reclaimed after the chase. Our hunting camps have been fired into, and we have been warned that we shall no longer be permitted to pursue the deer in those forests which were so lately all our own."[41]

---

[38] Hough, ed., *Proceedings of Commissioners of Indian Affairs*, 2:279.

[39] William L. Stone, *The Life and Times of Red-Jacket, or Sa-go-ye-wat-ha; Being the Sequel to the History of the Six Nations* (New York, 1841), pp. 56–59.

[40] Speech of Cornplanter to Gen. George Washington in Philadelphia, Feb. 28, 1797, O'Reilly Papers; also in *Iroquois Indians*, roll 44.

[41] Proceedings of Councils Held at Geneseo River; also in *Iroquois Indians*, roll 44. Stone, *Life and Times of Red-Jacket*, p. 325.

These concerns were expressed through metaphors that reflected an understanding of livelihood sharply different from the Jeffersonian model of economic life. European physiocrats and their counterparts in America expected conformity to what they observed as the mechanistic laws of nature. They talked about increasing the productivity of the land, converting products into property, and moving society through material stages. Iroquois and other Indian voices defended a social order in which the natural world mirrored social relationships between people. The Great Spirit spread animals over the land and caused the earth to produce corn, in the form of a gift, while humans provided each other with material goods. Reciprocal relations between men and women depended upon the ability of men to exchange products of the hunt for those of the harvest. To intensify production in the fields at the expense of production in the forests threatened both society and nature with disorder by potentially undermining interdependency.[42]

The categorical language used by Indian leaders to lament the decline of hunting in the late eighteenth century, therefore, was directed inward as much as outward. Although Iroquois communities were already adapting livestock to their way of life, cattle, hogs, and sheep did not easily assimilate into their belief system. More time was needed to replace culturally the products of hunting with the products of herding. As in other eastern woodlands societies, women seemed to be more eager than men to incorporate domestic animals into village husbandry—adding stress to the division of labor between the sexes.[43]

To understand the economic hazards and social dilemmas facing the Iroquois at the dawn of the nineteenth century, we must shift from utterances to circumstances or, if you will, from the language of models and metaphors to the material process

[42] My thinking here has been influenced by Greg Dening, *Islands and Beaches: Discourse on a Silent Land, Marquesas, 1774–1880* (Honolulu, 1980), Maurice Godelier, *The Mental and the Material: Thought, Economy, and Society*, trans. Maurice Thom (London, 1986), and Stephen Gudeman, *Economics as Culture: Models and Metaphors of Livelihood* (London, 1986).

[43] Marvin Thomas Hatley, *The Dividing Paths: Cherokees and South Carolinians through the Era of Revolution* (New York, 1993), pp. 162–63, 214.

of social and economic change.[44] Western New York, especially the Genesee River Valley, was then a chaotic frontier of commercial agricultural expansion. The 1797 Treaty of Big Tree, by which the Senecas lost most of their territory west of the Genesee, was signed in the midst of rampant land speculation and political corruption characteristic of rapid economic development. The Holland Land Company and other speculators attempted to accelerate migration into the region in order to boost the value of their holdings and to launch production of staple crops. Families of little means were offered land on credit, and, when unable to meet their debts, moved out of the area.[45] Frequent turnover of settlers, speculation and indebtedness, and even tenancy made many early white communities—in the words of Anthony F. C. Wallace—"slums in the wilderness." On the most fertile bottomlands around the lakes and along the rivers, meanwhile, successful farmers began to grow wheat and corn and to raise livestock and cut timber for the expanding commercial market. Much of this production, it must be noted, took place on the abandoned fields of former Iroquois towns. By the 1810s the Genesee Valley was fast becoming a leading grain-export region of the United States, the city of Rochester shipping some 26,000 barrels of flour in 1818.[46]

This was the general setting in which Iroquois leaders had to respond to the agricultural reform offered them by the United States government. In May 1798 representatives from the Philadelphia Society of Friends began to implement the agrarian component of Indian policy among the Allegany Senecas, having already met some success with the Oneidas. The Quakers

---

[44] For a critical analysis of the "linguistic turn in social history," see Bryan D. Palmer, *Descent into Discourse: The Reification of Language and the Writing of Social History* (Philadelphia, 1990).

[45] William Wyckoff, *The Developer's Frontier: The Making of the Western New York Landscape* (New Haven, 1988).

[46] Anthony F. C. Wallace, *The Death and Rebirth of the Seneca* (New York, 1970), pp. 179–96. For additional information on the expansion of commercial agriculture in the area, see Neil Adams McNall, *An Agricultural History of the Genesee Valley, 1790–1860* (Philadelphia, 1952), pp. 11–95; and Paul E. Johnson, *A Shopkeeper's Millennium: Society and Revivals in Rochester, New York, 1815–1837* (New York, 1978), pp. 16–24.

brought plows, hoes, spades, and shovels, paid half the costs for constructing a gristmill, and offered cash incentives for the production of wheat, rye, corn, potatoes, hay, and cloth. They never missed an occasion to preach the Jeffersonian dogma about different modes of subsistence, calling it "unreasonable" to "suffer their women to work all day in the fields & woods with the hoes & axes, whilst the Men & Boys were at the same time playing with their bows & arrows."[47]

To some extent the Iroquois took the advice of these outside reformers, intensifying agricultural production with new technology and dispersing settlement into nuclear farmsteads. Cornplanter of the Senecas became an enthusiast behind such changes, and his brother Handsome Lake even incorporated elements of agrarian reform into his gospel for cultural revitalization. Gerald Hopkins observed among Buffalo Creek Senecas in 1804 "a large plough at work drawn by three yoke of oxen, and attended by three Indians. They all appeared to be very merry, and to be pleased with our visit." By 1820 the agricultural revolution seems to have taken hold in some of the Iroquois communities. One Quaker estimated that the average Indian family around the Allegany mission had ten acres of corn, oats, potatoes, vegetables, and meadow fenced in and owned a plow, a yoke of oxen or pair of horses, five cows, and eleven pigs.[48]

But before we too quickly conclude that the Iroquois conformed to the Jeffersonian model of economic life, a closer look at changes in livelihood is in order. Indian initiatives and responses during the early nineteenth century, in fact, prove how dubious the Enlightenment's theoretical opposition between farming and hunting actually was. They reveal, moreover, an American Indian resilience and resourcefulness in adjusting to adverse economic conditions that defied the agrarian prescrip-

---

[47] Wallace, *Death and Rebirth of the Seneca*, p. 226.

[48] "Visit of Gerald T. Hopkins, A Quaker Ambassador to the Indians Who Visited Buffalo in 1804," ed. Frank H. Severance, *Publications of the Buffalo Historical Society* 6 (1903):221; Wallace, *Death and Rebirth of the Seneca*, pp. 310–15; Marilyn Holly, "Handsome Lake's Teachings: The Shift from Female to Male Agriculture in Iroquois Culture. An Essay in Ethnophilosophy," *Agriculture and Human Values* 7 (1980):80–94.

tion for social change. The Iroquois remained skeptical toward agricultural reform, viewing acceptance of new farming technology in return for cessions of hunting territory as no guarantee against continuing land grabs. In 1790 Cornplanter had issued a very mixed signal to President George Washington about the prospects for Iroquois livelihood under increasingly precarious conditions: "The Game which the Great Spirit sent into our Country for us to eat is going from among us. We thought that he intended that we should till the Ground with the Plow, as the White People do." But before committing themselves to such a change, Cornplanter and his people wanted to know "whether you mean to leave us and our Children any Land to till." The general security of the people and the needs of future generations had to be taken into account.[49] Acceptance of new agricultural methods hardly encouraged adoption of private property, as Iroquois leaders relentlessly defended their communities' collective ownership of the land. "Dividing lands into farms, and holding them as individual property," Captain Pollard of the Senecas told Jedidiah Morse in 1820, "will not do for us. Holding our lands in common, as we now do, keeps us together." Pollard discerned all too well the consequences of allotting tribal lands among individuals: "As Indians want goods of white people and buy them on credit, we fear difficulties would arise in collecting these debts, according to your laws, and our lands would be taken to pay them."[50]

The Senecas accepted Quaker instructors not without division and suspicion among themselves, but association with the Society of Friends was seen by many as a potential buffer against the pressures of speculators and settlers. And the Quakers often defended the land rights of Iroquois communities. Nevertheless, there was reason to take precautions against becoming too dependent upon the advice and assistance of any outside group. Halliday Jackson recalled the "very cautious method" employed by the Allegany Senecas when they first began to use plows in

[49] Hough, ed., *Proceedings of Commissioners of Indian Affairs*, pp. 165–71.

[50] Jedidah Morse, *A Report to the Secretary of War of the United States, on Indian Affairs, Comprising a Narrative of a Tour Performed in the Summer of 1820* (New Haven, 1822), Appendix 4.

the spring of 1801: "Several parts of a large field were ploughed, and the intermediate spaces prepared by their women with the hoe, according to former custom."[51] As the "mistresses of the earth," Iroquois women had an important stake in the effects of plow agriculture. For this period Diane Rothenberg has ably chronicled and explained the selective responses of Seneca women to Quaker efforts at teaching them spinning and weaving. While seeing gains in the knowledge of new household skills, they also resisted displacement from their traditional place in the fields by limiting the extent to which new agricultural methods were adopted.[52]

Adoption of new agricultural methods was by no means a panacea for the problems faced by Iroquois communities during the Jeffersonian era. More intensive production of one or two crops and greater reliance upon livestock for food and energy occasioned some unfortunate incidents. Tuscaroras who had been promised implements of husbandry by the federal government found themselves at the mercy of the Chapin brothers, who charged them dearly for everything, including items that were expected as gifts.[53] The federal government's practice of rewarding selected individuals and communities for adopting its plan more rapidly than others threatened to divide Iroquois people with inequality and jealousy. "If you do right," advised Red Jacket early in the process, "you will give to all something to work with as fast as they learn, so that all may be supplied; otherwise a strife will arise."[54] Ownership of livestock exposed

[51] Wallace, *Death and Rebirth of the Seneca*, p. 311.

[52] Diane Rothenberg, "The Mothers of the Nation: Seneca Resistance to Quaker Intervention," in Mona Etienne and Eleanor Burke Leacock, eds., *Women and Colonization: Anthropological Perspectives* (New York, 1980), pp. 63–87. Also see Joan M. Jensen, "Native American Women and Agriculture: A Seneca Case Study," *Sex Roles: A Journal of Research* 3 (1977):423–41, reprinted in her *Promise to the Land: Essays on Rural Women* (Albuquerque, N.M., 1991), pp. 133–52; and Nancy Shoemaker, "The Rise or Fall of Iroquois Women," *Journal of Women's History* 2 (1991):39–57.

[53] Communication from Tuscarora Chiefs, Apr. 26, 1799, enclosed in James McHenry to Israel Chapin, May 10, 1799, O'Reilly Papers. Also in *Iroquois Indians*, roll 44.

[54] Stone, *Life and Times of Red-Jacket*, pp. 84–85.

Indians to frequent acts of theft, as indicated in the many reports of horses and cattle lost to white poachers. Periodic setbacks in farm production, like damage to crops from frost or
drought, painfully alerted the Iroquois to the risks involved in
letting agriculture supersede other means of procuring food.[55]

Contrary to impressions left by national leaders, hunting in
western New York remained a viable economic activity in the
early nineteenth century. As Red Jacket remarked in October
1800, "You white people are very fond of our skins."[56] Traders
at Pittsburgh, Niagara, and Syracuse continued to buy skins,
bear oil, and other products from Iroquois hunters. Summer-
time hunting by men and wintertime expeditions by family
groups were still part of the seasonal cycle of subsistence and
trade. When the Rev. Roswell Burrows visited Cattaraugus in
late October 1806, most of the villagers were away hunting. In
1809 John Norton was told by his host at Allegany "that the
Friends had taught several of their people to plow, and to do
Blacksmith work, and some of their women to spin, so that the
people of the Village had made some advances in industry; but
that many found it more their interest to hunt than to work;
that for his part, he had acquired all his property by hunting, and that with the produce of the Chace, he had hired
people to build and to work for him."[57] Describing the Tona-
wanda Senecas in 1818, Estwick Evans reported: "They employ
the principal part of the summer in the chase. In autumn they
again engage in the business. This is their most important season, on account of the greater relative value of furs. During the
winter they return home, laden with peltry, smoaked flesh of

---

[55] Charles M. Snyder, ed., *Red and White on the New York Frontier, a Struggle for
Survival: Insights from the Papers of Erastus Granger, Indian Agent, 1807–1819*
(Harrison, N.Y., 1978), pp. 31–34; "An Act for the Relief of the St. Regis,
Oneida, Onondaga, and Seneca Indians" [1817], *Laws of the Colonial and State
Governments, Relating to Indians and Indian Affairs, from 1633 to 1831, Inclusive*
(Washington, D.C., 1832), p. 92.

[56] "Letters of Holmes," p. 199.

[57] "Visit to Buffalo, in 1806, of the Rev. Roswell Burrows," ed. Frank H. Severance, *Publications of the Buffalo Historical Society* 6 (1903):235; Carl F. Klinck
and James J. Talman, eds., *The Journal of Major John Norton, 1816* (Toronto,
1970), p. 9.

various kinds, and the fat of bears. Last season they were very successful."[58]

For as long as possible, many Iroquois families tried to preserve hunting as one of their sources of income in an annual round of farming, gathering, and fishing. But there is also plenty of evidence that Indians in western New York sought to incorporate new economic activities into their traditional pattern of livelihood in order to maximize flexibility. Herding livestock and timbering, even plowing and harvesting for wages, allowed men to tap into the encroaching commercial economy without sacrificing their physical mobility. Allegany Senecas cut timber at their own sawmill and floated the boards down to Pittsburgh during high water season. On rafts formed from cut boards, as merchant John Wrenshall noted in 1816, "they bring their peltry, furrs, and good canoes, to push up their return cargoes . . . and sometimes shingls, the latter of which I have bought for one dollar and fifty cents per thousand and paid for them in merchandise." Quaker reformers inquired the following year whether the Indians "would not have been in a better situation generally if you had employed the same time which you have spent in cutting and rafting timber in cultivating your good land." They concluded, as we might expect, that such activity "has much retarded their progress in agriculture."[59]

The forms of economic adaptation improvised by the Iroquois in the face of Jeffersonian agrarianism contributed in the long run to their endurance through the nineteenth century and to the present. In his census of the New York Iroquois communities published in 1847, Henry Schoolcraft described a livelihood that mixed a diversity of activities: the cultivation of various crops, hunting and gathering, the raising of livestock, and harvest work on neighboring white farms.[60] This and other evidence, nevertheless, did not stop American intellectuals

---

[58] Estwick Evans, *A Pedestrious Tour, of Four Thousand Miles, through the Western States and Territories, during the Winter and Spring of 1818*, in Reuben Gold Thwaites, ed., *Early Western Travels, 1748–1846*, 32 vols. (Cleveland, 1904–7), 8:155.

[59] Rothenberg, "Mothers of the Nation," pp. 71–79.

[60] Henry Rowe Schoolcraft, *Notes on the Iroquois; or, Contributions to American History, Antiquities, and General Ethnology* (Albany, 1847), pp. 10–21, 32–38.

and politicians from continuing to portray Indian economies as fundamentally in a hunter state. Carroll Smith-Rosenberg has recently explained how intertwined such a construction of negative Others was with the definition of citizenship during the early national period of the United States. Like the white middle-class woman and the African-American slave, the American Indian warrior was represented in contrast to the idealized male, middle-class citizen—veiling contradictions in the new nation's political ideology and rhetoric.[61]

The increasing drive for more Indian lands helped popularize the Jeffersonian model, with both friends and foes of American Indians invoking the image of nomadic hunters. In proposing his Indian removal bill before Congress in 1830, Andrew Jackson declared that "philanthropy could not wish to see this continent restored to the condition in which it was found by our forefathers. What good man would prefer a country covered with forests and ranged by a few thousand savages to our extensive Republic."[62] Henry Thoreau, whose romantic sympathy for Indians clashed with Jackson's policy, accepted that for survival the Indian "must seize hold of a plow-tail and let go his bow and arrow." But he confessed remorse over this choice: "They seem to me a distinct and equally respectable people, born to wander and to hunt, and not to be inoculated with the twilight civilization of the white man."[63] In the first ethnographic study of the Iroquois, Lewis Henry Morgan concluded that "the passion of the red man for the hunter life has proved to be a principle too deeply inwrought, to be controlled by efforts of legislation."[64]

From this kind of rhetoric, historians must now rescue the

[61] Carroll Smith-Rosenberg, "Dis-Covering the Subject of the 'Great Constitutional Discussion,' 1786–1789," *Journal of American History* 79 (1992): 841–73. Also see Eve Kornfeld, "Encountering 'the Other': American Intellectuals and Indians in the 1790s," *William and Mary Quarterly*, 3d ser. 52 (1995):287–314.

[62] Frederick M. Binder, *The Color Problem in Early National America as Viewed by John Adams, Jefferson, and Jackson* (The Hague, 1968), p. 150.

[63] Robert F. Sayre, *Thoreau and the American Indians* (Princeton, 1977), p. 21.

[64] Lewis Henry Morgan, *League of the Ho-dé-no-sau-nee, or Iroquois* (Rochester, N.Y., 1851), p. 57.

more complex means of livelihood and forms of socioeconomic change that were invented by American Indians. During the early national period of United States history, when Jeffersonians imposed a very narrow definition of agriculture on the scene, the Iroquois nations had to make some difficult adjustments. While government agents and religious emissaries promoted agricultural reform, land speculators and land-hungry settlers demanded further cessions. But while the Iroquois people struggled to adapt their livelihood to a shrinking land base, no amount of accommodation to the federal government's prescriptions seemed to deflect pressures for more Indian territory. When Red Jacket learned in 1819 that President James Monroe was recommending removal from Buffalo Creek, the Seneca leader angrily pointed to the plows, fences, and livestock successfully adopted by his people over the years. "The different claims you tell us of," Red Jacket quipped, "I cannot understand. We were placed here by the Great Spirit for purposes known to him. You can have no right to interfere. You told us that we had large and many unproductive tracts of land. We do not view it so. Our seats we consider small; and if left here long by the Great Spirit we shall stand in need of them. We shall want timber. Land after the improvements of many years wears out. We shall want to renew our fields; and we do not think that there is any land in any of our reservations, but what is useful."[65]

---

[65] Snyder, ed., *Red and White*, p. 94.

JOEL W. MARTIN

Cultural Contact and Crises in the Early Republic

Native American Religious Renewal, Resistance, and Accommodation

IN THE DAYS of the early republic, white settlers invaded the southeastern interior in unprecedented numbers and introduced a new order hostile to the very existence of Indians in the region. Southeastern Indians responded with a variety of strategies. Some emigrated. A small and highly visible elite turned toward white ways and became commercial planters and slave owners. A much larger number pursued alternative paths designed to prevent the extinction of their cultures. As residents of homelands being occupied by a hostile, alien force, this group relied increasingly upon a kind of cultural "underground," a hidden set of beliefs and practices that reinforced their identity as Indians and strengthened their will to survive and resist. This essay unearths the underground developed by Cherokees and Muskogee Creeks.[1]

This essay benefited from comments by Mary Elizabeth Young, Frederick E. Hoxie, Peter H. Wood, Stephen Aron, and James H. Merrell.

[1] This new order replaced an older one characterized by mutual accommodation. For stimulating works that focus on cross-cultural exchange in the colonial Southeast, see Daniel H. Usner, Jr., *Indians, Settlers, and Slaves in a Frontier Exchange Economy: The Lower Mississippi Valley before 1783* (Chapel Hill,

The necessity for a cultural underground emerged earlier among the Cherokees, a people who, unlike the Creeks, were defeated militarily during the American Revolution. Before the Revolution, Cherokees, like other large groups of southeastern Indians in the interior, had succeeded fairly well in requiring the English to accommodate to indigenous cultural and political expectations. Cherokee men and women traded frequently and successfully with the English. While Cherokee men traded deerskins, human captives, and horses for guns, paint, rum, mirrors, and many other items that they adapted to their own ends, Cherokee women traded food, herbs, and cane baskets for clothes, money, bread, and butter. Cherokee women formed sexual liaisons with English traders and gave birth to and raised métis children who later played a very important role in Cherokee society. In sum, Cherokee men and women had handled cross-cultural contact and exchange very successfully. They had accommodated to material, economic, social, and political changes within traditional patterns and routines.[2]

It required several generations of English and Cherokee efforts to build this "middle ground,"[3] a set of relationships, inter-

---

N.C., 1992), Tom Hatley, *The Dividing Paths: Cherokees and South Carolinians through the Era of Revolution* (New York, 1993), Peter H. Wood, Gregory A. Waselkov, and Marvin Thomas Hatley, eds., *Powhatan's Mantle: Indians in the Colonial Southeast* (Lincoln, Nebr., 1989), and Kathryn E. Holland Braund, *Deerskins and Duffels: The Creek Indian Trade with Anglo-America, 1685–1815* (Lincoln, Nebr., 1993).

[2] James H. Merrell, "'Our Bond of Peace': Patterns of Intercultural Exchange in the Carolina Piedmont, 1650–1750," in Wood, Waselkov, and Hatley, eds., *Powhatan's Mantle*, pp. 198–204; Gary C. Goodwin, *Cherokees in Transition: A Study of Changing Culture and Environment prior to 1775* (Chicago, 1977), p. 94. Hatley argues that Carolinians and Cherokees developed "a trading vernacular, which combined cross-cultural civilities and specific accommodations" (*Dividing Paths*, p. 47).

[3] As Richard White demonstrates, in a place beyond the effective control of empires and world-systems, the Algonquians and French cocreated a multidimensional network of cross-cultural ties that enabled them to engage in reciprocal forms of exchange. This network White calls the "middle ground." It depended upon political innovation. New kinds of political figures, alliance chiefs, emerged to mediate between nonhierarchical Algonquian villagers. The network also depended upon other kinds of relationships, including

actions, and altered identities, but it took only a single generation to destroy it. Two wars did the fatal damage. During the first, the Cherokee-Carolina war of 1759–61, many Cherokee towns were burned by white troops, their stores of corn and beans ruined. This caused Cherokees to reappraise their relationship with Carolinians. After the war the Cherokees curtailed their economic contact and political engagement.[4] Meanwhile, Carolinians also devalued trade with Cherokees, their former enemies. During the 1760s English refugees from Indian attacks in Virginia settled in the Carolina backcountry in great numbers. They had no tolerance for Indians or those who traded with them. They ostracized and attacked traders. Intercultural exchange, the main bridge between Carolinians and Cherokees, was dismantled as new forms of cultural and racial

---

some that were not strictly political. A rich range of cross-cultural exchanges, focused on sex, violence, and trade, was pursued. In dealing with each other, the Algonquians and French discovered that they could advance their own interests by appealing to the values of the other culture. Cultural congruences, whether actual or only perceived, provided mutual intelligibility. New or significantly modified rituals and myths emerged to represent and structure life on the middle ground. By the eighteenth century, the middle ground shaped human existence in the Great Lakes region. No one could escape the historical pressure to negotiate and compromise. When Algonquian alliance chiefs, like Pontiac, presumed to act as if they had supreme power, they failed miserably. When French authorities tried to substitute force for mediation or corrupt gifts into loans, they lost influence among the Algonquians (*The Middle Ground: Indians, Empires, and Republics in the Great Lakes Region, 1650– 1815* [Cambridge, 1991], pp. 38–40, 79, 84–90, 114–15, 175, 179–80, 202, 312–13). White says the metaphor of the middle ground can be applied to other regions (p. x). It certainly describes the colonial Southeast. During the colonial period, Europeans gained much from accommodation with the large interior groups of southeastern Indians, and these peoples gained much from accommodation with Europeans. Participation in the middle ground linked southeastern peoples to powerful allies; brought them large supplies of gifts; great quantities of cloth and later rum; introduced them to novel animals, foodstuffs, technologies, and social practices; and gave them sustained exposure to new ideas, religious visions, and expressive cultures. Great changes ensued. Over time, political, material, and cultural hybridity became the norm, not the anomaly.

[4] John R. Alden, *John Stuart and the Southern Colonial Frontier* (Ann Arbor, Mich., 1944), pp. 208, 298–301; Hatley, *Dividing Paths*, pp. 160–66.

hatred became the norm. How the Cherokees responded to this new situation was shaped in large measure by their decentralized, noncoercive form of governance.[5]

Throughout the eighteenth century, both villages and villagers operated with considerable autonomy. Although Cherokees seemed somewhat closer to creating a state than were other southeastern Indians, Cherokees of this period gave their primary political loyalties to their individual villages. Although some national organizations existed, villages had a great say in shaping their relations with the rest of the world. Influenced by regionalism, local leadership, unique historical experiences, and a host of other variables, villages often adopted divergent stances toward the English. Additionally, within any given village, no individual leader or governing body could coerce people to obey their decisions. Headmen might decide to promote neutrality, but groups of villagers might decide for war.[6]

During the 1760s and 1770s, Cherokee headmen ceded great quantities of land to the English to cover trade debts. Not surprisingly, Cherokees who disliked these cessions did not hesitate to express their frustrations.[7] The most bitter opposition came in response to treaties signed in 1771, 1775, and 1777. Since these treaties ceded millions of acres north of the Cumberland River, they most directly affected Cherokees living in the western section of Cherokee country, the so-called Overhills villages, many of which were on the Tennessee River or its tributaries. In these villages, many young Cherokee men felt that the loss of these prime hunting lands would force a change in Cherokee subsistence, a shift away from hunting and toward

[5] David Cockran, *The Cherokee Frontier, 1540–1783* (Norman, Okla., 1962), pp. 194, 256–65; Hatley, *Dividing Paths*, pp. 141–90.

[6] Duane Champagne, *Social Order and Political Change: Constitutional Governments among the Cherokee, the Choctaw, the Chickasaw, and the Creek* (Stanford, Calif., 1992), pp. 25, 28, 39, 57–59, 74–77.

[7] Alden, *Southern Frontier*, pp. 187, 208, 298, 303; Louis DeVorsey, *The Indian Boundary in the Southern Colonies, 1763–1775* (Chapel Hill, N.C., 1966), pp. 102, 116, 126, 128, 133, 135; Duane H. King, "Long Island of the Holston: Sacred Cherokee Ground," *Journal of Cherokee Studies* (1976):113–27; Hatley, *Dividing Paths*, pp. 216–28.

raising livestock. They also feared that whites were surrounding them. A leader named Dragging Canoe declared, "It seemed to be the intention of the white people to destroy them from being a people."[8] Speaking for young Cherokee men, he said his people did not want to rely upon domesticated animals for subsistence. The Maker had given tame animals to whites and wild ones to Indians. Not wanting to be penned up like hogs by encircling white settlers, Dragging Canoe and his followers determined to maintain open access to traditional hunting grounds. During the mid-1770s they went on the offensive. Seceding from the rest of their people, they left their respective villages and formed a new settlement on the Tennessee river called Chickamauga.[9]

The people of Chickamauga maligned those Cherokees who did not join them with the hated name of "Virginians." They called themselves *Ani-yuni'wiya*, or "real people."[10] Because they opposed white domination, emphasized the cultural division between whites and Indians, and rejected certain aspects of European civilization, we might call them "nativists." Yet that label is too simplistic, and it is pejorative.[11] The Chickamaugans

---

[8] Henry Stuart, "Account of His Proceedings with the Indians, Pensacola, August 25, 1776" [C.O. 5/7, 333–78, Public Record Office], in William L. Saunders, ed., *The Colonial Records of North Carolina, 1662–1776*, 30 vols. (Raleigh, 1886–1914), 10:764.

[9] Samuel Coles Williams, ed., *Adair's History of the American Indians* (Johnson City, Tenn., 1930), pp. 138–39; DeVorsey, *Indian Boundary*, pp. 74–85; Hatley, *Dividing Paths*, pp. 218–28; Gregory Evans Dowd, *A Spirited Resistance: The North American Indian Struggle for Unity, 1745–1815* (Baltimore, 1992), p. 54.

[10] James Paul Pate, "The Chickamaugas: A Forgotten Segment of Indian Resistance on the Southern Frontier," Ph.D. diss., Mississippi State University, 1969, p. 81; John P. Brown, *Old Frontiers: The Story of the Cherokee Indians from Earliest Times to the Date of Their Removal to the West, 1838* (Kingsport, Tenn., 1938), pp. 165–67.

[11] *Nativism* has negative connotations. Contemporary scholars associate nativism with closed-mindedness, ethnocentrism, racist attitudes, and a surrender of reason. See the way the word is used in current abstracts in *Dissertation Abstracts International, Part A: Humanities and Social Sciences* (Ann Arbor, Mich., 1969–).

showed considerable openness to cultural pluralism. They fostered direct ties to other indigenous groups and to the British in Pensacola. Chickamauga's inhabitants included Cherokees, Cherokee métis, Muskogees, and British loyalists. In 1776 the Chickamaugans attacked the Virginians who had settled in the Watauga Valley, and during subsequent years many bloody exchanges followed.[12]

Most Cherokees did not join the Chickamaugans. Nevertheless, they were caught up in the warfare of the American Revolution. During the summer of 1776, thousands of whig troops invaded Cherokee country. Motivated by the rhetoric of genocide and enslavement, they destroyed Cherokee habitations, orchards, and crops. Several subsequent campaigns attested to the determination of whites to destroy the Cherokee people. While they did not succeed in this goal, whites did destroy the middle ground once and for all. By 1777 the old patterns of mutual accommodation were gone. Whites no longer showed Cherokees respect, and Cherokees could not forget how whites had stained their hands with the blood of Cherokee women and children.[13]

After their defeat in the American Revolution, most Cherokees in the Carolinas adopted a strategy of nonmilitant separatism. They developed a cultural underground, a set of practices and beliefs that reinforced linguistic, cultural, ethical, and religious boundaries between themselves and whites. If they could not preserve physical distance and political independence, they could at least bolster symbolic distinctions in many areas of life and protect the core of their identity. For instance, Cherokees fluent in English pretended they did not understand it when addressed by Americans. As they had long done, Cherokees

[12] Dowd, *Spirited Resistance*, pp. 48–56. Although Dowd argues that it is appropriate to use the term *nativism* to describe several movements of Indian resistance (pp. xxi–xxii), he does not apply the term to the Chickamaugans. He asserts that their movement occurred during a period when religious nativism was "muted" (p. 49).

[13] For the 1776 intercolonial expedition and its consequences, see James H. O'Donnell III, *Southern Indians in the American Revolution* (Knoxville, Tenn., 1973), pp. 34–69, 118–19; Hatley, *Dividing Paths*.

continued to keep their sacred rituals secret. Additionally, it may have been around this time that they began performing a dance that satirized negative traits associated with whites. Among themselves, Cherokees danced the Booger Dance, in which masked Cherokee men pretended to be Europeans: "awkward, ridiculous, lewd and menacing."[14]

Just as the dance dramatized the difference between whites and Indians, myths describing the separate creation of human races became widely popular among the Cherokees. Originating among Indian prophets in the eighteenth century, the theory of racial polygenesis held that "red" people were fundamentally different from "white" people. Some Cherokees were proponents of the theory as early as 1799. In 1811 a Cherokee prophet promoted a small revitalization movement saying the following: "You yourselves can see that the white people are entirely different beings from us; we are made of red clay; they, out of white sand." Evidently, by that time at a popular level Cherokees had come to assume the difference between whites and Indians to be ontological: sacred and permanent.[15]

On a less metaphysical plane, many post-Revolutionary Cherokees created distance between themselves and whites by relying increasingly upon métis individuals to serve as cultural intermediaries. These individuals were perfectly poised to play such a role. Bicultural progeny of English fathers and Cherokee mothers, they owned a disproportionate number of slaves and increasingly modeled their lifestyle on that of white planters. At

[14] For the Booger Dance and secret rituals, see Frank G. Speck and Leonard Broom, *Cherokee Dance and Drama* (Berkeley, Calif., 1951), pp. 36–39; Raymond D. Fogelson and Amelia B. Walker, "Self and Other in Cherokee Booger Dances," *Journal of Cherokee Studies* 5 (1980):88–102; Hatley, *Dividing Paths*, pp. 235–36.

[15] For stories of separate creation and distinct destinies, see Edmund de Schweinitz, ed. and trans., "The Narrative of Marie Le Roy and Barbara Leiniger," *Pennsylvania Archives*, 2d ser., 19 vols. (Harrisburg, 1874–90):7; James Mooney, *The Ghost-Dance Religion and Wounded Knee* (New York, 1973), p. 677; William G. McLoughlin, *Cherokees and Missionaries, 1789–1839* (New Haven, 1984), pp. 91, 97; idem, *The Cherokee Ghost Dance: Essays on the Southeastern Indian, 1789–1861* (Macon, Ga., 1984), pp. 253–60; Dowd, *Spirited Resistance*, pp. 21, 63.

a time when many Cherokees were trying to differentiate themselves symbolically from whites, these individuals were identifying more openly with white ways. Their role as cultural brokers was crucial for several decades.[16]

The métis elite accepted Protestant missionaries into their midst, became producers of crops and livestock for white markets, and eventually reorganized the Cherokee polity by forming a constitutional government (1827).[17] During the 1820s the Cherokee elite attracted national praise. Anglo writers heralded their agrarian, mercantile, religious, and social achievements. In his *Remarks on the Practicability of Indian Reform* (1828), Isaac McCoy, eager to convince policymakers and church officials that Indians could be civilized, pointed to the Cherokee countryside. "Numerous flocks of sheep, goats, and swine, cover the vallies and hills. . . . The natives carry on a considerable trade with the adjoining States. . . . Apple and peach orchards are quite common, and gardens are cultivated. . . . Butter and cheese are seen on Cherokee tables. There are many publick roads in the nation, and houses of entertainment kept by natives. Numerous flourishing villages are seen in every section of the country. . . . The population is rapidly increasing. . . . Some of the most influential characters are members of the church, and live consistently with their professions. Schools are increasing every year; learning is encouraged and rewarded. The fe-

---

[16] For métis mediators, see Ronald N. Satz, "Cherokee Traditionalism, Protestant Evangelism, and the Trail of Tears, Part II," *Tennessee Historical Quarterly* 44 (1985):380–402; Hatley, *Dividing Paths*, pp. 61, 207–10, 220–21, 228. For métis slaveowning, see Theda Perdue, *Slavery and the Evolution of Cherokee Society, 1540–1866* (Knoxville, Tenn., 1979), pp. 57–60.

[17] See William G. McLoughlin, "Who Civilized the Cherokees?" *Journal of Cherokee Studies* 13 (1988):55–81; Douglas C. Wilms, "Cherokee Acculturation and Changing Land Use Practices," *Chronicles of Oklahoma* 56 (1978): 331–43; Marguerite McFadden, "The Saga of 'Rich Joe' Vann," *Chronicles of Oklahoma* 61 (1983):68–79; Michelle Daniel, "From Blood Feud to Jury System: The Metamorphosis of Cherokee Law from 1750 to 1840," *American Indian Quarterly* 11 (1987):97–125. Cherokee slave owners, like Muskogees, were usually lenient when compared to whites. See Theda Perdue, "Cherokee Planters, Black Slaves, and African Colonization," *Chronicles of Oklahoma* 60 (1982):322–31; William G. McLoughlin, *Cherokee Renascence in the New Republic* (Princeton, 1986); Champagne, *Social Order and Political Change.*

male character is elevated and duly respected."[18] McCoy concluded that the Cherokees as a whole were "a *civilized* people." Another commentator agreed, saying that the "Cherokees have the aspect, and the elements, at least, of a regular, civilized, Christian nation."[19] The Cherokees, it was implied, were exceptional Indians.

But when white commentators like McCoy described Cherokee society, they were really only describing the lifestyle and values of the Cherokee elite. As one missionary admitted, he worked primarily with "persons who speak both languages; as half-breeds, whites brought up in the nation, or married into Indian families, or otherwise dependent on them. This class of people have always been *the connecting link* between the Indians and the whites."[20] Dependent upon this class of mediators, whites inevitably knew the members of that class better than they knew the majority of Cherokees with whom they had less direct contact. This state of affairs may have been precisely the one ordinary Cherokees desired. Métis mediators provided them with a very useful and effective screen behind which they could continue to lead traditional lives beyond the gaze of whites. In effect, Cherokees used the métis to connect them to and shield them from a dominant public order organized around threatening values.

A comparison of elite and nonelite responses to Christianity underscores the difference between the two groups. During the 1820s Cherokees were missionized more than any group of interior Indians. Four denominations (Presbyterian, Moravian, Baptist, and Methodist) vied for converts. In 1827 these denominations supported eight Indian schools and seventy-one teachers who directly affected the lives of two hundred Cherokee boys and girls. Nevertheless, in 1830, these denominations

[18] Isaac McCoy, *The Practicability of Indian Reform, Embracing Their Colonization* (Boston, 1827), pp. 27–28.

[19] Review of *The Practicability of Indian Reform, Embracing Their Colonization,* *American Baptist Magazine* 137 (1828):151. See also, McLoughlin, *Cherokee Renascence,* pp. 277–301.

[20] Letter from Evan Jones, May 1, 1828, *American Baptist Magazine* 139 (1828):213 (emphasis mine).

could only claim thirteen hundred members out of a total Cherokee population exceeding fifteen thousand. Within the pool of converts, one would find almost all of the members of the Cherokee elite.[21]

Ninety percent of the Cherokee people did not have significant contact with Christian missionaries. Among the 10 percent of Cherokees who were exposed directly to Christianity, many were persuaded by arguments circulating among the Cherokees against the alien religion. An epistemological argument held that Christians' stories were "mere legendary tales." An ontological argument reasoned that since "the Cherokees were a different race from the whites," they could have "no concern in the white people's religion." And an ethical argument, after observing how Christians acted, concluded Christians were hypocrites. Rather than adopt the new religion, they continued to tell sacred stories, participate in rituals, and practice values cherished by their ancestors. Even among the small number of Cherokees who attended Christian services regularly, most refused to forsake entirely their traditional practices.[22]

The great majority of Cherokees did not convert to Christianity, attend school, hold elected office, run houses of entertainment, own slaves, or publish newspapers.[23] Literacy, another aspect of "civilization" embraced by the elite, also elicited nega-

[21] "Official Statement of Indian Schools," *American Baptist Magazine* 134 (1828):64; McLoughlin, *Cherokees and Missionaries*, p. 175.

[22] For mere legends and hypocrites, see *American Baptist Magazine* 132 (1827):364. For a different race, see *American Baptist Magazine* 100 (1825): 111. For majority participation in a traditional rite (a new year ceremony), see *American Baptist Magazine* 141 (1828):269. For simultaneous participation in Christianity and traditional religion, see Isaac Proctor to Jeremiah Evarts, Dec. 11, 1827, American Board of Commissioners for Foreign Missions, Houghton Library, Harvard University, Cambridge, Mass.

[23] When he read Isaac McCoy's essay on Indian civilization, Lee Compere commented that he thought McCoy was correct in general but that he had "viewed the Cherokees in a too favourable light." Compere did not want to minimize the cultural distance between the Indians and the surrounding white population, or underestimate the prejudice of the latter (Journal of Lee Compere, postscript, March 1828, American Indian Correspondence, American Baptist Foreign Mission Societies, Records, 1817–1959, American Baptist Historical Society, Rochester, N.Y.).

tive responses from ordinary Cherokees. Cherokees and other southeastern Indians experienced literacy as an essential part of white domination.[24] Literacy was associated primarily with missionaries, government agents, treaty negotiators, land speculators, and powerful traders. Literacy was linked to people who routinely denigrated Cherokee religion, tried to control Cherokee politics, and defrauded Cherokees of their lands. Given these associations, it is not surprising that most Cherokees did not try to learn to read and write. As one of their myths revealed, they felt that literacy, like Christianity, belonged exclusively to white people. According to the myth, in the beginning, the Maker had given the book to the Indian, the real or genuine man. When the Indian was not paying attention, however, the tricky white man stole the book. As a consequence of that primordial theft, the white man has since had an easy life, and the Indian has been compelled to gain his subsistence by hunting.[25]

[24] Muskogees, for instance, felt alienated from literacy. In the Redstick movement, prophets and warriors were concerned to show access to and mastery over the signs and tools of civilization, including literacy. During the summer of 1813, prophets claimed they had a letter from a commanding officer of the British in Detroit: "If they would Carry it to Pensacolah that the Spaniards or British would furnish them with Arms and aminition or anything that they wanted" ("Testimony of James Moore," July 13, 1813, Creek Indian Letters, Talks, and Treaties, 1705–1839, p. 785, Department of Archives and History of the State of Georgia, Atlanta; see also Benjamin Hawkins, *Letters, Journals, and Writings*, 2 vols., ed. C. L. Grant [Savannah, 1980], 2:655). On another occasion, one of the inspired Muskogee prophets claimed that he could speak and write all languages. With this single dramatic gesture, the prophet undermined European claims to superiority based on literacy and the historic linkage of writing with domination. Literacy had often been used against the Muskogees' interests or lorded over them, but, in both of these instances, the inspired prophets sought to use the sign and symbol of literacy for anticolonial purposes. See Theron Nunez, "Creek Nativism and the Creek War of 1813–1814," *Ethnohistory* 6 (1958):151.

[25] The myth is related in Grant Foreman, *Sequoyah* (Norman, Okla., 1938), p. 21: "In the beginning God created the Indian, the real or genuine man, and the white man. The Indian was the elder and in his hands the Creator placed a book; in the hands of the other he placed a bow and arrow, with a command that they should make good use of them. The Indian was very slow in receiving the book, and appeared so indifferent about it that the white man came and stole it from him when his attention was directed another way. He was

All of this changed in 1821 when Sequoyah, the son of a European man and a Cherokee woman, created a syllabary, a set of written symbols representing the basic sounds of the Cherokee language.[26] The syllabary was a cultural hybrid. It was European in form (the symbols were written and read) and Cherokee in content (the symbols represented spoken Cherokee). But if we would appreciate fully Sequoyah's achievement we need to go beyond noting its bicultural roots. Sequoyah's syllabary precipitated a movement of significant cultural renewal in the early 1820s among common Cherokee men and women.[27]

When Sequoyah through his syllabary made literacy in Cherokee possible, Cherokee men and women thought initially he had done something magical. Because they associated literacy with a use of power for destructive purposes, they thought Sequoyah's efforts were delirious or idiotic.[28] Soon, however,

---

then compelled to take the bow and arrow, and gain his subsistence by pursuing the chase. He had thus forfeited the book which his Creator had placed in his hands and which now belonged to his white brother." Another version of the myth, recorded by a Moravian in 1815, is reprinted in Clemens de Baillou, "A Contribution to the Mythology and Conceptual World of the Cherokee Indians," *Ethnohistory* 8 (1961):100–102. So thorough was the association of the English language and oppression that many Cherokees not only avoided literacy, they pretended they could not speak English, even if they were fluent. Better to avoid speaking it, lest you were forced to reveal something you wanted to hide. See Hatley, *Dividing Paths*, p. 234.

[26] Historians are uncertain of Sequoyah's paternity. Possible fathers include George Gist, who was said to have been "an unlicensed German peddler," and Nathaniel Gist, an English soldier and trader. See Albert V. Goodpasture, "The Paternity of Sequoya, the Inventor of the Cherokee Alphabet," *Chronicles of Oklahoma* 1 (1921):121–30; and Samuel Cole Williams, "The Father of Sequoyah: Nathaniel Gist," *Chronicles of Oklahoma* 15 (1937):3–20. At the time of Sequoyah's birth, his mother resided in Tuskegee. Sequoyah grew up among "fullbloods in the Lower Town region" (William G. McLoughlin, *Cherokees and Missionaries*, p. 183).

[27] See McLoughlin, *Cherokee Renascence*, pp. 350–54. During a conversation in July 1991 in Lexington, Kentucky, Theda Perdue directed my attention to this subject.

[28] "During the time he was occupied in inventing the alphabet, he was strenuously opposed by all his friends and neighbors. He was frequently told

Sequoyah convinced them through public demonstrations that he had done nothing magical or crazy, that anyone could learn to write the Cherokee language. Cherokees realized that here was new power that could be employed to preserve the core of Cherokee identity. From that point on, they showed zeal in learning and teaching the syllabary. White observers were astounded at how the new mode of writing caught on. In 1824 they reported that "the Knowledge of Mr. Guess's Alphabet is spreading through the nation like fire among the leaves." By 1825 the majority of Cherokees had learned the system, and "letters in Cherokee were passing in all directions."[29] With every letter written, nonelite Cherokees strengthened their own culture and implicitly refuted white claims to superiority. White culture was no more sacred than was the culture of the Cherokees. Or, to put it another way, Cherokee culture was no less sacred than that of whites. By taking the tools and symbols associated with the invading culture and turning them to countercolonial purposes, Sequoyah produced a written language that served as "virtually a code to sustain the traditional community *beyond the perception* of the authorities, red or white." Sequoyah had given nonelite Cherokees a valuable way to nurture and preserve Cherokee identity during the very period when whites were invading their lands in unprecedented numbers. Though in theory whatever was written was public and could be read by whites literate in Cherokee, in practice the overwhelming majority of letters were never seen by whites.

---

that he was throwing away his time and labour, and that none but a delirious person, or an idiot, would do as he did" ("Invention of the Cherokee Alphabet," Aug. 13, 1828, *Cherokee Phoenix*). A subsequent biography implies that Sequoyah was accused of conjure. "By this time he had become so abstracted from his tribe and their usual pursuits, that he was viewed with an eye of suspicion. His former companions passed their home without entering it, and mentioned his name as one who was practicing improper spells, for notoriety or mischievous purposes" (Samuel Lorenzo Knapp, quoted in Foreman, *Sequoyah*, pp. 24–25).

[29] McLoughlin, *Cherokee Renascence*, pp. 352–53. For knowledge of the alphabet, see William Chamberlain's Journal, Oct. 22, 1824, American Board of Commissioners for Foreign Missions; for letters in Cherokee, see Isaac Proctor to Jeremiah Evarts, Jan. 25, 1825.

In effect, this kind of literacy nurtured, without betraying, the Cherokee underground.[30]

Literate or not, all Cherokees, including the elite, could not prevent the invasion of their land by thousands of outsiders. Whichever strategy of resistance or accommodation they employed, they were unable to overcome the fundamental power relations shaping their world during the period of the early republic. Whites entered their land by the thousands during the Gold Rush of 1829; Georgia extinguished Cherokee sovereignty on June 1, 1830; whites stole Cherokee property with impunity and drove Cherokees from their farms. In 1838 the great major of Cherokees (sixteen thousand people) were forced to remove west in a murderous march that cost them thousands of lives.[31] Two years earlier their Native neighbors to the south, the Muskogees, had been compelled to travel their own "Trail of Tears."[32] In essence, both southeastern peoples were forced to leave their ancestral homes by whites who wanted Indian lands for cotton culture.

If Muskogee and Cherokee experiences of dispossession and removal in the 1830s seem very similar, their earlier experiences with the white invasion were distinct in some very important ways. Geography was key. Because the Muskogees were situated

---

[30] McLoughlin, *Cherokees and Missionaries*, p. 186 (emphasis mine). Precisely because nonelite Cherokees used the syllabary to express cultural autonomy, Cherokee literacy threatened Protestant missionaries (p. 185).

[31] Harold David Williams, "The North Georgia Gold Rush," Ph.D. diss., Auburn University, 1988; Mary Elizabeth Young, "Racism in Red and Black: Indians and Other Free People of Color in Georgia Law, Politics, and Removal Policy," *Georgia Historical Quarterly* 73 (1988):492–518; Russell Thornton, "The Demography of the Trail of Tears Period: A New Estimate of Cherokee Population Losses," in William L. Anderson, ed., *Cherokee Removal: Before and After* (Athens, Ga., 1991); David Kleit, "Living under the Threat and Promise of Removal: Conflict and Cooperation in the Cherokee Country during the 1830s" (Paper presented at the 1993 Conference of the Society for Historians of the Early American Republic, Chapel Hill, N.C., July 22, 1993).

[32] Mary Elizabeth Young, *Redskins, Ruffleshirts, and Rednecks: Indian Allotments in Alabama and Mississippi, 1830–1860* (Norman, Okla., 1961); Marvin L. Ellis III, "The Indian Fires Go Out: Removing the Creeks from Georgia and Alabama, 1825–1837," M.A. thesis, Auburn University, 1982.

much farther from the Carolina backcountry and because their trade was essential to backcountry Georgia, the Muskogees, unlike the Cherokees, were not targeted for massive anti-Indian violence during the 1760s or during the American Revolution. Muskogee towns survived the entire eighteenth century without being attacked by Europeans or Euro-Americans, a remarkable record for the eastern half of North America.

Nevertheless, if they successfully avoided the wars with whites that hurt Cherokees so badly, the Muskogees had faced some tough challenges during the eighteenth century. Beginning in the 1760s, Augusta merchants and traders had dramatically expanded the rum trade with the Muskogees. Over the next five decades, this trade increased the Muskogees' economic dependency, encouraged violence among villagers, promoted overhunting, precipitated an ecological crisis, and increased intertribal conflicts.[33] Eventually, the trade would provide whites

[33] Williams, ed., *Adair's History*, p. 35; Edmond Atkin, *Indians of the Southern Colonial Frontier: The Edmond Atkin Report and Plan of 1755*, ed. Wilbur Jacobs (Columbia, S.C., 1954), p. 35; William Bartram, *Travels* (1791; reprint ed., New York, 1988), pp. 53–62; David Taitt, "Journal of David Taitt's Travels from Pensacola, West Florida, to and through the Country of the Upper and Lower Creeks, 1772," in Newton D. Mereness, ed., *Travels in the American Colonies* (New York, 1916), pp. 507, 513, 524–25; Joel W. Martin, *Sacred Revolt: The Muskogees' Struggle for a New World* (Boston, 1991), pp. 65–69; Samuel J. Wells, "Rum, Skins, and Powder: A Choctaw Interpreter and the Treaty of Mount Dexter," *Chronicles of Oklahoma* 61 (1983–84):422–28; Blue Clark, "Chickasaw Colonization in Oklahoma," *Chronicles of Oklahoma* 54 (1976): 44–59; Richard White, *The Roots of Dependency: Subsistence, Environment, and Social Change among the Choctaws, Pawnees, and Navajos* (Lincoln, Nebr., 1983), pp. 69–92, 122. White places great weight on the role of rum in the destruction of the middle ground of the *pays d'en haut* (*Middle Ground*, pp. 238, 322, 334, 423, 491, 497–98). Compare Hatley, *Dividing Paths*, pp. 49, 89, 170; see also, William B. Taylor, *Drinking, Homicide and Rebellion in Colonial Mexican Villages* (Stanford, Calif., 1979), pp. 28, 59–72, 156–58. Liquor drinking seems to have been something that occurred primarily at the conclusion of the winter hunt and in the woods. Rum dealers intercepted hunters before they could return to their towns and exchange their skins with resident traders (Taitt, "Journal," p. 505; Williams, ed., *Adair's History*, p. 35; Atkin, *Indians of the Southern Colonial Frontier*, p. 35). This pattern of seasonal hard drinking in the woods apparently remained dominant during the first decade of the nineteenth century. Writing in 1805, the Quaker surveyor Isaac Briggs reported he had warned the Muskogees of "the pernicious effects of spirituous liquors."

with the means to force large cessions of land, cessions that would in turn inspire a movement of violent resistance among the Muskogees, the Redstick revolt of 1812–14. Only then would the Muskogees experience the kind of crushing military invasion that the Cherokees had faced decades earlier. This difference in timing is significant. It underscores the fact that the stories of Cherokee and Muskogee resistance are not identical. Rather, these stories converge and diverge in ways that warrant closer examination.[34]

Before the Redstick revolt, most Muskogees avoided massive conflicts by employing a range of small-scale modes of resistance. While less spectacular than the Redstick movement, these forms of resistance were very important throughout the period of the early republic, a time when domination was on the rise but not yet complete. Many elementary forms of resistance were performed in secret, in the woods, under the cover of darkness, or in a state of intoxication. During the 1790s, for example, as white encroachment made hunting on the Georgia-Muskogee frontier more difficult and dangerous, gangs of young Muskogee men began stealing whites' horses and slaves and selling them to complicit traders in Tennessee and Florida. Young men justified their acts as retaliation for white encroachment. When white hunting parties poached

---

He told Muskogees he had witnessed "traders on the frontiers selling this poison to some of their people." Liquor, he declared, "was indeed their most dangerous enemy, because not much suspected; and that if they indulged themselves in the use of it as they had done, it would destroy more of them than the gun, the sword, and the Tomahawk" (Isaac Briggs to Hannah Briggs, Mar. 16, 1805, Briggs-Stabler Collection, Ms. 147, Manuscripts Division, Maryland Historical Society, Baltimore). In appraising these and other sources, historians should consider the words of Moshulatubbee, a Choctaw chief during the 1820s, who tired of the negative judgments of missionaries. "I never can talk with you good missionaries without hearing something about the drunkenness and laziness of the Choctaws. I wish I had traveled over the white man's country; then I would know whether my people are worse than every other people" (Horatio Bardwell Cushman, *History of the Choctaw, Chickasaw, and Natchez Indians* [1899; reprint ed., Stillwater, Okla., 1962], p. 78).

[34] Peter H. Wood, "The Changing Population of the Colonial South: An Overview by Race and Region, 1685–1790," in Wood, Waselkov, and Hatley, eds., *Powhatan's Mantle*, pp. 35–103, esp. pp. 59–60; Martin, *Sacred Revolt*, pp. 46–113.

their game, the Muskogees responded by killing the settlers' cattle. In a few instances, they murdered individual whites, took women and children captive, plundered the stores of traders, and burned settlers' farm buildings and houses. When white authorities demanded justice, headmen said they were powerless to provide it. They blamed the unruliness of young men whose "mischief" they could not prevent. Furthermore, many of the accused men said they had committed their crimes while drunk and therefore were not accountable.[35]

Muskogees found creative ways to frustrate dominating whites. Proselytized by Moravian missionaries, they dissembled and said they already knew everything about the Savior. Lectured by the United States agent on the merits of patrilineal kinship patterns or commercial agriculture, they turned silent or pretended they could not understand. Advised to cede land at treaty conferences, they recalled the great quantity of lands already lost, reminded United States officials of the promises of previous presidents, invoked the ways of their own ancestors,

[35] The primary documents abound with references such as "a horse stolen and a cow killed." White observers wrote frequently concerning "gangs of young men doing mischief." For stealing horses, abducting slaves, and killing cattle, see Timothy Barnard to Gov. George Hanley, Jan. 18, 1789, May 27, 1789, Nov. 6, 1789, Unpublished Letters of Timothy Barnard, 1784–1820, pp. 86, 94, 98, Dept. of Arch. and Hist. of Ga.; Barnard to James Seagrove, July 13, 1792, Apr. 19, 1793, June 20, 1793, ibid., pp. 120, 149, 174; Barnard to Maj. Henry Gaither, Mar. 4, 1793, ibid., p. 130; Daniel Stewart to General Gunn, Nov. 2, 1796, Creek Indian Letters, Talks, and Treaties, 1705–1839, p. 420, Dept. of Arch. and Hist. of Ga. For white traders dealing in stolen horses, see "A Talk Delivered by Mr. Barnard to the Indians Assembled at the Cussetahs," Mar. 22, 1793, Unpublished Letters of Barnard, p. 132; Barnard to Gaither, Apr. 20, 1793, ibid., p. 154; and "A Talk from the Big Warrior of the Cussetahs," May 2, 1793, ibid., p. 164. For white poaching of Indian game and plundering of Indian property, see Barnard to Seagrove, Mar. 26, 1793, ibid., p. 136; and Proceedings of the Court of Enquiry, July 22, 1794, Creek Indian Letters, pp. 387–90. For murder of individual whites, see Barnard to Seagrove, May 10, 1792, Unpublished Letters of Barnard, p. 116, and Barnard to Seagrove, Apr. 9, 1793, ibid., p. 142. For captives, see Barnard to Seagrove, June 20, 1793, ibid., p. 172. For the plunder of traders' stores, see Barnard to Gaither, Apr. 10, 1793, ibid., p. 143. For intoxication as exonerating circumstance, see "Journal of Thomas Bosomworth," Aug. 25, 1752, in *Documents Relating to Indian Affairs, May 21, 1750–Aug. 7, 1754*, ed. William McDowell (Columbia, S.C., 1958), p. 286.

and pleaded the future needs of their progeny. Acts of theft, arson, and murder, the strategic use of flattery, equivocation, procrastination, lies, and dissimulation, careful appeals to high moral principle or the exonerating circumstance of intoxication—these were but a few of the ways Muskogees resisted white aggression and settler incursions without risking everything in a direct conflict.[36]

What is striking is that many of these less dramatic and small-scale modes, because they were performed in secret or involved purposeful obfuscation, allowed Muskogees and other southeastern Indians to express deep-seated resentments while keeping the wellsprings of resistance underground, partially hidden from whites and collaborating Indians. Unfortunately for us, this had the additional effect of ensuring that the full depth and range of the Muskogees' responses to domination would not be clearly recorded in the historical documents. Since most of these documents were written by whites who were kept partially in the dark, it is difficult to establish precisely the Muskogees' true feelings, motivations, ideas, and rationales. In anthropologist James C. Scott's terms, the documents do a good job of showing us the "public transcript," the ways Muskogees and other southeastern Indians acted in the presence of powerful Europeans. The documents do a much less satisfactory job of revealing the "hidden transcript," the discourses, gestures, rituals, and symbols southeastern Indians cultivated among themselves to justify, promote, and perpetuate resistance.[37] Like other schol-

---

[36] For dissimulation with missionaries, see Johann Christian Burckhard, *Partners in the Lord's Work: The Diary of Two Moravian Missionaries in the Creek Indian Country, 1807–1913*, trans. and ed. Carl Mauelshagen and Gerald H. Davis, Georgia State College Research Paper no. 21 (Atlanta, 1969), p. 22; see also pp. 30, 72. For silence and feigned ignorance, see Hawkins, *Letters, Journals, and Writings*, 1:47–48. For negotiating strategies, see ibid., 2:562; James F. Doster, *The Creek Indians and Their Florida Lands, 1740–1823*, 2 vols. (New York, 1974), 2:16; and Hoboheilthlee Micco [Hopoithle Miko] to the President of the United States [Madison], May 15, 1811, Records of the Secretary of War Relating to Indian Affairs, Letters Received (microfilm M271), roll 1, 554, Record Group 75, National Archives, Washington, D.C.

[37] See James C. Scott, *Domination and the Arts of Resistance; Hidden Transcripts* (New Haven, 1990). Scott defines the "public transcript as a shorthand way of describing the open interaction between subordinates and those who domi-

ars who deal with documents produced in situations of domination, we find there are no transparent windows into the consciousness of the oppressed.[38] This lack, however, should not lead to skepticism or agnosticism. If not exactly transparent, some windows nonetheless exist. The Redstick revolt is such a window. Because the Redsticks risked everything and dared to resist openly, their movement provides historians with one of our best glimpses at the hidden transcript developed by southeastern Indians resisting domination.

Like the Chickamaugan movement, the Redstick movement attracted people who were angry with their headmen for authorizing massive land cessions to whites. Intended to cover debts incurred in the deerskin trade, these cessions signaled for Muskogees a profound change in Indian-white relations. Everything hinged on the interpretation and handling of debt. Essential to the everyday transactions of the deerskin trade, debt for generations had signified ties between individual hunters and traders. Hunters went into debt to obtain what they needed

---

nate" (p. 2). Hidden transcripts, in contrast, are not expressed so openly. On the one hand, "every subordinate group creates, out of its ordeal, a 'hidden transcript' that represents a critique of power spoken behind the back of the dominant." On the other, "the powerful, for their part, also develop a hidden transcript representing the practices and claims of their rule that cannot be openly avowed" (p. xii). Scott's approach can be faulted on several grounds— it draws upon examples with little regard to cultural or historical context and it seems to imply that the oppressed can locate a "pure" space away from power (despite Scott's denials that this is his intention)—yet the approach is valuable; it provides a vocabulary for describing the complexity of historical struggles and the nuances of the historical record.

[38] Major theoretical and historiographic issues involved in studying oppressed groups have been engaged with considerable sophistication by the Subaltern Studies group. See Ranajit Guha, ed., *Subaltern Studies: Writings on South Asian History and Society, III* (Oxford, 1984); and Gayatri Chakravorty Spivak, "Subaltern Studies: Deconstructing Historiography," in idem, *In Other Worlds: Essays in Cultural Politics* (New York, 1987), pp. 197–221. Spivak's essay and several essays from the subaltern group have been reprinted in Ranajit Guha and Gayatri Chakravorty Spivak, eds., *Selected Subaltern Studies* (New York, 1988). For an eloquent statement on the epistemological problems inherent to ethnohistory, see Jennifer S. H. Brown, "Ethnohistorians: Strange Bedfellows, Kindred Spirits," *Ethnohistory* 38 (1991):113–21.

for a season's hunt and to supply their kin with goods. They negotiated with traders whom they knew personally. In the new system, debt was abstracted from personal relationships and made into a commodity that could itself be traded on the market. The debts owed small traders were purchased at discount by the largest trading firm in the region, Panton, Leslie and Co.—later John Forbes and Co. This firm then aggregated the debts of entire communities of hunters, indeed of all Muskogee hunters, to produce one astronomical lump sum which the firm charged against the Muskogee people. By 1803 the firm claimed the Muskogees owed $113,000.[39]

This extraordinary debt would have been impossible for the firm to collect if not for the cooperation of the United States. Such cooperation was novel. In previous years, hostility and competition had characterized the relations of United States officials and Pensacola merchants. In 1793, for instance, William Panton of Pensacola encouraged the Muskogees to resist the advance of the Georgians through whatever means possible, including violence. United States officials said Panton "would rather see the whole state of Georgia in flames, and women and children massacred by the savages, than lose one hundred deer skins."[40] By 1803 Panton was dead, and the interests of the United States and the Pensacola merchants coincided. During the first decade of the nineteenth century, United States agents

---

[39] William Simpson, Aug. 20, 1803, Records of the Secretary of War Relating to Indian Affairs, Letters Received, roll 1; William S. Coker and Thomas D. Watson, *Indian Traders of the Southeastern Spanish Borderlands: Panton, Leslie and Company, and John Forbes and Company, 1783–1847* (Pensacola, Fla., 1986), p. 228. The major precedent for such a settlement dated back to the Second Treaty of Augusta, 1773. Through this treaty, Augusta rum traders gained over one million acres above the Little River. A map representing this and other cessions is provided in Edward Cashin, "'But Brothers, It Is Our Land We Are Talking About': Winners and Losers in the Georgia Backcountry," in Ronald Hoffman, Thad W. Tate, and Peter J. Albert, eds., *An Uncivil War: The Southern Backcountry during the American Revolution* (Charlottesville, Va., 1985), p. 243; see also Albert J. Pickett, *History of Alabama, and Incidentally of Georgia and Mississippi for the Earliest Period* (Charleston, S.C., 1851), pp. 328–29.

[40] Barnard to Seagrove, July 2, 1793, Unpublished Letters of Barnard, p. 188.

compelled Muskogee headmen to cede millions of acres of land to the United States. In exchange for the land, the United States paid off some of the Indians' aggregate debt. Thus, thousands of small, face-to-face exchanges between traders and hunters were transmuted by a multinational company and an expanding nation-state into massive land cessions that affected an entire people. These cessions signaled the end of play-off politics, expanded United States sovereignty, took from the Muskogee people many of their best hunting grounds, and undermined the deerskin trade, the central economic basis of the middle ground.[41]

This example shows how Americans, working with Pensacola merchants, exploited an established practice, the giving of credit, for new ends antithetical to the trading system itself. A similar tale of ex post facto transmutation can be told by examining what happened to the institution of alliance chiefs after the departure of the French and the defeat of the British. During the 1790s and early 1800s, intercultural diplomacy did not work as it had in the past. Earlier alliance chiefs like Malatchi had struggled to find a compromise between European demands and the expectations of his people. Later alliance chiefs did the same thing, but now the white side of the balance weighed far more heavily upon them. The Americans were far too numerous and far too strong and no longer needed to listen to or compromise with their Indian interlocutors. Chiefs found themselves compelled to execute or legitimize policies that signified not mutual accommodation but United States domination. They were required to sign treaties permanently ceding massive quantities of land, to authorize the building of roads through their people's territories, and to enforce justice against their own people even when this meant violating sacred cultural values. Some chiefs such as Hopoithle Miko of Tallas-

---

[41] For U.S. collection efforts, see Hawkins, *Letters, Journals, and Writings*, 2 : 476, 483, 505, 526–27; Coker and Watson, *Indian Traders*, pp. 227–30, 243–72; Florette Henri, *The Southern Indians and Benjamin Hawkins, 1796–1816* (Norman, Okla., 1986), pp. 219–20, 244–53; White, *Roots of Dependency*, pp. 95–96; and Samuel J. Wells, "Federal Indian Policy: From Accommodation to Removal," in Carolyn Keller Reeves, *The Choctaw before Removal* (Jackson, Miss., 1985), pp. 181–213, esp. pp. 186–87, 208 n. 17.

see refused to comply and tried to set up alternative governments. Other chiefs such as Tustunnuggee Thlucco (Big Warrior) of Tuckabatchee promised to comply but dissimulated in speech or procrastinated in action. Still others such as William McIntosh of Coweta profited personally from their mediating role and adopted the lifestyle of white settlers or planters. Was a chief like McIntosh a true intermediary or a colonial collaborator? It was becoming hard to tell.[42]

As Americans and complicit Indians corrupted the institutions that supported cross-cultural exchange and mutual accommodation, and as white populations grew and settled closer to the Indians of the interior southeast, white authorities and intellectuals developed a coherent narrative that legitimated and depoliticized these great changes. According to this narrative, the United States was the great benefactor of southeastern Indians, and if Indians could only make a few adjustments, they would be much happier. The old system of gift-giving was dead, the rules of the market applied now, and cessions were necessary to pay trade debts. Although these cessions deprived the Muskogees and other Indians of ancestral game lands, hunters need not despair. They could cease "savagery" to become commercial agriculturalists and raise livestock. Men should stay home, accumulate property, and pass it on to their children. Chiefs should police their people and enforce white justice. All

---

[42] By the summer of 1812 the Muskogee town chiefs, pressured by Indian agent Benjamin Hawkins and obligated by the Treaty of New York, were putting to death their own people for crimes against Anglo-American settlers in the Ohio country, on the Duck River, and in Muskogee itself. Chief William McIntosh and others carried out these executions in the open, personally shedding the blood of their fellow Muskogees, even though these acts outraged many Muskogee men and women. See "Report of J. C. Warren," Apr. 13, 1813, Creek Indian Letters, pp. 775–76; Hawkins, *Letters, Journals, and Writings*, 2:612, 615–16; Hassig, "Internal Conflict in the Creek War of 1813–1814," p. 256; Gregory A. Waselkov and Brian M. Wood, "The Creek War of 1813–1814: Effects on Creek Society and Settlement Pattern," *Journal of Alabama Archaeology* 32 (1986):7; Hawkins, *Letters, Writings, and Journals*, 2:631–34; and Frank Lawrence Owsley, Jr., *The Struggle for the Gulf Borderlands: The Creek War and the Battle of New Orleans, 1812–1815* (Gainesville, Fla., 1981), pp. 15–16. See also Douglas Barber, "Council Government and the Genesis of the Creek War," *Alabama Review* 3 (1985):163–74; Martin, *Sacred Revolt*, p. 125.

would benefit. Whites would gain and use the land to its full potential, and Indians would become civilized. The plan of civilization, as represented to the Muskogees by Indian agent Benjamin Hawkins, was for the Muskogees' own good.[43]

Muskogees did not have to obey the Indian agent, but they had to listen to him and show respect. Because he controlled the federal annuities paid to Muskogees, could materially reward and punish villagers, and increasingly monopolized the execution of justice in Muskogee country, Hawkins could enter Muskogee villages with impunity and presume to tell the Muskogees how they had to change. His influence signaled that a new set of power relations was shaping Indian-white encounters. The United States, and for that matter individual states such as Georgia, possessed vastly more economic and military power than the Muskogee people. By the turn of the century, Muskogees could no longer compel cultural, political, or economic reciprocity.[44]

As Muskogees experienced the rise of domination and witnessed its effects, they created their own narratives to explain what was happening. Just as whites told stories, proposed plans, and developed institutions to impose their will, Muskogees told stories, created movements, and developed practices to resist the loss of territory, economic dependency, political domination, and cultural imperialism. Usually this subversive cultural activity went on out of the sight of whites, in the southeastern underground. In the Redstick revolt it came into almost full view when thousands of Muskogees decided to revolt against the United States. Because Muskogee resistance took a massive and open form in the Redstick prophetic movement, study of

[43] Martin, *Sacred Revolt*, pp. 87–113; Henri, *Southern Indians*, pp. 83–111.

[44] In 1793 Georgians considered going to war without congressional help. Timothy Barnard felt that the Georgians alone would have a hard time subduing the Muskogees (Barnard to Seagrove, Oct. 17, 1793, Unpublished Letters of Barnard, p. 215). In May 1794 Georgia militiamen, determined to "destroy any party of Indians" they encountered, attacked Muskogees who were being protected by United States troops at Fort Fidius. A violent conflict between the Georgia militia and the U.S. army was barely avoided. See Constant Freeman to the Secretary of War [Henry Knox], May 10, 1794, ibid., p. 234, and the Report of Dr. Frederick Dalcho, May 10, 1794, ibid., p.236.

this movement provides one of our best documented glimpses of the otherwise hidden transcript of southeastern Indians.

When the New Madrid earthquake violently shook their lands in 1811–12, Muskogees cast about for a meaningful and useful interpretation of the unprecedented events.[45] In shaping their interpretations, the Muskogee people, unlike whites, did not turn to the Book for guidance.[46] As a Muskogee man put it, "White people have the old book from God. We Indians do not have it and are unable to read it."[47] Even so, he averred, his people still possessed insight into the order of things. "The Indians know it without a book; they dream much of God, and therefore they know it." Instead of turning to Scriptures, Muskogees turned to their spiritual leaders, their shamans. Inspired shamans trembled and convulsed as if vibrated by an earthquake

[45] H. S. Halbert and T. H. Ball, *The Creek War of 1813 and 1814,* ed. Frank L. Owsley (1895; reprint ed., University, Ala., 1969), p. 71. Geologists refer to this event as the New Madrid earthquake and estimate that it would have measured 8.2 on the Richter scale, thus making it the largest such event to have occurred in North America in the last several centuries. See Moravian Mission Diary entry, Springplace, Ga., Feb. 10, 1811, Moravian Archives, Winston-Salem, N. C., quoted in McLoughlin, *Cherokee Ghost Dance,* Appendix E, p. 142; Francis Howard to Dr. Porter, Feb. 14, 1812, Louise Frederick Hays, ed., "Creek Indian Letters, Talks, and Treaties, 1782–1839," Georgia Department of Archives and History, Atlanta; Burckhard, *Partners in the Lord's Work,* p. 68; Moravian Mission Diary entry, Springplace, Ga., Dec. 17, 1811, Moravian Arch., quoted in McLoughlin, *Cherokee Ghost Dance,* Appendix E, p. 143; and R. A. Eppley, *Earthquake History of the United States, Part I* (Washington, D.C., 1965), pp. 67–68. Martin, *Sacred Revolt,* presents much of this material but does not employ Scott's theory to interpret its significance.

[46] Homi Bhabha theorizes the problematic of the Book in the colonial context in his articles "Signs Taken for Wonders: Questions of Ambivalence and Authority under a Tree outside Delhi, May 1817," *Critical Inquiry* 12 (1985): 144–65, and "Of Mimicry and Man: The Ambivalence of Colonial Discourse," *October* 28 (1984):125–33; see also Peter Worsley, *The Trumpet Shall Sound: A Study of "Cargo" Cults in Melanesia* (New York, 1968), p. 241.

[47] Burckhard, *Partners in the Lord's Work,* p. 53. In some Native American millenarian movements, prophets constructed "Books." For a description of the Delaware Prophet Neolin and the "Indian Bible," see John G. Heckewelder, *History, Manners, and Customs of the Indian Nations Who Once Inhabited Pennsylvania* (Philadelphia, 1876), pp. 291–93.

or seized by a spirit. These shamans, or "shakers," traveled to and from the spirit worlds.[48] They declared a charismatic event revelatory of sacred forces was at work and interpreted historical events and the earthquake through the template of Muskogean religious myth.

Muskogees imagined the cosmos divided into three primordial worlds: the Upper World, This World, and the Lower World. Just as the sun and moon illumined the earth, manifested order in their movements, and helped demarcate temporal boundaries, the Upper World released the powers of perfection, order, permanence, clarity, and periodicity. Pitted against the Upper World and releasing exactly contrary powers was the Lower World, the realm of reversals, madness, creativity, fertility, and chaos. In the Lower World, there lived a major order of sacred beings. Not to be taken lightly, these included the most dangerous spirit beings. Foremost among these was the Tie-Snake, a primeval dragonlike antlered monster snake. Although most Europeans denied the existence of Tie-Snakes, some traders like James Adair were not sure. Adair accepted southeastern Indians' accounts of snakes "of a more enormous size than is mentioned in history" that could bewitch their prey with their eyes and tongues, change color, and dazzle spectators with "piercing rays of light that blaze from their foreheads."[49]

Muskogees strongly affirmed the reality of these creatures. According to Muskogees, these great snakes could stretch themselves across a channel and practically dam a stream. During the early nineteenth century in Muskogee, the Tie-Snake was closely associated with a particularly dangerous rocky stretch of the Chattahoochee River and could often be seen there. "It had the appearance, when floating on the water, of a large number of

[48] The following discussion of shamans is based upon Bartram, *Travels*, p. 390; Jean-Bernard Bossu, *Travels in the Interior of North America, 1751–1762*, trans. and ed. Seymour Feiler (Norman, Okla., 1962), p. 149; Williams, ed., *Adair's History*, p. 90; Swanton, "Creek Ethnographic and Vocabulary Notes"; idem, *Indians of the Southeastern United States*, p. 774; J. Leitch Wright, Jr., *Creeks and Seminoles: The Destruction and Regeneration of the Muscogulge People* (Lincoln, Nebr., 1986), pp. 157–59; Waselkov and Wood, "Creek War of 1813–1814," p. 4.

[49] Williams, ed., *Adair's History*, p. 250.

barrels strung together, end to end, and could, almost at any time, be seen catching its prey by folding its helpless victims in the coils or 'tie' of its tail and instantly destroying life by a deadly hug."[50] In addition to making water travel dangerous, these Snakes brought numerous sicknesses to humans. Merely looking at the creature could cause insanity or death. And yet, it was difficult for a human not to look, for the Tie-Snake was strangely beautiful. Dreadfully alluring, its body was armored with crystalline scales that shone iridescently, its forehead crowned with an extraordinarily bright crystal. Highly prized as aids in divination, these dazzling scales and crystals could only be obtained by a shaman purified for contact with the dangerous powers of the Lower World.

In 1812 a Muskogee shaman Captain Sam Isaacs related to Upper Muskogees his vision of "diving down to the bottom of the river and laying there and traveling about for many days and nights receiving instruction and information from an enormous and friendly serpent that dwels there and was acquainted with future events and all other things necessary for a man to know in this life."[51] As Captain Isaacs revealed, it was the powerful Tie-Snake who recklessly shook the earth and unleashed a new force for recreating the world. Based upon this vision, the special knowledge and power that it provided him, and his familiarity with Tecumseh and the Shawnee Prophet, Isaacs acquired the veneration of a large number of people, perhaps sev-

---

[50] F. L. Cherry, "History of Opelika," *Alabama Historical Quarterly* 15 (1953): 184; see also, Charles Hudson, "Uktena: A Cherokee Anomalous Monster," *Journal of Cherokee Studies* 3 (1978):62–75; Raymond D. Fogelson, "Windigo Goes South: Stoneclad among the Cherokees," in Marjorie M. Halpin and Michael M. Ames, eds., *Manlike Monsters on Trial: Early Records and Modern Evidence* (Vancouver, B.C., 1980), pp. 132–51.

[51] Nunez, "Creek Nativism," p. 149. Nunez's article is a reprint of the George Stiggins narrative. Stiggins was born in Muskogee in 1788, the son of a Nauchee (Natchez) woman and an Anglo-American man. Although he wrote his account between 1831 and 1842, many of its chronological and biographical details are independently confirmed. Captain Sam Isaacs, for example, is identified as a rebel leader in contemporary documents. What makes the Stiggins account invaluable is that it provides a good glimpse into the way the Muskogees interpreted their history.

eral hundred.[52] As the movement grew, however, a younger group of shamans came to the fore. Borrowing from the fiery tales of apocalypse told by runaway Afro-Christian slaves, they said the Upper World power known as the Maker of Breath was about to destroy the present colonial order. This prophecy of cosmological upheaval provided the metaphors, symbols, and values that justified revolt against seemingly insurmountable odds. By identifying with these cosmic forces, the Muskogee rebels gained courage and felt they could purge their land of colonizers. Allied with the Shawnees and other Indians, they would "make the land clear of the Americans or loose their lives."[53]

Just as the Muskogees interpreted earthly events through the symbolic template of sacred stories, so they acted politically in a way directly patterned after rituals of purification and world renewal. Homologies between rituals and revolutionary acts were strong. As they had always done in traditional initiation ceremonies, the rebels withdrew to the woods, fasted, consumed purifying beverages, and danced. When they attacked an enemy town, the shamans said it would fall on the eighth day, for eight was a sacred number. Eight days was also the length of time it took the Muskogees to perform their most important collective ceremony, the *póskita*, or Busk, an annual ritual celebrating the primordial origins of corn and the rebirth of the social order. Muskogee rebels performed a dance borrowed from the Shawnees to symbolize solidarity with other Indians and their utter determination to resist white civilization's hegemonic power. If this meant attacking collaborating Muskogees or coercing people to join their movement, the Redsticks were willing to do so. "The declaration of the prophets [was] to destroy every thing received from the Americans, all the Chiefs and their adherents who are friendly to the customs and ways of the white

---

[52] Isaacs had visited Tecumseh in the Northwest. According to Woodward, Isaacs was a Muskogee from the town of "Coowersortda [Coosaudee]" (Thomas S. Woodward, *Woodward's Reminiscences of the Creek, or Muscogee Indians* [Tuscaloosa and Birmingham, 1939], pp. 36–37).

[53] John Innerarity to James Innerarity, July 27, 1813, Creek Indian Letters, p. 797. For a much fuller development of the different shamans' interpretations, see Martin, *Sacred Revolt*, pp. 114–49.

people." They were directed by the prophets "to kill any of there [*sic*] own People if they do not take up the war Club."[54] The rebels ritually assassinated collaborating chiefs and targeted Hawkins and his assistants for execution. They waged war on cattle. Central to the subsistence base of invading settlers, cattle symbolized white civilization itself. The Muskogee rebels agreed with their Chickamaugan predecessors. These tame animals were the very antithesis of the wild animals given to real Indians by the Maker of Breath. As they had always done in traditional initiation ceremonies, the rebels withdrew to the woods, fasted, consumed purifying beverages, and danced. Through these and many other acts, Muskogee rebels turned an upside-down world right side up. With prophetic declarations, new dances, purification ceremonies, wars on certain animals and people, and humorous inversionary gestures, the Muskogee rebels rejected domination and showed that they were indeed the masters of the land and all of its symbols.[55]

As historian Gregory Evans Dowd notes in his study of earlier, pantribal revolts, prophetic messages spread very fast in Indian country.[56] One of the main ways prophecies were disseminated was through rumors. As scholars of anticolonial movements have shown, rumors can elaborate, distort, and exaggerate information regarding events of vital importance, can spread with incredible speed, and can give voice to popular utopian longings. Since rumors have no identifiable authors, people can spread them while disavowing responsibility for their contents

[54] Hawkins, *Letters, Journals, and Writings*, 2:652; "Testimony of James Moore," July 13, 1813, Creek Indian Letters, p. 785. For Redstick coercion, see Hawkins, *Letters, Journals, and Writings*, 2:666, 669. The Redsticks were not the only ones who refused to let Muskogees remain neutral. In October 1813 Hawkins "ordered the Indians to take sides, all who are not for the Chiefs are hostile and will be treated accordingly. There is to be no neutrals. The evidence required of their having joined the Chiefs is to give battle to the adherents of the prophets" (2:673).

[55] "Report of Alexander Cornells, Interpreter, to Colonel Hawkins," June 22, 1813, *American State Papers: Indian Affairs*, 2 vols. (Washington, D.C., 1832–34), 1:845–46; Hawkins, *Letters, Journals, and Writings*, 2:641; Owsley, *Struggle for the Gulf Borderlands*, p. 17; Martin, *Sacred Revolt*, pp. 114–49.

[56] Dowd, *Spirited Resistance*, pp. 34, 138.

and effects. Rumors circulated rapidly in the southeastern underground. After the New Madrid earthquake, among the Muskogees "flying tales daily multiplied and were exaggerated in all parts of the [Muskogee] nation, told and received as truth by every one. . . . [These] Tales had no Father for they were said to be told by first one and then another and no body could ascertain who, but the relators were at a distance in general and hard to be detected." In many of these "flying, fatherless tales," Tecumseh, the great Shawnee leader of pan-tribalism, figured prominently. Indeed, according to some of the popular narratives, Tecumseh had stomped his foot and caused the earth to shake. In others, Tecumseh did not cause the earthquakes, but he prophesied how the Lower World would release awesome power, collapse the old order, and allow a new one to emerge. Responding to these rumors and other stories, seven to nine thousand Muskogees revolted against the United States.[57]

An equal number did not revolt. Why not? If several thousand Muskogees living on the Chattahoochee (Lower Muskogees) did not take up the red club, it does not mean that they were not religious or even less religious than the Redsticks. People can share the same religion but interpret its implications differently. They can cherish the same myths and rituals and still come to blows. When the Redsticks called for revolt, the Lower Muskogees listened, hesitated, and decided against joining their more militant cousins. They felt there were better ways to resist white domination. Since the Lower Muskogees lived very close to Georgians, they feared they would suffer catastrophic losses if they joined the revolt. But fear was not the only factor shaping their response.

By 1811 the Lower Muskogees had already dealt with the major economic and social challenges caused by the loss of their ancestral hunting lands. Like their Cherokee neighbors, they had shifted their secondary subsistence cycle away from hunting toward the raising of livestock and the trading of agricul-

---

[57] Nunez, "Creek Nativism," p. 146. For the importance of rumor in anti-colonial movements, see Kenelm Burridge, *New Heaven, New Earth: A Study of Millenarian Activities* (New York, 1969), pp. 106–7; Shahid Amin, "Gandhi as Mahatma: Gorakhpur District, Eastern UP, 1921–22," in Guha, ed., *Subaltern Studies*, pp. 1–61; Scott, *Domination and the Arts of Resistance*, pp. 144–48.

tural products. Women gained greater direct access to the market. Old men also benefited. A Coweta chief said he had "more pleasure . . . in carding and dying his cotton and making his clothing [with a loom] than he ever had in his young days hunting. 'I am old . . . and as such according to our old ways useless but according to the new way more useful than ever.'"[58] As for the young men, the Lower Muskogees most directly affected by the loss of hunting lands, many of them had emigrated, relocating in northern Florida. A region where settlers were rare and game was plentiful, northern Florida had served as a kind of escape valve for generations of Lower Muskogees frustrated with white encroachment. As a consequence, in 1811, among Lower Muskogees living on the Chattahoochee, there was no critical mass of angry young men determined to keep the traditional hunting grounds free of whites. Excepting the ethnically distinct town of Yuchis, Lower Muskogee towns determined to side with the Georgians against the Upper Muskogees. They expected to be amply rewarded for this alliance.[59]

Neither the Upper or Lower Muskogees saw their expectations fulfilled. The Redsticks were devastated utterly by their war with the United States. The Lower Muskogees, although the allies of the victorious United States, were forced by Andrew Jackson to cede millions of acres of their land. After the war the influx of white settlers accelerated. Nevertheless, Upper and Lower Muskogees continued to resist. Muskogees had employed a wide range of subtle and not so subtle forms of resistance before the Redstick movement. They did so afterwards as well and learned much from the Cherokees. In the decades following the Redstick war, Muskogees increasingly relied upon métis individuals, including educated Cherokees, to serve as cultural intermediaries. Cherokee métis involved themselves quite visibily in Muskogee affairs during the 1820s. For in-

---

[58] Hawkins, *Letters, Journals, and Writings*, 2 : 562.

[59] Ibid., pp. 612, 636, 646, 648, 650–51, 654–57, 664, 666, 672. For the migration of Lower Muskogees to Florida, see William C. Sturtevant, "Creek into Seminole," in Eleanor Burke Leacock and Nancy Oestreich Lurie, eds., *North American Indians in Historical Perspective* (New York, 1971); Bartram, *Travels*, pp. 181–82. For descriptions of ample game in Florida, see ibid., pp. 165, 170, 172.

stance, in 1826 John Ridge and David Vann provided counsel and served as secretaries to Muskogee headmen during treaty negotiations with the United States.[60]

There is also evidence that Muskogees, like Cherokees, made special efforts to hide their culture of the sacred from Anglo scrutiny. For instance, during the 1820s the Tuckabatchees would not let any white person see their ancient copper plates, sacred items displayed during that town's Busk ceremony. Although Lee Compere, a Baptist missionary, lived among the Tuckabatchees from 1822 to 1828, he "would never get to see them. . . . The Indians were reluctant to talk about them." Compere did succeed in persuading Tustunnuggee Thlucco to relate some of the Muskogees' sacred history, including how they had defeated the indigenous inhabitants of the southeast. However, when Compere made an insensitive comparison between this ancient story of conquest and the ongoing Anglo-American invasion, the chief turned silent. Compere had crossed the line. "From that time I could never after induce him or any of the other chiefs to give me any more of their history."[61]

In addition to hiding their most sacred relics and keeping much of their oral tradition secret, Muskogees tried to protect their ceremonies from white civilization. They created new rules governing the consumption of alcohol and the use of manufactured goods during the Busk. In some towns, both were banned. At least in one square ground it was "considered as a desecration for an Indian to allow himself to be touched by even the dress of a white man, until the ceremony of purification is complete."[62] This could have been the case earlier, but the fact that the rule was enforced in 1835 reveals an active concern to protect sacred ceremonies from white meddling.

[60] McLoughlin, *Cherokee Renascence*, pp. 372–75; Edwin C. McReynolds, *Oklahoma: A History of the Sooner State* (Norman, Okla., 1954), pp. 122–23.

[61] Notes furnished A. J. Pickett by the Rev. Lee Compere of Mississippi relating to the Creek Indians among whom he lived as a Missionary, Albert J. Pickett Papers, Notes upon the History of Alabama, sec. 24, Alabama Department of Archives and History, Montgomery.

[62] John Howard Payne, "The Green-Corn Dance," *Continental Monthly* 1 (1862):24.

In addition to protecting their own religion, Muskogees tried to check the influence of the Christian religion in their country. Most chiefs would not permit preaching in their towns. When Compere (through a Muskogee interpreter named John Davis) began conversing on the Gospel in the square ground of Tuckabatchee, the men ignored him and concentrated on cutting sticks and rubbing their pipes. On another occasion they protested that they were too old to learn such things and "did not want to hear them." In another town Muskogees told Compere to avoid the square altogether as many Indians were intoxicated and would cause trouble.[63]

Not surprisingly, Compere's mission was not successful. Except for Davis, he converted almost no "full-bloods." He simply did not have access to the Muskogees' inner lives. They kept their sacred life secret, as an incident in the spring of 1828 revealed. When clearing land for cultivation, Compere killed a hickory, unwittingly violating a Muskogee rule of propriety. A Muskogee woman informed him that he had "broke in upon some of the secrets of the Indians' superstition . . . which is that the Indians consider such trees when they happen to be found in the Townfield as sacred to the Great Spirit." Informed of his error, Compere was "not very sorry." Aware that he was being kept in the dark about major aspects of Muskogee life, Compere was pleased the accident had happened. It had served as "the means of dragging out a secret which I might never have learned without."[64] Muskogees simply did not trust Compere. Not surprisingly, the mission failed. Within a few years, the Muskogees were forcibly removed from Alabama.

In the decades before removal, Muskogees and Cherokees alike had experienced the invasion of their lands by missionaries, miners, government agents, settlers, and slaves. Although they had occasionally responded with violence, much more common were the everyday nonviolent means they used to protect their feelings, rituals, identities, and cultures. Confronted

[63] For ignoring, protesting, and delaying, *American Baptist Magazine* 125 (1827):143–46.

[64] Journal of Lee Compere, Apr. 25, 1828, American Indian Correspondence.

with hostile whites in their midst, Muskogees and Cherokees kept important things—values, beliefs, practices, and ideas—secret. They developed alternative stories and myths to explain the origins of the diverse races, performed rituals and dances that celebrated their identities as Indians, and carefully controlled whites' access to their interior lives. By developing and hiding an underground cultural life, they retained their sense of their separate identity even as their land was being invaded.

To be sure, sometimes the Cherokees and Muskogees used violent means to repel whites, most spectacularly in the Chickamaugan and Redstick revolts. Even these revolts, however, were linked to the southeastern underground. The revolts simply concentrated in a vivid, explicit manner what was already present in a more diffuse, less visible way among the Cherokees and Muskogees. Symbols, practices, and narratives emphasizing Indian distinctiveness were underscored, exaggerated, dramatized, and, most important, made public. Like geysers, the violent character of the Chickamauga and Redstick revolts attracted a lot of attention from shocked whites. But, also like geysers, these revolts owed their existence to larger underground currents flowing out of sight. If the revolts deserve attention, surely deserving equal or greater attention is the cultural underground that made them possible. Southeastern Indians found much of value there: powerful symbols of a separate Indian identity, opportunities to vent frustrations, and a rich repertoire of strategies to resist domination. Although purposefully hidden by its creators and long overlooked by historians, the southeastern Indians' underground should be unearthed at last and ignored no longer, for it exercised significant influence in the days of the early republic.

III

Native American
Images

ELISE MARIENSTRAS

The Common Man's Indian

The Image of the Indian as a Promoter of National Identity in the Early National Era

IN THE EARLY national era, the American nation, which had been born, in the words of John M. Murrin, an "unexpected, impromptu, artificial, and therefore extremely fragile creation of the Revolution,"[1] had yet to assure its political legitimacy, its territorial boundaries, and the unity of its citizens. It had yet to acquire a specific culture made out of a common past and destiny, a common lore, and common cultural products. The image of the Indian as it appeared in early American stories, in songs, paintings and engravings, on domestic or commercial objects provided an important answer to the American quest for a national identity.

In order to root itself firmly on the continent, the United States at once created a vacuum by removing or destroying the indigenous inhabitants and absorbed them into its nascent national culture. The images white Americans formed of the vanquished Native peoples helped them form an original concep-

---

[1] John M. Murrin, "A Roof without Walls: The Dilemma of American National Identity," in Richard R. Beeman, Stephen Botein, and Edward C. Carter II, eds., *Beyond Confederation: Origins of the Constitution and American National Identity* (Chapel Hill, N.C., 1987), p. 344.

tion of the world and of themselves as a collective entity. The representations of Indians in early American culture are part of a process that is well summarized by Roger Chartier, when writing about the role of ideology in the formation and evolution of societies: "There is no action nor any structure which is not the product of the contradictory, sometimes clashing representations by which individuals and groups give a meaning to their own world.[2]

Representations of Indians, either as hereditary, fierce, and wild enemies or as exotic, strange savages and illegitimate roamers of the new continent, were not only a one-sided justification of their spoliation and decimation: their image became an integral part of the national culture and identity, providing meaning and impetus to the new nation's deeds and politics. As the country grew stronger, the old American Indian nations who lived on the eastern side of the continent became more and more fragile, losing, as it were, their substance to the benefit of their white invaders. It took some time before they yielded ground, but they never completely disappeared from the eyes, or rather from the minds, of the American citizens.

The purpose of this essay is to study the means by which, alongside the rhetorical use of Indians by the nation's intellectual leaders, the image of the Indian also permeated the ordinary citizen's mentality, contributing to the sense of belonging to the new nation. Presented as a formidable foe who stood in the way of the forward march of history, the Indian provided legitimacy for the conquest of the continent, for the ultimate sovereignty of the United States over most of North America, and for the Indian wars whose participants became vital players in the national drama. At the same time, the new nation found in former Indian-white conflicts, as well as in the pre-Columbian American past, a way to make up for its too short span of history. The image of the Indian became a means for white Americans to identify themselves in opposition to what they deemed to be the savage, ferocious, uncivilized nature of the Natives. The image of the Indians was thus a vision of the Other that delineated in refraction the image of the new, national self. However, as

[2] Roger Chartier, "Le monde comme représentation," *Annales* 44 (1989): 1508.

the Indians of the East became less and less physically visible, their presence became more a part of popular culture. More and more a benign figure, or an abstract or imaginary idea, the Indian of the Jacksonian era became, in the common man's culture of the 1830s, an incidental although ever-present, and more or less unconscious, part of the daily life and culture of the American nation.

NATIVE AMERICANS AND POPULAR EXPANSION

Locating the image of the savage, whether noble or ignoble, in the common man's "profit and amusement," and wondering how much it was present by the firesides of modest homes, requires an unorthodox methodology.[3] This image may be discovered in all sorts of items of vernacular and folk culture such as songs and illustrations (etchings, prints, cartoons, advertisements), material representations (weather vanes, figureheads, tobacco store figures),[4] popular magazines, newspapers and almanacs, children's and schoolbooks, anecdotes and proverbs, and numerous stories of war and captivity, as well as in works of fiction that were published as "blue-back books" and sold both in the countryside and the cities.[5]

[3] In my first inquiries, I have been helped by Rayna D. Green's excellent article "The Indian in Popular American Culture," in Wilcomb E. Washburn, ed., *History of Indian-White Relations*, Handbook of North American Indians, vol. 4 (Washington, D.C., 1988), pp. 587–606.

[4] Kenneth L. Ames, *Beyond Necessity: Art in the Folk Tradition: An Exhibition from the Collections of the Winterthur Museum* (Winterthur, Del., 1972), p. 46; Ken Fitzgerald, *Weathervanes and Whirligigs* (New York, 1976); Anthony W. Pendergast and William P. Ware, *Cigar Store Figures in American Folk Art* (Chicago, 1953). Artifacts with Indian representations were rather rare before the mid-nineteenth century. The cigar store advertising figure generally alluded to Indians through its feathered headdress. Otherwise the Indian figure was somewhat confused with the plantation black slave. The weather vanes in the shape of a kneeling Indian with a bow date from the second half of the nineteenth century. A number of cast metal store plates representing Indians were manufactured in the late eighteenth and early nineteenth century (Green, "Indian in Popular American Culture").

[5] Among the 150 early national era almanacs I have consulted, 35 contained articles dealing with Indians. The guide to the almanacs is Milton

The question whether in the eighteenth and nineteenth centuries one can distinguish between "high culture" and "low culture" has been frequently discussed.[6] It is obvious that the back-country farmers and the urban mechanics had neither the time nor the intellectual and financial means to avail themselves of books dealing with law, politics, history, or philosophy. Yet certain cultural artifacts were more readily available both to the common man and to the elite: In all classes, the reading of newspapers and almanacs, broadsides and ballads, novels for adults and children's books benefited from "a new marketing situation, with very short-term, but high-volume, sales."[7]

Drake, *Almanacs of the United States*, 2 vols. (New York, 1962). See also James A. Bear, Jr., and Mary Caperton Bear, *A Checklist of Virginia Almanacs* (Charlottesville, Va., 1962), Albert C. Bates, "Checklist of Connecticut Almanacs, 1789–1850," *Proceedings of the American Antiquarian Society* 24 (1914), and James S. Wenrick, "Indians in Almanacs, 1783–1815," *Indian Historian* 8 (1975):36–42. For schoolbooks, the best study is Ruth Miller Elson, *Guardians of Tradition: American Schoolbooks of the Nineteenth Century* (Lincoln, Nebr., 1964). The American Antiquarian Society, Worcester, Mass., owns an extensive collection of pre-1876 juvenile literature (17,000 titles). Access has been made easy by making a database: research was conducted under the entry "Indians of America"; the pedagogical subcollection is also listed. Among the titles the librarians helped me to find, some of the most significant are: Maria Edgeworth, *The Parents' Assistant; or, Stories for Children*, 2 vols. (New York, 1820), E. P. of Providence, *Tales for Doncas from Well-Known Facts* (New York, 1823), *Julia, or, The Pet Lamb; or, Good Temper and Compassion Rewarded* (Portland, Maine, 1827), A Lady, *Lights of Education; or, Mr. Hope and His Family: A Narrative for Young Persons* (Baltimore, 1825), Rev. Isaac Taylor, *Scenes in America, for the Amusement and Instruction of Little Tarry-At-Home Travellers* (Hartford, 1825), Emily Taylor, *Letters to a Child, on the Subject of Maritime Discovery* (New York, 1821), Hoseah Hildreth, *A Book for New Hampshire Children* (Exeter, N.H., [1823]).

[6] Eve Kornfeld, "Culture and Counter-Culture in Post-Revolutionary America," *Journal of American Culture* 12 (1989):71–76. Richard L. Bushman, "American High-Style and Vernacular Cultures," in Jack P. Greene and J. R. Pole, eds., *Colonial British America: Essays in the New History of the Early Modern Era* (Baltimore, 1984), pp. 345–84. Winfried Fluck, "Popular Culture as a Mode of Socialization: A Theory about the Social Functions of Popular Cultural Forms," *Journal of Popular Culture* 12 (1989):31–46.

[7] Robert B. Winans, "Bibliography and the Cultural Historians: Notes on the Eighteenth-Century Model," in William L. Joyce et al., eds., *Printing and Society in Early America* (Worcester, Mass., 1983), p. 175.

The form of those widely diffused literary, material, or pictorial artifacts remained familiar. At the same time, although it had been a part of colonial life, popular culture became, after the Revolution, the carrier of a new, national ideology. That ideology transcended local particularisms all the more easily as literacy became widespread, reaching approximately 70 to 75 percent of the American population, a much larger proportion than in England or France.[8] Moreover, a great number of Americans could often afford to buy books now published for a few shillings.[9] The technology of iconography also improved, enabling illustrators like Alexander Anderson to draw clearer and finer images. Material culture also lost some of its local and vernacular character, both in architecture and in domestic objects. And finally, as Richard D. Brown has shown,[10] the cultural and economic exchange network had been expanding since the second half of the eighteenth century, thanks to circulating libraries and book peddling, as well as public reading in taverns and clubs. Writers, politicians, teachers, clergymen, self-advertising composers of songs and others used these means to engender a sense of nationalism among the citizens.

During the colonial era, the mental horizon of the common man had been restricted to his parish, township, or, at best, the province. After the Revolution the sense of belonging to a national community became more familiar. Culture started to be Americanized, referring less to European memories than to indigenous traditions, tales, or images. Since, in the early nineteenth century, the number of Native Americans was dramatically decreasing in the Atlantic area—that is to say, at the core of the young republic—Indians no longer constituted an object of immediate terror. But their presence at the frontier

[8] Kenneth A. Lockridge, "Literacy in Early America, 1650–1880," in Harvey J. Graff, ed., *Literacy and Social Development in the West: A Reader* (Cambridge, 1981), pp. 183–200; William Gilmore, *Reading Becomes a Necessity of Life: Material and Cultural Life in Rural New England, 1780–1835* (Knoxville, Tenn., 1989).

[9] Cathy N. Davidson, *Revolution and the Word: The Rise of the Novel in America* (New York, 1986); Winans, "Bibliography and the Cultural Historians."

[10] Richard D. Brown, *Knowledge Is Power: The Diffusion of Information in Early America, 1700–1865* (New York, 1989).

still formed an obstacle to the expansionist project of the nation and to the territorial ambition of the settlers.[11] Although Jeffersonian leaders claimed that their Indian policies were based more on philanthropic than expansionist motives, the pioneers and small farmers still regarded the Natives as an endemic threat.[12] At the same time, they could not erase Indians from the memory and traditions they conveyed to the next generation.

For several decades the new nation was an ambiguous political entity. In spite of the solemn international guarantees provided by the Treaty of Paris in 1783, ultimate sovereignty was not to be achieved at once. A considerable part of the territory that the United States assumed to be theirs continued to be in the possession of Indian tribes. Even after 1830, when Chief Justice John Marshall formulated his famous definition of Indian tribes as being "domestic, dependent nations"—implying that their territory and sovereignty were included inside and dependent upon United States dominion—the reality of the concept would never go uncontested. For a long time treaty negotiators, political officials, and courts reckoned that the Native nations held a conception of sovereignty that was different from the Euro-American one. They simultaneously denied it and dealt with it as being valid.[13] For several reasons (including the contradiction between colonialism and republican ideology), some confusion about American sovereignty persisted and the very meaning and extent of United States domestic sov-

[11] In "A General Description of America," Francis Bailey asserted and deplored that "a great part of this territory is not under the jurisdiction of any particular state, but belongs to the confederacy [of Ohio Indian nations]" (*Bailey's Pocket Almanac . . . for . . . 1785* [Philadelphia, 1784]).

[12] Bernard W. Sheehan, *Seeds of Extinction: Jeffersonian Philanthropy and the American Indian* (Chapel Hill, N.C., 1973); Richard Drinnon, *Facing West: The Metaphysics of Indian-Hating and Empire-Building* (Minneapolis, 1980), chaps. 6–9.

[13] Dorothy V. Jones, *License for Empire: Colonialism by Treaty in Early America* (Chicago, 1982); Vine Deloria, Jr., and Clifford Lytle, *The Nations Within: The Past and Future of American Indian Sovereignty* (New York, 1984); William R. Swagerty, *Indian Sovereignty: Problems and Issues concerning American Indians Today* (Chicago, 1979).

ereignty was blurred. Never would the United States government be in possession of a sovereignty comparable to that of Western European nations, whose territories and internal colonized peoples had long since been fused into nation states.

Within the boundaries that had been allocated to the new nation, Native Americans, gradually decimated, dispossessed, and deprived of their dignity and identity, did not lay down arms easily. They retreated after actual military battles, and later the symbolic combat in which cultures, mentalities, and opposing world visions confronted each other. During the American War for Independence, the majority of the eastern tribes, aware that independent colonists would be a greater threat to their land and freedom than the former British empire, had taken sides with the British against the Revolutionaries.[14] After 1783 new forces coalesced against the American imperialist government and invading settlers.[15] And after the 1795 Treaty of Greenville deprived the Indians of most of their territory in the Ohio area, new Indian confederacies were formed. Indian combatants took advantage of the War of 1812 in the North, while bloody wars, expeditions, and reprisals were fought against the white settlement in the South. Finally, Andrew Jackson, "the Indian fighter" and the herald of the common man, became president of the United States in 1829 and declared himself the champion of expansion.[16]

Although eventually defeated on the battlefield, Native nations' very presence at the frontier, the mere memory left by those who had been destroyed by colonization, and the images that they imprinted on the minds and cultural productions of the former colonists enabled them to take a symbolic revenge as

[14] Barbara Graymont, *The Iroquois in the American Revolution* (Syracuse, N.Y., 1972); Elise Marienstras, "Les réprouvés de la Révolution américaine: nations indiennes et guerre d'indépendance," in Bernard Vincent and Elise Marienstras, eds., *Les oubliés de la Révolution américaine* (Nancy, 1990).

[15] Wiley Sword, *President Washington's Indian War: The Struggle for the Old Northwest, 1790–1795* (Norman, Okla., 1985).

[16] Ronald N. Satz, *American Indian Policy in the Jacksonian Era* (Lincoln, Nebr., 1975); Reginald Horsman, *Expansion and American Indian Policy, 1783–1812* (East Lansing, Mich., 1967).

well as to testify in the eyes of history to the particular nature of the new republic. When the young nation started to develop a culture of its own, the Native Americans' presence asserted itself. The role they played in the symbolic world of the new nation provided sufficient evidence that the process of colonization still existed, not only in the memory of the past, but in the political present and in the planned future of the nation.

The Federalists and Jeffersonians both justified the future removal of the southeastern tribes.[17] They argued that the new nation, preoccupied with its economic development and the establishment of a strong republic, did not need to be encumbered with the primitive savage. He was wild in his manners, ferocious in his social relations, and unable to take part in the economic and ideological impetus of the nation. Let him move farther west, pleaded President Thomas Jefferson, where the "empire for liberty" had not yet set foot.[18] But let him, at the same time, be used as proof that the newly formed nation was not lacking one of those elements that elsewhere are essential parts of a national culture: a legitimate territory, a common past made of glorious deeds and ancient heroes, and a hereditary enemy.

The Indian image at once enabled American citizens to legitimize their conquest of the continent and helped them to forge a counterimage of themselves. The fact that the image misrepresented reality was not important. What counted was its presence in the cultural productions of the nation and the fact that the citizenry believed it.

Native Americans, being altogether rejected and sometimes even denied their humanity, became emblematic of a national geography, of the antiquity of the continent on which the nation was taking its roots. They reminded the nation's citizens of the common history of military exploits and hardships they shared. By emphasizing their former military strength and ferocious nature, portraits of Indians testified to the bravery of the British-American soldiers, the fortitude of the pioneers on

[17] Sheehan, *Seeds of Extinction*.

[18] Thomas Jefferson, "Addresses to Indians," Saul K. Padover, ed., *The Complete Jefferson* (Freeport, N.Y., 1943), pp. 476–85; "To the Ricara Nation," ibid., p. 480; "To the Chiefs of the Osage Nation," ibid., p. 486.

the frontier, and the pains and dangers all Americans had had to endure to master nature and its wild inhabitants.

Even the repeated defeats of the American army during the years shortly following Independence were turned into heroic deeds because they showed the Indian foe simultaneously as a formidable army and as a collection of wild savages. In the early nineteenth century, poems, ballads, and songs printed as broadsides or chapbooks recalled the defeats of William Crawford in 1782 at Sandusky and of Arthur St. Clair in 1791. They were sold in the backcountry, as a substitute for the epic of the new nation. In *A Song, Called Crawford's Defeat by the Indians*, the anonymous author started with a proud military picture of a somewhat classical battle:

> There was brave Colonel Crawford, an officer bold,
> The fourth day of June did the Indians behold;
> On the plains of Sandusky, at three the same day,
> Both armies did meet there in battle array.

The army of Crawford was overwhelmed by the military strength of the Indians. But then the military battle turned into a nightmare. The Indians, not content with their victory, took the wounded officers to their town, where they tortured and burned them:

> Now they have taken these men of renown
> And have dragg'd them away to the Sandusky town;
> Where in their council condemn'd for to be
> Burn't at a stake by most cruel Girtee.

St. Clair's defeat in 1791 is painted with less moderation. From the start, the fate of the American army is doomed by the very nature of "those young Diabolians":

> At Bunker's Hill and Quebec many a hero fell
> Likewise at Long Island, as I the truth can tell;
> But such a heavy carnage sure never did I see,
> As happened on the plains near the river St. Mary.[19]

[19] *A Song, Called Crawford's Defeat by the Indians, On the Fourth Day of June, 1782*, and *St. Clair's Defeat: A New Song*, Broadside Collection, Am. Ant. Soc. See also, Freeman Hearsey, *An Elegiac Poem, Composed by F . . . N H . . . Y, a Citi-*

Whether these ballads were sung or recited, they were part of a lore that common people would recall and transmit to the next generation. The Native American image thus entered the new American culture, foreshadowing the process that future colonial cultures would adopt in other parts of the world.[20] Indian symbols and metaphors that had been repeatedly and rhetorically mentioned by the elite were beginning to spread among the people, providing the grounds for a popular culture that would fully emerge in the era of the common man.

What is the relationship between popular culture and material identity? How did the former merge into the latter? Incorporating Native culture, at least a semblance of it, became a way of forging a common sense of American identity for the common man.

In the new republic there was no clear, definable, common identity among the Euro-Americans. As soon as imperial conflict arose, the Revolutionary leaders had used pamphlets, broadsides, sermons, and articles to assert a national British-American identity. But there were no ideological factors strong enough to make this unity permanent.[21] The citizens of the new nation still had to acquire a distinctive "character," a community of thought, morals, and values enabling them to adhere to the entity that had just come into being. The quest for a national identity, far from being achieved with the creation of the republic, continued during the first quarter of the nineteenth century.[22] But this process was not easy. Indeed, the nature attributed to the American nation had ironically to be instilled in

---

zen of Boston, and Published . . . as a Sacred Testimony of Gratitude and Regard to the Immortal Memory of Those Brave and Galant Heroes Who Fell Gloriously Fighting for Their Country in the Bloody Indian Battle at Miami, near Fort Washington, in the Ohio, Nov. 4, 1791 . . . (Boston, 1791), Broadside Coll., Am. Ant. Soc.

[20] Albert Memmi, *Portrait du colonisé: suivi du Portrait du colonisateur* (Paris, 1957).

[21] Elise Marienstras, *Les mythes fondateurs de la nation américaine: essai sur le discours idéologique de Pères fondateurs* (1976; reprint ed., Brussels, 1992).

[22] See for instance the efforts of linguistic nationalists—Noah Webster, Thomas Jefferson, William Cardell—as studied by Kenneth Cmiel, "'A Broad Fluid Language of Democracy': Discovering the American Idiom," *Journal of American History* 72 (1992):922.

the American people for that concept to become a reality. The nationalism expressed by the elite thus was both a justification and an act of creation. Its ideological content, its rhetoric, its rites and symbols have been described many times.[23] On the other hand, the diffusion of this nationalism among the common people has frequently been neglected.

The colonial image of Native peoples, as well as blacks, shackled in slavery, was carried over into the popular culture of the new nation.[24] In their attempt to give birth to a common identity, to create a respectable image of themselves, the former colonists, now American citizens, utilized those whose participation in their own society they at the same time rejected. Thomas Jefferson and John Adams had used the Indians as an argument in defense of their right to own land in freehold against the feudal claims of the king of England. Following the earlier arguments of Roger Williams, they pretended that the colonists possessed the land not through a royal grant but through their acquisition of it. The Indian tribes, not the king, had been the original owners of the soil. Acquiring the land from Native Americans reinforced the British-Americans' conviction that they were the only legitimate sovereign of the soil. However, the continent was still offering its expanse for them to conquer and

[23] For instance, Catherine L. Albanese, *Sons of the Fathers: The Civil Religion of the American Revolution* (Philadelphia, 1976); Marienstras, *Mythes fondateurs*; and idem, *Nous, le Peuple: les origines du nationalisme américain* (Paris, 1989).

[24] Elwood Parry, in *The Image of the Indian and the Black Man in American Art, 1590–1900* (New York, 1974), deals only with "high culture," which is to say oil paintings. In the examples he quotes, blacks and Indians never figure together in the same picture. They actually played different roles in the allegory or the implicit meaning of the higher and middle classes' paintings. In more popular illustrations, blacks and Indians sometimes figure together, such as one engraving by Alexander Anderson, the first American lithographer, which represents the giving of the Holy Bible by the missionary to all races of men around the world. At the fore, the black, dressed only with a rag, is visibly an African-American slave. He sits near a stereotyped American Indian recognizable by his feather bonnet and the hard racial traits usually attributed to Native Americans (Alexander Anderson Proof-Books, New York Public Library, New York City). More often, the representation of the Indian and the black are fused in one unique character: this was the case with the early Virginian cigar-store sculptures that only in the nineteenth century no longer alluded to blacks but only to the stereotyped Indian.

"settle." As Richard W. Van Alstyne first remarked, the War for Independence was actually the last colonial war for empire.[25]

During the colonial era the British settlers' identity as colonists was ambivalent: they were subjects of British power, and they were agents in the process of colonization. By gaining independence, that ambivalence disappeared. They were now rid of the imperial dominion. But their second function as colonizers, the former vanguards of British imperialism, now saved the interests of the new American empire. This is why it is legitimate to consider, as does Carroll Smith-Rosenberg, that George Washington and the Federalist leaders envisioned "Americans as imperialists first and as independent republicans second."[26] The nature of the republic was imperialist from the very beginning, and the Jeffersonians, no less than the Federalists, saw no contradiction in the dual nature of the new nation. Indians were part of the territory the American nation was to conquer. Both farmers and the people engaged in mercantile activities envisioned the Natives as being the main object of their common expansionist dreams. The common man, when referring to the Indian, was no less imperialist than his leaders— probably more so.

Furthermore, when confronting the British, the Revolutionaries had used the image of the Indian to adorn themselves with the virtues normally attributed to the Noble Savage—pre-Adamic innocence and untouched natural purity—in order to assert their moral superiority over old, corrupt Europe.[27] Simultaneously, by presenting a negative image of the Native peoples, they portrayed themselves as the heralds of civilization

[25] Richard W. Van Alstyne, *Empire and Independence: The International History of the American Revolution* (New York, 1967), and idem, *Genesis of American Nationalism* (Waltham, Mass., 1970).

[26] Carroll Smith-Rosenberg, "Dis-Covering the Subject of the 'Great Constitutional Discussion,' 1786–1789," *Journal of American History* 79 (1992): 841. See also Walter L. Williams, "American Imperialism and the Indians," in Frederick E. Hoxie, ed., *Indians in American History* (Arlington Heights, Ill., 1988), pp. 231–49.

[27] Walter Bromley, *An Appeal to the Virtue and Good Sense of the Inhabitants of Great Britain . . . in Behalf of the Indians* (Halifax, Nova Scotia, 1820); Ames, *Beyond Necessity*, pp. 64–65.

in a world of barbarism and bestiality. As Roy Harvey Pearce, Robert F. Berkhofer, Richard Slotkin, and many historians have demonstrated, the representation of the Indian was the reflection of the idealized self of the citizens as it had been for the colonists since they first settled on the new continent.[28] Both images—noble and ignoble—recalling the Alien's presence next to the American citizens, became intimately linked to the Euro-Americans' growing sense of national identity.

In the early national era, Native Americans thus played a conspicuous part in the nascent American culture. If the elite, not having to distance itself any longer from Europe, tried to emulate British and European literature and paintings,[29] the common man was more in need of a vernacular mode of expression. Thus popular culture used more local themes—including Native Americans—than did high culture.

COLONIZATION IN THE POPULAR MIND

One of the frequent fireside tales the common man and his children could listen to, or read in their textbooks, was the history of colonization. Even those Americans who could claim they and their forefathers had been born in this country, did not forget that their ancestors had once landed on a foreign shore that had been inhabited by other people.[30] For that matter, the difference between the theory and rationalization by the elite, on the one hand, and domestic objects, fiction or his-

---

[28] Roy Harvey Pearce, *Savagism and Civilization: A Study of the Indian and the American Mind*, rev. ed. (Baltimore, 1965); Richard Slotkin, *Regeneration through Violence: The Mythology of the American Frontier, 1600–1860* (Middletown, Conn., 1973); Robert F. Berkhofer, Jr., *The White Man's Indian: Images of the American Indian from Columbus to the Present* (New York, 1978).

[29] "Five Letters from Ebenezer Hazard to Jedidiah Morse," Jedidiah Morse Miscellaneous Manuscripts, New-York Historical Society, New York City; Noah Webster, *An American Selection . . . Calculated to Improve the Minds and Refine the Taste of the Youth . . .* (Hartford, 1789); Thomas Jefferson, *Notes on the State of Virginia*, ed. William Peden (New York, 1982), pp. 64–65.

[30] Wilcomb E. Washburn, "A Moral History of Indian-White Relations," *Ethnohistory* 4 (1957):47–61.

torical writings, and artistic creations for wide use on the other, is merely that of a difference of genre. The purpose and signifier of all these cultural productions applied to the same signified. In both kinds of iconography and writings[31]—high culture and low—colonization under the British was described as necessary and desirable. Nature and providence demanded it as the geography of the North American continent proved by itself: when described in laudatory words, it made clear that it would reward the colonists' efforts to improve it; when presented in gloomy terms, it explained the hardships the forefathers had encountered and surmounted.

In low as in high culture, the Indian was a reminder of the fact that the United States came to life after a colonial process and on land that had formerly "belonged" to the Indians. Imperialism had been the reason for conflict between peoples, of wars between nations, and the inspiration of murderous fights between whites and Indians. Behind the sufferings of the colonials at the hands of the Indians lay the idea that the new nation was heir to a necessary process of conquest. Sometimes, especially in history textbooks and in children's storybooks,[32] the "black legend" of Latin America was told, not, however, to deny the general colonial process, but to contrast Spanish colonization with the civilizing achievement of the English in North America. The author of *Sketches of the Moravian Missions*[33] explained how "shameful the way the Spaniards took advantage of their [Natives'] cowardice and ignorance. They would not so easily have subdued the North American Indian, who is fierce, active, and intelligent; wise in council, and of undaunted courage in battle." Many a story, like the one by Priscilla Wakefield, *A Brief Memoir of the Life of William Penn*, recalls the deeds of William Penn, the exemplary colonist, who "bartered with the

[31] Justifying exploration and conquest was obviously the aim of those popular articles and tales that summarized travelers' accounts; see, for instance, [Zadok Cramer], *The Ohio and Mississippi Navigator*, 3d corrected ed. (Pittsburgh, 1802); Alonso Decalves, *New Travels to the Westward or Unknown Parts of America* . . . , 1797, Broadside Coll., Am. Ant. Soc.

[32] A Lady, *Lights of Education*.

[33] *Sketches of the Moravian Missions* (Philadelphia, 1827), pp. 86–87.

Indians for their lands" and signed a treaty with "these simple sons of nature."[34]

Finally, the dual stereotype of the Indians as innocent or depraved "men of nature" was wonderfully plastic. If the author's intention was to praise the spread of civilization and Christianity, then the Indians' docile, simple, and native character was stressed to display their "exquisite nicety and [the] keen operation of their senses."[35] If it was to justify dispossession of lands and "Indian wars," then their nature would be described with the threatening epithets of "murderous savages," "superstitious," "barbarous," and "intractable."[36] What is most noticeable is that these tales about cruel encounters with the Native people provided the citizens with a sense of sharing a common history and reminded them that their common history was as different from others as it was linked to colonization.

Remembering colonization also meant introducing the prehistory of the United States into the present, thereby providing the new nation with an extended lifetime. Textbooks and children's books started the history of the young nation with remote events such as the arrival of the Pilgrims or even Christopher Columbus's discovery.[37] In that popular imagery, Native Americans were the incarnation of the past: "All those customs [of past Indians] however indifferently they may be related, are worth attending to as affording useful material for an authentic memorial of a people, whose manners will be totally changed before their race is exterminated."[38] When related to Columbus's discovery, the Natives, standing naked, either disarming or repulsive, were described with some ethnographic detail. Their primitivism proved that the nation was new and youthful. It sug-

[34] Priscilla Wakefield, *A Brief Memoir of the Life of William Penn, Compiled for the Use of Young Persons* (New York, 1821), pp. 17–35.

[35] Taylor, *Scenes in America*, p. 81; Rena Neumann Coen, "The Indian as the Noble Savage in Nineteenth-Century American Art," Ph.D. diss., University of Minnesota, 1969.

[36] Louise K. Barnett, *The Ignoble Savage: American Literary Racism, 1790–1890* (Westport, Conn., 1975).

[37] Taylor, *Scenes in America*, chap. 6; Taylor, *Letters to a Child*.

[38] A Lady, *Lights of Education*, p. 155.

gested that nature, like man, offered itself in its untouched state to exploration and conquest.

As a corollary, emphasis was put on the inventiveness of the discoverers and settlers and on the superiority of their industry and courage. Rarely can one find a critical view of colonization. Most often it was expressed by Quaker missionaries such as in a tale found in a Quaker collection,[39] which vigorously denounced the "Power makes right . . . motto of those princes who . . . parcelled out territories over which they could have no claims." The author warned "those who would assert the lenity of the Northern settlers" that although the northern colonists had acted like "men," contrary to the Spanish in South America, "they still have terminated in the same end." No other popular writings shared these views. All the rest globally praised the colonial cause for the sake of progress and religion.

Because they accepted the idea of colonization, writings rarely alluded to the spoliation of Indian lands. Sometimes official documents such as Fourth of July orations—which were reproduced in almanacs or separately sold as broadsides—mentioned that the Pilgrim Fathers "found a country swarming with its tawny sons, the lord proprietors of their native soil."[40] Similarly, in 1787 David Daggett made a rare "faux-pas," as Karl Lubbers calls it, and designated British colonization as guilty of land theft: "Let it be remembered, that even in this early period of our existence, we exhibited some specimens of that fraud and injustice which has been too conspicuous ever since—I mean in forcibly or fraudulently depriving the natives of their possessions."[41]

[39] *The Christian Indian, or, Times of the First Settlers* (New York, 1825). It must also be noted that the 1820s were an era of the Quakers' strong advocacy of the Indian cause; but more than an attack of colonization, their pamphlets express humanitarian and nostalgic feelings for the "dying race." See "William Penn" [Jeremiah Evarts], *Essays on the Present Crisis in the Condition of the American Indians* (Boston, 1829).

[40] William L. Atkinson, quoted in Karl Lubbers, "The Status of the Native American Indian in Fourth of July Orations, 1777–1876," in Renate von Bardeleben, ed., *Wege Amerikanischer Kultur* (Frankfurt am Main, 1989), pp. 97–110.

[41] Ibid., p. 102.

Although in reality it was "nearly reduced to insignificance," the territory formerly held by the Indians was frequently referred to as a "wilderness," "forest," or "dark woods." The captivity stories and their illustrations demonstrated how colonizing an indigenous land required that one step forth through the woods, through that shadowy wild space, where atrocities were taking place so often. The Indians were always represented in the forest or next to a tree. In every document where Indians are represented in their own space, the forest could only serve as a hiding place for nomads or to supply firewood for cannibal feasts. The fact that the woods were of no use to the Natives proved that they only waited for whites to clear them.

This assertion that America was "wild" contradicted the information contained in many almanacs regarding the continent's archaeological treasures. The contradiction was never apparent, however, because although almanac writers described or mapped the "tumuli" or "Ruins of a City [which have been] discovered near the River Miskingum,"[42] they made no mention of the nations who built it or lived there. These ruins reminded the reader that former civilizations and peoples had lived in America in ancient times, but those inhabitants could as well have been the Vikings, the English, or the French. Even the bones and carcasses along with the works of "exquisite art" found in the "earth pyramids about the great falls of the Mississippi," which suggest that the country has been "in ancient ages, as well cultivated, and as thickly inhabited as the country on the Danube or the Rhine," did not connect these traces of an antique past with a more recent history of still living, indigenous peoples.[43] The latter were said to be "roaming" or "hovering," that is, living without any legitimate abode that might have been taken from them.

The nomadism commonly attributed to Indians was also contradicted in most captivity narratives. For, after having been captured, the white victims are often taken to the village of the

[42] "A Description of That Part of the Ohio Country Where the Ruins of a City Was Discovered. A Plan of Which Is Here Given . . . ," *Weatherwise's Federal Almanack, for . . . 1788* (Boston, 1787).

[43] "Antiquities of Interior America," *Pittsburgh Almanack, for . . . 1801* (Pittsburgh, 1800).

tribe, where they watch the Indians lead a life which, though poor, is sedentary. But again, the contradiction was resolved because the *forest* was the setting for Indian villages; they were far away from any white settlement. To get there, the captives are dragged over long distances along which all kinds of horrors— depredations, thefts, looting, and murders committed by their abductors—take place.[44] In fact it is this suffering that is central to the captivity tales of the early republic. They form a sequel to former redemption stories such as the ones of Mary Rowlandson or John Williams.[45] Redemption, not a spiritual metaphor any more, is less important than the violent scenes displayed. In the post-Revolutionary era there is a luxury of detail—and the quasi-ritual unfolding of the action and of the scenery that takes place at the borderline of savagery and civilization. These stories appeared in broadsides, chapbooks, or almanacs. They had no didactic concern with the variety of Indian cultures. There was rarely any mention of names of tribes. All, except the Iroquois and Hurons, were simply called "Indians."

Native women were absent from the post-Revolutionary captivity stories. They only appear as "old squaws" who watch the scenes of torture and emulate the men. On the other hand, as June Namias makes clear in her book *White Captives*, white

[44] Joseph Bartlett, *A Narrative of the Captivity of Joseph Bartlett among the French and Indians, Written by Himself* (n.p., 1807); Archibald Loudon, *A Selection, of Some of the Most Interesting Narratives, of Outrages, Committed by the Indians, in Their Wars, with the White People*, 2 vols. (1808–11; reprint ed., Harrisburg, Pa., 1888); Samuel L. Metcalfe, *A Collection of Some of the Most Interesting Narratives of Indian Warfare in the West* (Lexington, Ky., 1821); *Murder of the Whole Family of Samuel Wells* ([New York, 1813]), Broadside Coll., Am. Ant. Soc.; *Shocking Murder by the Savages of Mr. Darius Barber's Family, 26 Jan. 1818*, Broadside Coll., Am. Ant. Soc.

[45] Mary Rowlandson, *The Sovereignty and Goodness of God . . . ; Being a Narrative of the Captivity and Restoration of Mrs. Mary Rowlandson* (Cambridge, Mass., 1682); John Williams, *The Redeemed Captive Returning to Zion* (Boston, 1706). For a classic discussion of early captivity narratives, see Richard Slotkin, *Regeneration through Violence: The Mythology of the American Frontier, 1600–1860* (Middletown, Conn., 1973), chaps. 3 and 4; and Roy Harvey Pearce, "The Significance of Captivity Narratives," *American Literature* 19 (1947): 1–20. For a feminist interpretation, see June Namias, *White Captives: Gender and Ethnicity on the American Frontier* (Chapel Hill, N.C., 1993).

women played a conspicuous part, often the central part, in these stories. Rarely did the pitiful victims of the savages, like Jemima Howe or Jane McCree, continue as representatives of the "Frail Flowers" who earlier brought romance and sentiment to more elaborate visual arts and novels. In the popular writings and pictures of the early nineteenth-century, women were "Amazons," "deputy husbands," redemptioners.[46] Spiritual redemption is no longer what matters: the bold farmer's spouse is the rescuer of the family, the Indian fighter, often the retriever of the men's lost bravery and honor. If there was a "private female sphere" on the frontier, it is clear that in popular ideology, women were in no way despised for their domestic role: the domestic sphere as conceived through the captivity or Indian murder stories played as great a part in the history of colonization as the battlefield and the usual men's activities did.[47]

The new captivity story generally began in the poor, isolated lodging of a frontier family. Sometimes the episode started at night and spread over several days. The members of the family, fewer in numbers than their attackers, were asleep. In the recurrent imagery displayed in stories by Mrs. Dustan, Mrs. Davies, Massy Harbison, Mrs. Armstrong, Mrs. Clendenin, and many others,[48] the young mother is the most interesting character. Either she is taken captive and has to marry an Indian chief and

[46] For an elaborate study of the Frail Flower and Amazon types, see Namias, *White Captives*, pp. 25–48, 92–97.

[47] I agree here with Eve Kornfeld, who points at the gap between the ideology of the elite leaders and popular culture, the latter being "inspired, consumed, and even largely produced by American women." The intellectual discourse "is representative in its link of women, popular culture, and social authority" ("Culture and Counter-Culture," pp. 71–79).

[48] *A Genuine and Correct Account of the Captivity, Sufferings, and Deliverance of Mrs. Jemima Howe, of Hinsdale, in New Hampshire* (1792; reprint ed., New York, 1977); *A True and Wonderful Narrative of the Surprising Captivity and Remarkable Deliverance of Mrs. Frances Scott* (1786; reprint ed., New York, 1978); *A Narrative of the Sufferings of Massy Harbison* (1825; reprint ed., New York, 1977); Loudon, *A Selection of Narratives of Outrages*, vol. 1; Mrs. Merrill, "White Mothers," *Family Magazine* 5 (1843), quoted in Namias, *White Captives*, p. 298. For more references on women's captivity narratives, see Namias, *White Captives*, pp. 294–302.

live with him until she escapes, or, more often, she is the fighter who may or may not manage to rescue her children from death. Interestingly, in these popular stories, no mention is ever made of rape. Either the female captive is rescued just in time, or she successfully fights for her honor,[49] or, more often, the texts omit sex as an explicit issue while the drawings that illustrate the stories allude clearly to the erotic aspect of the white woman. In illustrations her breast is partially exposed and her attractive legs are visible through the folds of her transparent skirt.

Generally, in order to make the captivity story more pitiful, the man, the defender of the family, is either absent or the first one to be killed. It is the wife who is forced to fight, and she overcomes the savages not because of her technical superiority (often she kills the Indians with a knife or a simple ax) but because of her moral superiority and her cleverness. The archetype of this kind of story may be Experience Bozarth, the heroine of the story called "Signal Prowess of a Woman, in a Combat with Some Indians."[50]

"Signal Prowess" tells how Experience became the victor over a company of Indians. The dangers of living on the frontier are highlighted in gruesome detail. The episode starts with the children rushing in from outside and saying they have just seen "ugly red men." At once, the attack by the Indians begins. One of the white men "stepped to the door, where he received a ball in the side of the breast, which caused him to fall back into the house," the other one engages in a fight with an Indian who has managed to enter the house and falls upon him on the bed. It falls to Mrs. Bozarth to kill two Indians with an ax: she "cut out the brains" of the first one "with one blow" of her ax, gives the second one "several large cuts, some of which let his entrails appear," while the first white man, who apparently has already recovered from the bullet he has received in his breast, rushes inside the house and helps her kill another Indian.

---

[49] As in *A Surprising Account of the Discovery of a Lady Who Was Taken by the Indians in the Year 1777, and after Making Her Escape, She Retired to a Lonely Cave Where She Lived Nine Years* (1785 and 1788; reprint ed., New York, 1978), quoted in Namias, *White Captives*, pp. 94–95.

[50] *Columbian Almanac . . . for . . . 1796* (Wilmington, Del., 1795).

Thrilling Adventure of two Girls.

Fig. 1 Mrs. Durham and Mrs. Macknight Escape from the
Indians. *John Frost,* Thrilling Adventures among the Indians,
1850. (Courtesy of the Newberry Library)

In this and other stories, the bodies of the victims, the husband, or the red attacker, killed by the heroine, lay in the cabin
doorway. In some stories, the body of the dead Indian has to be
moved inside the house so as to be able to close the civilized
shelter off from the attacks of barbarism. In every story, the pioneer hut is encircled by savagery. The narratives of war and cap-

tivity found in almanacs and chapbooks do not talk of conquest but of defense. Again, colonization is amply justified. No question is ever raised about the reason why the log cabin is situated in the midst of the woods—a ground which obviously belongs to the Natives. However, the two territories are visibly separated: the door of the cabin is the vulnerable spot through which barbarism threatens to invade the civilized space. On one side of the door is the intimacy of the home, the warm relations among the family, the innocence of the children, the courage of the women, and the technical aspects of civilization—comfortable furniture, protective guns, or else useful knives and axes; on the other, disorganized wild gangs who are united only by their greed and sadism.[51] Readers were so taken by these images that on a number of the originally published illustrations I consulted, spots of red ink were added on the images of the savages, thus giving them a bestial aspect, which fitted well with the words frequently used as metaphors in the accompanying texts: "vultures," "tigers," "buffaloes," and "wolves." On some drawings, other marks added blood flowing from the wounds caused by the savages.

The wild Indian image depicted in the early republic's captivity tales occasionally evolved into a cannibal. Generally, cannibalism appears indirectly: during an intertribal war, one group of Indians, after having put their Indian captive to torture, are said to "bring the kettle" on the scene.[52] Other implicit but more ambiguous references to cannibalism take place in several stories. One such narrative told the adventure of a man named Morgan, a "white man with two Indians." During the fight, Morgan "did the blow, and the Indian the throw, almost at the same instant, by which the little finger was cut off Morgan's left hand."

[51] *Horrid Massacre. An Authentic Account . . . on the North West Coast of America, Together with a Song* (1806), Broadside Coll., Am. Ant. Soc.; *The Affecting History of Mrs. Howe, the Wife of a British Officer in America . . .* (London, [1815]); "Narrative of the Massacre, by the Savages, of the Wife and Children of Thomas Baldwin" (1781), first published in 1837, *Magazine of History in Notes and Queries*, extra no. 171 (1931):107–29; Eunice Barber, *Shocking Murder by the Savages* ([Boston], 1818).

[52] "Behavior of the Indians, on Their Execution," *Columbian Almanac . . . for . . . 1791* (Wilmington, Del., [1790]).

Then Morgan caught the finger of "the [Indian] yelling most hideously" and "disconcerted him considerably by chewing it." With "a severe screw with his teeth," he "twitched it out through his hand, cutting it most grievously."[53] Symbolic of castration as well as of cannibalistic rites, these stories did not conceal that white and Indian protagonists shared the same methods. They appealed to the reader, more than the worn image of a boiling cauldron wherein the savages were preparing to throw their prisoners before eating them—a feast that is not described any further.[54]

From the 1780s to the 1840s, captivity narratives, often published in almanacs or in separate publications such as the Manheim Anthology,[55] sometimes summarized in the shape of anecdotes, belong to a special genre. One cannot confuse them with the novels read by middle-class women. At a time when captivity stories were so popular, novels were less frequently concerned with Indians than were captivity stories.[56] Until James Fenimore Cooper started to publish his Leatherstocking Tales, novel readers were more interested in love stories than in savage-civilized themes. It is only from the 1820s onward that captivity stories started influencing higher fiction literature. Then the interest among novel readers started to shift from the earlier British romance novel, depicting the sufferings of girls cruelly deceived by their lovers, toward American stories of valiant and suffering female captives of Indians. Middle-class culture and popular culture then joined in a more American-centered, creolized fiction.

Although highly evocative, captivity and murder stories do not provide—as would the more elaborate Leatherstocking

---

[53] "Remarkable Encounter of a White Man with Two Indians. In a Letter to a Gentleman of Philadelphia," *Columbian Almanac for 1796.*

[54] Anthony Aufrere, *Cannibal's Progress* (Hartford, 1795).

[55] *Affecting History of the Dreadful Distresses of Frederick Manheim's Family* (New York, 1798).

[56] Frank Luther Mott, *Golden Multitudes: The Story of the Best Sellers in the United States* (New York, 1947); Winans, "Bibliography and the Cultural Historians," p. 173; Roger L. Nichols, "The Indian in the Dime Novel," *Journal of American Culture* 5 (1982).

Tales—an explicit justification of spoliation of Indian lands and encroachment on their aboriginal rights. James Fenimore Cooper's *The Pioneers*,[57] especially, contains such explicit demonstration: Templeton, where the action takes place, is the metaphor for the early colonial frontier, a community "poised between order and chaos," settled by Judge Marmaduke Temple.[58] Chingachgook is the last of the Mohican tribe who originally held Temple's land. Part of the story deals with the ambiguity of the colonial contest on land ownership. At the end of the book, Chingachgook appropriately dies, "rendering moot the issue of Indian rights."[59]

INDIANS AND THE AMERICAN FUTURE

While captivity stories and other forms of popular culture reassured white Americans about the righteousness of past colonization, they also reinforced the idea that the new nation would pursue the western expansion and improvement of civilization. Independence gave the process of conquest new impetus. While colonial history was mostly shown as a part of a general—at least British—process, modern expansion took on a rather different meaning: it was linked with the purpose and destiny of the new nation.[60]

Beginning at a time coincident with Jefferson's active exploration policy, books on travel, discovery, and distant trade multiplied. Although primarily scientific, they nevertheless explicitly aimed to "amuse and instruct" the general reader. They inspired the authors of children's books, who used them as didactic tools. Passages were reproduced in almanacs and magazines. Above all, they stressed the idea that the continent re-

[57] James Fenimore Cooper, *The Pioneers; or, The Sources of the Susquehanna: A Descriptive Tale* (New York, 1823).

[58] William P. Kelly, *Plotting America's Past: Fenimore Cooper and the Leatherstocking Tales* (Carbondale, Ill., 1983), p. 1.

[59] Ibid., p. 3.

[60] Ernest L. Tuveson, *Redeemer Nation: The Idea of America's Millennial Role* (Chicago, 1968); Myra Jehlen, *American Incarnation: The Individual, the Nation, and the Continent* (Cambridge, Mass., 1986).

mained to be discovered and settled, that the Natives had to be converted, and that the work accomplished thus far was only a prologue to the future. Borrowing from travel literature also allowed popular authors to better inform their readers about the various Indian cultures. Throughout, however, the old stereotypes remained intact. Among tribes encountered by the "Gentlemen of the Exploring Party,"[61] there were "villainous" Kaskaskia, Comanche, Sioux, Kiowa, and "handsome, friendly," and "brave" Pawnee or Kansas—and the Cherokee-type of the once noble Indian, now corrupted and weakened by European contact and diseases.

But the travel and discovery theme remained ambivalent. No matter how legitimate and grandiose such enterprises were shown to be, the dangers and the horrors accompanying them procured the required thrill and pleased the public. Going around Cape Horn to carry out "a trading with those savages N.W. of America" was something the supposed author of an 1806 song, "The Atahualpa,"[62] and his companions hoped never to do again "for fear we should be slain." After the first stanza of the song, when peaceful trading was apparently taking place, the treacherous Indian chief had already prepared to spill the blood of honest sailors:

It was to buy their furs of them our Captain he began,
While a number of those savages all on our decks did stand
We sold them powder, pistol, shot, and swivel-guns also,
But little did we think they'd prove our overthrow.

Their Chief he being anxious to begin his bloody fray,
He tried several projects our Captain to betray.

More often cruel and treacherous than hospitable and noble, the Indian image never caused the common man to regret the

---

[61] Edwin James, *Account of an Expedition from Pittsburgh to the Rocky Mountains, Performed in the Years 1819 and '20 . . . Under the Command of Major Stephen H. Long*, ed. Howard R. Lamar (Barre, Mass., 1972).

[62] *The Atahualpa* (1806), Broadside Coll., Am. Ant. Soc. See also *A Journal of the Travels and Sufferings of Several Persons, Who Were Shipwrecked in the Gulf of Florida*, 9th ed. (Stamford, N.Y., 1809).

deeds of his ancestors or even to renounce trading with the Natives. For in the eyes of the ordinary citizen as well as of his leaders, the conquest of the continent had its justification in the teleological concept of the American nation. While the wording "manifest destiny" could not yet be found anywhere, and while precise references to the millennium had become obsolete, the idea that the American nation was endowed with a civilizing mission and that it was to bring on the advent of happiness for mankind underlined both high and popular cultures.

Especially in the eyes of pioneers and of frontier settlers, the legitimacy of future territorial appropriation did not need justification. It only had to be stated that the Natives "beheld with a grudging eye [the Americans' ancestors] reaping the fruits of their honest industry" and that they constantly threatened the newcomers with "outrages, hostilities, and rapines,"[63] to understand that the Natives did not deserve such profits, for they lacked the eagerness for hard labor and the capacity to cultivate their minds. Even benign representatives of the Natives were presented in a derogatory tone. Children learned for instance, that the "peoples encountered by the first European settlers were of a brown color." The hierarchy of values and ways of life between lighter and darker races were unequivocal. White American superiority was taken for granted.[64]

The alleged inferiority of the Natives was one reason the image of the Indian could no longer be an official symbol of America after the Revolution, despite the fact that Indians were still used as a metaphor. Another reason is that the image was also less important once Americans no longer needed to base their legitimacy on the Indians' ownership of the continent. Thus, after Independence, and more and more in the nineteenth century, the image of the Indian, while persistent in popular culture, played a different role in national life. Native Americans, like slaves, were seen as the antithesis of the American citi-

[63] Thomas Fessendent, 1802, quoted in Lubbers, "Status of the Native American Indian," p. 100.

[64] Hoseah Hildreth, *A Book for Massachusetts Children* (Boston, 1829), pp. 106–7.

zen. As the common farmer, the mechanic, the sailor, the merchant, the planter, and the professional entered an era of mass politics, where everybody (except blacks, Indians, and women) could share in and contribute to a flourishing mercantile economy, the need for sharing a common identity became more acute. The common identity emerged in contrast to those who continued to be alienated from the republic. From the 1820s onward, race, ethnicity, and gender were more than ever the criteria upon which American citizens—called by the Jacksonian ideologues "The People"—could define their collective identity. "The People" were everything slaves and Indians were not: white and not black or "tawny," civilized and not wild, free but situated in society. They were the legitimate inhabitants of the American continent, not an exotic, erratic group. "The People" believed in the sacredness of private property and made profit out of the bounty of nature.

THE ALLEGORICAL INDIAN

In the first quarter of the nineteenth century, the Indian image became an integral part, not only of stories, but of the very domestic life of citizens. He did not always have to figure as a villain to play his part as a countermarker of white American identity. Here and there, with a growing frequency as time passed, the Indian was presented as a harmless figure in poems, anecdotes, sermons, vignettes, and cartouches at the top of geographic maps, in the decoration of ships and tobacco stores. During the years of imperial conflict, throughout the War for Independence and down to the Battle of Fallen Timbers, the negative image of Indians predominated. Sometimes, though, as in the stories about the terrible defeat of the American army confronting the confederated tribes at Sandusky, or St. Clair's humuliating defeat, the authors were almost silent about the "fierce Indians" at the hands of whom numerous white heroes had lost their lives and the American army its honor. Then, in literature and official representations, the "Indian Princess" who had figured on British maps as a symbol of America for more than a century, was replaced by Minerva, the "Roman goddess." She appeared on elaborate American prints, as well as on the peace medals presented to Indian chiefs at treaty encounters.[65] When intended for Indian use, the engraved figure of a dignified woman facing an Indian chief on the peace medals could allude to the American benevolence towards the Natives. But the Roman goddess was somewhat too abstract and literate to be an ingredient of popular nationalism. Moreover, proud American citizens needed to present an image of themselves that should be, not only at par with but also different from, that of other countries. Therefore, in addition to the Roman goddess who embodied republican ideology, the Native image—Pocahontas or some more or less legendary chief—was recalled, though now subordinated, in the popular writings, songs, and illustrations. The female and male Indian heroes thus played an organic if subsidiary role, providing the required roots for the citizens' quest of national identity.

A poem reproduced in *The Balloon Almanach for 1790* depicts "beauteous Pocahonta" with languid, preromantic accents. With her "sparkling brown complexion, not the lilly pallid hue," and "her jetty tresses loosely flowing," she fuses with the "crystal" pure nature. While she anxiously waits for her lover, who may have been killed by a hostile weapon, she deplores the tragic fate of her "bloody race." She is both the incarnation of the American forest in its untouched purity and the witness of the disappearance of the Natives. A solitary, exceptional, and admirable figure of faithfulness and delicacy, this new version of "Pocahonta," the Indian princess, is easy to admire and identify with.[66]

[65] The first peace medals known are dated 1789. "They show the figure of an Indian wearing a feather headdress and draped in a blanket. He is dropping a tomahawk with his right hand, and with his left he is receiving a pipe of peace from a female figure in the garb of Minerva, undoubtedly meant to signify America" (Francis Paul Prucha, *Indian Peace Medals in American History* [Madison, Wis., 1971], p. 73).

[66] "An Indian Eclogue," *Balloon Almanach, for . . . 1790* (Pennsylvania, [1789]); John Higham, "Indian Princess and Roman Goddess: The First Symbols of America," *Proceedings of the American Antiquarian Society* 100 (1990):45–79; E. McClung Fleming, "The American Image as Indian Princess," *Winterthur Portfolio* 2 (1965):65–81; Rayna D. Green, "The Pocahontas Perplex: The Im-

Fig. 2   George Washington Peace Medal. Distributed to Indian tribes in 1789 to commemorate peace agreements and treaties. The front of the medal carried an image of an Indian chief shaking hands with Columbia; the reverse carries the seal of the United States.

As the Indian image took on some familiarity in popular culture, it lost part of its former formidable stature. Echoing the paintings of the Hudson School, where Indians appeared significantly tiny, far in the background or very small in the foreground, some cartouches in the corners of almanacs, newspapers, and broadsides depicted the Natives as one more element of the American landscape: as in Edward Hicks's paintings, the indigenous men and women drawn in popular illustrations give more life by their presence to the luxuriousness, the rich creativity of God's promised land.

Now almost completely absent from the familiar neighborhood of the East, the Indian more and more took on an allegorical meaning. Presented as a fictional, emblematic figure, he was also directly identified with exoticism, often associated with

age of Indian Women in American Culture," *Massachusetts Review* 16 (1975): 698–714.

other very remote strangers, such as Asians, Fuegans, or more familiar Scots or Jews.[67]

In a poem designed to instruct the "little tarry-at-home travellers,"[68] Isaac Taylor describes the various climates in which the different tribes have resided. From "panting" under a vertical sun, to freezing "in fierce and stormy weather," the Fuegans, as well as the Eskimo are not able to master their environment. "The very climate" makes primitive people of them, unable as they are to invent artifacts and to live otherwise than "in clumsy modes" like the wild beasts, which use of words such as "prey" helped the reader imagine.[69]

The almanacs were rich with those kinds of stories: throughout the 1830s anecdotes and amusing episodes abound and partly replace the captivity stories, revealing the astonishing modes of living of exotic and barbarian peoples. Interestingly, at the same time as white women were described as "Amazons," apparently revered by their male counterparts, the Native peoples were accused of debasing, exploiting, and bullying their wives. One story "pathetically describes the miserable slavery" in which women were held by their South American Native husbands, and how "married women frequently destroy their female infants" in order to spare them such an awful fate.[70] Another tale took place in Greenland, where the "slavish and dependent state of the wives" does "not derive from nature, whose dictates and influence are nearly the same in all regions and climates" but from the primitive and fierce manner of their culture.[71] "In Terra del Fuego," writes the author of a geography book, "the natives are fat, short, ill-formed. . . . A few branches of trees bent down, and spread over their skins, are their only defence from inclemency of the weather." When it comes to the United States,

<hr />

[67] "Mode of Courtship in Greenland," *Farmer's Almanack, for . . . 1799* (Norwich, Conn., [1798]).

[68] Taylor, *Scenes in America.*

[69] *People and Customs of Various Nations, Designed for the Amusement and Instruction of Young People* (New York, 1828).

[70] "Slavery of Married Women in South America," *New-Jersey and Pennsylvania Almanac, for . . . 1796* (Trenton, 1795).

[71] "Mode of Courtship in Greenland," *Farmer's Almanack for 1799.*

this long book never mentions any other inhabitants than the English who had immigrated there, even though the author quotes at length the names of all the tribes who lived in Upper and Lower Canada.[72]

Almost as exotic as the faraway Natives was the Indian chief whom American citizens were often urged to emulate. In this function, he replaced the antique Roman figures who played such an important part in the rhetoric of the Revolutionary era. The courage displayed by Indian men or women, who could face the most unheard of tortures imposed on them by their enemies and show such "an inflexible conformity to the principles in which they are bred," is said to "distance the most celebrated stories of antiquity."[73] The name of Tecumseh, more familiar to nineteenth-century Americans than Cato or Brutus, strangely provided the occasion for enthusiastic poems and stories. After the War of 1812, the captivity genre was transformed as it inspired children's books. The great Shawnee chief is the hero of one such story intended for children. Although unmistakably shown as an Indian, his character differs distinctly from that of his race.[74] His compassion, his elevated spirit, his natural leadership of men contrast with the predatory and base nature of the Indians he encountered: "Tecumseh was returning slowly and thoughtfully from the chase, when a shriek, as of nature's last and most dreadful extremity, burst on the stillness of the forest. He turned and beheld, through a vista of the trees, a party of marauding savages, loaded with the spoils of war. A female form, whose fair though faded countenance bore a strong

---

[72] Mary Anne Venning, *A Geographical Present; Being the Descriptions of the Principal Countries of the World, with Representations of the Various Inhabitants in Their Respective Costumes*, 1st American, from 3d London, ed. (New York, 1829). Better informed are articles about "The American Aborigines" published in the *Western Magazine and Review*, July 1827, and in *Niles' Register* 15 (1818). Some other ethnological studies were published at that time, such as Albert Gallatin's *A Table of Indian Tribes of the United States, East of the Stony Mountains* ([n.p., 1826]). These elite-oriented writings help us to remark how little effort was made to spread a more scientifically accurate knowledge of Native Americans among a popular audience.

[73] "Behavior of the Indians, on Their Execution."

[74] *Julia, or, The Pet-Lamb*.

contrast to the swarthy and painted features of the savages . . . had just fallen to the earth." Tecumseh came too late to help the young woman avert the tomahawk, but he was able to save an infant girl, and he bartered her for "his load of furs." "His olive cheek reddened with the glow, his eye radiant with the fire of youth," "never had [he] felt a purer pleasure than that which warmed his heart when the poor infant . . . smiled like a cherub in his face . . . and the angel of mercy, like the pillar of fire that guided the wandering Israelites, went before him in light, through the darkness of the forest." Of course when taken collectively, the Indians were displayed with the same cruel manners as in former captivity narratives. It was the exceptional individuals, such as Tecumseh and Pocahontas, who were praised.[75] And Tecumseh's deed was the more admirable as he saved a "blue-eyed baby" from "dark distorted featured savages."

In another children's book, Tecumseh's "famous speech" is reproduced, adding both to the well-known genre of "Indian oratory" and to enhancing his patriotic virtue. Many "Indian Speeches" were published in the form of chapbooks and sold well. The "Farmer's Brother's Speech" was considered "an interesting specimen of boldness of figure and [sublime]." "The Speech of Red Jacket, I think," wrote the editor, "discovers the beauties of imagery, united with the shrewdness of remark and an extent of information, far, far beyond what we could have expected to find in the wandering tribes of Indians." Following Thomas Jefferson's use of Chief Logan's speech in his writing, the Native American's reputation for oratory played a part in the republican rhetoric, a genre that praised eloquence as one of the foremost Roman civic virtues.[76] It is worthy of note, how-

[75] "Specimen of Indian Heroism," *New-Jersey and Pennsylvania Almanac, for . . . 1797* (Trenton, 1796); *Ontwa, The Son of the Forest: A Poem* (New York, 1822).

[76] Jefferson, *Notes on the State of Virginia*, pp. 62–63. See the frequent reproduction of Red Jacket's speeches: A Lady, *Lights of Education*, p. 46; *Farmer's Brother: Seneca Chief Speeches* (Canandaigua, N.Y., 1809); Farmer's Brother, *Speech of Farmer's Brother* (Boston, [bet. 1810 and 1814]), Broadside Coll., Am. Ant. Soc.; *An Indian Speech in Answer to a Sermon Preached by a Swedish Missionary at Conestoga* (Stamford, N.Y., 1804).

ever, that Noah Webster's children's textbooks as well as the other textbooks intended to teach rhetoric and virtue by the example of great orators, never quoted any but Roman, Greek, or English texts. If Western white culture was considered the heir of Greek and Roman culture, Americans did not think the achievements of a race that was vanishing were part of their legacy. In the American culture of the time, real Indian life and culture were rejected; instead, an imaginary, symbolic Indian was created to serve the needs of the new nation. The more Indians were used as a symbol for America, the more they disappeared from the world. Here an extract of Pope's *Essay on Man* was reproduced to give more credence to the image of the "poor Indian! whose untutor'd mind / Sees God in clouds" and lives alone with "his faithful dog."[77] Here, too, it is a poem by Philip Freneau that talks of the retreat of "the unsocial Indian" confronted with European immigration.[78]

More often the great Indian chiefs and prophets were shown as if lost in a faraway haze or disappearing slowly from sight, as in the shape of *Alknomook*, the Dying Cherokee. In this nostalgic, dignified song, Alknomook on the point of dying admonishes his son never "to complain" but to "remember the Arrows he [the father] shot from his Bow," the "Chiefs by his Hatchet laid down," and all the glorious actions that allow Alknomook to join the ghosts of his forefathers in the sun. One of the rare songs dealing with Indians in the early nineteenth century, this one had "the popularity of a national air" and was widely known.[79]

Rarely do dying Indians of popular poems or tales complain about death.[80] Often they meet it as a deliverance from the

[77] Eben W. Judd, *An Astronomical Diary for . . . 1785* (Hartford, 1784).

[78] "Stanzas on the Emigration to America and Peopling the Western Country," *Bailey's Pocket Almanac for 1785*.

[79] *Alknomook, the Dying Cherokee*, Broadside Coll., Am. Ant. Soc. Also quoted in Oscar G. T. Sonneck, *A Bibliography of Early Secular American Music* (Washington, D.C., 1945).

[80] Abraham Shoemaker, *The New-Jersey and New-York Almanac, for . . . 1800* (Newark, [1799]); "The Dying Indian," Eben W. Judd, *The United States Almanack; for . . . 1789* (Elizabethtown, N.J., 1788); Hearsey, *Elegiac Poem; Mr. Oc-*

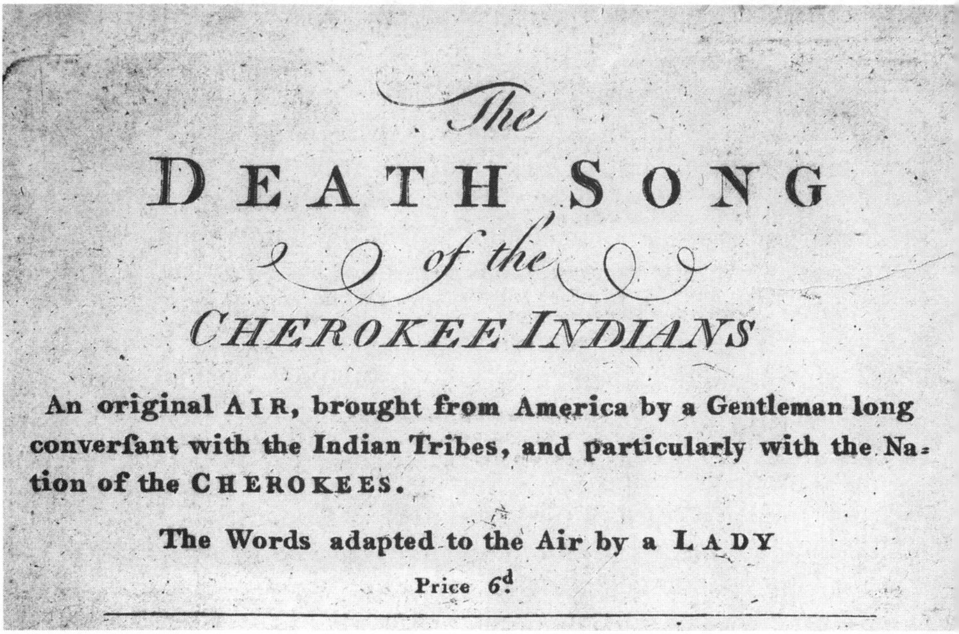

The

DEATH SONG

of the

CHEROKEE INDIANS

An original AIR, brought from America by a Gentleman long converſant with the Indian Tribes, and particularly with the Nation of the CHEROKEES.

The Words adapted to the Air by a LADY

Price 6d.

Fig. 3 Title page of The Death Song of the Cherokee Indians. *Early nineteenth century. (Courtesy of the Newberry Library)*

hardships of a miserable life: the Indian who is dying from a "poised dart" in a story of Judd's *United States Almanack for . . . 1789* envisions the world of death as "the blest island," prosperous and secure, "where my forefathers feast daily on the hearts of Spaniards." The "Dying Indian" boasts of never having "worshipped with those that eat their God."[81] Apart from Cooper's *Last of the Mohicans*[82] and his other Leatherstocking Tales,[83] there are few accounts of a massive disappearance of Native Americans in popular literature. Epidemics, alcohol,

---

com's Address to His Indian Brethren, Broadside Coll., Am. Ant. Soc., reproduced in Georgia Barnhill, *American Broadsides* (Worcester, Mass., 1984).

[81] Judd, *United States Almanack for 1789*.

[82] James Fenimore Cooper, *The Last of the Mohicans: A Narrative of 1757* (Philadelphia, 1826).

[83] Although widely read, the works of Fenimore Cooper have an ambiguous status. We cannot compare them to the popular literature represented by the almanacs, chapbooks, or broadsides, which were aimed at "amusement and instruction" rather than at literary perfection. Moreover, the authors of the

and especially massacres of tribes at the hands of the whites (except for the Spanish massacres) are rarely alluded to directly.[84] Several poems published in almanacs show Pocahontas or a noble chief sighing over the fate of their vanishing race.[85] Then the noble image reappears, with recollections of past deeds, emphasizing politeness, hospitality, and courage.[86]

As the Jacksonian era approached, carrying with it the prospect of the Removal, the Indian appeared more and more frequently in anecdotes and tales, in decorative domestic objects, in front of cigar stores, or as weather vane figures. The Indian had become a familiar, incidental presence. No longer a frightful and beastly savage, he was now quiet and benign, or else carved out of iron or wood in the most abstract unrealistic shape. The Indian image had become naturalized. It seemed natural to adopt Tammany as "America's patron saint" and to give this legendary character's name to an almanac.[87] In the 1820s the Indian represented fortitude in children's books.[88] But more often the Indian's broken English[89] (to be compared

---

chapbooks and broadsides were often the very simple peddlers who sold them and had no connection with high-class and literary circles.

[84] In "An Account of the Plague and Yellow Fever in Europe and America," *Farmer's Almanack for 1799*, there is only one mention of the epidemic fever of 1645, which *"raged among the Indians of Martha's Vineyard."*

[85] See the opera by James Nelson Borker, *The Indian Princess; or, La Belle Sauvage: An Operatic Melo-Drame in 3 Acts* (Philadelphia, 1808); *A Death Song of an Indian Chief* (Boston, [bet. 1810 and 1814]), Broadside Coll., Am. Ant. Soc.

[86] Nicholas M. Hentz, *Tadeuskund, the Last King of the Lenape* (Boston, 1825).

[87] Nicholas Varga, "America's Patron Saint: Tammany," *Journal of American Culture* 10 (1987). [Benjamin Workman], *Father Tammany's Almanac. For . . . 1786* (Philadelphia, [1785]), and [idem], *Father Tammany's Almanac, for . . . 1787* (Philadelphia, [1786]); A. J. Hatton, "The Songs of Tammany; or, The Indian Chief. A Serious Opera" (1790), *Magazine of History with Notes and Queries* 43, no. 2 (1931).

[88] Elias Cornelius, *The Little Osage Captive* (Boston, 1822).

[89] "How do do do, broder" are the only English words known by the "poor savage" in the story about a "Remarkable Encounter of a White Man with Two Indians."

with similar anecdotes about Negroes' language), the involun-
tary jokes he provokes when he mistakes one word for the other,
or does not know how to behave in polite or embarrassing situations, make of him a ridiculous, lazy, despised, sometimes pitiful
mongrel, inferior even to dogs.[90]

More related with missionaries than with the army in popular
writings, the Natives' dialogues with their benefactors were of
various kinds.[91] These encounters suggested that Indians were
incapable of understanding true religion or of acquiring civilized mores. Indians conveyed the impression that they were
only partly acculturated and that they had nothing to offer in
exchange for the material and spiritual goods Americans offered them. Ultimately their representation by white authors
and artists "proved" that they were unfit to belong to the American republic.

On the eve of the Jacksonian era, when the task of appropriating the continent had only started, when the common man
was just at the beginning of his career as the central figure of the
republic, the Native American had almost fully played his part
as a promoter of nationalism among plain citizens. In the popular mind his image as a real, flesh-and-blood person was fading,
as if absorbed by the white American nation. He had become
the emblematic sign of a remote past, allowing America to assert in front of the other nations of the earth that it was a nation
quite like the others—with its own territory, its own past, and its
own destiny. Indeed, America could also claim that it was superior to others because of its sacred duty to destroy the wilderness and spread civilization—*and* because America was the heir
of that imaginary, noble, innocent pre-Adamic creature who
had once lived on the new continent.

[90] "The Faithful American Dog," *Columbian Almanac for . . . 1798* (Lancaster, Pa., 1797); Richard M. Dorson, "Comic Indian Anecdotes," *Southern
Folklore Quarterly* 10 (1942):113–28; Mary Fleming Mathur, "The Tale of
the Lazy Indian," *Indian Historian* 3 (1970):14–18; Rayna D. Green, "Traits
of Indian Character: The Indian 'Anecdote,'" *Southern Folklore Quarterly* 39
(1975):233–62.

[91] "Anecdotes," *Farmer's Almanack for 1799*; "Humor" [two anecdotes dis-
playing Indians and clergymen], *Stoddard's Diary, or, The Columbia Almanack,
for . . . 1800* (Hudson, N.Y., 1799).

VIVIEN GREEN FRYD

Imaging the Indians in the United States Capitol during the Early Republic

THE VISUAL CONSTRUCTION of the Indian as both the noble and ignoble savage was codified during the early republic in four bas-reliefs executed in the Rotunda of the United States Capitol. Completed between 1825 and 1828, these works are Antonio Capellano's *Preservation of Captain Smith by Pocahontas* of 1825 above the western entrance, Enrico Causici's *Landing of the Pilgrims* of 1825 over the east door, and his *Conflict of Daniel Boone* executed between 1826 and 1827 over the south door, and Nicholas Gevelot's *William Penn's Treaty with the Indians* of 1827 over the north door. In rendering episodes of discovery, conquest, and colonization in the New World, these Rotunda reliefs emphasize through dress and physiognomy the differences between the European emigrants and the continent's original occupants, providing an excuse for the latter's subjugation by what the general public believed was a superior, civilized culture. The four sculptures resonate with ideological meanings and reflect changes taking place in federal Indian policy that were occurring in Washington while the artists worked.

PLANS FOR THE ROTUNDA DECORATION

The person most responsible for the federal commission of these four artworks was Charles Bulfinch, architect of the Capi-

This material is reprinted with revisions and with permission from the publishers of *Art and Empire: The Politics of Ethnicity in the United States Capitol, 1815–1860* by Vivien Green Fryd (New Haven, 1992).

tol from 1818 to 1829. This Harvard-educated and European-trained architect had been hired by the president and the commissioner of public buildings to take over what had been a piecemeal construction of the Capitol building under two previous architects. When Bulfinch began working on the Capitol, he inherited a structure only partially complete. Even the central Rotunda still awaited a decision regarding the display of John Trumbull's four large Revolutionary War paintings, originally commissioned in 1817. Bulfinch had called for a staircase and a separate gallery for the paintings, but Trumbull instead had wanted a simple architectural setting with unbroken wall space. Bulfinch agreed, eliminated the flight of steps, and situated Trumbull's works inside the Rotunda between prominent pilasters that supported an entablature ornamented with twenty olive wreaths. Trumbull's *Declaration of Independence* was in place in 1818, and the other four paintings were completed between 1820 and 1824.[1]

A sketch from around 1818 (fig. 1) reveals that Bulfinch also planned for horizontal rectangular reliefs of floral patterns above Trumbull's pictures and vertical reliefs above the north and south doors. According to this drawing, the vertical panels would have contained an eagle perched on the fasces, but for reasons unknown the architect decided to replace these abstract symbols with scenes that would narrate specific events from America's colonial past. He also decided to expand the two plaques to four, one over each Rotunda doorway.

Materials survive that document the four historical sculptures, allowing us to reconstruct the process of their creation. Bulfinch seems to have had free reign in selecting the artists and subject matter for the Capitol, provided he obtained the approval of the commissioner of public buildings, Joseph Elgar, who never disagreed with Bulfinch's plans.

---

[1] For a more detailed explanation of the collaboration among John Trumbull and the architects, see Egon Verheyen, "John Trumbull and the U.S. Capitol: Reconsidering the Evidence," in Helen A. Cooper, ed., *John Trumbull: The Hand and Spirit of a Painter* (New Haven, 1982), pp. 260–71. See also Fryd, *Art and Empire*, pp. 14–16, and Pamela Scott, *Temple of Liberty: Building the Capitol for a New Nation* (New York, 1995), pp. 60–67.

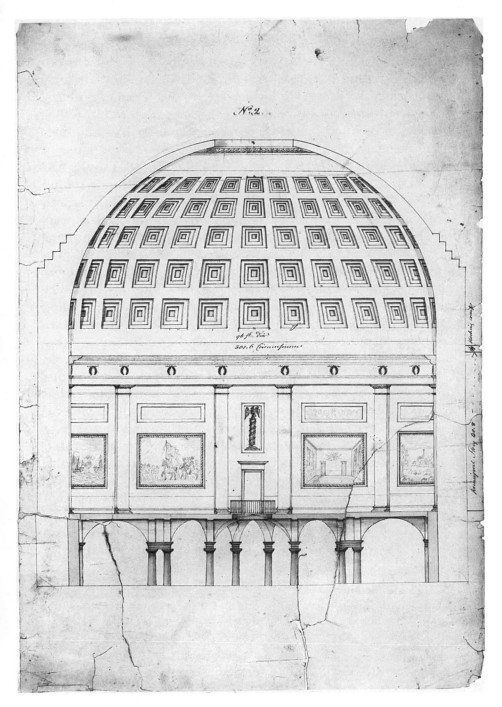

Fig. 1   U.S. Capitol sectional elevation. Charles Bulfinch, between 1817 and 1828. (Massachusetts Institute of Technology. Courtesy of the Library of Congress)

Despite his power, however, the creation of the new decorations was not a simple task. In July 1822, four years after conceiving the Rotunda's interior decorative scheme, Bulfinch contacted Enrico Causici about plans for sculpture in the Rotunda, explaining that the commissioner of public buildings had delegated the relief sculpture to the architect. A native of Verona who was purported to be a pupil of Canova, Causici had arrived in the United States earlier in the year. He first settled in New York City and then moved to the capital city in search of patronage. Presumably someone had introduced Causici to Bulfinch or informed the architect of the Italian sculptor's search for work. In a letter to Causici in 1822, Bulfinch proposed four subjects, hoping the sculptor would choose two for the east and west doors, "one to represent, either the discovery of America by Columbus, or which I should prefer, the landing of Capt. Smith in Virginia; & the other, the Declaration of Independence, or the adoption of the Federal Constitution."[2]

Apparently, Bulfinch had decided to replace the eagle and the fasces with historical subjects that concerned America's discovery, colonization, and federation, as well as the codification of its legal system. The one panel, representing either Columbus's discovery or Smith's landing, would document instances of the early European arrival and settlement of the New World. The second relief would echo subjects found in two of John Trumbull's large history paintings, *The Declaration of Independence* and *The Resignation of General Washington*. It seems that Bulfinch wanted another civic scene like those created by Trumbull, in which the painter documented momentous occasions of the republican triumph over Great Britain's monarchy.[3]

[2] Charles Bulfinch to Henry Couceci [Enrico Causici], July 8, 1822, Records of the Commissioner of Public Buildings, Record Group 42, National Archives, Washington, D.C. "Enrico Causici," *Niles' National Register* 45 (1833): 53, reported that Causici had died in Havana of Asiatic cholera.

[3] In some ways it is surprising that Bulfinch did not recommend the more dramatic scenes from the Revolutionary War that he had witnessed as a youth, such as the Battle of Bunker Hill. For general information about Bulfinch's life and career, see Rexford Newcomb, "Charles Bulfinch, First American-Born Architect of Distinction," *Architect* (1927):290–93, Claude M. Fuess, "Charles Bulfinch, 1763–1844: His Life and His Connections with Phillips

Writing three years before the placement of Trumbull's paintings in the Rotunda, the architect was determined to create a unified interior decorative scheme in which the paintings and reliefs would relate thematically to one another.

Despite Bulfinch's original plan, the four reliefs, when completed, represent scenes from the colonial history of the United States. Instead of illustrating any of the four subjects that Bulfinch had recommended in his letter of 1822, Causici executed *Landing of the Pilgrims* in 1825 (fig. 2) and *Conflict of Daniel Boone and the Indians* between 1826 and 1827 (fig. 3). It appears that Causici had for a time considered the first subject that the architect had recommended, for on February 25, 1823, the Speaker of the House presented a memorial from Causici in which the artist proposed to represent in "alto relievo for the centre building of the capitol . . . the landing of Columbus on the new continent."[4] It is unclear why the Italian never translated his design into stone, but Bulfinch's preference for the Smith subject probably discouraged Causici from pursuing the Columbus relief. Perhaps he replaced the landing of Columbus with the landing of the Pilgrims as a way to satisfy the architect's preference for a subject from the early seventeenth century.

Foreigners also executed the other two reliefs for the Rotunda. An Italian, Antonio Capellano, carved *Preservation of Captain Smith by Pocahontas* (fig. 4) in 1825, and a Frenchman, Nicholas Gevelot, executed *William Penn's Treaty with the Indians* (fig. 5) in 1827. Capellano, a Florentine sculptor, had first settled in Baltimore in 1815, where he carved the figure of Washington for the battle monument. By 1824, however, the immigrant apparently wanted to be hired by the federal government, for he wrote Joseph Elgar that if he could not find employment in Washington, he would return to Italy. Offering to "execute two drawings on stone," the Italian proposed motifs that related thematically to those Bulfinch had suggested to Causici. "The subjects I have thought most appropriate were first, when Columbus, the Indians refusing to give him the ac-

---

Academy," *Phillips Bulletin* 21 (1926):9–20, and Charles A. Place, *Charles Bulfinch, Architect and Citizen* (1925; reprint ed., New York, 1968).

[4]*Niles' National Register* 23 (1823):415.

Fig. 2 Landing of the Pilgrims. *Enrico Causici, 1825. U.S. Capitol Rotunda, above east door. (Courtesy of the Architect of the Capitol)*

customed provisions, announced to them that the God, whom he served, to manifest his indignation against them for their conduct would cover the Moon with a veil." When an eclipse appeared the next night, Capellano elaborated, the Indians in fear brought him abundant supplies. The artist also proposed a scene "when [Captain John] Smith received provisions from the Indians on the banks of the river Shecoughtan in return for their Okee or God, which had been taken from them." Capellano did not illustrate either of these topics even though he sent

Fig. 3 Conflict of Daniel Boone and the
Indians. *Enrico Causici, 1826–27. U.S. Capitol
Rotunda, above south door. (Courtesy of the
Architect of the Capitol)*

Fig. 4 Preservation of Captain Smith by Pocahontas. *Antonio Capellano, 1825. U.S. Capitol Rotunda, above west door. (Courtesy of the Architect of the Capitol)*

sketches for the landing of Columbus to Elgar. Instead, he depicted a subject that had strong appeal to nineteenth-century Americans: Pocahontas's rescue of John Smith.[5]

The few details about Gevelot's life and career that are known allow only a sketchy reconstruction of his single commission for the Capitol's ornamentation. The Frenchman had submitted two small clay models for the competition held in 1825 for the central pedimental decoration on the east facade. President

---

[5] Antonio Capellano to Joseph Elgar, Jan. 29, 1824, and Capellano to Elgar, Feb. 28, 1824, Records of the Commissioner of Public Buildings.

Fig. 5   William Penn's Treaty with the Indians.
Nicholas Gevelot, 1827. U.S. Capitol Rotunda,
above north door. (Courtesy of the Architect of the
Capitol)

John Quincy Adams had rejected all thirty-six proposals, declaring that they failed to express adequately a new national mythology. Elgar nevertheless offered to employ Gevelot, not for the central pedimental statuary that was executed by Luigi Persico, but to assist Capellano in finishing the Pocahontas-Smith tablet. Because the two sculptors worked in divergent styles, Capellano understandably objected to Gevelot's assistance.[6] As compensation, the commissioner of public buildings allowed Gevelot to create a relief over the north door. The artist himself probably chose the subject of Penn's treaty with the Indians.

THE ROTUNDA RELIEFS

Antonio Capellano's *Preservation of Captain Smith by Pocahontas* (see fig. 4) presents the earliest historical incident among the four Rotunda narratives. The work alludes to Raleigh's explorations of the New World that had led to the settlement of Virginia by the Virginia Company of London, a business established under the temporary leadership of Capt. John Smith, whose record of the colony's early history contains the anecdote pictured in Capellano's relief. On April 26, 1607, Smith and his party arrived in the tidewater region of Virginia with a mandate from James I to explore the area, fortify a settlement, search for natural resources, and discover a route to the Indian Ocean.[7] Unknown to these emigrants, however, several villages united under the leadership of a chief whose wealth and prestige enabled him to dominate other groups in the tidewater region. Not surprisingly, shortly after the Europeans arrived in Powhatan's ter-

[6] Bulfinch to Elgar, Jan. 29, 1829, Records of the House Committee on Public Buildings, 20 AG 16.1, Natl. Arch.

[7] Grace Steele Woodward, *Pocahontas* (Norman, Okla., 1969), p. 48. Other sources that detail the Pocahontas–John Smith legend are Philip Young, "The Mother of Us All: Pocahontas Reconsidered," *Kenyon Review* 24 (1962):391–415, Philip L. Barbour, *Pocahontas and Her World* (Boston, 1970), Rayna D. Green, "The Pocahontas Perplex: The Image of Indian Women in American Culture," *Massachusetts Review* 16 (1975):698–714, Frances Mossiker, *Pocahontas: The Life and the Legend* (New York, 1976), and Marilyn J. Anderson, "The Best of Two Worlds: The Pocahontas Legend as Treated in Early American Drama," *Indian Historian* 12 (1979):54–64.

ritory, the chief's followers attacked the colony, leading to further altercations between the two races.

In December 1607 (not 1606, as the relief designates),[8] Smith undertook an expedition on the Chickahominy River to procure corn and to explore the river to its headwaters. Powhatan's followers took Smith captive, offering him freedom only if the emigrant would assist the tribe in attacking the Jamestown fort. Smith refused. The Indians then paraded the Englishman before various villages and tried other tactics to frighten him into compliance, but he persisted. Finally, Smith was brought before Powhatan. According to the adventurer's own account (told in the third person), "two great stones were brought before Powhatan: then as many as could layd hands on him, dragged him to them, and thereon laid his head, and being ready with their clubs, to beate out his braines." The chief's daughter, Pocahontas, immediately intervened, taking Smith's "head in her armes, and laid her owne upon his to save him from death."[9] This event, described in Smith's *Generall Historie of Virginia* of 1624, is embellished in numerous poems, plays, and books, some of which contain illustrations such as Theodore de Bry's engrav-

---

[8] The date of 1606 inscribed on the relief is thus incorrect. In Rembrandt Peale's reminiscences of Capellano, whom he knew in the 1830s, the painter reported that the Italian "was a most industrious man—and so devoted to his marble that he could not spare an hour to learn either French or English" ("Reminiscences," *Crayon* 3 [1856]:6). Since Capellano's letters to the Commissioner of Public Buildings are in English, the sculptor either knew the language or asked someone to translate his correspondence. If the latter, then Capellano could not have read the books on Pocahontas. This does not negate my argument, however, for someone could have conveyed the content of the texts to the artist and, in doing so, made revisions or simplifications, which would account for his departure from Smith's account and the mistake in the date inscribed "1606" in the lower left-hand corner of the relief.

[9] This passage is published in Mossiker, *Pocahontas*, p. 341. Mossiker theorizes that Pocahontas's rescue of Smith constituted a portion of the adoption ceremony characteristic among northeast woodlands tribes in the seventeenth and eighteenth centuries (p. 81). Francis P. Jennings, in *The Invasion of America: Indians, Colonialism, and the Cant of Conquest* (Chapel Hill, N.C., 1975), p. 152, suggests the act derived from an Indian custom that allowed widowed women to adopt a prisoner to replace her deceased husband. Helen C. Roundtree, on the other hand, rejects these suggestions, arguing that Smith

ing from *General Historie* and the frontispiece from John Davis's *Captain Smith and Princess Pocahontas, an Indian Tale,* published in 1817 (fig. 6).[10]

Capellano did not derive his composition from Smith's account of his rescue (except for the detail of Indians ready with clubs); nor did he copy these images, even though one 1830 guidebook to the Capitol asserted that the "design is partly taken from a rude engraving of this event, in the first edition of Smith's History of Virginia."[11] Nonetheless, the pictures in combination with various texts must have influenced the artist's conception. In Capellano's composition, Chief Powhatan forms a central axis symmetrically framed by Indians facing inward. The Indians' upright poses parallel the vertical framing margins, left and right, and the reclining figure of Capt. John Smith reinforces the base. The chief, slightly smaller than the two other standing Indians, raises his left arm in a forceful gesture that causes his tribesmen to stop their violence.

At first Pocahontas may seem secondary in importance, owing to her location in the left corner of the panel, her suppliant form, and her diminutive size created by her crouching. But the twelve-year-old girl's elongated, outstretched arms lead

---

did not write the event as if it belonged to a ritual sequence and that only the Iroquois are known to have had such adoption ceremonies. See Roundtree, *Pocahontas's People: The Powhatan Indians of Virginia through Four Centuries* (Norman, Okla., 1990), p. 39.

[10] Among the nineteenth-century poems, plays, and books about Pocahontas are John Davis, *Captain Smith and Princess Pocahontas, an Indian Tale* (Philadelphia, 1817), *Virginia; or, The Fatal Patent: A Metrical Romance* (Washington, D.C., 1825), Samuel Griswold Goodrich, *Stories about Captain Smith, of Virginia, for the Instruction and Amusement of Children* (Hartford, 1829), George Washington Custis, *Pocahontas; or, The Settlers of Virginia* (Philadelphia, 1830), Robert Dale Owen, *Pocahontas: A Historical Drama in Five Acts* (New York, 1837), and Seba Smith, *Powhatan: A Metrical Romance in Seven Cantos* (New York, 1841). Both Jonathan Elliot, in *Historical Sketches of the Ten Miles Square Forming the District of Columbia* (Washington, D.C., 1830), p. 114, and Robert Mills, in *Guide to the Capitol and to the National Executive Offices of the United States* (Washington, D.C., 1834), p. 26, quote Smith's account of Pocahontas's rescue. For more information about this theme in American culture, see Robert S. Tilton, *Pocahontas: The Evolution of an American Narrative* (New York, 1994).

[11] Elliot, *Historical Sketches,* p. 114.

Fig. 6 Pocahontas Ran with Mournful Distraction to the Block. *1817. Engraving from John Davis,* Captain Smith and Princess Pocahontas, an Indian Tale. *(Courtesy of the Library of Congress)*

up toward her father's commanding gesture, suggesting that Powhatan's action derives from his daughter's entreating pleas. Following Smith's own interpretation, as well as the self-serving assessments concocted in the nineteenth century, Capellano presents Pocahontas as an intercessor whose actions made possible both the Jamestown settlement and the subsequent birth of the United States.[12]

The Pocahontas-Smith sculpture telescopes a first-person historical narrative of violence into a vivid, theatrical image that summarizes the relationship between the earliest English colony and the Powhatans. As Richard Brilliant has noted about the viewer's participation in the visual narrative process, "In seeing or registering that work of art, the viewer must employ an inductive method of analysis, not only to recognize the subject represented but also to integrate it within a larger context, especially through the operation of memory."[13] Anyone familiar with the Pocahontas-Smith story could identify the specific episode that Capellano portrayed. Numerous books and plays in the early republic, such as Davis's *Captain Smith and Princess Pocahontas* and George Washington Custis's *Pocahontas; or, the Settlers of Virginia* (1830), would have helped Americans locate Capellano's image within a larger narrative discourse. Consequently, the viewer of the Pocahontas relief establishes "a narrative context of greater dimension than the narrative bit presented."[14] Although the English arrival on the Virginia shore is not depicted, the viewer quickly understands that Smith's rescue was the catalyst for a chain of events that enabled the English settlement to proceed. And those familiar with Pocahontas's life would remember that she went on to marry an Englishman, John Rolfe, sealing the alliance between Jamestown and Pocahontas.

Capellano's relief alludes to these later events. Pocahontas's prayerlike gesture and beatific facial expression seem to foreshadow her conversion to "civilization" and Christianity. The close connection between Pocahontas and Smith—both figures are on the ground, while the woman shelters the captive beneath her arms and torso—suggests the future incorporation

---

[12] Davis suggested this interpretation in his 1817 biography of Smith in which he recognizes that "the race of Indians has been destroyed by the inroads of the whites" (*Captain Smith and Princess Pocahontas*, p. 65).

[13] Richard Brilliant, *Visual Narratives: Storytelling in Etruscan and Roman Art* (Ithaca, N.Y., 1984), p. 23.

[14] Ibid.

of a peaceful Pocahontas within the Jamestown settlement that occurred with her later marriage and baptism. The U-shaped composition, created by the two framing Indians who link up with Pocahontas and Smith, hints at the amicable relationship that resulted, albeit briefly, from the Indian princess's intercession. *Preservation of Captain Smith by Pocahontas* thus reconstructs one episode from the story of the seventeenth-century European expansion and makes clear that peaceful submission was a reaction that the colonists' heirs preferred. Pocahontas's marriage to John Rolfe and the birth of her mixed-race son demonstrated that amalgamation could occur, even though current events portended otherwise. In Capellano's work, the selfless Pocahontas and heroic John Smith stand out in greater relief than the ignoble Powhatan and his henchmen. Their projection outward and Powhatan's recession inward enact the future prominence of the white man and all compliant Indians over those who resisted the Euro-American invasion.

In moving from Capellano's *Pocahontas* relief to Causici's *Landing of the Pilgrims* (see fig. 2), we shift from a scene of peaceful assimilation to one fraught with potential conflict. John Quincy Adams had introduced the Pilgrims into national mythology in a speech he delivered in December 1802 to commemorate the first English landing in New England. Subsequent oratory and books of the early republic that focused on the Separatists' pilgrimage, such as Michael Corne's *Landing of the Pilgrims at Plymouth Massachusetts* (ca. 1803) and Henry Sargent's *Landing of the Pilgrim Fathers* (1813), transformed this obscure landfall into a rite of passage—from ocean to land, past to future, Englishman to American. In the hands of Adams and his contemporaries, the event came to portend the course of empire in North America. When Daniel Webster delivered an oration in 1820 that commemorated the Pilgrim settlement of New England, he claimed the English had transformed the region by establishing "smiling fields" and villages there, along with "the patrimonial blessings of wise institutions, of liberty, and religion." According to Webster, all these blessings extended from the Plymouth Rock westward to "the murmur of the Pacific seas," fulfilling the nation's providential mission. Twenty years before the term *manifest destiny* became current,

Webster's speech expressed and located its source in the Pilgrim voyages.[15]

Causici's relief reflects the growing popularity of Pilgrim imagery in the early nineteenth century. In his hands, the colonists form a compact group whose interrelationships are conveyed through pose and gesture. The son stands in profile, reaching toward his father with his left arm and looking up toward his mother, who embraces him with her right arm. The woman unites the group through her frontal position and massive form. The father does not turn to his family and enclose the group but instead faces the opposite direction, toward the Indian. The line of the high boot around the European's knee leads toward the Indian's right hand, which in turn points to the settler's foot.

The composition of this tranquil scene suggests that the two cultures meeting here will never merge as equals, despite the Indian's gesture of tribute and conciliation in providing an ear of corn to the travelers. The gift-giver symbolically offers the crop that became a staple in the colonial New Englander's diet and early economy, often enabling the transplanted Europeans to survive in the strange land.[16] The two large ears of corn beneath the Indian's bent leg indicate that the New World will

---

[15] For John Quincy Adams's speech, see *An Oration, Delivered at "Plymouth," December 22, 1802. At the Anniversary Commemoration of the First Landing of Our Ancestors, at That Place* (Boston, 1802). Robert D. Arner, in "Plymouth Rock Revisited: The Landing of the Pilgrim Fathers," *Journal of American Culture* 6 (1983): 25–35, identifies Adams's speech as the beginning of the Plymouth Rock mythology, analyzes the pilgrimage as a symbolic rite of passage, and discusses Daniel Webster's oration. The rock's mythic significance is suggested by Elliot, in *Historical Sketches*, who, in discussing Causici's relief, concluded, "the identical rock on which the Pilgrims first landed, has been broken up into fragments, and one part of it placed in the centre of the town of Plymouth, where it is known by the name of 'Forefather's Rock,' and is visited with a degree of veneration by all New Englanders" (p. 117). See also George Watterston, *A New Guide to Washington* (Washington, D.C., 1842), p. 38, for another reference to the rock's meaning.

[16] Historians have identified Squanto as the Indian who had taught the emigrants in the Plymouth colony to plant corn. It is unlikely, however, that Causici intended to portray this Patuxet Indian or to record his crucial role in helping the settlers survive. For information on Squanto, see Leonard A. Adolf, "Squanto's Role in Pilgrim Diplomacy," *Ethnohistory* 2 (1964): 247–61.

become a garden of plenty for the newcomers. In the relief, the Indian's gesture to sustain the aliens' bodies contrasts with the pose and gesture of the woman, whose nourishment and salvation come from above. The family group of the arriving Pilgrims echoes the familiar subject of the Holy Family's flight into Egypt, an association that emphasizes the Pilgrims' contrast with the non-Christian Indian.

The Plymouth composition is divided into two parts, emphasizing the cultural and religious distinctions between the races. Whereas the Pilgrims form a solid mass of smooth surfaces, the Indian's uneven contours and rough surfaces—created by the musculature and animal-skin robe—underscore the differences between the two cultures. The Indian is almost a caricature of the noble savage, whose childlike innocence, naïveté, and goodness show through as he straddles a stone that signifies Plymouth Rock. The English father's left leg with bent knee and the paternalistic gesture of his hand raised in greeting are juxtaposed by the Indian's outstretched left arm, right hand pointing downward, and bent right knee; unlike a jigsaw puzzle, where angles, curves, and notches interlock, the contours of these two figures do not match. This disparity is heightened by the space between giver and taker: although the Indian's gesture with his left hand reaches out toward the Pilgrim, the two men never touch.

The Native American, though larger and more muscular than the Pilgrim father, is clearly subservient, for his crouching position diminishes his towering size and strength. His contours are not the smooth curves that unify the colonists. Instead they are a combination of broad arches (evident along his back) and jerky angles (created by his bent knees, arm gestures, and profiled facial features). That the Indian points downward with his right hand toward the European's foot—drawing the viewer's eye to this motion—suggests the Indian's prescient recognition of the future course of events and emphasizes the Pilgrim's movement from left to right (though not from east to west), from ocean to land, from Europe to the New World, from civilization to a country inhabited by people perceived as primitives. The movement of the Englishman toward the Indian and the presence of the Pilgrim child presage the supplanting of the native inhabitants by the European white man, who begins, using Robert C. Winthrop's metaphor from his 1839 oration, "the triumphal entry of the New England Fathers upon the theatre of their glory."[17] (What happened in actuality is that the Pilgrims, like the Puritans, claimed title of the land by virtue of *vacuum domicilium* because the area had been temporarily vacated upon their arrival and they relied on Native foods for survival.) [18]

The message in Capellano's Pocahontas-Smith relief is that of reconciliation and peaceful assimilation. The conflict between Powhatan and the Europeans is mediated by Pocahontas, who brings peace to the two groups through her intercession on behalf of Captain Smith and her later conversion and marriage. Causici's *Landing of the Pilgrims*, on the other hand, suggests war in peace. A peaceful scene in which the Indians welcome the Pilgrims nonetheless intimates compositionally that the Natives will become subservient to the superior race. The third relief, *William Penn's Treaty with the Indians* (fig. 5), by Nicholas Gevelot, shows egalitarian relations between the Indians and the colonial English, although in this case the peace between them exists because of the Quakers' desire for more land. This work is unique because it represents peace as a feature of the encounters outlined by the other three Rotunda reliefs.

Early nineteenth-century popular biographies of William Penn described his life in England and the colonies. They explained, among other things, his role in protecting and sustaining the Quaker movement, in founding Pennsylvania, and in negotiating successful land sale and peace agreements. Nevertheless, the Great Treaty with the Delawares, declared by William Clarkson in 1813 as "the most glorious of any in the annals of the world," which was depicted by Gevelot in his relief, became the most celebrated agreement and event in Penn's career. According to tradition, the Quaker had met chiefs of the Delaware tribes in 1682 under the "wide-spreading branches" of an "elm tree of prodigious size" at Shackamaxon to sign a

[17] Robert C. Winthrop, "The Pilgrim Fathers, an Address, Delivered before the New England Society, in the City of New York, December 23, 1839," in idem, *Addresses and Speeches on Various Occasions* (Boston, 1852), p. 10.

[18] Robert F. Berkhofer, Jr., *The White Man's Indian: Images of the American Indian from Columbus to the Present* (New York, 1978), p. 130.

treaty in which the natives agreed to sell land in exchange for gifts. As *Niles' Weekly Register* concluded in 1825, instead of using the sword as "the instrument of gaining ascendancy over the natives," Penn employed "the even scales of justice and mild persuasion of Christian love . . . [to sway] the mind."[19]

A series of peace medals issued between 1764 and 1766 memorialized Penn's Indian diplomacy.[20] These medals, given to tribal chiefs as "symbols of allegiance from the new Great Father,"[21] contained a bust of a British authority on one side and an Indian scene on the other. Although early nineteenth-century biographies provided information about many of the agreements Penn signed with various tribes in Pennsylvania, peace medals such as the Richardson Medal of 1757 (fig. 7) usually depict a treaty under an elm tree, suggesting that Penn's famous compact with the Delawares along the river served to signify all treaties between the two cultures.

In Gevelot's relief, the position of Penn and the Indian who faces him on the left, the handshake between the two, and the Quaker's features and clothing all seem to derive from the reverse of Silvanus Bevan's William Penn Medal of 1720. The sculptor added a second Indian, in the center in lower relief, and the elm tree marking what Clarkson identified as the "Treaty of eternal Friendship."[22] The harmonious coexistence between the Quakers and the Delawares that resulted from the

[19] For discussions about the other treaties, see, for example, Thomas Clarkson, *Memoirs of the Private and Public Life of William Penn*, 2 vols. (London, 1813), 1:240–56, and Mason Locke Weems, *The Life of William Penn, the Settler of Pennsylvania* (Philadelphia, 1836), pp. 146–56. Clarkson's book was revised in 1849 with illustrations, including an engraving of West's famed painting of the treaty (Clarkson, *Memoirs of the Public and Private Life of William Penn*, new ed. [London, 1849]). For the quotes cited here, see the 1813 edition, vol. 1, pp. 334–39, and *Niles' National Register* 28 (1825):226.

[20] Ann Uhry Abrams, "Benjamin West's Documentation of Colonial History: *William Penn's Treaty with the Indians*," *Art Bulletin* 64 (1982):69–72, discusses these medals.

[21] Francis Paul Prucha, *Indian Peace Medals in American History* (Madison, Wis., 1971), p. 3.

[22] Clarkson, *Memoirs* (1813), 1:338.

Fig. 7   Richardson Medal. Reverse. 1757. (Courtesy of the Historical Society of Pennsylvania)

agreement held in Penn's left hand is emphasized by the compact, semicircular arrangement of the stationary figures and by the firm handshake that links the Englishman on the right and the Indian chief on the left. The enclosed grouping of the three figures—united by their gestures and glances—is created in part by the device of Penn's hat, which leads to the central Indian. This figure's position away from the Quaker but facing his tribesman directs our view to the Indian on the left, whose outstretched right arm points to Penn's left hand grasping the treaty. Penn's downward-pointing forefinger directs us to the inscription on the scroll, "Treaty 1682."[23]

[23] The pointing finger literally acts as an "indexical sign" that points to the treaty. The relationship among the figures merely underscores the impor-

The handshake functions as an iconographic reference to peace. Although not all of the nineteenth-century books about Penn indicate that such a ritual occurred during the meetings between the Quakers and the Indians, the gesture found in the Bevan Medal became codified first in the Thomas Jefferson medals (fig. 8) and then in such later ones as the James Madison medals and the Zachary Taylor medals.[24] In these, two clasped hands float against a flat, unornamented surface. The inscription, "Peace and Friendship," and the crossed ax and pipe above the hieroglyph are the only additional motifs found on the coins. The text identifies the meaning of the image that Gevelot has included in his relief: the handshake and the pipe grasped by one Delaware symbolize friendship and peace.[25]

The composition splits into a lower portion that contains the human figures, planted firmly on the ground and involved in a civilized activity, and an upper area, in which the branches allude to the elm tree and thus to the Great Treaty in the wilderness. Two subsidiary lines within the figural grouping lead the eye upward and downward: the peace pipe points to the three feet in the middle, each of which touches the other, thereby suggesting assimilation and integration. The central figure's upward-pointing finger—an echo of Penn's downward

---

tance of the document as the beginning of peace between the two races. In referring to "indexical sign," I am deriving the terminology from semiotics, in this case, Wendy Steiner, *Exact Resemblance to Exact Resemblance: The Literary Portraiture of Gertrude Stein* (New Haven, 1978), p. 6.

[24] For example, Clarkson's more factual biography of William Penn never mentions such a ritual. However, Parson Weems's anecdotal biography published in 1836 narrates that the handshake occurred more than once during the meeting between the Quakers and the Delawares. Upon finishing his speech to the Indians and their "cordially shaking hands all around," the group then smoked a peace pipe (Weems, *Life of William Penn*, p. 154). According to Weems, the two races also shook hands earlier during the ceremony (p. 148).

[25] According to Francis P. Jennings, in Indian diplomacy a chain of friendship was a political bond created by a treaty ("Brother Miquon: Good Lord!" in Richard S. Dunn and Mary Maples Dunn, eds., *The World of William Penn* [Philadelphia, 1986], p. 200). I wonder if the handshake on the peace medals intentionally applied to the native tradition or if this is merely a coincidence.

Fig. 8   Jefferson Indian Peace Medal. Reverse. 1801. (Courtesy of the American Numismatic Society)

gesture—directs our gaze to the tree in which two centralized, symmetrical kissing birds symbolize peace. Except for the differences in clothing and headgear—the Indians wear feathered headdresses and animal fur while Penn wears a Quaker suit and hat—the three men are equal in size, with similar physiques and amicable mannerisms.

Gevelot's conception in fact corresponds to the good savage and the good Quaker first detailed by Voltaire in his *Lettres*

Philosophiques (1734), in which the French philosophe gave an account of Penn's Quaker colony.[26] John Galt, in his biography of Benjamin West, discusses the significance of the Great Treaty, noting Voltaire's observation that the treaty between the Indians and William Penn had constituted "the first public contract which connected the inhabitants of the Old and New World together" and "the only treaty that has never been broken." Voltaire asserted that Pennsylvania was "the first country which has not been subdued by the sword, for the inhabitants were conquered by the force of Christian benevolence."[27]

Voltaire was correct. Penn, unique among colonial leaders in the seventeenth century, demonstrated justice and decency in his treatment of the Native Americans. But as the historian Francis P. Jennings has pointed out, Penn's motivation also derived from his desire to expand his territorial claims in New York and Maryland and to obtain trading profits at the expense of his rivals.[28] Although the Quaker succeeded in establishing his colony without conflict, he nevertheless negotiated with the Indians in order to expand his empire and wealth, a reality ignored by nineteenth-century books and images. As Michael Paul Rogin has aptly stated, treaties "engaged Indians in consent to their own subjugation."[29]

Nicholas Gevelot created a word that adheres to Voltaire's assessment of the Quaker-Delaware relationship in Philadelphia, but the subtext takes on a new meaning in light of a twentieth-

---

[26] Richard Slotkin identifies the French symbolic figures of the good savage and good Quaker as originating in Voltaire in *Regeneration through Violence: The Mythology of the American Frontier, 1600–1860* (Middletown, Conn., 1973), p. 204.

[27] John Galt, *The Life, Studies, and Works of Benjamin West* (London, 1820), pp. 14–15.

[28] Jennings, "Brother Miquon," pp. 195–214.

[29] Michael Paul Rogin, "Political Repression in the United States," in idem, *"Ronald Reagan," the Movie, and Other Episodes in Political Demonology* (Berkeley, Calif., 1987), p. 47. Rogin also summarized, "Treaties presented a fiction of Indian freedom to disguise the realities of coerced consent, bribery, deception about boundaries, agreements with one faction enforced on an entire tribe, and the encouragement of tribal debts—real and inflated—to be paid off by the cession of land" (p. 46).

century view of Penn's motivations. The composition implies equality, but a different set of circumstances existed from that which Gevelot was willing to reveal or could have understood. According to Gevelot's relief, the Native Americans amicably forfeited their land. But what is not apparent is Penn's motivation for peaceful negotiation. He avoided conflict yet achieved the same result that war would have accomplished: the exploitation and subjugation of the Delawares.

As we move to the final relief in the group, we shift from the seventeenth to the eighteenth century, from a peaceful scene fraught with suggestions of European dominance, to one that shows what came to be perceived as an inevitable conflict between the two races. In Causici's *Conflict of Daniel Boone and the Indians* (see fig. 3), the Anglo-Saxon and Native American are again facing one another in profile, but now the gap between pioneer and Indian is closed as they engage in combat, forming the apex of a triangle whose base is created by the one dead Indian. The stability established by the triangular figural composition, a prevalent format in Renaissance and Baroque art, is countered by the diagonal lines of the rifle and tomahawk held by Boone and the Indian. Their right and left legs press isometrically as they crush against the defeated Indian, forming an angle that leads the eye first to Boone's chest and then to his face and rifle. The swag of drapery beneath the Indian's left arm extends the line of Boone's rifle, pointing toward the compressed legs, one naked, the other in a high boot. The Indian's bulging, muscular thigh and calf are countered by the knife Boone holds in his right hand. The settler is poised to strike his opponent.

John Filson's popular biography of Boone, published in 1784 and reissued several times, had first recounted the pioneer's "dangerous, helpless situation, exposed daily to perils and death amongst savages and wild beasts . . . in the howling wilderness,"[30] thereby transforming the historical person into an exemplar of white settlers on the frontier. Later authors during the early republic, such as Daniel Bryan in his 1813 epic poem, *The Mountain Muse*, and Timothy Flint in his 1833 *Biographical*

---

[30] John Filson, *The Discovery of Kentucke and the Adventures of Daniel Boone* (1784; reprint ed., New York, 1978), p. 53.

Memoir of Daniel Boone, perpetuated the notion of Boone as a mythic hunter-adventurer who led the Chosen People westward and acted as an agent of civilization.[31] Causici's relief freezes Boone's struggles against the Indians in his attempt to subdue savagery and the wilderness, the latter symbolized by the tree that branches over the figures. According to Robert Mills, the future architect of public buildings who wrote a guide to the Capitol in 1834, the foliage identifies the setting as "the deep lone forest of the 'far west,'" the far west where the Dangerfields in James Kirke Paulding's *Westward Ho!* of 1832 moved to become, like the great "patriarch . . . of 'Old Kentuck,'" the "founders of a new empire."[32]

Located toward the center of the lowest branch is the date 1773, allowing us to identify the specific episode illustrated by the artist. As Filson recorded in his biography of Boone, on October 10 the settler penetrated the Kentucky frontier with at least five other families: "The rear of our company was attacked by a number of Indians, who killed six, and wounded one man. . . . Though we defended ourselves, and repulsed the enemy . . . we retreated forty miles."[33] Rather than portray the death of white settlers and their retreat from battle, Causici instead distorted reality by showing Boone struggling with an Indian equal in physical strength. The prominent musculature and ferocious grimace of this fighting Indian identifies him as an ignoble savage who threatens civilization's progress. Taller and brawnier than his opponent, the Indian will nevertheless succumb to Boone, who is empowered and supported by moral strength (indicated by the serene expression on his face) and by the superiority of his rifle—evidence of an advanced civili-

---

[31] Daniel Bryan, *The Mountain Muse: Comprising the Adventures of Daniel Boone, and the Power of Virtuous and Refined Beauty* (Harrisonburg, Va., 1813); Timothy Flint, *Biographical Memoir of Daniel Boone, the First Settler of Kentucky: Interspersed with Incidents in the Early Annals of the Country* (Cincinnati, 1833). For more information on the iconography of Daniel Boone in American art, see J. Gray Sweeney, *The Columbus of the Woods: Daniel Boone and the Typology of Manifest Destiny* (St. Louis, 1992).

[32] Mills, *Guide to the Capitol,* p. 28, and James Kirke Paulding, *Westward Ho! A Tale,* 2 vols. (New York, 1832), 1:70 and 55.

[33] Filson, *Discovery of Kentucke,* p. 57.

zation. The impending defeat of the indigenous people is suggested by the vanquished Indian at the base, who, according to William Force's 1848 guidebook to Washington, "admirably expresses the proud spirit of a fallen savage, unsubdued even in death."[34] The relief thus transcends the specific episode to become an icon of the frontier experience.

STEREOTYPES OF NATIVE AMERICANS

These images in the Capitol follow stereotypes that had existed before the founding of the Republic. Noble and ignoble savages can be found in novels, poems, plays, book illustrations, and paintings. "Noble" images predominated among eighteenth-century French philosophes who described the American Indian as a being who lived apart from civilization's corrupting influences and enjoyed a primitive state of harmony with nature.[35] Benjamin West, the American-born colonial artist who became the president of the Royal Academy in England and the court painter to the king, especially gave form to the noble savage in numerous paintings such as *Savage Warrior Taking Leave of His Family* of 1760, in which he depicted a seminude, standing figure with outstretched arm derived from the Hellenistic *Apollo Belvedere*. The appropriation of this antique male form enabled West to create a heroicized and idealized Indian with bulging muscles and perfect proportions as a noble savage. The ignoble savage, on the other hand, is an indigenous construction created by Puritan captivity narratives[36] and carried on by the texts

[34] William Q. Force, *Picture of Washington and Its Vicinity, for 1848* (Washington, D.C., 1848), p. 61.

[35] For a summary of the noble savage in literature and art, see Hoxie Neale Fairchild, *The Noble Savage: A Study in Romantic Naturalism* (New York, 1928), Roy Harvey Pearce, *Savagism and Civilization: A Study of the Indian and the American Mind* (Baltimore, 1967), Rena Neumann Coen, "The Indian as the Noble Savage in Nineteenth-Century American Art," Ph.D. diss., University of Minnesota, 1969, p. 3, Gaile McGregor, *The Noble Savage in the New World Garden: Notes toward a Syntactic of Place* (Toronto, 1988), and Stelio Cro, *The Noble Savage: Allegory of Freedom* (Waterloo, Ontario, 1989).

[36] Louise K. Barnett, *The Ignoble Savage: American Literary Racism, 1790–1890* (Westport, Conn., 1975), p. 73.

and illustrations of eighteenth- and nineteenth-century captivity novels. Hostile savages were not found in American oil painting until 1804 with John Vanderlyn's *Death of Jane McCrea*. In this painting (fig. 9) commissioned by Joel Barlow to provide engravings for his epic poem, *The Columbiad*, Vanderlyn also appropriated ancient prototypes for his male Indians, but rather than depict benign and peaceful people, he rendered dangerous and brutal heroic men who threaten the helpless and terrified woman who stands for white civilization.

The sculptors who carved the Rotunda reliefs similarly render noble and ignoble savages, although with the exception of Gevelot's panel, their works reiterate the awkward poses, flattened compositions, angular features, distorted scale, and caricatured facial expressions found in earlier illustrations of Native Americans. These appeared in such books as Theodore de Bry's *America* (1591) and Captain John Smith's *Generall Historie of Virginia*.[37] Only Capellano's *Preservation of Captain Smith by Pocahontas* represents both the innocent savage and the unremitting one.

The Capitol reliefs thus reconstruct and represent historical realities as filtered through the imagination of nineteenth-century European artists who themselves became transplanted emigrants outside the mainstream of Anglo-Saxon culture, producing works for that culture in the Capitol building. These outsiders clearly studied previous images in order to create their visions of the nation's colonial past. In hindsight, it seems significant that Europeans executed the Rotunda reliefs that initiated the stereotyping of Native Americans in the Capitol decoration. True, Bulfinch had no choice but to commission foreigners because there were no professional sculptors at that time in the United States. Antonio Capellano, Enrico Causici, and Nicholas Gevelot came to the States from Italy and France in the hopes of establishing their reputations, probably recognizing that they could not surpass the leading sculptors in Europe. But they did not become American citizens assimilated

[37] Vivien Green Fryd, "The Italian Presence in the United States Capitol," in Irma B. Jaffe, ed., *The Italian Presence in American Art, 1760–1860* (New York, 1989), pp. 138–40.

Fig. 9 The Death of Jane McCrea. *John Vanderlyn, 1804. (Courtesy of the Wadsworth Athenaeum, Hartford. Purchased by Subscription)*

into American culture. Instead they remained visitors, leaving this country sometime after completing their congressional commissions.

THE INDIAN PROBLEM

It is significant that the Capitol reliefs, which contain both inherited stereotypes and images of native subjugation, were carved during a decade of rapid change in federal Indian policy. In the 1780s and 1790s, Euro-Americans had believed that the continent's Native population could become incorporated into the settlers' transplanted culture. For this reason, missionaries and agents under the direction of the Department of War taught Indians white agricultural practices and domestic arts. Thomas Jefferson adhered to this tradition during his administration, promoting the civilization, education, and assimilation of Indians with a philanthropic plan that called on them to abandon the hunter-warrior culture and communal ownership of land. Hoping that the Indians would become yeoman farmers and intermix with the white population, Jefferson advocated federally supported instruction in agriculture and the English language. Just as the wilderness had been transformed into burgeoning villages and farms, Indian communities would be molded into units of the new republic.[38]

But the third president was not only concerned about Indian advancement. He realized that a shift to agriculture would reduce the territory Native people would require for their livelihood. "While they are learning to do better on less land," Jefferson reasoned, "our increasing numbers will be calling for more land, and thus a coincidence of interests will be produced between those who have lands to spare, and want other necessaries, and those who have such necessaries to spare, and want lands." The architect of the Louisiana Purchase believed that Indian "progress" would allow for the further increase of the nation's geographical domain.[39]

[38] Bernard W. Sheehan, *Seeds of Extinction: Jeffersonian Philanthropy and the American Indian* (Chapel Hill, N.C., 1973).

[39] Three books are especially helpful in understanding Thomas Jefferson's attitudes toward the Indians: Brian W. Dippie, *The Vanishing American: White*

Jefferson's strategy won wide support, but events during the first two decades of the nineteenth century gradually led the government to take a different approach. First, the alliance various tribes formed with the British during the War of 1812 convinced many Americans that war with the Indians was inevitable. Second, a seemingly unbridgeable conflict between Georgia and the Cherokee nation led some government officials to embrace the concept of Indian Removal. In 1802 the federal government had agreed to terminate its agreements that had recognized the Cherokees' claim to land in Georgia in exchange for a cession of the state's western land claims. But in the ensuing years the national government did not carry out its promise to the state. Georgians began to demand that Indian ownership in the state be abolished. In 1827 the Cherokees drafted a constitution modeled after that of the United States and declared themselves an independent nation with sovereignty over their territories. Frustrated by federal inaction and Indian intransigence, Georgia responded with measures that curtailed Indian rights within its boundaries. The conflict raised the same issue of states' rights that would bedevil national politics for the rest of the pre–Civil War era.[40]

The War of 1812 and the Georgia-Cherokee crisis caused Indian Office officials to vacillate over the "Indian problem." They began to question their assumption of eventual Indian assimilation and to consider the alternative of segregation. As

Attitudes and U.S. Indian Policy (Middletown, Conn., 1982); Michael Paul Rogin, Fathers and Children: Andrew Jackson and the Subjugation of the American Indian (New York, 1975); and Ronald T. Takaki, Iron Cages: Race and Culture in Nineteenth-Century America (New York, 1979). For Jefferson's quote, see Thomas Jefferson to Benjamin Hawkins, Feb. 18, 1803, Paul Leicester Ford, ed., The Writings of Thomas Jefferson, 10 vols. (New York, 1892–99), 8:214. For the relationship between the United States' market economy and Indian policy, see Takaki, Iron Cages, pp. 57–60.

[40] Information about Indian-white relations during this period is extensive, but most helpful are Dippie, Vanishing American, Richard Drinnon, Facing West: The Metaphysics of Indian-Hating and Empire-Building (Minneapolis, 1980), Reginald Horsman, Race and Manifest Destiny: The Origins of American Racial Anglo-Saxonism (Cambridge, Mass., 1981), Francis Paul Prucha, American Indian Policy in the Formative Years: The Indian Trade and Intercourse Acts, 1790–1834 (Madison, Wis., 1971), and Sheehan, Seeds of Extinction.

the Indian agent and ethnologist Henry Schoolcraft wrote in 1828, "Nobody knows really what to do."[41] Until the Georgia-Cherokee conflict brought the issue to a resolution—one in which white Americans profited and the Natives were forced to leave their ancestral homeland—the government continued Enlightenment policies of civilization. This is evident in President James Monroe's approval of the 1819 Indian Civilization Act, which provided for the acculturation of Indian tribes adjoining the frontier settlements by appropriating ten thousand dollars annually to employ people to instruct the Indians in agriculture and to educate their children. By the 1820s, however, the incorporation of southeastern Indians into white society presented an obstacle to expansion and a threat to the white supremacy that underlay the region's rapidly growing slave economy. The actions of the defiant Cherokees, Georgia's unhappiness over the federal government's apparent sympathy for the tribes, and the fear of many humanitarian observers that the Indians would be destroyed in any confrontation conspired to produce a new policy of removal. President Monroe first urged tribes to move west of the Mississippi in a special message to Congress in March 1824, and his successors picked up the theme over the following decade.[42]

The idea of removal had circulated through Washington since the Louisiana Purchase, when Thomas Jefferson viewed the new territory as perfect for the relocation of Indian tribes. Although Presidents Monroe and Adams endorsed this approach as well, it was not until 1830 that the Jackson administration won congressional approval for a comprehensive program of relocating eastern tribes to new lands west of the Mississippi. The Indian Removal Act Andrew Jackson signed into law on March 28, 1830, provided for the exchange of lands between the Indians and white Americans and for all Indian tribes to move beyond the borders of the states. During the 1830s the federal authorities negotiated with and bullied the tribes and moved them onto the

[41] Quoted in Dippie, *Vanishing American*, p. 48.

[42] Francis Paul Prucha, "Indian Removal and the Great American Desert," in idem, *Indian Policy in the United States: Historical Essays* (Lincoln, Nebr., 1981), pp. 100–101.

Great Plains. Perhaps the most notorious result of the Indian Removal Act was the Trail of Tears, in which the Cherokees experienced extreme hardships and suffered many deaths during the long trek from Tennessee to Oklahoma.[43]

Old Hickory had justified the relocation of the Indians by arguing that the policy would ensure the eventual civilization and acculturation of people that he called "savage dogs." Nevertheless, despite the bill's enactment, some Jacksonian opponents believed that the Indian tribes had rights to self-government and to their lands, even though they also shared their rivals' belief in white America's superiority. The Indian Removal Act prepared the way for the market revolution in the United States, in which enslaved African Americans were moved onto the abandoned Indian land to cultivate cotton. Unlike the Indians, blacks would not be expelled. The new order demanded their labor, and so, as Ronald T. Takaki has written, slaves were "securely chained to white society and its political economy."[44]

CONCLUSION

Although Bulfinch clearly influenced the subject matter of the Capitol relief panels, there is no hard evidence to document his views concerning Native Americans. Bulfinch himself was a Boston politician, having served as chairman of the Board of Selectman of the Town of Boston (the equivalent of being a mayor) for nineteen years beginning in 1799. But his role was to run government affairs of the city, not to resolve differences with the Native peoples who had earlier been relocated from the region. It is known that Bulfinch entertained President

[43] The exact number of deaths is disputed. See ibid., pp. 7–8. In addition to the sources cited previously, Philip Borden's "Found Cumbering the Soil: Manifest Destiny and the Indian in the Nineteenth Century," in Gary B. Nash and Richard Weiss, eds., *The Great Fear: Race in the Mind of America* (New York, 1970), pp. 71–97, provides a succinct summary of the Indian Removal policy, linking it into the ideology of Manifest Destiny.

[44] For Andrew Jackson's degrading nickname for the Indians, see Takaki, *Iron Cages*, p. 96. Takaki analyzes the relationship between racial domination and the development of capitalism in nineteenth-century American society, providing the basis for my references to what Takaki calls the "Market Revolution" and the importation of slaves into former Indian territory (p. 110).

Monroe in 1817 for a week when he visited the city and that this experience contributed to his position the following year as architect of the Capitol, but whether they discussed or even agreed about political issues is unknown. Certainly, Bulfinch as a loyal party man approved of images that buttressed the removal philosophy.

It is also possible that President Monroe had some suggestions for the reliefs, given the evidence that during the next administration in 1825 President John Quincy Adams influenced the iconography of Luigi Persico's *Genius of America* for the central pediment of the Capitol.[45] Certainly his concern over the "Indian problem" may have contributed to his approval of the works executed under Bulfinch's office. Monroe was confronted directly with the problem of resolving the Cherokee-Georgia dispute, and he believed that resolving the issue without conflict required removal of the tribes beyond the Mississippi. He believed that the West offered the only hope for their improved "civilization," and improved "security and happiness."[46] Monroe, in fact, had advocated removal throughout his tenure as president, believing that the "progress" of white settlement westward could not be prevented—"the rights of nature demand [it]." "It is our duty to make new efforts for the preservation, improvement, and civilization of the native inhabitants," he explained in his first annual message on December 2, 1817, elaborating later in 1821 that the government "should perform the office of their Great Father."[47] President John Quincy Adams continued Monroe's removal philosophy, although his secretary of war, James Barbour, advocated the removal of individuals rather than tribes.[48]

---

[45] Fryd, *Art and Empire*, pp. 180–82.

[46] "Message from the President of the United States, Transmitting Certain Papers Relating to the Compact between the U. States and the State of Georgia of 1802," 18th Cong., 1st sess., Apr. 2, 1824, S. Doc. 63, p. 8.

[47] James Monroe, "First Annual Message," Dec. 2, 1817, in James D. Richardson, ed., *A Compilation of the Messages and Papers of the Presidents*, 20 vols. (New York, 1897–1917), 2:585; Monroe, "Second Inaugural Address," Mar. 5, 1821, p. 661.

[48] Prucha, "Indian Removal," p. 102.

Whether the foreign sculptors understood the changes in official Indian policy that were occurring as they carved the Capitol reliefs is unknown, but the works do resonate with the emerging official ideology of the 1820s and 1830s. They hint at the influence of Bulfinch, Monroe, Adams, the artists, or any combination of these. By showing the initial meeting between the two cultures in the colonial New World and the inevitable subjugation or incorporation of the Indian race, these reliefs present situations from the past that seem to condone the policies being enacted by the Congress and the presidents who commissioned them. As John Elliott, a member of the Committee on Indian Affairs, expressed it during a debate in 1825 over the bill to preserve and civilize the Indian tribes:

> So long as the Indian tribes within our settlements were strong enough to wage war upon the States, and pursue their trade of blood with the tomahawk and scalping-knife, it was neither the policy nor the duty of the Federal Government to consult their comfort, or to devise means for their preservation. The contest, then, was for the existence of our infant settlements, and for the attainment of that power by which a civilized and Christian people might safely occupy this promised land of civil and religious liberty. It was, then[,] to be regarded as a struggle for supremacy between savages and civilized men, between infidels and Christians. But now, sir, when, by successive wars, and the more fatal operation of other causes, hereafter to be noticed, their power has departed from them, and they are reduced to comparative insignificance, it well becomes the magnanimity of a humane and generous Government to seek out the causes of their continued deterioration, and, as far as practicable, to arrest its progress, by the application of the most appropriate remedies.[49]

The Indians' overscaled size in the Rotunda reliefs thus may reflect the exaggerated threat they posed and their mythical status in the eyes of white Americans. These works had been created in the decade when the Indian Removal policy was being formulated, when the battle, in the words of Senator Elliott, raged between civilized Christians and infidel savages.

[49]Senate, *Register of Debates*, 18th Cong., 2d sess., Feb. 22, 1825, pp. 639–40.

Afterword

JAMES H. MERRELL

American Nations,
Old and New

Reflections on Indians
and the Early Republic

NOT SO LONG ago neither this volume nor the conference that was its earlier incarnation would have been possible. A scholarly gathering—conceived, say, in the early 1980s—to consider Indians in the new nation probably would have been called off for lack of interest and expertise.[1] When, little more than a decade ago, Native peoples did appear in the historical literature on post-Revolutionary America at all, they generally were cast as problems to be solved by federal policymakers or objects of study by intellectuals.[2] Those few scholars interested in taking a look at Indians themselves tended to become preoccupied with

[1] My assessment of the lack of work in the field differs from that of Gordon S. Wood, who has asserted that since World War II work on Indians in the new nation has generated "a huge literature" ("The Significance of the Early Republic," *Journal of the Early Republic* 8 [1988]:2 n. 4). In support of his contention, Professor Wood cited only a book by William G. McLoughlin, Robert F. Berkhofer's study of white attitudes toward Indians from Columbus to the present, and Bernard W. Sheehan's treatment of Jeffersonian philanthropy toward Native Americans.

[2] Walter Harrison Mohr, *Federal Indian Relations, 1774–1778* (Philadelphia, 1933); Randolph C. Downes, *Council Fires on the Upper Ohio: A Narrative of Indian Affairs in the Upper Ohio Valley until 1795* (Pittsburgh, 1940); Roy Harvey Pearce, *Savagism and Civilization: A Study of the Indian and the American Mind* (Berkeley, Calif., 1988); Francis Paul Prucha, *American Indian Policy in the Formative Years: The Indian Trade and Intercourse Acts, 1790–1834* (Cambridge, Mass., 1962); Reginald Horsman, *Expansion and American Indian Policy, 1783–1812* (East Lansing, Mich., 1967); Bernard W. Sheehan, *Seeds of Extinction: Jeffersonian Philanthropy and the American Indian* (Chapel Hill, N.C., 1973);

the Native experience during the great events—the American Revolution and Indian Removal—bracketing these decades.[3] Anthony F. C. Wallace's classic study of the Senecas stands all but alone in grounding itself in Native villages and Native lives during the early national period.[4]

Even the social and political earthquakes of the 1960s, whose aftershocks redirected scholarly approaches to America's past— pushing historians to examine poor as well as rich, slaves as well as masters, women as well as men—did little to spark interest in Alexander McGillivray as well as George Washington, Tecumseh as well as Thomas Jefferson, Sequoyah as well as James Fenimore Cooper. The pathbreaking work of the 1970s and early 1980s on Natives in colonial times by Francis P. Jennings, James Axtell, and others had few counterparts for the descendants of those Indians living after the Revolution.[5] For the early national period al-

---

Robert F. Berkhofer, Jr., *The White Man's Indian: Images of the American Indian from Columbus to the Present* (New York, 1978).

[3] Barbara Graymont, *The Iroquois in the American Revolution* (Syracuse, N.Y., 1972); James H. O'Donnell III, *Southern Indians in the American Revolution* (Knoxville, Tenn., 1973); the best study of Indians in these times, which appeared after this was written, is Colin G. Calloway, *The American Revolution in Indian Country: Crisis and Diversity in Native American Communities* (New York, 1995); Grant Foreman, *Indian Removal: The Emigration of the Five Civilized Tribes of Indians* (Norman, Okla., 1932); Angie Debo, *And Still the Waters Run* (Princeton, 1940); Mary Elizabeth Young, *Redskins, Ruffleshirts, and Rednecks: Indian Allotments in Alabama and Mississippi, 1830–1860* (Norman, Okla., 1961); Arthur H. DeRosier, Jr., *The Removal of the Choctaw Indians* (Knoxville, Tenn., 1970); Ronald N. Satz, *American Indian Policy in the Jacksonian Era* (Lincoln, Nebr., 1975); a more recent study of Removal is Anthony F. C. Wallace, *The Long, Bitter Trail: Andrew Jackson and the Indians* (New York, 1993).

[4] Anthony F. C. Wallace, *The Death and Rebirth of the Seneca* (New York, 1969). Articles by William G. McLoughlin on Cherokees in the early republic began appearing in the 1970s, but his books on this subject did not appear until after 1980. For the articles, see McLoughlin, *The Cherokee Ghost Dance: Essays on the Southeastern Indians, 1789–1861* (Macon, Ga., 1984).

[5] In 1982 Reginald Horsman, studying trends over the past decade, included almost no work on Indians in this period (Horsman, "Well-Trodden Paths and Fresh Byways: Recent Writing on Native American History," *Reviews in American History* 10 [1982]:234–44). For the historiography on Indians in colonial times, see Bernard W. Sheehan, "Indian-White Relations in Early

most the only noticeable effect of the new directions in scholarly inquiry was that works on white attitudes and federal policies—long the staple of the literature—took on a more critical tone.[6] Penetrating and perceptive as these works were, nonetheless Washington, Jefferson, Cooper, and their kind remained the center of attention. It was their eyes, and their pens, that informed modern views of Indian life between 1780 and 1830.

This habit of ignoring Indians after the American Revolution has a long pedigree. During the War for Independence itself J. Hector St. John de Crèvecoeur began writing the Natives' obituary, announcing that Indians "appear to be a race doomed to recede and disappear before the superior genius of the Europeans."[7] Crèvecoeur's nineteenth-century intellectual heirs in explaining this new nation shared his assumptions about where Natives fit into the story of America. Francis Parkman argued that "the victory of Quebec [in 1759] was the signal of their [the Indians'] swift decline. Thenceforth they were destined to melt and vanish before the advancing waves of Anglo-American power, which now rolled westward unchecked and unopposed."[8] Another influential nineteenth-century interpreter of America and its Native peoples, James Fenimore Cooper, carried the story of Indian-white relations only a little farther than Parkman did. In Cooper's version of the American past, the hero, Natty Bumppo, headed west to the

---

America: A Review Essay," *William and Mary Quarterly*, 3d ser. 26 (1969):267–86; James Axtell, "The Ethnohistory of Early America: A Review Essay," *William and Mary Quarterly*, 3d ser. 35 (1978):110–44.

[6] Richard Slotkin, *Regeneration through Violence: The Mythology of the American Frontier, 1600–1860* (Middletown, Conn., 1973); Michael Paul Rogin, *Fathers and Children: Andrew Jackson and the Subjugation of the American Indian* (New York, 1975); Richard Drinnon, *Facing West: The Metaphysics of Indian-Hating and Empire-Building* (Minneapolis, 1980).

[7] J. Hector St. John de Crèvecoeur, *Letters from an American Farmer, and, Sketches of Eighteenth-Century America*, ed. Albert E. Stone (New York, 1981), p. 122.

[8] Francis Parkman, *The Conspiracy of Pontiac, and the Indian War after the Conquest of Canada* (1851), 2 vols. (Boston, 1903), 1:ix.

prairie shortly after the Revolutionary War, as if in the East his life with Indians—and America's history with Indians—had come to a close.[9]

That until recently most scholars have been content to don blinders fashioned so long ago by Crèvecoeur and others is astonishing, because—except for the first generation or two of direct contacts between worlds—the early national period is the most important era in the history of North America's Native peoples. Comparing the lay of the land at the beginning and end of these pivotal decades helps to measure the extent of the transformation. In the 1780s most of the continent north of the Rio Grande was what it had been before the European colonial enterprise: Indian Country. Spanish and French colonists held beachheads in the South and West; other French folk dotted the shores of the Great Lakes; England's mainland provinces, by far the most populous of the colonial peoples, were still largely confined to the Atlantic coast.[10] Few Anglo-Americans had breached the Appalachian wall because beyond it lived Native peoples that, in the face of drastic changes wrought by European contact, maintained their military power, their political independence, and their cultural integrity. Those peoples did so in part with an old habit of playing off one colonial power against another—English and Dutch, English and French, English and Spanish (not to mention New York and Pennsylvania, Virginia and South Carolina, South Carolina and Georgia). At the close of the Revolutionary War the English and Spanish were still very much a presence in the East, and the newly independent states showed few signs of being united in anything but

[9] James Fenimore Cooper, *The Pioneers; or, The Sources of the Susquehanna: A Descriptive Tale* (1823; reprint ed., Albany, 1980); idem, *The Prairie: A Tale* (1827; reprint ed., New York, 1859).

[10] David J. Weber, *The Spanish Frontier in North America* (New Haven, 1992); Richard White, *The Middle Ground: Indians, Empires, and Republics in the Great Lakes Region, 1650–1815* (Cambridge, 1991); Daniel H. Usner, Jr., *Indians, Settlers, and Slaves in a Frontier Exchange Economy: The Lower Mississippi Valley before 1783* (Chapel Hill, N.C., 1992); Jack P. Greene, *Pursuits of Happiness: The Sociology of Early Modern British Colonization* (Chapel Hill, N.C., 1988); D. W. Meinig, *The Shaping of America: A Geographical Perspective on Five Hundred Years of History*, vol. 1, *Atlantic America, 1492–1800* (New Haven, 1986).

name; Indians had reason to think that some sort of play-off regime would continue.

But the most marked feature of the American landscape in the 1780s was not that the vast center of the continent remained Indian Country. Rather, it was the ubiquity of the Indian presence everywhere in America. As Colin G. Calloway observes in this volume's Prologue, Natives—both those in the interior and those still living among Anglo-American settlements—were a part of everyday life to an extent difficult to imagine today. As a boy Thomas Jefferson became acquainted with Outassete and other Cherokees who routinely camped at the Jefferson plantation on their way to and from Williamsburg. Jefferson's long-time rival and occasional ally, John Adams, was perhaps even more familiar with Indians, knowing in his youth many who lived near the Adams home in Braintree, Massachusetts.[11] Such contact was the rule, not the exception. Indian hunters, Indian farmers, Indian slaves, Indian traders, Indian ambassadors—all could be found in virtually every corner of the American land.[12]

Consider now that American land at the close of the early national period. By 1840, from what was Anglo-America, white settlers and their black slaves had not only crossed the mountains by the millions, they had pushed past the Mississippi River. This flood of people spilled over the Appalachians because Native control of the interior was shattered by military defeat, which in turn was a sign that the Indians' old play-off system had fallen apart as first the French, then the individual American states, and finally the Spanish and English stopped playing. With defeat on the battlefield came a loss of autonomy and, of-

---

[11] Jay Fliegelman, *Declaring Independence: Jefferson, Natural Language, and the Culture of Performance* (Stanford, Calif., 1993), p. 99; Drinnon, *Facing West*, p. 74.

[12] James H. Merrell, "Some Thoughts on Colonial Historians and American Indians," *William and Mary Quarterly*, 3d ser. 46 (1989):93–119; idem, "'The Customes of Our Countrey': Indians and Colonists in British America," in Bernard Bailyn and Philip D. Morgan, eds., *Strangers within the Realm: Cultural Margins of the First British Empire* (Chapel Hill, N.C., 1991), pp. 117–56; Calloway, *American Revolution in Indian Country*, Prologue.

ten, of homeland, as victorious Americans pushed many Native groups west.

By the end of this era, widespread face-to-face contacts between Natives and whites were a thing of the past; never again would Indians occupy so central a place in American life.[13] From friends and foes, customers and acquaintances, Natives were reduced in American eyes to curios and artifacts, specimens often lumped, as Elise Marienstras notes, with Asians, Fuegans, and other "exotic" peoples. In 1833 the defeated Sauk leader, Black Hawk, confronted this new American world when the federal government sent him and some of his men home from Washington, D.C., by way of several Eastern cities. Time and again, thousands of people—people whose parents and grandparents had found nothing remarkable about crossing paths with Indians in Philadelphia or Boston—crammed the streets and lined the riverbanks to catch a glimpse of these strange creatures.[14]

The stark contrast between the 1780s and the 1840s suggests a story so dramatic, so essential to an understanding of America's past, that it makes the scholarly indifference to it nothing less than a profound failure of the historical imagination. Fortunately, this curious neglect shows signs of ending, as during the past decade or so scholars—swimming against the current generated by Crèvecoeur, Cooper, Parkman, and their followers—have begun to rescue from obscurity Indian lives of the

[13] It was in this era, as Roy Harvey Pearce has noted, that Indians were "forced out of American life and into American history" in a process that involved "psychological as well as physical Removal" (*Savagism and Civilization*, pp. 58, 76). Surveying those same decades, Michael Paul Rogin argues that "Indians had not mattered so much, in the history of Europeans in the English new world, since the colonial settlements. They would never matter so much again" (*Fathers and Children*, p. 4). See also Robert H. Wiebe, *The Opening of American Society: From the Adoption of the Constitution to the Eve of Disunion* (New York, 1984), p. 346; Calloway, *American Revolution in Indian Country*, Epilogue.

[14] Donald Jackson, ed., *Black Hawk: An Autobiography* (Champaign, Ill., 1990), pp. 9–15, 143–50. For the routine of seeing Indians in eastern cities before 1800, see Carl Bridenbaugh, ed., *A Gentleman's Progress: The Itinerarium of Dr. Alexander Hamilton, 1744* (Pittsburgh, 1948), pp. 110, 112–14, 141, and John F. Watson, *Annals of Philadelphia and Pennsylvania, in the Olden Time . . .* , 2 vols. (Philadelphia, 1845), 2:163.

late eighteenth and early nineteenth centuries. Indeed, the rapidly expanding shelf of works on the Native experience has made the early national period arguably the most exciting field of Indian history today.[15]

Thus the contributors to this volume are in the vanguard of an important new chapter in Native American studies. At first glance, however, the volume may seem a curious sort of vanguard, for most of the essays here owe much to the older "policies and attitudes" school of work on Indians in the early republic. Reginald Horsman on federal policy, Vivien Green Fryd on white images, Elise Marienstras on white attitudes—these are only the most obvious debtors to more traditional perspectives. In fact, almost all of the authors hitch their research to one or both of those reliable nags, policies and attitudes, that for so long have hauled the interpretative freight on Indians in the early republic.[16] And yet a closer look at these chapters reveals that they are more complicated than that. While many of the authors do indeed use policies and attitudes as their starting point, they liberate those timeworn topics from the narrow, Eurocentric constraints in which the two had long been confined. To pursue the equine metaphor a bit further, instead of beating a couple of dead horses, the authors have revived the old beasts and put them to work at innovative and productive tasks.

[15] Besides the earlier work of the contributors to this volume, see Michael D. Green, *The Politics of Indian Removal: Creek Government and Society in Crisis* (Lincoln, Nebr., 1982); William G. McLoughlin, *Cherokees and Missionaries, 1789–1839* (New Haven, 1984); idem, *Cherokee Renascence in the New Republic* (Princeton, 1986); J. Leitch Wright, Jr., *Creeks and Seminoles: The Destruction and Regeneration of the Muscogulge People* (Lincoln, Nebr., 1986); Gregory Evans Dowd, *A Spirited Resistance: The North American Indian Struggle for Unity, 1745–1815* (Baltimore, 1992); Stephen Aron, *How the West Was Lost: The Transformation of Kentucky from Daniel Boone to Henry Clay* (Baltimore, 1996). My own attempt to tell the Indians' story in these years, written before much of the new literature on the subject appeared, is "Declarations of Independence: Indian-White Relations in the New Nation," in Jack P. Greene, ed., *The American Revolution: Its Character and Limits* (New York, 1987), pp. 197–223.

[16] With apologies to J. H. Hexter (*Reappraisals in History: New Views on History and Society in Early Modern Europe*, 2d ed. [Chicago, 1979], p. 77).

AFTERWORD

Take, for example, the new light shed here on government policies. Daniel K. Richter's dissection of Pennsylvania Indian affairs after the Revolution not only adds a new chapter to our understanding of policies at the state level, not only shows how the arguments of state leaders found their way into the national discourse on Indians, but also suggests just how bleak were the prospects for Native Americans in those years. If "the climate of sleaze" pervaded even the land of William Penn—if the heirs of Onas could rob, swindle, and shoot Indians—then the Natives' chances of fair treatment anywhere in the new nation were remote indeed.

At the national level, too, the intricate diplomatic negotiations with Natives—a story traditionally served up treaty by treaty, and from the federal side of the table—are considered in novel ways by Richard White, who approaches the subject from "the middle ground" between one world and another. This vantage point enables White to explore the fictions, memories, and expectations that *all* parties brought to the council table. The result is a perspective that helps illuminate Indian as well as white behavior in those conversations.[17]

The same imaginative search for a way out of what Daniel H. Usner, Jr., in a slightly different context, calls a "historiographical hall of mirrors" is evident in the work on white attitudes toward Indians. The scholars here have not discarded the study of the white mind as a waste of time, a barren field that will produce little that is new. Rather, they bring to that topic a determination to—quoting Usner again—"reach behind" the metaphors in order to deconstruct the rhetoric. This approach yields not only a better understanding of whites but also of Indians, for to that conventional rhetoric the authors add Native words and actions. White and Richter, for example, consider *Father*, *Brother*, and other terms both sides used to plumb the depths of misunderstanding in their cross-cultural conversations.

Using similar sensitivity to language, Theda Perdue uncovers hidden dimensions in the lives of Native American women. Resisting the temptation to abandon as hopelessly biased the observations of white men who wrote about those women, she uses

[17] For their fuller interpretations, see Joel W. Martin, *Sacred Revolt: The Muskogees' Struggle for a New World* (Boston, 1991), and White, *Middle Ground*.

the distorted accounts as a vehicle for showing how Indians and whites defined words like *labor, incest,* and *promiscuity* in fundamentally different and revealing ways. Daniel Usner does much the same thing with bias of a different sort: the Jeffersonians' inability to "see" Indian agriculture. Usner helps to account for that blindness; then, like Perdue, he goes on to survey the chasm between white perceptions and Native realities.

This technique of using traditional themes as points of departure for a journey into new realms of understanding can also be found in the chapters on images of Native Americans. Elise Marienstras considers cartoons, songs, advertisements, proverbs, and even jokes in her determination to "reach behind" the elite and glimpse the notions average citizens had about Indians.[18] In this deliberate eclecticism Marienstras—like White, Perdue, Usner, and others in this volume—heralds a new approach, an approach that takes into account what Indians said and did as well as what preoccupied whites. As Richter notes, the Seneca leader Cornplanter once said that "we count Ourselves a people Capable of Speaking and Acting for Ourselves."[19] The essays here, taking Cornplanter at his word, listen to what people like him have to say. And that is as clear a measure as any of how far the scholarship has moved beyond standard accounts of government policies and white attitudes.

The end result of all these imaginative ventures, when combined with the more general renaissance in the field over the past decade or so, is a much more interesting, but also a much more confusing, picture of Indians in the early republic. The story used to be fairly straightforward: setting Native nations in the background, one started with the Jeffersonian mind or the blueprints drafted by Henry Knox and George Washington and proceeded from there down the road to Removal, a road laid out along a route dictated by white attitudes, marked by federal

[18] Martienstras notes her debt to Rayna D. Green, "The Indian in Popular American Culture," in Wilcomb E. Washburn, ed., *History of Indian-White Relations*, Handbook of North American Indians, vol. 4 (Washington, D.C., 1988), pp. 587–606.

[19] As Richter observes, the meaning of Cornplanter's remark is difficult to decipher, since he was vague on whom "we" represented. I employ his words here in their widest possible sense, to denote Indians generally.

policies and federal agents, and paved by treaties. Nowadays it is harder to trace a single plot line, pick a single perch from which to view the landscape of encounter, or hear a single, harmonious account of these years; the sounds emerging from the recent research are polyphonic and multilingual. It turns out that whites themselves said different things, depending on whether they spoke from Washington, a state capital, or the frontier. In addition, to this discord we must now hearken to the songs Native Americans themselves sang, songs also marked by dissonance. Pan-Indian movements competed with nascent Cherokee or Shawnee nationalism, and both tugged against traditional attachments to town or kin. Those Natives urging war against the United States had to argue with men like Cornplanter and Black Hoof, who wanted a different approach. Amid this cacophony, Native women—and African Americans—had their own stories to tell, stories that only now are beginning to be heard.

Even as we delight in the discoveries of the new work, even as we try to sort out the tangle of stories emerging from that work, the recent scholarship also brings home how far we are from fully appreciating Indian life in eastern North America two centuries ago. Much remains to be done before Natives are restored to their proper place in this chapter of American history. Paradoxically, those intent on effecting that restoration must follow lines of inquiry that point in opposite directions: deeper into Indian Country and, turning around, closer still to white society.[20]

However successfully they have freed the study of attitudes and policies from its former Eurocentric confines, scholars continuing to plot their investigations using attitudes and policies

---

[20] It should also be noted that another new direction of the scholarship is to connect the lives of Indians in eastern North America with those farther west. For some of the work being done, see Elizabeth A. H. Johns, *Storms Brewed in Other Men's Worlds: The Confrontation of Indians, Spanish, and French in the American Southwest, 1540–1795* (Lincoln, Nebr., 1975), Ramón Gutiérrez, *When Jesus Came, the Corn Mothers Went Away: Marriage, Sexuality, and Power in New Mexico, 1500–1846* (Stanford, Calif., 1991), James P. Ronda, *Lewis and Clark among the Indians* (Lincoln, Nebr., 1984), and Usner, *Indians, Settlers, and Slaves.*

as their benchmarks are missing a great deal. Too much of the recent literature fixes its attention on the public realm, the very realm that most preoccupied whites. Thus we are, for the most part, seeing what whites themselves saw, and what white record-keepers wanted *us* to see—looking at it in new ways, certainly, but nonetheless letting whites direct our gaze and point out the important sights. Treaty negotiations, Indian leadership and government, Native reactions to federal agents and Christian missionaries, the interplay between white perceptions and Indian realities—the skill involved in recovering these is considerable, the results well worth the effort. But those diplomats and leaders, those myopic white perceptions still garner an inordinate share of scholarly attention and energy. To come to terms more fully with the Indian experience in these tumultuous and pivotal years, we must wander away from the familiar confines of the council ground, the agent's plantation, and the missionary's model farm in order to poke around in the shadows.

In those shadows lived the vast majority of Indians. During the early national period, for example, the Cherokee Nation was renowned for its adoption of white ways. Owning slaves and growing cotton, building roads and mills, welcoming missionaries and schools, producing a constitution and a newspaper— Cherokees were a model of the civilizing enterprise. Yet, as William G. McLoughlin has noted, in these years more than "three-quarters of the Cherokees were full bloods who spoke no English" and for the most part "stayed by themselves, eschewing contact with whites."[21]

Among the Cherokees and other Indian nations, the shadowy corners contain fascinating stories waiting to be told, "hidden transcripts" (to borrow a phrase of James C. Scott's) waiting to be discovered. Joel W. Martin is on the right track when he uses those transcripts to explore the Indian "underground" of resistance to white rule. Following McLoughlin's lead in pointing out the limits of the white presence, Martin listens to the

---

[21] McLoughlin, *Cherokee Renascence*, pp. 69, 329. See also idem, *Cherokee Ghost Dance*, p. 22 n. 30, and Tom Hatley, *The Dividing Paths: Cherokees and South Carolinians through the Era of Revolution* (New York, 1993), pp. 233–34.

silence and secrecy, the myths and dances, thereby opening up new worlds of possibility for the study of Natives. Even so, however, it can be argued that exploring the Native American underground does not go far enough into Indian Country, for it still takes as its focus Native "responses to domination" by whites rather than the character of Indian culture and society itself. Martin's study of resistance is as crucial to an understanding of the Indian experience as studies of slave resistance are to African-American history. But just as slave resistance was only part of plantation life, so the Native underground takes us only part of the way into the heart of Indian Country, where a silent majority held sway.[22]

If most Natives lived in obscurity, tucked away deep in Indian Country remote from curious whites, it is reasonable to ask how historians are supposed to find them in order to recover what McLoughlin called the "quiet quality of their lives."[23] In addition to Martin's insights, a quick look at the Catawbas of Carolina suggests that it is indeed possible to recover fragments of Native social history from these years. Catawbas in the early national period did not *have* much of a public life—missionaries tended to steer clear of them, both the state of South Carolina and the federal government ignored them, Tecumseh left them off his itinerary when he traveled through the South recruiting allies— so their story can only be pieced together from folklore, land records, the occasional petition or traveler's account, and the reminiscences of white neighbors. No doubt the backcountries of more prominent tribes can yield many more such hidden transcripts. But to harvest those sources, scholars must direct their attention away from the spotlight that shines so brightly on intercultural and intertribal affairs.[24]

---

[22] As Michael Meranze has written, such "alternative perspectives . . . run the risk of . . . interpreting everyday life as a terrain of continual resistance" ("Even the Dead Will Not Be Safe: An Ethics of Early American History," *William and Mary Quarterly*, 3d ser. 50 [1993]:370).

[23] McLoughlin, *Cherokee Renascence*, p. 329.

[24] James H. Merrell, *The Indians' New World: Catawbas and Their Neighbors from European Contact through the Era of Removal* (Chapel Hill, N.C., 1989), chaps. 5– 7. For an example of the kinds of sources awaiting scrutiny, see the Cherokee

The rewards of exploring the remoter recesses of Indian Country are many, but so are the risks. Perhaps the greatest risk is that as students of Indian history move away from the arena where Natives mingled with whites, they will end up still farther out of the mainstream of American historical studies, even more parochial than Reginald Horsman, in 1982, said Indian history was.[25] Unfortunately, Horsman's assessment is as true today as it was then. Virtually none of the standard accounts of the new American nation's trials and triumphs published during the past generation includes the Indians' story. Indeed, the modern neglect of Native Americans by scholars of the early republic is so complete that Henry Adams's classic study of the administrations of Thomas Jefferson and James Madison, written a century ago, devoted more space to Indians than do any of the more recent surveys.[26] If Indians are to find their way into the larger chronicle of the American past, students of Native American history must show the way; scholars paddling along in what they consider the American mainstream are not inclined to do so. Hence, while we ought to head deeper into Indian Country, we must also chart a course that goes in precisely opposite direction: connecting Natives to broader patterns of American life.

---

inventories of goods left behind when they were forced west (Mary Elizabeth Young, "The Cherokee Nation: Mirror of the Republic," *American Quarterly* 33 [1981]:517, 519).

[25] Horsman, "Well-Trodden Paths," p. 234.

[26] Henry Adams, *History of the United States of America during the Administrations of Thomas Jefferson and James Madison*, 9 vols. (1891–96; reprint ed., New York, 1962). The syntheses I have consulted are John C. Miller, *The Federalist Era, 1789–1801* (New York, 1960), Charles M. Wiltse, *The New Nation, 1800–1845* (New York, 1961), Daniel J. Boorstin, *The Americans: The National Experience* (New York, 1965), George Dangerfield, *The Awakening of American Nationalism, 1815–1848* (New York, 1965), Marshall Smelser, *The Democratic Republic, 1801–1815* (New York, 1968), John Mayfield, *The New Nation, 1800–1845* (New York, 1982), Jack Larkin, *The Reshaping of Everyday Life, 1790–1840* (New York, 1988), Gordon S. Wood, *The Radicalism of the American Revolution* (New York, 1992), and Stanley Elkins and Eric McKitrick, *The Age of Federalism* (New York, 1993). Exceptions to this neglect are John R. Howe, *From the Revolution through the Age of Jackson: Innocence and Empire in the Young Republic* (Englewood Cliffs, N.J., 1973), and Edward Countryman, *Americans: A Collision of Histories* (New York, 1996).

Some students of Indians in this era already have begun that task. In 1981 Mary Elizabeth Young pointed out that the Cherokee Nation was a "Mirror of the Republic." More recently, William McLoughlin noted parallels between the Cherokee experience and that of the young United States.[27] In this volume, too, Daniel Usner takes a similar tack, turning a critical eye on Jeffersonian agrarianism from his vantage point in Iroquoia, while Theda Perdue and Richard White deftly join the familial languages of Indians and whites.[28] All of this is a start, but only that. Scholars need now to forge these interpretive links more solidly and more explicitly. They can do so in two different ways.

The first is to take a closer look at certain important correspondences in the histories of Indians and other Americans. Consider, for example, the matter of racial attitudes. In these years both whites and Indians were groping their way toward views in which racial traits came to play a vital role in making sense of the world. Just as whites were formulating a "rational" and "scientific" school of thought that placed Europeans atop a hierarchy of races, so Natives were revising their perceptual universe to explain why they, and not Europeans or Africans, were a favored people. We know a great deal about these intellectual journeys among whites, and something about them among Indians; but as yet no one has laid the two lines of thought side by side in order to see how they compared and, perhaps, how they influenced one another.[29]

[27] Young, "Cherokee Nation," pp. 502–24; McLoughlin, *Cherokees and Missionaries*; idem, *Cherokee Renascence*.

[28] For the familial language of whites, see Jay Fliegelman, *Prodigals and Pilgrims: The American Revolution against Patriarchy, 1750–1800* (New York, 1982).

[29] For white attitudes, see William Ragan Stanton, *The Leopard's Spots: Scientific Attitudes toward Race in America, 1815–1859* (Chicago, 1960), Winthrop D. Jordan, *White over Black: American Attitudes toward the Negro, 1550–1812* (Chapel Hill, N.C., 1968), Ronald T. Takaki, *Iron Cages: Race and Culture in Nineteenth-Century America* (New York, 1979), Reginald Horsman, *Race and Manifest Destiny: The Origins of American Racial Anglo-Saxonism* (Cambridge, Mass., 1981), and Alden T. Vaughan, "From White Man to Redskin: Changing Anglo-American perceptions of the American Indian," *American Historical Review* 87 (1982):917–53. For Indian attitudes, see McLoughlin, *Cherokees and Missionaries*, p. 9, Martin, *Sacred Revolt*, pp. 183–84, Dowd, *Spirited Resistance*,

Another common experience inviting closer attention are the spiritual revivals that tore through Indian villages and American communities alike during these years. Recent work on Natives by Gregory Evans Dowd, Joel W. Martin, and others points to the importance—indeed, the centrality—of the religious dimension in Native life.[30] Similarly, scholarship on the Second Great Awakening has recovered the enormous popularity and the radical thrust of this tidal wave of religious fervor in the new republic. Yet even though some students of the Second Great Awakening call that revival a revitalization movement,[31] none consider in any depth how—or if—camp meetings like Cane Ridge resembled what struck Senecas, Shawnees, Creeks, and others in Indian Country.[32] Even as they were killing each other with unparalleled ferocity, frontier folk—Native and newcomer—were flocking to hear good news brought by dreams and visions, to listen to spiritual explanations for the chaos, the sense of loss, the painful uncertainties of their lives.[33] It would be useful to compare the messages prophets and preachers imparted and the forces that made those messages popular.

Religion was certainly fundamental to both societies at this time, but perhaps the most important parallel during these decades was the quest for a common identity in the United States

---

pp. 30, 37, 44, 63, 108, 141, 167, 175, and White, *Middle Ground*, p. 507. The best study of Indian thinking about matters of color, which appeared after this was written, is Nancy Shoemaker, "How Indians Got to Be Red," *American Historical Review* 102 (1997):625–44.

[30] Martin, *Sacred Revolt*; Dowd, *Spirited Resistance*.

[31] John B. Boles, *The Great Revival, 1787–1805* (Lexington, Ky., 1972), p. 24; William G. McLoughlin, *Revivals, Awakenings, and Reform: An Essay on Religion and Social Change in America, 1607–1977* (Chicago, 1978), chap. 1; Nathan O. Hatch, *The Democratization of American Christianity* (New Haven, 1989).

[32] For suggestions of the parallels, see Anthony F. C. Wallace, "Handsome Lake and the Great Revival in the West," *American Quarterly* 4 (1952):149–65 (I am grateful to Charlene Akers for bringing this article to my attention), idem, *Death and Rebirth of the Seneca*, pp. 215–17, McLoughlin, *Cherokees and Missionaries*, p. 84, and Aron, *How the West Was Lost*, chap. 8.

[33] For whites' belief in dreams and visions, see Hatch, *Democratization*, pp. 10, 36–37, 40.

and in the Indian countries, the effort to come up with a set of values or institutions that would give shape to that identity. Richard White has pointed out how during the 1780s the fledgling United States and the Indians of the Ohio country tried to build confederations, both with mixed results.[34] Similarly, William McLoughlin has suggested how the growth of Cherokee nationalism had much in common with the flowering of American nationalism.[35] But neither they nor anyone else has studied the issue in the depth it deserves.

The comparison is rich in possibility. The contest between assertions of authority from the center and the enduring pull of local attachments; the campaign to form a cohesive society with firm cultural boundaries even as that society was increasingly divided along lines of race, region, and status; the role of ritual, of law, of language in encouraging a national spirit— none of these matters were the exclusive province of the new American nation.[36] Many *old* American nations—Cherokee, Creek, Shawnee, Iroquois—were involved in the same sorts of adventures.[37]

Drawing such political or religious parallels would do much to illuminate how Indians and other Americans shared certain common experiences in the generation or two after the Revolution. But setting the Shawnee Prophet beside such revivalists as Lorenzo Dow, Joseph Brant alongside American statesmen like Alexander Hamilton, or the cultural nationalist Sequoyah with his white counterpart Noah Webster still risks leaving Natives off the American stage—intriguing comparisons, perhaps,

[34] White, *Middle Ground*, pp. 413, 416, 442.

[35] McLoughlin, *Cherokees and Missionaries*, pp. 3, 6, 10, 190; idem, *Cherokee Renascence*, p. xvii.

[36] For public ritual, see Susan G. Davis, *Parades and Power: Street Theatre in Nineteenth-Century Philadelphia* (Philadelphia, 1986), and David Waldstreicher, *In the Midst of Perpetual Fetes: The Making of American Nationalism, 1776–1820* (Chapel Hill, N.C., 1997). For language, see E. Jennifer Monaghan, *A Common Heritage: Noah Webster's Blue-Back Speller* (Hamden, Conn., 1983), and David Simpson, *The Politics of American English, 1776–1850* (New York, 1986).

[37] McLoughlin, *Cherokee Renascence*, pp. 219, 326; Martin, *Sacred Revolt*, p. 107.

but not fully part of the main currents of our national past. The problem with the comparative approach is that it fails to show how intimately Indians were a *part* of that collective past. Just as one cannot understand the Shawnee or Cherokee experience during these years without considering the influence of the new United States, so understanding of the early republic will remain elusive unless those Shawnees and Cherokees are included, somehow, in the larger American chronicle.

Among possible avenues of approach to this challenge,[38] perhaps the most promising connects the work on Indians with recent trends in the historiography of this period in America's past.[39] Thirty years ago John Higham termed this period "the age of boundlessness," and others have picked up this theme. Robert H. Wiebe calls the years after 1790 "the opening of American society"; Gordon S. Wood, considering the broad sweep of the Revolutionary era, writes of "loosening the bands of society."[40] Whatever the term—*boundlessness, opening, loosening*—the point is much the same: this era witnessed the crum-

---

[38] Another specific approach would be to include relations with Indians in the study of diplomacy in the new republic. Were policies, personnel, and strategies different in kind when the federal government faced west instead of east? The standard accounts do not consider diplomatic relations between the United States and the Indian nations across the mountains as well as with countries across the Atlantic. See Frank T. Reuter, *Trials and Triumphs: George Washington's Foreign Policy* (Fort Worth, Tex., 1983), Reginald Horsman, *The Diplomacy of the New Republic, 1776–1815* (Arlington Heights, Ill., 1985), and Daniel George Lang, *Foreign Policy in the Early Republic: The Law of Nations and the Balance of Power* (Baton Rouge, La., 1985).

[39] I have made this point briefly before, in "Indians and the American Survey: Thoughts on Supplementary Readings," The D'Arcy McNickle Center for the History of the American Indian, Newberry Library, Occasional Papers in Curriculum Series, no. 4, *The Impact of Indian History on the Teaching of United States History: Washington Conference, 1985* (Chicago, 1986), pp. 252–53. More recently, others have developed parts of the argument more fully. See William L. Barney, *The Passage of the Republic: An Interdisciplinary History of Nineteenth-Century America* (Lexington, Mass., 1987), chap. 2, and Jean W. Mathews, *Toward a New Society: American Thought and Culture, 1800–1830* (Boston, 1991), pp. 77–79, 86–93.

[40] John Higham, *From Boundlessness to Consolidation: The Transformation of American Culture, 1848–1860* (Ann Arbor, Mich., 1969); Wiebe, *Opening*

bling of geographic, social, political, and economic barriers, thereby offering unparalleled opportunities for a pell-mell pursuit of the main chance by large segments of the population.

Less prominent in the recent literature is the fact that most of those pursuing their own versions of happiness were white men. For many in America, this was not an age of boundlessness but one of new boundaries, not the opening of American society but its closing.[41] Indeed, the widening field of opportunity was accomplished in part by removing, in various ways, certain elements of the population, leaving white men free to play out their intensely competitive contests in the economic, social, and political arena.

The roster of those removed from American life in one way or another is long. The poor, formerly supported as much as possible in their own homes, were placed in workhouses. The mentally ill, formerly kept by family or friends, were put into insane asylums. Criminals, formerly dealt with summarily and—if not executed—returned to the community, were sentenced to penitentiaries.[42] Women, too, were confined after a fashion, at once uplifted and restricted by the doctrine of republican

---

of American Society; Wood, *Radicalism of the American Revolution*, chap. 8 (and p. 358: "a . . . boundless nation"). See also Steven Watts, *The Republic Reborn: War and the Making of Liberal America, 1790–1820* (Baltimore, 1987), p. xxii.

[41] But see Wiebe, *Opening of American Society*, p. xv.

[42] This argument has been developed by David J. Rothman, *The Discovery of the Asylum: Social Order and Disorder in the New Republic* (Boston, 1971). More recent scholarship has disagreed with Rothman on some points—pushing the movement's origins back in time to the late eighteenth century and tracing the connections with similar developments in Europe—without undermining the integrity and utility of his central argument. See John K. Alexander, *Render Them Submissive: Responses to Poverty in Philadelphia, 1760–1800* (Amherst, Mass., 1980), Michael Meranze, *Laboratories of Virtue: Punishment, Revolution, and Authority in Philadelphia, 1760–1835* (Chapel Hill, N.C., 1996), Michael B. Katz, *In the Shadow of the Poorhouse: A Social History of Welfare in America* (New York, 1986), Thomas L. Dumm, *Democracy and Punishment: Disciplinary Origins of the United States* (Madison, Wis., 1987), Robert E. Cray, Jr., *Paupers and Poor Relief in New York City and Its Rural Environs, 1700–1830* (Philadelphia, 1988), and Louis P. Masur, *Rites of Execution: Capital Punishment and the Transformation of American Culture, 1776–1865* (New York, 1989).

motherhood, which gave them the vital role of raising the next generation of the republic's citizens but insisted that they stay home to carry out this task.[43]

Blacks after the American Revolution faced the prospect of different sorts of removals. One was colonization to Africa, the West Indies, or—after the Louisiana Purchase in 1803—across the Mississippi River. Thomas Jefferson was among the first to contemplate "Negro removal," more than twenty years before he began, as president, to consider Indian Removal.[44] James Monroe, too, was exploring the possibility of finding or creating what he called an "asylum" for blacks, and as president he endorsed the efforts of the American Colonization Society— founded in 1816, the year he took office—to accomplish that goal.[45] In retirement Jefferson lent his support to the new society's program of black removal; one of its first vice-presidents

[43] Mary Beth Norton, *Liberty's Daughters: The Revolutionary Experience of American Women, 1750–1800* (Boston, 1980); Linda K. Kerber, *Women of the Republic: Intellect and Ideology in Revolutionary America* (Chapel Hill, N.C., 1980); Nancy F. Cott, *The Bonds of Womanhood: "Woman's Sphere" in New England, 1780–1835* (New Haven, 1977). For some of the work that expands and deepens our understanding of women in this era without altogether overturning earlier notions of restrictions on women's freedoms, see Jan Lewis, "The Republican Wife: Virtue and Seduction in the Early Republic," *William and Mary Quarterly*, 3d ser. 44 (1987):689–721, Linda K. Kerber et al., "Beyond Roles, beyond Spheres: Thinking about Gender in the Early Republic," *William and Mary Quarterly*, 3d ser. 46 (1989):565–85, esp. 567–68, and Joan M. Jensen, *Loosening the Bonds: Mid-Atlantic Farm Women, 1750–1850* (New Haven, 1986).

[44] Jordan, *White over Black*, chap. 15; Ira Berlin, *Slaves without Masters: The Free Negro in the Antebellum South* (New York, 1974), pp. 104–7; P. J. Staudenraus, *The African Colonization Movement, 1816–1865* (New York, 1961), chap. 1; Floyd J. Miller, *The Search for a Black Nationality: Black Emigration and Colonization, 1787–1863* (Urbana, Ill., 1975); Gary B. Nash, *Race and Revolution* (Madison, Wis., 1990), pp. 42–49, 146–65. The link between Indian Removal and black colonization has been made before. See Wilcomb E. Washburn, "Indian Removal Policy: Administrative, Historical, and Moral Criteria for Judging Its Success or Failure," *Ethnohistory* 12 (1965):277, and Wallace, *The Long, Bitter Trail*, pp. 38–39.

[45] Staudenraus, *African Colonization Movement*, pp. 51–53; Jordan, *White over Black*, p. 568 (quotation).

was the rising star in the political firmament, Andrew Jackson, later the architect of Indian Removal.[46]

Despite enlisting such prominent backers and gaining considerable popularity during the 1820s, the American Colonization Society declined by 1840, a victim of white ambivalence, black resistance, and the sheer impracticability of its schemes.[47] Perhaps it also declined because blacks were effectively being removed from American society by other means. In the South the spate of manumissions after the Revolution declined, lingering dreams of wholesale emancipation had been crushed, and free blacks lived under ever tighter restrictions.[48] In the North, too, African Americans increasingly found themselves pushed to the margins of society.[49] North or South, free or slave, blacks had been effectively removed without actually going anywhere.

Seen against this backdrop of opening and closing, of the expansion and contraction of opportunity, it becomes clear that Indian Removal was not some aberrant episode best treated separately or ignored. It was, in fact, part of a wider culture of removal in American life, removal that was sometimes physical, sometimes psychological, sometimes social, but almost always justified by its authors as assistance to those being shunted aside. The poor, confined to workhouses, were to learn habits of industry that would ultimately make them useful members of society. The insane and the criminals, isolated from the social conditions that had robbed them of their sanity or drove them to a life of crime, would be cured and returned to the larger world. Women would be protected from the evils of American life—the competitiveness, the vulgarity, the ruthlessness. Blacks would be happier in their African "homeland." And Indians? Indians after removal would be protected from the evils of

[46] Staudenraus, *African Colonization Movement*, pp. 30, 48, 171–72.

[47] Berlin, *Slaves without Masters*, pp. 199–207, 355–56; Leon Litwack, *North of Slavery: The Negro in the Free States, 1790–1860* (Chicago, 1961), pp. 20–29.

[48] Berlin, *Slaves without Masters*, esp. chap. 3.

[49] Litwack, *North of Slavery*; Gary B. Nash, *Forging Freedom: The Formation of Philadelphia's Black Community, 1720–1840* (Cambridge, Mass., 1988), chaps. 6–8; Leonard P. Curry, *The Free Black in Urban America, 1800–1850: The Shadow of a Dream* (Chicago, 1981), esp. chaps. 5 and 6.

American society (the Indian-hating frontier folk), like women; they would be happier, like African Americans; they might even, in time, be "cured," like the poor, the insane, the criminal—and, cured, could join American society at last.

It did not work out that way. The Indian asylum in the West was as much a failure as the other asylums constructed in America during the first half of the nineteenth century. It is not the failure that should surprise us, perhaps, but the fact that so few people have seen the early national period for what it was: the Age of Removal. In that era Indians belong not in the wings, not in the audience, and not only in the first act of the American pageant; they belong at center stage, for only by positioning Indians there can we appreciate their importance to the history of the early republic. If we lose sight of these Native peoples, if we fail to weave the threads of the new tales being spun about them into the American fabric made from the old stories, those who marched Indians west will have won a second, greater victory: not only removing these peoples from their homelands, but from our history as well.

Contributors

COLIN G. CALLOWAY wrote his paper while teaching at the University of Wyoming. He is currently Professor of History and Native American Studies, Chair of Native American Studies, and John Sloan Dickey Third Century Professor in the Social Sciences at Dartmouth College. His books include *New Worlds for All: Indians, Europeans, and the Remaking of Early America* (1997), *The American Revolution in Indian Country* (1995), *The Western Abenakis of Vermont, 1600–1800* (1990), and *Crown and Calumet: British-Indian Relations, 1783–1815* (1990). He has also edited several collections of essays and documents, including *After King Philip's War: Presence and Persistence in Indian New England* (1997) and *The World Turned Upside Down: Indian Voices from Early America* (1994). He is currently working on a volume for the University of Nebraska Press's new series on the history of the American West.

R. DAVID EDMUNDS is the Anne Stark Watson and Chester Watson Professor in American History at the University of Texas at Dallas. He has written or coauthored biographies of Tecumseh and the Shawnee Prophet, tribal histories focusing upon the Potawatomis and the Mesquakies, and has edited two volumes that examine Native American leadership. He currently is writing a history of Native American entrepreneurs on the Great Plains, editing a volume that discusses cultural change among the Great Lakes tribes, and is co-authoring a textbook in Native American history.

VIVIEN GREEN FRYD, associate professor of fine arts at Vanderbilt University, has published *Art and Empire: The Politics of Ethnicity in the U.S. Capitol, 1815–1860* (1992) and articles on various topics, including nineteenth-century American sculpture, Benjamin West's *Death of Wolfe*, and Thomas Hart Benton's *Sources of Country Music*. She is currently writing a book entitled *Marriage and Modernity: The Art and Lives of Georgia O'Keeffe and Edward Hopper*.

REGINALD HORSMAN is Distinguished Professor of History at the University of Wisconsin–Milwaukee. He is the author of eleven books and numerous articles. Among his books are *Race and Manifest Des-*

355

tiny: The Origins of American Racial Anglo-Saxonism (1981), *The War of 1812* (1969), and *Expansion and American Indian Policy, 1783– 1812* (1967). He is currently writing a volume on the New Republic in the Longman History of America series.

ELISE MARIENSTRAS is a professor of American history and civilization at the University of Paris. She is director of the Centre de Recherches sur l'Histoire américaine, which centers its work and resources on early American history and Native American history and culture and has organized several international conferences on early American history. She has published extensively in French on colonial and early national American political and cultural history and on relations between Euro-Americans and Natives throughout the colonial and national periods. Among her publications are *1890. Wounded Knee: L'Amérique fin de siècle* (1992), *Nous le Peuple: Les origines du nationalisme américain* (1988), *Naissance de la République fédérale, 1783–1828* (1987), *La résistance indienne aux Etats-Unis* (1980), and *Les mythes fondateurs de la nation américaine: Essai sur le discours idéologique aux Etats-Unis à l'époque de l'indépendance* (1976, 1992). She is currently working on intercultural comparisons and exchanges between Europe and America in the eighteenth and nineteenth centuries.

JOEL W. MARTIN is associate professor, Department of Religious Studies and Program in American Studies, Franklin and Marshall College. He is the author of *Native American Religion* (1999) and *Sacred Revolt: The Muskogees' Struggle for a New World* (1991), and coeditor with Conrad E. Ostwalt, Jr., of *Screening the Sacred: Religion, Myth, and Ideology in Popular American Film* (1995). His current research focuses on the origins of southern nationalism during the era of Indian Removal.

JAMES H. MERRELL, Lucy Maynard Salmon Professor of History at Vassar College, is the author of *The Indians' New World: Catawbas and Their Neighbors from European Contact through the Era of Removal* (1989) and *Into the American Woods: Negotiators on the Pennsylvania Frontier* (1999).

THEDA PERDUE is professor of history at the University of North Carolina. She is author of *Cherokee Women: Gender and Culture Change, 1700–1835* (1998), *The Cherokee* (1988), *Native Carolinians* (1985), and *Slavery and the Evolution of Cherokee Society, 1540–1865* (1979), editor of *Cherokee Editor* (1983) and *Nations Remembered* (1980), and coeditor of *The Cherokee Removal* (1995), *Hidden Histories of Women in the New South* (1994), and *Southern Women: Histories and Identities* (1992).

DANIEL K. RICHTER, professor of history at Dickinson College, is the author of *The Ordeal of the Longhouse: The Peoples of the Iroquois League in the Era of European Colonization* (1992) and the coeditor, with James H. Merrell, of *Beyond the Covenant Chain: The Iroquois and Their Neighbors in Indian North America, 1600–1800* (1987). Among the scholarly journals in which he has published articles are *The William and Mary Quarterly, The Journal of American History, Ethnohistory,* and *American Indian Quarterly.* He is at work on a book of essays on narrative perspectives in eastern North American Indian history as well as an ongoing study of cultural interactions between Pennsylvanians and Native Americans after the American Revolution, of which "Onas, the Long Knife," is a part.

DANIEL H. USNER, JR., professor of history at Cornell University, is the author of *American Indians in the Lower Mississippi Valley: Social and Economic Histories* (1998) and *Indians, Settlers, and Slaves in a Frontier Exchange Economy: The Lower Mississippi Valley before 1783* (1992). His current research projects include a volume on Mississippi for the Indiana University Press series on transappalachian frontiers and a study of colonial Louisiana's representation in American history and culture.

RICHARD WHITE is Margaret Byrne Professor of American History at Stanford University. His major works are *The Middle Ground: Indians, Empires, and Republics in the Great Lakes Region, 1650–1815* (1991), *"It's Your Misfortune and None of My Own": A New History of the American West* (1991), *The Organic Machine: The Remaking of the Columbia River* (1995), and *Remembering Ahanagran: Storytelling in a Family's Past* (1998). He is currently working on a book about the transcontinental railroads.

Index

Italicized page numbers refer to illustrations.

359